AN ESPN BOOK CLUB SELECTION

P9-CZV-493

"ASTONISHING."
—Mike Vaccaro, *New York Post*

"Compelling.... Hard to put down."
—Christian Swezey, *The Washington Post*

"Wojnarowski's sensitive, insightful look at the social backgrounds and emotional development of the varsity players will keep readers riveted throughout this book....One of the best recent pieces of sports journalism." —*Publishers Weekly*

"A great book. I couldn't stop reading. I highly recommend it."
—Regis Philbin

"The story he wishes to impart is less basketball than real life....Wojnarowski handles the material deftly."
—*The New York Times*

"Wonderful...You won't soon forget it."
—Joe Posnanski,
The Kansas City Star

"One of the best sports books in years."
—Dan Wetzel, Yahoo! Sports national columnist and coauthor of *Sole Influence*

"FASCINATING."
—Scott Fowler, *The Charlotte Observer*

"Part *Bad News Bears*, part *Hoosiers*, and absolute entertainment for anyone who cares about kids, basketball, education, and any combination thereof."
—Gregg Doyel, CBS Sportsline.com

"Hurley's calling was always to do for St. Anthony what Coach Carter, Ken Carter, did for his Richmond, California, team, a truth laid out poetically in Adrian Wojnarowski's book, *The Miracle of St. Anthony*."
—Ian O'Connor, *USA Today*

"EXCELLENT."
—Frank Dascenzo,
The Herald-Sun (Durham, NC)

Praise for *The Miracle of St. Anthony:*

"Part *Bad News Bears*, part *Hoosiers*, and absolute entertainment for anyone who cares about kids, basketball, education and any combination thereof."   —Gregg Doyel, CBS Sportsline.com

"After more than eight hundred wins and in excess of one hundred players placed in four-year colleges, Bob Hurley may have thought he'd seen it all. But then St. Anthony's tough-love coaching legend encounters a group of players he regards as the most clueless and unmotivated bunch he's dealt with in thirty years of winning state and national titles. Bob Hurley deserves a great basketball writer to tell this story and he has one in Adrian Wojnarowski."

—Bob Ryan, *Boston Globe* columnist and panelist
for ESPN's "The Sports Reporters"

"Hurley's calling was always to do for St. Anthony what Coach Carter, Ken Carter, did for his Richmond, California, team, a truth laid out poetically in Adrian Wojnarowski's book, *The Miracle of St. Anthony.*"   —Ian O'Connor, *USA Today*

"Wojnarowski . . . has matched Feinstein's effort with *The Miracle of St. Anthony. . . .* It reads like a novel, with the players' characters so fully developed that you felt personally connected."

—Joe Sullivan, *The Boston Globe*

"Through the eyes and words of players, coaches, and nuns, Wojnarowski tells their story in a kind and compelling manner. But *Miracle* is more than a hoops history lesson; Wojnarowski also chronicles the devotion and motivation of Hurley and the sometimes harrowing life experiences of the young men he is trying to reach and teach."

—Steven Goode, *The Hartford Courant*

"Wojnarowski provides a powerful, poetic look at an old-school disciplinarian. He makes it clear Hurley's mission isn't so much to win games as it is to change lives, to take boys from difficult urban backgrounds and turn them into men."

—Jerry Sullivan, *The Buffalo News*

"An honest, sometimes startling peek into the workings of the most storied high school hoops program in the country. . . . Basketball junkies will love the book."

—Jerry Carino, *Courier News* (Bridgewater, NJ)

"In [Wojnarowski's] words, the entire tale becomes a melding of *Hoosiers* and *Hoop Dreams*. . . . St. Anthony's is a story of passion and dedication and drama told well and true here."

—Mike Sielski, Calkins Newspapers

"[An] enormously readable take on one of the game's great teachers. . . . Wojnarowski has captured the Hurley life, one that along with producing winning basketball teams and successful kids also saves St. Anthony from closure and, some would say, saves a way of life in Jersey City."

—Cormac Gordon, *Staten Island Advance*

THE MIRACLE
OF
ST. ANTHONY

A Season with Coach Bob Hurley
and Basketball's Most Improbable Dynasty

ADRIAN WOJNAROWSKI

GOTHAM BOOKS

GOTHAM BOOKS
Published by Penguin Group (USA) Inc.
375 Hudson Street, New York, New York 10014, U.S.A.
Penguin Group (Canada), 90 Eglinton Avenue East, Suite 700, Toronto, Ontario, Canada
M4P 2Y3 (a division of Pearson Penguin Canada Inc.); Penguin Books Ltd, 80 Strand,
London WC2R 0RL, England; Penguin Ireland, 25 St Stephen's Green, Dublin 2, Ireland
(a division of Penguin Books Ltd); Penguin Group (Australia), 250 Camberwell Road,
Camberwell, Victoria 3124, Australia (a division of Pearson Australia Group Pty Ltd);
Penguin Books India Pvt Ltd, 11 Community Centre, Panchsheel Park, New Delhi – 110
017, India; Penguin Group (NZ), cnr Airborne and Rosedale Roads, Albany, Auckland
1310, New Zealand (a division of Pearson New Zealand Ltd); Penguin Books (South
Africa) (Pty) Ltd, 24 Sturdee Avenue, Rosebank, Johannesburg 2196, South Africa

Penguin Books Ltd, Registered Offices: 80 Strand, London WC2R 0RL, England

Published by Gotham Books, a division of Penguin Group (USA) Inc.

Previously published as a Gotham Books hardcover edition.
First trade paperback printing, January 2006
10   9   8   7   6   5   4

Gotham Books and the skyscraper logo are trademarks of Penguin Group (USA) Inc.

LIBRARY OF CONGRESS CATALOGING-IN-PUBLICATION DATA
has been applied for.

ISBN: 1-592-40186-4

Photo credits:
Inside front cover, top: Ray Lundgren
Inside front cover, bottom: John Munson, *The Star-Ledger*

Stepback cover, top: Noah K. Murray, *The Star-Ledger*
Stepback cover, bottom: Tony Kurdzuk, *The Star-Ledger*

Front cover photograph by James Cotier/Getty

Printed in the United States of America
Set in Bembo with News Gothic
Designed by Daniel Lagin

For my parents, Edward and Lillian Wojnarowski, whose sacrifices for Bryan, Brenda, and me taught us the value of family.

For Amy, the love of my life.

For Annie and Ben, who make it all worthwhile.

"We were in Vegas at the AAU event last summer, recruiting some kids on a South Dakota team. They come in, all white kids, beautiful uniforms, four coaches, parents in tow, running all kinds of offenses and defenses. So, I told my assistants, 'Now, watch this. See this team here? Eight black kids from Jersey City. Shitty uniforms, no parents, not even a coach. Just a chaperone somewhere there.'

"So, I tell my assistants, 'Watch these Jersey City kids kick the shit out of that team.'

"They're like, 'Why? What's special about them?'

"I told them, 'They will not say a word to the refs. They will not say a word to the other kids. They'll get on each other's backs for not taking the charge, not closing out, not stopping penetration.'

"So the game starts, and they were huddling at the free-throw line, one or two kids were yelling about not closing on penetration. They're coaching themselves.

"My assistants finally said to me, 'Holy shit, these kids play like they're possessed, like they're freaking animals. Who are they?'

"I said, 'Well, they're Bob Hurley's kids.'"

—Pat Kennedy, former Florida State and DePaul coach,
currently at Towson University

"To some extent, we're all 24/7 with basketball, but Bob takes it to a level I've never really seen anywhere in the game. I mean, this guy takes his vacations to go coach basketball. Good luck finding any of us doing that in college. I've never seen anyone, on any level, more dedicated than him."

—Jim Boeheim, Syracuse University,
2003 national championship coach

"Everybody knows that Bob Hurley is the total package. The presence, the organization, the style of play, he's one of the great teachers in the game. He captivates people when he's talking. What he's done at St. Anthony—with no gymnasium, no funding—the success speaks for itself. It's staggering."   —Hubie Brown,
2003–2004 NBA Coach of the Year

"I think that Bob Hurley teaches the game of basketball better than anybody in the country. In the purest sense, a coach is a teacher. And he's the best I've ever been around."

—Phil Martelli, St. Joseph's University,
2003–2004 NCAA Coach of the Year

PROLOGUE

In the old neighborhood, on the street corners in the Greenville section of Jersey City, in the playgrounds and the gymnasiums, Bob Hurley can still see him. Thirty-eight years have passed but Tommy Esposito will be forever eighteen years old, the kid the girls adored, the kid the boys wanted to be. He was Hurley's best friend, big and strong and smart, representing promise—the promise of every kid who Hurley someday would struggle to save, and the tragedy of those he would lose.

It happened late in the summer of 1965, in the fading innocence of his childhood, and it wouldn't be until years passed that Hurley understood that both of them had been desperately trying to hold onto something that was slipping away too fast.

Everything was changing, the way it had in the world beyond the borders of this jagged city in the shadows of the Statue of Liberty and Manhattan: the racial tensions, the growing anxiety about the Vietnam War, the drugs. Bob and Tommy had missed all of it while bouncing a basketball. Together, they had held courts from St. Paul's Parish to the No. 30 School to Audubon Park. Afterward, they would drop a quarter on the counter of Irv's Deli on the walk home to Greenville, on the southern tip of the city, buying pressed ham sandwiches on half a pizza loaf. On Friday nights, they would cross Kennedy Boulevard for the Friday night dances at Sacred Heart Academy, where fluid footwork on the gym floor remained secondary to flailing fists outside in the parking lot.

It was one of those gorgeous summer nights when young men feel untouchable, like nothing could ever stop them. Bob, Tommy, and a few of the fellas had gone down to Roosevelt Stadium to watch Bucky Rineer, a buddy from the neighborhood, play quarterback for a minor-league football team.

In just a few weeks, Hurley would begin his sophomore year at St. Peter's College, over on Kennedy, where he had played freshman basketball. Tommy was a bright student and had a chance to play football in college, but no one had ever steered him that way at home. He had been a year behind Bob in school because he had run away as a kid and had been kept back at Snyder High. After enlisting in the army that summer, he would soon be leaving for basic training, and after that, Vietnam. Everyone was sure he would come home a war hero. Tommy Esposito could be a little crazy, but he always landed on his feet.

As they walked to the corner of Danforth and Fowler, Hurley told his buddies that his family was away for the night and invited them over to watch the Mets game.

"Nah," Esposito told them, "we're gonna go swimming in the channel."

Now, on a bright October afternoon in the fall of 2003, Bob Hurley, the coach of the nationally renowned St. Anthony High School boys basketball team, was pulling up in his Toyota Camry to that same corner. His thoughts went back again to that night in 1965.

"So we get to the corner, and a couple of us made the right and walked over to my house," Hurley said. "Tommy and two others guys decided to turn down toward the water. They walked up and bought some beer, and now they were going to go swimming in the pitch black down by the channel. They decided to hop a train. Two kids hopped up. Tommy was carrying the beer. He tried to hop on while the train was going.

"He lost his balance. The one kid couldn't grab him."

While Bob had been sitting in his living room, Lindsey Nelson and Ralph Kiner flickering on the television set, Tommy Esposito ended up under that train, pieces of his body scattered down the tracks by the Morris Canal.

Hurley tapped the pedal in his old neighborhood, looked into his rearview mirror, and turned right, down Fowler. Window down, elbow dangling, he could feel the chilled autumn air through his blue nylon New Jersey Nets windbreaker. It meant that the start of basketball season wasn't far off. And it guaranteed to tighten the knot in his stomach, that edge to his disposition that always came with the beginning of practice, with the uncertainty of it all.

He made his way down Fowler, toward the gym, toward the basketball season and those St. Anthony kids looking as strong and young and alive as

Tommy once had. He tugged on his baseball cap, snug to the edge of his forehead. His eyes were on the road, but his mind was back where Danforth met Fowler, where one boy had turned toward manhood, another toward a cautionary tale.

"You get older and you realize that something was going to happen to the poor guy," Hurley continued. "He didn't have much at home. He just didn't have the benefit of people helping him through things. Tommy Esposito had managed to fight everything. He was invincible."

That night, Hurley had learned the lesson about invincibility and these Jersey City streets, about what a kid needed growing up to give him a shot at getting on his way to a good life.

"I guess you just know sometimes that a guy's in danger, that someone has got to save him."

Thirty-eight years had passed, but on the streets outside his window, there were kids who now believed themselves to be just as invincible, who had no idea how vulnerable they were.

That was something that never changed in Jersey City. There was always a corner, and there was always a choice.

SEEN FROM THE steel arches suspending the Casciano Bridge over Newark Bay, Jersey City stands with a skyline of steeples and smokestacks, leaving the ill-informed the impression that it has stayed largely untouched and unchanged over the years. Still, everything had moved such a long way from those days when Bob Hurley's old man had walked the streets as a beat cop.

As crime and poverty remained on the rise in Jersey City, as the public school system grew into such disarray that the state of New Jersey had to strip control from the local board of education, Hurley and the two Felician nuns, Sister Felicia and Sister Alan, wouldn't let the doors of the tiny brick school on Eighth Street in downtown close for good, even when the parish church had pulled its funding, even when the archdiocese would do little but wish them the best and privately predict its demise. For a quarter of a century now, the three of them had been trying to keep St. Anthony High School open for the poorest of the poor in Jersey City. Each year, with limited resources—without even his own gymnasium—Hurley constructed a national powerhouse program out of an enrollment that struggled to stay at 200 students for four grades. And every year, as St. Anthony balanced on the brink of financial ruin, that basketball team and coach would find a way to rally everyone and raise the money so another class could graduate and keep the school's decade-long streak of 100 percent college acceptance. Most of all, Hurley just wouldn't let that school die in a Jersey City where so much else he had held sacred was gone.

Today, the varsity letter sweaters have turned to gold chains, the fists to firearms, and it breaks Hurley's heart to see that the Jersey City that raised him has grown so complicated and treacherous for the kids under his watch now. High school basketball has changed, too, growing corrupt and commercialized, but its greatest dynasty never budges because Bob Hurley is determined to stay the most stubborn S.O.B. ever to walk into the gym with a whistle. In thirty-one seasons as St. Anthony coach, his teams had 796 victories and 91 losses, twenty-one Parochial state titles, eight of the fifteen New Jersey Tournament of Champions titles ever held, two *USA Today* national championships and five runner-up finishes. And most of all, all of it had been done the St. Anthony way. His way.

"What I have here is a formula to get kids out of Jersey City," Hurley says, and it begins with his foot on their throats, commanding them completely until they get out of high school, until they've gone to college like each of his players but one has since he started coaching at St. Anthony in 1972.

Hurley has sent more than a hundred players to full basketball scholarships, and five to the NBA as first-round picks, including his son, Bobby. It stands as an odd juxtaposition: Hurley has stayed so that they can get out. Somehow, Hurley is still the biggest bargain in sports—$6,800 a season to win championships year after year, to mold men and raise the revenue to save the school and its student body, to save a way of Catholic school education that is fading fast in urban America.

To him there is something so pure about high school basketball. In Hurley's practice gym, it is always 1965. There are no tattoos on his players, no cornrows, no facial hair. The most improbable dynasty in basketball has survived against the longest odds because Hurley has kept watch on these streets when he could've left to be a famous college coaching star, with a million-dollar-a-year package, a shoe deal, and racks of Armani suits. Yet on game nights, he wore that same maroon sweater-vest, those gray slacks, and his dulled brown loafers. And his kids still play the fiercest man-to-man in basketball, treating opponents like they've broken into their homes and threatened their families.

He drives his team with a tenacity taken from thirty years on the job as a Hudson County probation officer. Thirty years of walking into housing projects and gutted-out apartments where cops didn't dare go without a partner and a piece. Trusting his instincts to think on his feet, Hurley had hardened himself to deal with whatever lurked in the stairwell shadows.

The fear, the sheer uneasiness that his figure strikes into his players— what he uses to push his teams—is borne out of his own fear of the influence of the streets, out of the understanding that as soon as compromise and concession reach his gymnasium, he's lost everything. "I grew up in a neighborhood where you crossed the street to avoid somebody, or you just kept walking toward him, saying to yourself, 'Screw it, I've got to deal with it *today*,'" Hurley says.

Yet something still drove him that people couldn't see, couldn't possibly understand unless they had seen the innocence of Tommy Esposito's face, unless they had sat at Hurley's probation desk to witness the wasted lives and broken promise of two generations. Until his retirement from probation two years ago, he had done the best he could sifting through the carnage of Jersey City's lost souls.

"If they went to jail, it was because I had exhausted every other avenue with them," he says. "It was because that's where they belonged."

Hurley had been too late for most of them. He was picking up the pieces of families and lives that had already been shattered. It deepened his own resolve, a belief that coaching was a calling, a responsibility, the last line of defense between kids and the streets, between getting out and getting left behind.

"I would sit and listen to these men's stories for thirty years, and almost always it was the same: Somewhere in the eighth, ninth grade, when they were just starting to make decisions, they got off course," Hurley says. "At the end of the day, when it was time for me to go practice, I would want to run to those kids on my team. They all had the potential to rise above this, and I would do anything to see that they would. They would be behind academically, or need more discipline, and I would tell myself, 'I can't let them fall by the wayside, too.'

"There were an awful lot of days where I would stagger to practice and tell my kids, 'I had a brutal day today, boys.' Friday was sentencing day in the county, where it became the ultimate frustration of watching men go inside for years of their lives. And Monday would be the day where the ones on probation would come in and tell me their stories. Those would just take the life out of me. We would practice from 3:00 to 4:30 on those days, and it would be a catharsis for me, just to get out of there for those one and a half hours. After that, I would go back to the office and meet with more men from 5:00 until 6:30.

"But I would always bring these stories back to practice—and I still tell them now. I would point to a kid and tell him a story about a man going back to jail out of the housing project where the player was growing up. And once in a while, too, I'd have a story of someone who had turned his life around."

THIS WOULD BE the season of survival for Bob Hurley. The showdown of a street fighter's life awaited in the winter of 2003–2004. Everything was on the line this year, the history, the tradition, the lives of a senior class threatening to sink back into the city's streets.

This would be the fight to save St. Anthony High School, the fight against the change in the culture of kids, the fight to prove that this basketball team—the one constructed around seniors he calls the "most dysfunctional class that I've had in thirty-two years"— would rise to meet a standard of St. Anthony Friars basketball greatness that they seemed determined to lower every day.

They would have to do it on the basketball court, because he was going to be on this team like nothing they'd seen at St. Anthony in years. He is known as the greatest high school basketball coach in the country, but maybe there is no stopping there, because no one teaches the game like Bob Hurley. No one inspires kids like him, and no one anywhere in basketball comes closer to perfection under the most imperfect of circumstances. Almost anyone who's watched his teams play through the years comes away convinced that they play harder than any team, on any level, that they've ever seen. And this promised to be a season where those seniors could expect him to keep coming at them every day.

Yet, going into this season, Hurley had already given this team so many second chances, letting kids back whom he would never have before. He feared that it tore at the fabric of his authority, undermined his ability to lord over this basketball program—this dominance—with an iron fist. Sometimes, he knows, one player needs to be cast aside to spare the rest. Because once anyone sees a crack in the foundation, once the discipline is dulled, once the fear of God that his players feel when Bob Hurley walks into the gymnasium is done, this dynasty is dead. They might as well deflate the balls, barricade the doors to the high school, and understand that St. Anthony basketball will have lost its edge, lost its usefulness, and ultimately, lost its way.

This worry wasn't just on his mind now, it was torturing him. But what was his choice anymore? Once more, Hurley was the last line of defense. The tiny school was dying, the money had dried up again, and most of the fund-raising and donations that had come in were because people believed in him, in his values from a different time, a different Jersey City. They knew that if Hurley ever left, if the school ever closed, a whole way of life would go down too.

Now, the relentlessly troubled seniors on his team were messing with the St. Anthony mystique, messing with Bob Hurley. They were daring him to a street fight that brought him back to the old days. They still didn't get it, but there was time. He knew that somehow, if he could just get through, they would understand. He just hoped it wouldn't be too late to save them, and maybe, save this senior class the dubious distinction of being the biggest bunch of screwups in school history.

Someday, he knew, Marcus Williams and Ahmad Mosby, Lamar Alston Otis Campbell and Shelton Gibbs—all of them—would hear his voice and it would resonate. Because that voice never leaves his players.

For better or worse, it stays with them forever.

BOB HURLEY'S BALLPLAYERS will even hear his voice far from the basketball court, long after they have left his watch, the way Mark Harris, a firefighter out of Jersey City Ladder No. 12, had heard it on the roof of those burning row houses on Harmon Street years after he had shared the Friars backcourt with Hurley's son Bobby, back in the late 1980s.

His partner, Donald Stembridge, had been cutting a ventilation hole in the roof, and his foot got caught in the hole. Beneath them, they could see the flames exploding into the rafters and through the roof.

"When we played, we used to get guys in traps and look at their facial expressions—just to see how scared they were," Harris remembers. "As a kid, you're not supposed to be thinking like that, but the game used to slow down that much for us. As players for Coach Hurley, we were so prepared that we began to see everything at a different speed. So I was standing in the middle of this, and the flames are everywhere and the roof is giving way and we're close to falling into the fire. . . .

"And right away, all that flashed into my mind was: *Think before you react. Awareness. Alertness.* And it was just like Coach had trained us. Everything turned to slow motion. It was like I was playing ball again."

After freeing his partner, Harris and Stembridge navigated across the crumbling footing, leaping to a safe area on top of a row house next door. A moment later, the blaze exploded through the rafters, engulfing the roof they had just abandoned.

As Mark Harris stood against the Jersey City sky, as flames spit into the air, the chills ran up and down his spine. It had hit him, like it would for so many old St. Anthony basketball players.

He looked into the inferno and thought: "Coach Hurley just saved my life."

THE MIRACLE
OF
ST. ANTHONY

CHAPTER 1

ED SZALKIEWICZ KEPT coming down the third-floor corridor of St. Anthony High School, insisting that Ahmad Mosby—the senior everyone called "Beanie"—turn around and talk to him. Beanie wouldn't take his do-rag off. That's all the teacher wanted. Just take the damn thing off your head.

"I'm going to call Coach Hurley," Szalkiewicz warned.

"Go ahead," Beanie said, still walking away from him. "I don't care."

This was one of those moments when working at the high school felt like working in a mental ward, because Beanie was losing his mind again. Actually, Beanie was being Beanie. It was a damned do-rag. Beanie wouldn't dare to wear it into Hurley's gymnasium, and he knew he shouldn't be wearing it in the corridors of the school.

This was Beanie at his worst: acting out, convinced that the world was out to get him, that he was just the last in a line of Mosby men doomed to self-destruction. Bob Hurley never called him Beanie, the nickname his family gave him when, as a baby, he looked as tiny as a bean. Hurley called him Ahmad. "Beanie was always the guy getting in trouble," Hurley explains. "I want him to grow up and become 'Ahmad.'"

It was a Friday morning, November 21, just a week until practice started, and it looked like Beanie was trying hard to throw away the last chance he had to redeem himself. He was an elastic five-foot-eleven, all gangly arms and legs. At times, he could be one of the most charming kids in the school, but too often, Beanie just brooded. He had a long, thin face, often wearing a tired, troubled look—like a forgotten old man sitting alone on a park bench.

Beanie kept moving to his next class—psychology class, of all places—and dropped his books on the desk inside and sunk into the seat. Beanie remained defiant, telling the trailing teacher that he didn't want to be yelled at, that he just wanted to be left alone.

Between periods of teaching his environmental science class, a young assistant basketball coach named Darren Erman had heard it all unfolding from down the hall and rushed into the classroom to defuse the kind of mindless confrontation that had cost Beanie a week's suspension at the start of the month.

"Beanie, you're so close," Erman said, standing over him. "You're too damn close to screw this up."

Beanie's eyes stared defiantly straight ahead. Erman stayed on him.

"You're almost there. You're getting the grades, the test scores. You're playing great. You can taste it.

"Don't blow it, Beanie."

How many times had he heard that?

Don't blow it.

His whole life, his mother and older sisters had shielded him like an endangered species, because, well, he was just that. The last Mosby man standing.

The first-marking-period grades had just come out and all the hard work and concentration that Beanie invested had been rewarded: all B's, and an A. He had been a good student in elementary school, pulling mostly B's, and even winning science and math awards. He had done the absolute minimum—and often even less—for his first three years in high school. It was too late in his high school career to raise his marks high enough for a Division I scholarship, but this marking period had shown promise. There was so much unfulfilled promise within him, and Hurley prayed staying with Ahmad Mosby was worth the trouble.

If only he could glide past his life's strains like he could a defender—with one of his stop-on-a-dime, stutter-step moves to freedom. Every star high school guard in the state of New Jersey had a story about Beanie embarrassing him somewhere—against St. Anthony, in summer ball, at a camp—somewhere. He was the guard that just kept coming for you, again and again. He was a pain to play against, and when his head was on straight, a quintessential Hurley player.

He was the youngest child of Cornelius and Beverly Mosby's three daughters and two sons. Growing up, they had never told Beanie the reasons his father was constantly in and out of the hospital near the end of his life, why he was finally gone when Beanie was just in the second grade. Cornelius had been a drug dealer, and it had cost him his life.

"Those years were so confusing for him," his older sister, Crystal, says. "He was the baby, and we tried to protect him from my father dying." She had gone away to college on a basketball scholarship, to the University of South Alabama, where after the constant telephone conversations with her little brother, and her mother's reports on the way it seemed Beanie was slowly, surely getting sucked into Jersey City's streets, Crystal had transferred back to Kean College in New Jersey for her final two years.

"It didn't hit him until he was thirteen and really realized his father was gone," she says. "He needed him, and he realized that he wasn't there. It hit him all at once: the acting out, the behavior, the mood changes."

Beanie escaped with basketball. Traveling constantly with the Jersey City Boys Club team, winning tournaments and trophies throughout the Northeast and the nation, basketball kept him on course. Basketball kept him going when an uncle had gone in and out of prison due to drugs, and basketball kept him going when his older brother ended up behind bars for pushing, too.

"It put a lot of pressure on me," Beanie says. "My father was in the drug game, and my uncle, and now my brother is locked up for it. It was like all the males in my family. Everyone is relying on me . . . 'I want him to go to college . . . I want him to do this,' and it's pressure. It's pressure I can handle, because I want to go to college. It's like I shouldn't mess up, because everyone is relying on me.

"But it falls on my head. It's like, 'How am I going to keep myself on track, and not fall into the drug game like them?' I think about it at times, and then I just tell myself, 'No, you can't even let yourself think of that, because you're going to fall, too.'"

Crystal says, "When you're growing up and that's what you've seen out of your role models, there's that identity crisis that a young man will go through, trying to find out who he is, and where he fits. With what my brother has seen and been through, it's remarkable that he's never dabbled in that life. Never did."

And maybe it had been too much last year, when Hurley and the basketball team counted on him as a junior. Twenty games into the season, with the stretch run for the state tournament looming, Hurley had started to turn up the heat on his kids. He was on Beanie, the way he was on everyone. He kept telling him that he was only on the floor until Sean McCurdy came back from his injury, just keeping his spot warm.

At home, in the Hudson Gardens projects, the pressure continued. His mother was watching a young grandson for a few hours a day, but the boy's mother was constantly coming back late to take over the responsibilities. When Beanie would arrive home, he felt like his mother was taking her frustrations out on him. "She would start to yell at me, just after I came home from practice," he says. "Coach Hurley was yelling at me there. I just couldn't take it."

So he missed a practice in February and didn't call anyone. And then another. In his mind, he was just going to walk away. Yet, as he sat home that second day, the confusion slowly gave way to clearer thinking and he reached out to Hurley's assistant coaches with some tale about an injury, and then the snow. Nobody bought it. For thirty years, Hurley had listened to professional con men sell him stories every day in the probation office. The kids on his basketball teams could never get over on him. Never. Had he just told the truth, Beanie would've suffered a suspension and made it back to the season. He didn't, so he was tossed.

"In other schools, what he did would not have warranted what happened to him, but he's in a different place," Hurley says. "Instead of just admitting that he made a mistake, he tried to build some more stories to cover himself. The thing was, he was caving. We were coming to the pressure time of the year and there was some real performance anxiety there."

And then, Beanie made the mistake of trying to talk to Hurley after the next game, a sluggish victory over St. Peter's of Staten Island in Jersey City. After witnessing Hurley's fury in the postgame locker room, his top assistant coach, Ben Gamble, was mortified to see Beanie walking toward him outside. "I wish I could've stopped him," Gamble says.

Beanie tried to explain himself, only to have Hurley unload on him. "Get out of my face," Hurley screamed. He was done, Hurley told him. He was suspended for the rest of the season. After flunking off the team as a sophomore, Beanie would fail to complete his second straight season. There was no guarantee that he'd ever play basketball at St. Anthony again.

Looking back, Hurley had wished the assistants had stopped Beanie, told him to come to practice the next day and talk to Hurley after he had cooled down. He would've reinstated him for the state tournament, but it was too late, in the coach's mind. The deed was done. Beanie was gone for the season.

"At that point, he went from double secret probation to off the charts," Hurley says. "There is a little bit of social worker in me. I had counseled him. It's not like out of the clear blue that I'm going to chop someone's head off. This is a sentencing. And the sentencing up in Superior Court is going to be based on the charge and the previous record.

Judge Olivieri and Judge Callahan, good friends of mine, are very fair judges. And I think I'm a very fair judge."

In the end, St. Anthony had lost to number-one-ranked St. Patrick's, its archrival, when sophomore point guard Derrick Mercer was overcome by St. Pat's ball pressure. He kept turning the ball over, and everyone couldn't help but think that Beanie would've made the difference in that game. They still lost by just four points.

"The whole team brought that up to me," Beanie says. "All of them were saying, 'If you had played in that game, we would've won.' "

When Beanie kept showing up at games at the end of last season, Gamble was afraid of what he saw in the stands. More and more, Beanie looked like he was slipping into the thug life. Because without basketball, the kid would to try to fit in somewhere, with someone else. "He was walking around with that hard image, thinking he needed that to be accepted," Gamble says.

Ten years ago, Hurley never would've considered bringing Beanie back to the team. The relentless—twelve months a year—commitment was what separated St. Anthony—the conditioning, the camps, the summer leagues. Once he let one kid slide on it, the others would think that they could come and go as the mood struck them, and the championship foundation promised to crumble. But when the season was over, the coaches talked a lot about Ahmad Mosby and kept coming back to the same thing: He had nowhere else to go.

They told Beanie that his grades had to come up, and as long as those did, he could start coming to open gym in the springtime. He had to start over with Hurley, but for better or worse, he was back together with his graduating class for a final run at redemption at St. Anthony, a final chance to chase what Hurley had always promised was waiting for them beyond the rainbow, a state championship and a scholarship. His family wanted to get him out of the Hudson Gardens, out of Jersey City, and away.

Between now and then, Hurley would still call him Ahmad. To him, Beanie was the screwup, the baby, and Mosby needed to leave all that behind.

"Everyone thinks that I'm a head case," Beanie says. "I've gotten into trouble, but I can keep myself out of it. I can hit the books hard this year, and I can dedicate myself to the team. Since he let me back on the team, I haven't missed an open gym yet. I'm gonna have to work harder than everybody else on the team. I have to prove that I've committed myself to them, to coach.

"This is it for me now."

* * *

Now DARREN ERMAN was standing over him in Darryl Powell's psychology class, pleading with him, and Szalkiewicz was still seething in the hallway, threatening to call Coach Hurley. It just seemed like so many demons tugged at him, so much anger and fear and uncertainty conspired inside him.

Beanie took the do-rag off.

It wouldn't be long until basketball practice would begin and Hurley would be back in his face, testing his commitment, his resolve. No one could be sure if in that bony little point guard a man would emerge who could step out of the shadows of the Mosby men, of the troubled St. Anthony seniors, and give Beanie a shot to finally find Ahmad.

IT WAS GROWING late on a chilly, overcast November afternoon, late in the autumn and far too late in the seniors' careers for them to be messing with the man, with the start of practice still three weeks away. Eyes narrowing beneath that graying, cropped hair, Bob Hurley moved quickly over the sidewalk on Montgomery Street and up the cement stairs of the Jersey City Armory. Once he burst through the steel doors and into the loud, bustling gymnasium, Hurley had that twitch going good. He was rubbing his right hand over the watch on his left wrist, like he was tightening the band to his arm—a warning to get out of his way now, because he didn't just want someone's ass, he wanted everyone's ass.

Hurley wanted to bring them back to the old days, the old rules, bring them back to a time when the code of the street could've corrected this kind of disrespect. He wished he could take care of them the way his father had taken care of him. Somehow, his seniors still believed they could get away with giving a St. Anthony teacher volunteering to tutor them on the SATs attitude during the final period of the day—or just walk out early, or blow it off—and somehow think that it wouldn't get back to the coach. Every day, it was something else with this crew. So now Hurley stormed into the Armory, stalking straight for his basketball team when a most satisfying sight softened the ferocity in his face.

Someone else had beaten him to it. Someone else was pounding on his players. Greeting him were the pained groans of his players crawling like crabs across the Armory floor, wearing wire-braced contraptions that connected arms and legs and created resistance. The sweat leaking looked like an oil spill on the floor. Standing in the middle of the floor, delivering his weekly torture chamber to the St. Anthony players, was a shiny-domed conditioning guru, Burke Spencer. The shrieking was a sweet symphony to Hurley's ears, and he wished only that his old friend Carmine Salerno, the St. Anthony teacher who ran the SAT session earlier that day, could've had a front row seat for the seniors' suffering. Truth be told, this would be a popular spot to hold a St. Anthony faculty meeting.

Hurley considered the Class of 2004 the most academically, athletically and socially underachieving in St. Anthony basketball history.

Marcus Williams. Otis Campbell. Ahmad Mosby. Lamar Alston. Shelton Gibbs. Together, they were the cornerstone of an unprecedented five-time Athletic Amateur Union (AAU) state championship team representing the Jersey City Boys Club, winning thirteen-, fourteen-, fifteen-, sixteen- and seventeen-year-old-and-under age group titles. Twice, they had reached the final eight of the national tournament. None were considered blue-chip college prospects, none stood taller than six-foot-three, and still they had managed to vanquish thirty opponents without a loss in state tournament games. In an era when sneaker companies bankrolled traveling AAU teams, stocking them with all-star talent and sending them on expense-paid trips to tournaments throughout the country, the Jersey City Boys Club team remained a tribute to neighborhood basketball teams. They won with an innate sense of playing together, a bond built back in grade school. Most of all, they won with the principles of St. Anthony basketball: unselfish passing, unforgiving defense and unparalleled toughness.

All the basketball they played together revolved around a twelve-month-a-year commitment to their high school program. For St. Anthony, these seniors had been the driving force for running roughshod over teams in the spring and summer of 2003. After losing to archrival St. Patrick's High School of Elizabeth in the Parochial B North championship game in March, the Friars had returned to work with a vengeance for the 2003–2004 season, lifting weights almost daily in the dimly lit basement of White Eagle Bingo Hall and playing ball upstairs on the creaky, warped court.

Over the spring and summer, St. Anthony had gone unbeaten in sixty-one tournament and recreation-league games. Most promising of all had been the team's performance in the AND 1 sneaker company's national high school tournament. Two hundred fifty-six teams in eight regional brackets started across the country, with St. Anthony beating the best teams in the Northeast to reach the final eight at St. Joseph's University in Philadelphia in late June.

St. Anthony and AND 1 were an unlikely marriage of basketball past and present, old school and new school. AND 1 tapped into the basketball street culture, separating itself from the Nike and Adidas empires with a marketing slogan that crystallized a clarion call for an antiestablishment basketball revolution: *Get Yours*. It was a middle finger flung in the face of tradition, the hip-hop generation colliding with old-time values on the basketball battleground.

AND 1 turned the old school of basketball into a new school of showmanship, where the biggest stars and the biggest reps were manufactured by style over substance, humiliation over humility. In AND 1's vernacular, the F-word is fundamentals. When America turned on Fox Sports Network that Sunday afternoon in June to watch St. Anthony beat Booker T. Washington, 72–60, they witnessed something of far greater consequence than the championship game of a national summer tournament. Between the contrast of the fundamentally sound St. Anthony game set against the company's commercials celebrating the decline of civility in American basketball, the game had unwittingly morphed into a basketball culture war.

In one moment, AND 1's circus basketball ads flickered on the screen, where balls whipped between legs like the Globetrotters meeting PlayStation, where passes bounced off the heads of defenders, inspiring the heckling, taunts and belly laughs of teammates and fans. In the next moment, returning to the game, it was a trip back in a time machine. There was St. Anthony running its meticulous offense: setting screens, backcutting and always deferring the shot to the open man; playing its fabled man-to-man defense, swallowing up dribblers, full-court pressing, trapping and holding the two-time Mr. Basketball in Tennessee to just ten points. The Anti-AND 1 was winning the rebel company's championship. With Hurley home in Jersey City, letting his assistant and ex-player, Ben Gamble, coach the summer team, St. Anthony had conducted a clinic. To Hurley, the ultimate judge of his teaching came not always when he was there to direct his players, but when they were on their own.

If only this senior class could incorporate the discipline and clearminded choices from the gym into a world beyond the court. If only the summer's success could carry over into the start of the seniors' final year at St. Anthony. If only they could push past the sordid array of dysfunctions borne out of broken homes and emotional frailties and a shared appetite for self-destruction. At once, the St. Anthony seniors and Jersey City Boys Club crew were the best of friends and each other's worst enemy.

"When one of us gets in trouble, it's like the rest of us has to find a way to go down with him," Beanie said.

The Boys Club's director, Gary Greenberg, has steered his eighth graders to St. Anthony for twenty years, believing the best chance any Jersey City kid has is with Hurley and the Sisters at St. Anthony. "But we never had a group that needed them as much as this one did," Greenberg says. "I don't want to think where they would be without them." Still, there were too many times Greenberg and Hurley huddled, picking up the pieces of the latest letdown.

"Do they understand the opportunity in life they're blowing?" Greenberg would ask Hurley over and over.

On the night of Bobby Hurley's annual charity golf tournament and dinner auction at the Montclair Country Club in late September, Marcus, Otis and Shelton were turned in to school officials for raising hell on the bus ride back to Jersey City. For Hurley, it was the ultimate kick in the stomach. Here it was at the end of a long day and night, when so many people had invested the time and energy to raise $200,000 to help save the school, and his seniors had gone and shamed everyone in the worst way possible.

The three seniors and two junior starters, Barney Anderson and Derrick Mercer, had been suspended for a month from working out with the team and punished with thirty hours of community service. For Hurley, one of the most disturbing parts was how the seniors dragged Derrick and Barney into the mess with them. Those two had never been in trouble.

Beanie and Lamar had spared themselves a role in that drama, but found trouble elsewhere for themselves. Beanie lost his temper toward a teacher, his old jayvee basketball coach, Tony DiGiovanni, and it won him a week's suspension. In September, Lamar had disappeared for three days, AWOL without telling his parents or his coach where he had gone.

As a junior, Otis had quit the team in the preseason for two weeks, partly because of an inability to handle the heat Hurley directed toward him, and partly because he had lost a starting job to the most unique transfer in school history, Sean McCurdy. One of the reasons Hurley had been so hard on Otis in the preseason a year earlier had to do with what had happened late in his sophomore year, after Otis had been instructed to make the move up to varsity for the state tournament. He had spread glue on a teacher's pet rock and then watched as her hand got stuck to it. "Just a way to self-destruct and keep himself from handling the responsibilities of coming to varsity practice," Hurley would theorize.

From one day to the next, Hurley never knew how the seniors' demons and defects would manifest themselves. They had tested Hurley in new ways, causing him to reflect on the leadership decisions of balancing second chances and accountability, saving a life and costing himself the credibility to instill the fear of consequences into his underclassmen.

This November afternoon was the first day of the National Collegiate Athletic Association's letter of intent signing period, which had slipped Hurley's mind until now. As far back as Hurley could remember, there hadn't been a fall when he hadn't had a steady stream of college coaches making presentations to his seniors. Just one year earlier, it had been three national championship winning coaches—Syracuse's Jim Boeheim, Connecticut's Jim Calhoun and Maryland's Gary Williams—courting the Friars six-foot-nine star, Terrence Roberts. Across thirty-one years as a coach, Hurley as averaged three scholarship players per graduating class. He has sent them to every major conference in the nation: the Big East, ACC, Big Ten, Pac-10, SEC and Atlantic 10. He had sent even more to Division II and Division III programs. Almost every player is so well coached, so well schooled in the fundamentals, that they arrive far more advanced than their classmates. This season, Hurley has ten of his ex-players playing Division I basketball. Hurley tries to never tell a kid where he should go, but does his best to guide him through a decision he calls the most important he would make to date in his life. In his twenty-five years of mining St. Anthony for Iona, Florida State and DePaul, Coach Pat Kennedy even confessed to getting tired of listening to himself make the same pitches over and over on visits to Hurley's prospects in Jersey City. But Bob Hurley never does.

"Bob knows exactly what I'm going to tell his kid, but he sits there in his shirt and tie with the same intensity as if it was the first time he had ever heard me," Kennedy says. "He sits there with such respect for you, such an interest on behalf of his kids. How many high school coaches do that anymore?

"He's the most consistent guy I've ever met in my life."

For the most consistent force of the most consistently great high school basketball program in the country, it had come to this in the November chill: Hurley had to rely on his most inconsistent collection of players to take its turn carrying the torch. If Otis and Lamar could make academic progress, they had a chance to earn Division I scholarships for next season. For Marcus and Beanie, they had grade point averages so low that it would be impossible to become Division I prospects. Because of this, they had limited options, mostly centering on two-year junior colleges, where, after earning associate degrees, they could transfer to four-year schools for the final two years of basketball eligibility. The backdoor route to university life was something that St. Anthony players had previously endured in isolated cases, but never before en masse with an entire class.

Whatever they would accomplish on the court this season, the embarrassment of the players' poor academic standing gnawed at him, leaving him wishing away the preseason *USA Today* Super 25 poll that had ranked St. Anthony fifth in the nation. Under Hurley, St. Anthony had been a consistent part of the poll for two decades, climaxing undefeated seasons in 1989 and 1996 with number-one rankings, and finishing number two in '88, '91, '93, '97, and 2002.

After going 29-1 and winning Parochial B and Tournament of Champions titles for the second straight time in 2002, St. Anthony struggled through an injury-riddled 21-5 before losing to St. Pat's last year. For now, Hurley had his eyes fixed on reclaiming state superiority this season. The Friars were the consensus preseason number one in New Jersey, a precarious perch, considering the checkered histories of the seniors.

The composition of this team made it an oddity among the elite. It didn't have that one blue-chip college basketball prospect to carry them. No consistent twenty-point scorer, no All-American. The best player was Marcus Williams, a four-year starter who was considered an under-sized high school forward at six-foot-two. For the purposes of the national polls, their coach was the superstar. He was the most comforting of high school difference makers: one who never graduated.

In some respects, this team had the chance to meld into the quintessential Hurley team. Built to dominate defensively, it would have to manufacture points by transforming turnovers into easy baskets. Beginning the season without a starter taller than six-foot-five, they were small but as quick as water bugs, physically strong and the beneficiaries of a deep bench of fresh legs.

"As much as any we've had, this will have to be a 'team,' in every sense of the word," Hurley would say.

Between November and March, Hurley's mission was to finally get these kids to buy into his program, into St. Anthony, into the tradition. Mostly, that meant Hurley had to get them to buy into Hurley. Maybe these soap operas were becoming standard operating procedure everywhere else in high school basketball, but Hurley was going to be damned to let it happen here.

Inside the Armory, as his weary players were finishing with the trainer, Hurley said softly, "Maybe I'm getting old, but if I have to drag their asses from point 'A' to point 'B' then that's what I'll have to do this year."

Soon Hurley called his team over, and thirteen varsity players surrounded him in a tight, closed huddle. Fifteen years earlier, the Armory floor they stood on had been brought back to life for the homeless St. Anthony basketball program, because Hurley and three friends sanded and varnished an area of 10,000 square feet, installed lights and even an electronic scoreboard. Like everything else they had at St. Anthony, it had been borne of his bare hands, and there was no way in hell he was going to stand on the sideline and watch them tear it all down.

As the team gathered, there were no eyes gazing in the distance, no wisecracking or whispers. However else they did things in school and at home, however else they treated parents and teachers and elders, they stood like soldiers when Hurley spoke to them.

Hurley started with the telephone call he'd gotten from Carmine Salerno about the SAT class, and went from there, his voice rising to be heard over the acoustics and noise in the busy building.

"I'm going to go out of my way this year to take you on," Hurley said. "I will not look the other way this year. I am coming straight for you people. I'm a basketball coach. It's not my job to raise you. You have no self-discipline. You don't set goals for yourself. You hear over and over how important it is to get an education. And you don't care. Since you've been here, kids quit the team, kids have been suspended, and now you're seniors and it's the same shit, different year."

He stopped for a moment, letting the words hang there. Marcus stood the closest to him, the indisputable leader of the old Boys Club crew. He had been listening to these speeches for four years, but this was supposed to be his team now, and Marcus knew Hurley was talking to him more than to any of his teammates.

"You seniors don't work hard. You aren't anything I want our underclassmen to see. I want to put up a wall around you, just to keep them away from you all. You still don't understand that what you do away from here affects you here. When are you going to learn that you can't be a shithead in school and go be a good player on the court? When are you going to learn that it doesn't work that way?"

Hurley's eyes rolled over Ahmad Mosby and Lamar Alston and Otis Campbell, and his glare met with sullen, blank faces. They understood that the slightest tic, the mildest sign of exasperation with his lecture, could turn what was merely an agitated disposition for the coach into a full-blown rage.

"The seniors are supposed to be leaders, but all you do is play ball and then try to cut corners. Why isn't anyone in this senior class in student government? I'll tell you why not: because nobody would listen to you."

Looking down, Lamar and Otis stubbed their feet into the floor, but Hurley's glare never left them.

"We've had to put up with your sorry asses for four years. I know you're all thinking that you can't wait to get out of here, that you can't wait to not have to put up with this anymore. But how do you think your coaches feel about you?

"Are you kidding me? Do you think we love coaching you? We can't wait for you to be gone."

Hurley breathed out and delivered one final dismissive glance around the circle. "Prove me wrong this year, but I don't think you will."

Hurley stalked off, leaving the kids to gather up their gym bags and winter jackets and head for the door.

Gamble turned to another assistant coach, Tom Pushie, and smiled a knowing smile.

"You can tell it's getting close to Thanksgiving," he said.

What he meant was this: It was getting closer to the start of the season. Hurley was becoming Hurley again.

CHAPTER 2

IF SISTER MARY Felicia Brodowski had expected an inspirational speech to send her off on the assignment doled out in the office of the Provincial Superior on that spring afternoon in 1982, her noble ideals were quickly extinguished. Sister Viterbia needed someone on the faculty at the Immaculate Conception School in Lodi to be appointed principal of St. Anthony, the dying Polish parish high school a few miles away in Jersey City.

For a fleeting moment, the word of her appointment to St. Anthony warmed Sister Felicia. She had taught English there for two years, starting in 1969, instilling within her a connection to the teachers and students. For the Felician Order's motherhouse to send her back there as principal was wonderful news.

The trouble was, the motherhouse community had a dimmer view of the future.

"They've got a lot of trouble there," Sister Viterbia said flatly. "You're going in to close that school."

The archdiocese had decided that St. Anthony had become an educational anachronism. It was never worth funding. The St. Anthony Catholic Church, located five blocks away, had stopped its support, leaving the school vulnerably independent. To many of the old guard in the parish community, St. Anthony belonged to someone else now. St. Anthony had already turned into an inner-city high school, its student body coming increasingly from the black and Hispanic families throughout Jersey City.

The school had been founded in 1952 to educate many of the first-generation children of Polish immigrants arriving at Ellis Island, but over the years St. Anthony had undergone the transformation that mirrored so many urban parochial high schools. The "white flight" of the 1970s had resulted in the exodus of families to the suburbs, and the children they brought with them began to fill the sprouting regional Catholic high schools.

A growing sentiment throughout segments of St. Anthony and the Archdiocese of Newark was that there was a reluctance to fight for urban high schools. One of the underlying reasons was undeniable: The inner-city students turning to Catholic education no longer represented the traditional Catholic parish student body. Or, more bluntly: These poor minority kids aren't our problem anymore.

As Sister Felicia listened to the Provincial Superior deliver St. Anthony its death sentence, she resolved that she would not close the school. To close the school would be going back on every vow of service she had made, upon joining the Felician Order. It wouldn't be long before she reached out to an old Villanova graduate school friend, Sister Mary Alan Barszczewski, who was still on the front lines of St. Anthony as teacher and athletic director. Everyone surrounding Sister Alan—the administration, the faculty, the students—was losing hope. The world had changed, but St. Anthony had stayed the same. It couldn't go on that way.

Without knowing that Sister Felicia had accepted the job of principal, Sister Alan warned, "Whoever takes this job is *crazy*."

Sister Felicia broke the news to Sister Alan and promised that, if nothing else, saving St. Anthony would be the hardest undertaking of their lives. This was a long way from the comfort of the motherhouse in Lodi, a long way from a quiet afternoon prayer in wooden pews with the sun streaming in through the stained-glass windows of the Immaculate Conception of the Blessed Virgin Mary.

How could they abandon these kids in Jersey City? It went against everything Sophia Truszkowska had set out to do in early nineteenth-century Poland when, as a child of privilege, her heart would sink upon seeing the packs of homeless children wandering the streets of Warsaw. After a life of boarding schools in the Alps, Sophia turned an apartment in downtown Warsaw into a warm, safe place to care for them. More women came to work side by side with her, educating, feeding and caring for the kids. Together, they created the beginning of something beyond a religious community. More than that, Sophia began a movement.

In November of 1855, a Franciscan priest dedicated Sophia's life to God's service before the icon of Our Lady of Czestochowa. Soon, Sophia became known as Sister Mary Angela. All around Warsaw, the people would see the Sisters and children praying at the nearby shrine of St. Felix of Cantalice. They began to call them the Sisters of St. Felix. Before long, they were simply the Felicians.

The legend of the Sisters' work spread throughout Poland and Europe, young women joining the order and soon caring for the sick and impoverished of every age. Five Felicians made the journey to the United States in 1874, settling in Polonia, Wisconsin. There the order's numbers swelled to 200 within ten years, with the Sisters creating homes for children and the elderly.

From the traditionally Polish-American bastions of Chicago and Buffalo, to Brazil, France, and England, the Felician Sisters have had a long history of going into the cities and neighborhoods and dwellings where no one else would care for the impoverished. At the community in Lodi, less than a mile from Jersey City, Sister Felicia had a good life teaching at the Immaculate Conception High School. The girls there were well-disciplined and polished products of the Catholic grammar-school system, many of them preparing for lives in the Felician order themselves. All in all, it was a far cry from the changing world of St. Anthony.

"When I arrived in Jersey City in the summer of '82, I had no teachers and a dirty building," Sister Felicia says. "I just said, 'Hi Alan, I'm here.' And we rolled up our sleeves and went to work."

In the beginning, the Sisters spent their days poring over résumés and interviewing teachers, cleaning the thirteen-room school, class by class. They would get on their hands and knees that summer, scrubbing the floors, cleaning bathrooms and painting peeling walls. They had to completely overhaul the curriculum, loading up classes on the basics of reading, writing and arithmetic. They were a classic good-cop, bad-cop pairing. Sister Alan was short, sturdy and feisty. She wore her gray hair short on top, and she never, ever backed down. She was the disciplinarian, the muscle. Sister Felicia looked the part of the traditional, genteel nun: neatly coifed and often speaking in a calming, hushed tone.

No one had stayed at St. Anthony longer than Sister Alan, except for the basketball coach, Bob Hurley. She had outlasted almost everyone. Raised in the working-class neighborhoods of the Fishtown section of Philadelphia, she had embraced the charge of educating kids in the changing urban world, even as her last principal and fellow Felician Sisters felt overwhelmed by the prospect. Before her assignment to St. Anthony in 1979, Sister Alan had taught at an elite Catholic girls school in Delaware, where "the biggest problem we ever had was that someone stole the Froggy soap dish out of the bathroom."

The St. Anthony parish itself was struggling to meet its own expenses, never mind the high school five blocks away. The parish cut its formal financial obligation to the school in 1981; it no longer even passed the basket for it during the second Sunday morning Mass collections. If the school had a fund-raiser, there were still some old-guard parishioners who could be counted on to buy a few boxes of cookies and a couple of raffle tickets. But it would bring nothing that was enough to sustain the school's operating budget.

Even so, St. Anthony had still been working to educate the kids coming out of a crumbling public school system, out of drug-riddled, crime-ridden neighborhoods and broken homes. Across Jersey City, the kids came on trains and buses and foot, from Curries Woods and Hudson Gardens and the Booker T. Washington projects. More than half of St. Anthony's students were annually denied admission into other parochial high schools, based largely on minimal academic test scores and achievement in elementary school. St. Anthony was the one parochial Jersey City school that would take them, the one keeping tuition costs down. They had no choice: More than 50 percent of the families sending children to St. Anthony lived under the poverty line of an income of $16,000 a year.

When St. Anthony officials had opportunities over the years to move into more functional structures closer to the housing projects and neighborhoods where most of the students came from, the parents objected. St. Anthony was nestled in a safe part of downtown, and they wanted to keep their kids there.

The kids at St. Anthony had dramatically changed in the years since Sister Felicia had first arrived back at the school. This had once been a high school for children with stronger academic credentials, who had been drilled in fundamentals in the city's bursting parochial grammar schools. The Marist brothers and Felician Sisters of St. Anthony could often count on well-nourished, well-loved children listening intently in class every day. It made educating easy. The students climbed on a college track, steering themselves to the National Honor Society, high standardized test scores, and prestigious college placements. "In the past, parochial schools had been a place for white people to go and hide," Sister Alan says. "Most of our city Catholic schools today are minority schools. We were the institutions that stayed and tried to help. The role of Catholic schools was changing, too. In the past, Catholic schools were these little bastions for their parishioners.

"The world around St. Anthony was changing, kids were changing, but we hadn't changed with it."

★ ★ ★

THE SECOND-BIGGEST city in the state, after Newark, with a population of roughly 240,000, Jersey City sits on the banks of the Hudson River, some fifteen square miles nestled in the shadow of the New York City skyline. For most of the nineteenth and twentieth centuries, Jersey City was a port and manufacturing center. It had long been an attraction for arriving Europeans due to its low housing costs, with the ferry from Ellis Island bringing largely Polish and Irish immigrants to Jersey City for the housing and the available jobs on the docks and in the factories. Some just climbed onto trains, using the city as a gateway to the United States, but some stayed forever.

"Coming to America through downtown Jersey City was like entering a big, beautiful restaurant through the service entrance," Helene Stapinski, born and raised in Jersey City, wrote in her best-seller, *Five-Finger Discount: A Crooked Family History*. "You passed the garbage and the stockroom along the way."

For those immigrants in search of the great American democracy, they would struggle to find life, liberty and the pursuit of happiness in the early to mid twentieth century. From 1917 to 1947, the Jersey City police were part of the powerful arm of dictatorial city mayor Frank Hague, who didn't so much govern the city for three decades as he did rule over it. Carrying out his agendas with a ferocious bent, he was known throughout the East for his famous mantras, "Justice at the end of a nightstick" and "I am the law." He counted President Roosevelt among his close friends, with FDR leaning on Hague to deliver him New Jersey and Northeast precincts in elections. Even when Hague left office in 1947, he simply transferred power to his nephew, Frank Eggers, and continued to rule the city for several years more.

Hague's foot soldiers carried out beatings on anyone considered a threat to authority: political opponents or protestors. Anyone deemed a danger to his dictatorship—real or perceived—could expect a bullying, or even a beat-down, from Jersey City's finest. There was never as much justice at the end of that nightstick as there was corruption and coercion. As one historian wrote, "[Hague's] use of Jersey City's police force rivaled Hitler's use of the [Gestapo] during the same period."

Around Jersey City, there was no taking on Boss Hague. When the *Jersey Journal* endorsed his opponent in the late 1920s, businesses were intimidated into pulling ads, circulation was disrupted and a $175,000 tax was levied on the paper. Hague even tried to change the name of Journal Square to Veterans Square, but no one in Jersey City would go along with it.

Hague inspired a generation of wise guys and wannabe gangsters, a city conditioned to work the angles of graft and gifts in exchange for blind loyalty to the emperor. Just about everyone was on his payroll and in his debt. Hague would never get busted, but corruption indictments did come down for mayors in 1971 and 1991. When Jersey City mayor Gerald McCann went down in the early 1990s, there rose out of the rubble a string of clean administrations that began the development boom in downtown Jersey City. The state eventually returned power to the city board of education, and since it was no longer necessary to grease politicians and contractors with kickbacks and bribes, it was suddenly profitable to do business in Jersey City. Now, corporations and housing developers could have the proximity to Manhattan without the cost of graft. Along the waterfront, Goldman Sachs built a skyscraper, and luxury high-rise apartments rose facing New York. Between 1997 and 2001, more than 2,700 residential units were constructed in Jersey City, as opposed to 221 in Paterson, the state's third-largest city.

There is still an old-world quality to Jersey City, except now it's the new immigrants passing into New York. It isn't the Polish, Irish and Italians arriving through Ellis Island, but first-generation Americans arriving out of the Middle East, the West Indies and Latin America. More than one out of every three people living in Jersey City was born outside of the United States. There are nearly as many Arabs as there are Poles now. Still, Jersey City belongs to its neighborhoods. It is still the reason people identify so strongly with it, why so many still have a hard time ever moving away.

There are five sections of town: Downtown, The Heights, Journal Square, Lafayette and Greenville. Where the boundaries of those neighborhoods and sections begin and end is a constant matter of interpretation and debate. Journal Square and its old palace movie theaters are surrounded by several blocks of restaurants and storefronts. It's considered the undisputed center of Jersey City life.

There was an uproar recently, when Our Lady of Czestochowa stopped saying masses in Polish, changed its named to "OLC on the Waterfront," and began marketing itself to the yuppie commuters living on the waterfront and working in Manhattan. For the church, it was a matter of survival. It was changing times in America's cities. If the thinning congregation wanted Polish masses, they could still go to St. Anthony. The mail carriers had come to rue the influx of workaholic young commuters, complaining that delivery routes had become burdensome with all the Eddie Bauer and Lands' End catalogues.

The Waterfront was the window to the Hudson and New York, but Jersey City was still largely a city of the poor and disenfranchised.

FOR YEARS, AS St. Anthony educated the children of the congregation, its blond-haired Polish kids would walk on one side of the street in the old days, just as the dark-haired Italian kids walked in a different direction to the Holy Rosary Parish around the corner. Within months of Sister Felicia's appointment as principal, the archdiocese, eager to consolidate some of the twenty-five parishes in Jersey City, was considering merging the two neighboring churches. It never happened.

St. Anthony stayed on its own—and it stayed needed. By 1989, the mismanagement of the city's public schools prompted the state to take over the school system, and the wave of bad publicity pushed parents to enroll kids at St. Anthony. In the 2000–2001 school year, according to Department of Education statistics, 78.3 percent of the student body would be suspended from Snyder High School at least one time during the year. And in 2002–2003, the same survey said, only 26.8 percent of graduating seniors could pass New Jersey's High School Proficiency Assessment, a test of minimal academic accomplishment. Statewide, public school percentages of those who did pass was 84.6.

Violence and unruliness in the schools were considered the major reasons for the low achievement. In November 2002 at Snyder High School, located in the southern part of the city where many St. Anthony students live, a gang fight involving roughly a dozen students during lunch break escalated into a battle of sticks and bricks, and eventually, the shooting of three students a block from the Grant Avenue school. This was a melee that followed a fifteen-year-old boy shooting a classmate in the basement of nearby Lincoln High School.

Every day, the Sisters picked up the *Jersey Journal*, read the horror stories and thanked God that they could still let kids through their doors in the morning without a metal detector.

"The Sisters who used to be here thought, 'We're Polish nuns, we have to be a Polish school,'" says Brother James Redunski, a St. Anthony assistant principal. "Felicia and Alan had a different vision. They thought, 'The world around us is changing, we can change with that, and we can serve the poorest of the poor.' And that's what's happened.

"I've seen how hard they worked. I know how hard they struggled. When I worked for the diocese, I was over here a lot, holding their hand sometimes, because they were so frustrated. They have literally kept this place alive and functioning.

"And here we are: We're serving the poorest of the poor."

SEEING THE HIGH school for the first time still stuns people. *This* is St. Anthony High School, home to high school basketball's greatest dynasty?

Across Eighth Street, between Marin and Manila avenues, just two blocks from the Holland Tunnel connecting New Jersey and New York City, the little brick school built in 1917 stands defiantly with its off-yellow brick facing and silver, steel double doors just four steps up from the sidewalk. Above a white stone archway, two crosses punctuate the beginning and end of the rusted bronze sign that declares ST. ANTHONY HIGH SCHOOL. If you stop on a quiet day, with school out of session, without students wearing those uniform maroon shirts in the parking lot, the structure looks like something abandoned long ago. In fact, it *was* abandoned long ago. Jersey City shut the building down as a middle school, declaring it unfit for public education in 1952. There was no gymnasium. No library. St. Anthony moved into the building that fall, and never left.

Through the front doors and up the staircase, greeting visitors in the school is a statue of St. Anthony. He wears his brown robe and sandals, and balances a young boy on a book in his left hand. Above his kind face, there is a new sign greeting the 236 students enrolled for the 2003–2004 academic year: YOU ARE ENTERING A SPECIAL AND SAFE PLACE. THE STREETS STOP HERE.

The main office sits to the left of the entrance, barely enough room for Sister Alan, assistant principals Brother James and Margie Calabrese and a secretary, Toni Bollhardt, to fit three desks into the open area. To the right of the front entrance, there is even less room in Sister Felicia's cubby office space. "Cozy" is the kind word for the atmosphere of the school itself, but "confining" is nearer to the truth.

The plumbing and heating are hit-and-miss. Kids wear winter jackets in classrooms where the radiators have stopped spitting out heat. Science experiments in the labs are limited in scope, because the pipes are known to back up and flood classroom floors. But walls are freshly painted, the glass cases in the hallways full of state championship trophies and commemorative basketballs. All the basketball memories have to be stored and hung on walls throughout the school, because there is no gymnasium to display the history like there is at other schools. Upstairs, on the second floor, the walls are covered with a photo diary of the 1989 national championship season, complete with private moments of the players sharing a laugh in a locker-room mirror, and Bob Hurley holding two teary-eyed players, his son, Bobby, and Jerry Walker, in a courtside embrace moments after completing their 32-0 season.

As the school year began in the fall of 2003, there was a collective sigh that, just one year earlier, St. Anthony had survived being on the brink of closing down. In the terrorist attacks of September 11, 2001, St. Anthony lost some of its most generous benefactors, who worked on Wall Street, with its lives and companies and an economy shattered. People were inspired to give to post–September 11 funds—not to the high school. For a school forever teetering on the brink, this began to push St. Anthony over the edge.

And then, on October 7, 2002, a sports section cover story in *USA Today*, written by Jill Lieber, told the story of Hurley and the dying school. It began this way:

> *Bob Hurley is a giver. As head basketball coach at St. Anthony's High School the past 31 years, he has given 24 hours a day, seven days a week, 365 days of the year to aspiring students from the downtrodden, drug-infested neighborhoods of this city.*
>
> *He has given as a coach, teacher, father figure, advisor, mentor and friend.*
>
> *Now the time has come for Hurley to switch roles, and he's in quite a quandary. Because of a decrease in charitable donations since the 9/11 attacks, St. Anthony's has fallen into such dire financial straits that it will probably be forced to close at the end of this school year.*

The story turned the tide for St. Anthony. It mobilized people in Jersey City and across the country. Letters and telephone calls poured into the school and into Hurley's Recreation Department office. Perfect strangers wrote checks, including a man from Kalamazoo named Edward Fletcher, who wrote a simple, "Dear Mr. Hurley. The work you are doing is truly God's work." Out fluttered a check for $10,000. Letters from as far away as Germany arrived, sometimes with two dollars, or five dollars, and always a note, always someone saying they were inspired that someone could do so much with so little. Grant Hill and Christian Laettner, who had won two national titles with Bobby at Duke and were now millionaire NBA players, each called to pledge $50,000 to the school. Kerry Kittles of the New Jersey Nets had never met Hurley, but he had been an altar boy, gone to a Catholic high school and university, and he called the coach with a $20,000 donation. He had read the story in the paper and wanted to give his money anonymously, but Hurley wouldn't allow it. He wanted everyone to know what a stranger had done out of the kindness of his heart.

In the archdiocese, Sister Dominica Rocchio, the superintendent, feared the wave of publicity could backfire on the school, scaring prospective students into thinking that the school was closing and it was pointless to register for fall 2003 classes.

Just the opposite happened: People wanted to help. Alums came flooding back for a benefit dinner. A board of trustees, led by a new, energetic and imaginative president, Tom Breen, formulated a plan to stabilize the school in the short-term, and eventually begin an aggressive campaign to make it solvent over the long run. In the fall of 2003, St. Anthony had to come up with $850,000 by July 2004 to close the gap on a $1.9 million operating budget. Every year, they played this kind of Russian roulette.

Because of Bob Hurley, what could've been a neighborhood story in downtown Jersey City became a national one. Together, the trustees and administration tried to turn St. Anthony into a fund-raising machine, but it came down to one indisputable truth.

"Bob Hurley is the ultimate draw," the school's new director of development, Bernie Fitzsimmons, says. "Without him, we're done."

Says Sister Alan: "Before us, it was almost like the basketball program was unto itself. People viewed it like, 'There was St. Anthony, and oh yeah, there was the team.' One of the first things we did was make the team part of the school—that they were the schoolkids. I mean, we weren't even buying basketballs for them before. We said, 'You're our team, we should be paying for these things.'"

The three of them sweated out a lot of years together in the 1980s, but they always found a way to see St. Anthony through to another year. "That's when Bob really became involved with us," Sister Felicia says. "He was always fighting for the survival of the team in the early years. It became easier because we were doing it together."

Sister Alan was his athletic director, and in a lot of ways, his extension in the schoolhouse. She knew which referees to submit for his "Not Wanted" list with the state association. She knew the slime-ball college coaches he didn't want recruiting his kids. She knew when to call him after a player had a bad day in school and tell Hurley to lay off him in practice. Most of all, she knew that Bob Hurley would never leave them. She believed he could never walk away from his mission of coaching and educating the Jersey City kids, of keeping St. Anthony alive.

Tuition for 2003–2004 was $3,350 for the school year, with the per-pupil cost of education $7,163. The mean teaching salary at St. Anthony was below $30,000 a year, nearly $23,000 below the state norm. And the trustees had just raised the teachers' salaries before the start of the 2003–2004 school year. St. Anthony teachers had a history of getting frustrated, leaving the school for bigger paychecks in better-funded public school systems, only to call the Sisters back and ask, "Any chance I can get my old job back?"

Even as the costs of education escalated, St. Anthony had raised tuition little through the years. "Our families can barely afford it now," Sister Alan says. With 60 percent of the students' families below the poverty line, three out of every four students gets financial aid to meet the costs. In the mid-1990s, Rashon Burno, a St. Anthony basketball player who lost both his parents to AIDS, had kept a shoe box full of tuition money under his bed. He had earned it working a summer job. When an uncle staying in his small, Jersey City apartment had caused a fire, the money was charred near to a crisp.

"We closed a classroom door, and spent hours piecing it back together," Sister Alan says. "We were matching serial numbers and taping the bills back together."

After that, Sister Alan and school finance secretary Margie Calabrese took him to a bank and helped him open his own account.

"When the summer is over, so many of our kids are just glad that they don't have to work anymore," she says. "We had a mother come in to start school this year, and she had lost her job in the spring. She still owed us money from last year. A real nice, bright girl. The mother came in and paid the money, and said, 'My daughter's going to be here in a bit with her check to pay the tuition bill.' That broke my heart. The kid worked all summer and just handed over her paycheck."

The Sisters can sit for hours and tell those stories. Truth be told, they start sentences and finish them for each other. They still view their mission the same way they did in 1982, still can't imagine any other kind of life for themselves.

"You get back from the kids here so much more than you'll get back from the kids in the suburbs," Sister Felicia says, "because these kids are so grateful for somebody who cares about them. They'll try and test their teachers. But once they know that person is there for them, they'll carry that person in the palm of their hands. There are certain people around here that walk on water for them."

"But the challenge is harder now," Sister Alan says. "Because you're getting the kids who are the sons and daughters of crack addicts."

Sister Felicia nodded.

"I mean, think about that," she says. "They've grown up with the fact that their mothers were on crack when they were carrying them. Parents don't let kids out in Jersey City, leaving a lot of our student body almost living life as prisoners. The only time they get out is to St. Anthony, where it's safe. They need us to protect them. They need us to be family."

"There have been times I've turned to Sister Alan and said, 'You better head over to 42nd Street in Times Square, because all we have left to make money with around here are our bodies," Sister Felicia says.

With that, they let out a long, warm laugh.

MOST OF ALL, it was wonderful that they were still together, that they could still laugh.

After all, Sister Alan should be dead by now.

Because of her history of kidney stones, her doctor had suggested in May 2001 that she stop into the office for a battery of kidney tests she had gone too long without. Noticing her liver enzymes were unusually high, they sent her to a specialist who saw something in the liver. "There's something wrong here," the doctor told Sister Alan, and soon she was sitting in the Jersey City office of a cancer doctor, listening to him deliver his diagnosis of doom.

When the doctor told Sister Alan that she was going to die, the rest was a blur, except for this: "I can just try to make you comfortable." The doctor held the X-rays in the air, pointing to the fuzzy, black spot on her liver. Sister Felicia and Margie Calabrese were sitting in the office chairs next to her, holding Sister Alan's hand, saying silent prayers that this was just a horrible, horrible dream.

Sister Alan had three months to live. Maybe six, if she was blessed. From appointment to tests to diagnosis, it had been just a couple of days. What made it hardest to accept was that Sister Alan had no symptoms. This made it so much more confounding, so much harder to accept. "If I felt sick, maybe," she says. "But I felt great."

Before that fateful appointment, Margie had called in a favor from a doctor in upstate New York who had studied at the renowned Memorial Sloan-Kettering Cancer Center in New York City. That contact called Dr. Yuman Fong, Chief of Gastric and Mixed Tumor Service at Sloan-Kettering, securing Sister Alan a swift appointment that next Monday morning. Dr. Fong was considered one of the best in the world at performing the delicate procedure of removing tumors from livers.

Still, they had the weekend to wait. Nobody could sleep. They simply sat inside the convent house on Danforth Avenue with Sister Alan curled up in a state of disbelief. For so long, they had immersed themselves in the struggle of sustaining St. Anthony, a relationship of unspoken devotion, a concentrated, consuming life centered on the school that, even after two decades together, never allowed for a measure of reflection. In the past, they had personal crises that pulled them away from Jersey City. Each had ailing parents to care for, but the problems always seemed to stagger themselves, so that one of the Sisters could stay back and oversee the school.

As Sister Felicia saw it, "When you're together with someone for such a long time, it's probably very similar to a marriage. You're two sisters living a religious life together and you live so closely, and you're so much involved in the school . . . I know Alan's first thought was, 'What's going to happen to the school?' And I thought, 'What's going to happen to the school?' Because that's where our energies were directed."

As long and excruciating as that weekend was, the Sisters would find something with Dr. Fong at Sloan-Kettering that lightened the load: hope. As it turned out, the Jersey City doctor had misdiagnosed the area of tumors, but they were still formidable. Two-thirds of Sister Alan's liver had been consumed with cancer, but the clean one-third had begun to regenerate itself.

A couple of things were going for Sister Alan: She hadn't turned a jaundiced shade of yellow, the way many liver patients did. And she felt fine. This made a difference, Dr. Fong said. This gave her a fighting chance in the operating room. He was the best in the world at getting in and getting out, but she needed to understand: She could bleed to death on that operating table. The tumors bordered the aorta.

"But I think we could be fine," he said.

Within a week, surgery was scheduled at Sloan-Kettering. Sister Alan's brother, Ted Barszczewski; her younger sister, Monica Lynam; and Monica's husband, Gene, made the drive to New York from Philadelphia. On the eve of the surgery, they stayed until 10:00 in her hospital room. No one wanted to leave her side. She was crying so uncontrollably, they thought someone should stay the night.

Sister Alan gave Monica her last will and testament.

And that next morning, at 5:00, they gathered for a final few minutes with Sister Alan before the orderlies wheeled her into surgery. Overcome with dread, Monica rushed out and threw up in the bathroom.

"I did not want to say good-bye to her," Monica remembered. "I didn't want to believe that could be good-bye."

But Monica came back and resolved to stay strong for her big sister. Before they took her into the operating room, Sister Alan said something just loud enough for Monica to hear.

"I want to fight."

Sister Felicia and Margie returned to Jersey City for the junior class ring ceremony that afternoon at the St. Anthony church. An annual rite of passage, the Mass was held at 11:00, so parents could leave work on lunch break and make it there. Everyone couldn't help but notice that Sister Alan was missing. She was such a part of the picture at these ceremonies, at every important turn a presence side by side with Sister Felicia that the parents and teachers and students had come to take for granted.

Stepping to the lectern, Sister Felicia recalls staring out into a sea of St. Anthony faces, the bright-eyed kids, the proud parents, and had no choice but to tell them the truth. Sister Alan, she told them, was undergoing life-threatening surgery in Manhattan, and they needed to say a prayer for her.

It was almost as if the air had been let out of the church, the way everyone gasped together. No one even suspected she was sick. There was an invincibility—almost an indestructible aura—surrounding Sister Alan. She played the heavy in the hallways, the disciplinarian that belied her modest stature. But they understood that she cared so deeply, that she had made St. Anthony and its students her life. They could count on her. They trusted her. In the inner city, where so little in life seemed certain, this was everything.

The sheer shock in the church pews dissolved into weeping, and Sister Felicia led a prayer for Sister Alan, as the bright, buoyant faces suddenly turned empty and frightened.

As soon as the Mass ended, Ray Page, an ex-Marist brother and one of the school's best teachers, hurried Sister Felicia to a waiting car outside the church, helping her into the backseat and speeding for the Holland Tunnel. At the hospital, everyone waited for Dr. Fong. After an hour, a nurse appeared to bring them upstairs.

The news was good: The doctor had contained the cancer. After five days, Sister Alan was released from the hospital and began an aggressive chemotherapy program. Soon, her doctors believed that they had controlled it. It wasn't long before she was able to make an appearance at a school function, the senior prom. The kids rushed across the dance floor to tell her how beautiful she looked in her dress.

"Sometimes, my role, and Sister Felicia's role, is to be the heavy," Sister Alan says. "Sometimes, you wonder: Do these kids realize that you really like them? But they do. And I sometimes think why we can get through to them and handle problems that teachers can't is because the kids don't trust them enough yet. And they know that we really care about them. We've been here a long time and we care. Sometimes, they will come in and say, 'I've got something I really want to talk to you about.' They want to talk to somebody who's been around."

The chemotherapy was a monster. Everything had happened so fast that she hadn't had time to feel anything but fear. Soon, anger set in. Sister Alan was so stubborn, she kept telling everybody that the cancer was not going to change her life. "But it had changed her life, and to come to terms with that was the hardest thing to understand," Monica says.

Through it all, Sister Felicia kept trying to pick her up. "On your sickest day," she told Sister Alan, "you'll do more than someone else when they're healthy."

"In the back of my mind," Sister Alan says, "I was thinking that I couldn't leave Felicia alone in this place. There aren't too many volunteers to come here. I went through the feeling of guilt that I couldn't do as much as I used to do. And the times I had to leave early. And I know that Margie has had to cover more things, and pick up more things, as well as Felicia. No matter how many times they say, 'You've got to do what you can do—because you know your body—it doesn't make you feel better. I still feel so guilty.

"When I force myself to come to school, even when I feel lousy, I'll just get so involved with the kids that it makes it easier to forget about your own personal problems. That's what's helped me fight through this.

"The kids get me from one day to the next."

As always, Sister Alan would dig in for the fight. She tried to fight the fatigue, but resistance was futile. There was an incredible internal struggle borne out of guilt, out of the sense that she was failing the kids at St. Anthony, the teachers, Sister Felicia and Margie. There were nights Sister Felicia would just sit with Sister Alan on the couch in the house, holding her hand as she cried. Just the idea that she wouldn't make it to school in the morning left her dazed and disillusioned. She had tried so hard to get through full days at school, but it was just impossible.

"You come when you can come, Alan," Sister Felicia assured her, but Sister Alan didn't want to hear it. For twenty-three years, her routine had been so interwoven with St. Anthony that she resisted the doctor's advice and dragged herself there at 7:00.

"There were days that you could see the circles under her eyes," Sister Felicia says. "You could actually see when she was fading out. Yet she was fighting it. You'd almost have to physically yell at her. 'Get out of here. Go, now.'

"I would yell at her. Margie would yell at her. And we would make her leave. And that was the hardest thing at the beginning."

After several grueling months of chemotherapy following the diagnosis in May 2001, Sister Alan was declared in remission. During that time, however, September 11 happened and the financial picture for St. Anthony had grown increasingly dire. Just when it felt like she had been getting past those miserable Monday visits to Sloan-Kettering for chemo, believing God had blessed her with a second act to be a driving force in the school's survival, a biopsy came back in May 2002.

The cancer had returned.

This time, it was worse.

Much worse.

CHAPTER 3

THE SUNLIGHT CASCADED through the high windows, tumbling past the banners on the walls of the Pascack Valley High School gymnasium in the affluent community of Hillsdale in New Jersey's Bergen County. This was home to a successful high school girls basketball power, but the pennants told the story of the world beyond Jersey City, where Hurley has come to give a two-hour coaching clinic.

Boys tennis champs.

Ice hockey league champs.

Golf sectional champs.

Carrying clipboards and sipping coffee on this Saturday morning in the middle of November, an eclectic gathering of coaches settled into the wooden bleachers, from ambitious young high school coaches to fathers commissioned to oversee their sons and daughters on grammar school and CYO teams. Before introducing Hurley, Jeff Jasper, the successful girls basketball coach at Pascack Valley, made time for a brief but impassioned plea to his audience. He implored the registered voters from the area to vote "yes" on a school referendum, so, as Jasper explained, "We can actually play in a gym that's for real.

"This was built in 1954, and it's exactly the same as it was when it opened," Jasper told them. "All of the other schools you coach at have beautiful gyms probably, but over here, if you have size thirteen shoes, there's no room between the end line and the out-of-bounds wall."

If this passed for coaching hardship, Hurley laughed to himself, where could he find the sign-up sheet? St. Anthony's first practice was less than two weeks away, and its coach was still scrambling for a gym. The Golden Door Charter School—a block away from St. Anthony High School, where they rented the gym for most practices and all its home games—had its court shut down for floor renovations. If that floor wasn't finished at the charter school, Hurley still wasn't sure where he could hold his double sessions on that first Friday after Thanksgiving. The charter school had been operating for four years, but in years past, St. Anthony players were accustomed to taking buses and running to every corner of the city to use an available gym.

Home court for St. Anthony had never been much about friendly rims, but a toughness and tenacity rising out of the vagabond ways. Through Hurley's three decades of coaching, St. Anthony had practiced in twenty-five different gymnasiums and played home games on nine different courts. What had long defined the program's mystique was the practice gym it had used, White Eagle Bingo Hall, next door to the St. Anthony church. Deep corner jumpers were impossible, because the arc of the shot would careen off the overhang. Within the crumbling wood-paneled walls, the warped floor with nails rising that Hurley had to constantly hammer back into the floorboards, and the half-exposed ceiling of dangling and missing tile, the St. Anthony mystique and mind-set had been manufactured every day.

Who else would've ever missed that dump? Well, St. Anthony had nothing else. And they missed White Eagle.

Here he was, introducing Bob Hurley to the audience for his twenty-one state championships, two national titles, and five first-round NBA draft picks, the coach with everything on his résumé in thirty-one years but this: a gymnasium to call his own. The irony was lost on his audience, just like the appeal of suburban life was lost on Hurley. He never would've lasted long coaching in the affluent, tree-lined towns of Bergen County, where high school coaches didn't worry about losing kids to the streets, but rather Christmas vacation ski trips to Aspen.

Hurley had always said, "I need to be needed," which was partly the reason these clinics invigorated him. For the wisdom he comes to impart, he's always convinced he gets more out of going to listen to other coaches than he ever believed he imparted himself.

"I'm one of the greatest stealers of all time," Hurley began, promising two hours of ideas borrowed from the chalkboards of Mike Krzyzewski and Bob Knight, John Wooden and Dean Smith.

Hurley came alive, his presence palpable while conducting the clinic. For two hours, Hurley preached practices and drills, meshing detailed teaching with a wiseass humor that was pure Jersey City. He was considered one of the best in basketball in these settings, the ultimate teacher conducting class in his laboratory.

At the beginning, he promised a brief break halfway through his lecture, but that would be a waste of time and Hurley hates wasting time. He's nothing if not efficient. Forty-five minutes into the clinic, he asked the coaches: "Anybody have a problem if I just go straight through this?" not even bothering to wait for them to shake their heads, because Hurley was on a roll now, and if someone needed to use the bathroom, well, tough. Hold it.

Since September, he had been to Illinois, Florida, and even Antigua to conduct clinics. For this day, Hurley was the first of three speakers that included the rising star young coach at Manhattan College. Bobby Gonzalez was smart and talented, one of the fast-talking, self-promoting characters dotting the coaching profession these days. Gonzalez had started out as a young coach at the Five-Star Basketball Camp in Honesdale, Pennsylvania, where the roster of clinicians had been a roll call of the game's greatest minds. Every summer, coaches gathered on the sun-baked courts to lecture campers on the fundamentals of the game. From Pitino to Krzyzewski, Chuck Daly to Hubie Brown, the coaching fraternity's most famous faces took turns teaching the campers at Five-Star. Tom Konchalski, a renowned high school talent evaluator, remembered Hurley had been one of the select coaches that the counselors would skip the post-lunch nap to listen to. St. Joseph's University coach Phil Martelli calls Hurley "the best pure teacher of basketball I've ever seen."

Hurley still thirsted for knowledge. Several months earlier, in the spring of 2003, he had been a lecturer in a two-day coaching clinic in Atlantic City that included several Hall of Fame and championship NBA and college coaches, including Connecticut's Jim Calhoun and ex–Detroit Pistons coach Chuck Daly. At the end of the final night, after almost everyone else had gone to dinner, grabbed a seat at a blackjack table, or just gone home, Hurley still scribbled notes furiously in his notebook.

"He told me that he was going to be back to the room by seven o'clock, but he didn't get back until ten," his wife, Chris, says. "He said, 'Oh my God, you won't believe how much stuff I got from Hubie Brown.' I'm looking at him like, 'You know all this stuff already,' but the thing about Bob is that he's as hungry for knowledge now as he was when he was first starting out in coaching.'"

To Hurley, it was never a big deal to have one of Rick Pitino's assistants with the New York Knicks, Brendan Malone, stop over at White Eagle Hall and check out his big-man drills to bring back to Patrick Ewing. Coaches were coaches, and they could learn something everywhere. One day, Hurley would be talking about Hubie Brown's fast break and the next, he would be going on and on about something the women's coach at Stephen F. Austin University had taught at a clinic.

"It was really no big deal at the time, because Bob always felt that high school coaches and good college ones focused on repetitive teaching," says John Duffy, an assistant coach for Hurley in the 1980s. "If you didn't have a drill, you'd pick one up. Or with Bob's imagination—you'd make one up."

His drills never made it into coaching manuals, never into a book. Mostly, they were scribbled on sheets of paper, buried in a box in his closet. Most of his offensive principles of passing and scoring balance had been learned studying Dean Smith on several visits to Chapel Hill, and his half-court defense studying Dick Bennett, the coach at Wisconsin-Stevens Point in the eighties. He picked up little things along the way, and incorporated them into the context of his own beliefs and systems.

It was amazing the lengths some coaches would go to hear Hurley speak on the game. Tony Staffiere, then a small college assistant at Maine Maritime Academy, used to sit on the porch of the Coach's house at his old camp in Sidney, New York, and over hot dogs and hamburgers and bottles of Coke listen to him talk basketball for hours. Under the stars, Hurley told stories and dragged out his clipboard, diagramming endless possibilities for them. After the first hour he heard Hurley lecture, Staffiere walked away saying, "I don't know anything about basketball." It wasn't long before Staffiere became something of a Hurley groupie, driving hours to different camps to catch his clinics. After a while, Hurley would see him sitting on a picnic table with Chris, and laugh, "You again, huh?"

"He just sees things that you would never see," says Staffiere, the women's coach at Regis College in Massachusetts. "They make you feel like you can do this, too. It's not that hard. It's not reserved for just two or three legends. Coach Hurley has a way of talking about the game, teaching it, that is almost conversational. He's human. You see it in him every day. With a lot of other big-time coaches, there's an air about them where you feel like you can't touch them. They're not real. Coach Hurley is right there. You can reach out and grab him. He's just this Jersey guy who will sit down and talk the game with you."

Beyond the X's and O's and the drills to bring back to practices and driveways, the two hours that day at Pascack Valley carried a theatrical quality, a kind of one-man off-Broadway show. The voice boomed off the walls of the gymnasium, one moment detailing the new rebounding drill that Calhoun used at Connecticut, and the next imploring his audience that at anytime during one of their team's practices, "Walk to a corner of the gym, close your eyes, and listen for the voices and squeaking of sneakers. If I don't hear it, I'll go off."

There was Hurley, standing on the baseline, back to the court, eyes closed and head tilted to the ceiling. There wasn't just a way the game ought to look, but a way it should *sound*. Kids communicating, feet meeting the floor for sure, hard cuts. As much as he swore this is a little Krzyzewski here, a little Wooden there, it was pure Hurley. They heard him tell the stories of his off-season conditioning, where his players wore gardening gloves while dribbling figure eights around traffic cones and folding chairs to improve ball control. They heard him tell everyone that St. Anthony players love attacking the best players on defense, insisting, "We don't come to get their autograph."

In the end, there was a rhythm and cadence to a Hurley coaching clinic that was unmistakably his own. And ultimately, Coach K and Wooden and Smith just hadn't had the life experiences to dispense this kernel: "Now, my feelings about steady girlfriends: I would rather one of my players be a member of the Latin Kings than have a steady girlfriend. When they get to college, they can have a steady girlfriend. In high school, I want them to be focused on just getting good grades and playing ball."

He explained his reasoning this way: "What happens is that a kid is a junior, becomes pretty good and has gotten some notoriety. One day, I'll come to practice and he'll be sitting out in the car with the girl. When I pull in, I'll see him running into practice.

"Those kids with the steady girlfriends are the ones who lose their jobs, because some hungry guy looked around and said, 'I saw him in the cafeteria with Joan at lunchtime, and saw him sitting in the car with her. That's the guy whose job I'm going to take.'"

The pens furiously scribbling in the notebooks stopped.

"So give him the gang colors and I know I'll have a better shot."

Everyone on the wooden bleachers dissolved into laughter.

Near the beginning, Hurley offered the coaches a chance to visit a St. Anthony practice on weekend mornings. Just call him at the Recreation office and he would be glad to open up his gym. Hurley Unplugged for inspection.

When the two hours were done, someone asked: "Can you repeat your telephone number again?" Hurley did, calling it out slowly. Seventy-five coaches' heads were down, writing it a second time, just to make sure they'd gotten it right.

On his way out, the clinic organizer asked Hurley to whom to make out the check for his appearance fee.

Bob Hurley's answer never changed, because the money went where it always did.

"St. Anthony High School," he said.

AT THE END of the school day on Wednesday, November 26, the final-period bell ended the countdown to Thanksgiving weekend break, and started the final thirty-six uneasy hours of the senior class of 2004's march toward the official start of preseason basketball practice on Friday. With Division I college coaches permitted to leave campus beginning that day for a window of evaluation of high school talent, several college coaches had called Hurley about taking a drive to Jersey City to check out Ahmad Nivins, a six-foot-nine junior transfer from nearby Hudson County Prep.

Once St. Joseph's Martelli arrived at the Boys Club gymnasium from Philadelphia, he considered all the different Jersey City addresses where he had scouted St. Anthony players through the years and decided this was a new one.

"We're running out of places, Phil," Hurley said, with a laugh.

Hurley had been driving over to the charter school every day to check on the progress of the refurbished floor, with school officials finally assuring him that it would be usable in two days for the double sessions of practice on Friday. For today, Hurley worked the telephones to get the Boys Club to stay open a little later on the start of a holiday weekend. With St. Joe's, Fordham and Rutgers wanting to watch Nivins, he felt compelled to find a gymnasium.

Ahmad had been a baseball pitcher for most of his life, a fabulous student and a gentle soul just starting to take basketball seriously after a growth spurt. His father, Larry, a basketball player himself at Lincoln High in Jersey City and later Slippery Rock University, figured that if he was going to take basketball seriously, Ahmad ought to go to a school where it was taken seriously: St. Anthony, under Hurley.

Hurley stopped to talk to Martelli for a moment about Dwayne Lee, a former St. Anthony guard now playing behind All-American Jameer Nelson at St. Joseph's. It was impossible to see Martelli, to talk about Dwayne, and have anything but the memories of White Eagle Bingo Hall come to Hurley's mind. It was just five years ago that Dwayne's father, Brian, was standing on the steps of White Eagle mere weeks before his son made the St. Anthony varsity. It had always been the father's hope, all the way back to those long hours with his boy on the neighborhood courts at the Curries Woods projects, one shot after another preparing Dwayne for a future in the Friars' backcourt.

Brian Lee had been a terrific basketball player at nearby St. Mary's High School, a Jersey City man understanding life on those city streets, and all of that made him uniquely qualified, at the age of thirty-eight and a father of three, to see into White Eagle and St. Anthony's soul.

Hurley still remembers the questions that Brian Lee had for him on the steps of the White Eagle, on the steps rising into something only a devoted Jersey City father could understand led to endless possibilities in life.

"Do these kids understand the opportunity they have here?" he asked that afternoon.

"Do they understand how lucky they are?"

The kids were inside White Eagle, lifting weights in the basement, and Brian was on his way back to his shift at the firehouse. About an hour later, he would close his eyes on a cot and never wake up. He had died of a heart attack.

And after all the years, all that heartache, all those long talks with his high school coach on the rides he'd catch with Hurley home from practice over the next three seasons, nothing could fortify Dwayne for taking that telephone call his freshman year at St. Joseph's, when someone told him that he had lost his mother, Rhonda, too. After each of these deaths, Hurley would go to the Leeses' house, sit down with Dwayne, and talk to him about staying the course with his education, that the best way to be there for two younger siblings was to get his degree, and get a good job.

There were so many memories at White Eagle Bingo Hall, so much the essence of the school's struggle, so much the source of the dynasty's desire. It was a gym, and it had belonged to them, though they had never played a high school basketball game there. After all, it would've been like holding a swim meet in a fish tank. The court was merely sixty-five feet long—twenty-nine feet short of regulation. The sidelines were just wide enough to fit long wooden benches between the court and the wall. Mostly, you discovered you were out-of-bounds when you were peeling part of your flesh off the wall. Take the ball hard and fast to the basket, and you could expect to end up crashing into the bingo stage behind it. And forget about calling the foul, because there were none here except to decide game point.

Bob Knight made the pilgrimage just once in his life, on a rare recruiting trip to the Northeast to observe the nation's number-one high school junior, St. Anthony's Rod Rhodes, work out in the spring of 1991. In the flow of a pickup game, Carlos Cueto, who would go on to the University of Richmond, was smacked in the nose. Blood started flowing, his nose twisting off center. The game never stopped. They just played on. Without a word, Cueto slipped into the bathroom and just as quickly reemerged, ramming tissue into his nostrils on his way back into the action.

Those thick, bushy eyebrows on Knight furrowed, and he turned incredulously to Hurley.

"I love this fuckin' place."

Everyone did. The Eagle was a Jersey gym, the way the Stone Pony in Asbury Park was a Jersey bar. The difference was: Springsteen had moved on, but Hurley never left. There wasn't an important coach in Eastern college basketball who had come to watch a Saturday morning practice and dared to stand idly as Hurley and his players broke down the sixty-three bingo tables and two hundred chairs from the past night's festivities to play on the court, and then exhausted, set them back up once practice was over. Duke coach Mike Krzyzewski closed the deal for Bobby on a weekend morning in 1988 when he pitched in with everyone else.

White Eagle *was* St. Anthony, the way Pauley Pavilion was UCLA. Something easily underestimated and dismissed, something out of nowhere turning into the most ferocious basketball scenes you had ever seen in your life. It was the epitome of St. Anthony basketball, of Hurley's resourcefulness and resolve.

The Eagle wasn't much of a place for those talking big games, but rather those delivering them. Reputations were made, and phonies exposed. Pros would come into the gym, get knocked to the floor, and find out fast that they didn't get foul calls, just like the last kid on the St. Anthony bench didn't get one. In all the years there, the most remarkable thing was that there was never a major injury suffered in White Eagle. Never a blown-out knee, nothing.

"Most of recruiting isn't much fun, but I loved going into that gym," Syracuse's Jim Boeheim says. "The kids just played so hard, busted their tails because they knew they had to. Bob will just say one word and they'll all immediately freeze where they are. Nobody will flinch. I loved watching that."

"You have to be a coach to fully appreciate the respect he commands from his players," Martelli says. "There was no pausing to debate calls, no out-of-bounds, and know what I loved best about it? In most all the gyms you go into recruiting, the kids are in charge. At White Eagle, the grown-up ran it."

IN THE LATE summer of 2003, White Eagle had gone silent. Hurley had barked his last word of instruction, the floor had absorbed its last squeaking sneaker, the flimsy basket standards had tipped forward on the last dunk.

To walk into White Eagle Bingo Hall now, you have to stop over at the rectory at St. Anthony Church and ask Walter, the custodian with the old-country Polish accent, to unlock the doors. It was dark and dusty and strangely untouched, almost like a museum. Below the balcony with brass rails, there were two basketballs still sitting on the floor. On the wooden bench along the wall, there was a stray pair of Reeboks and a gardening glove. Near that, an orphaned black sneaker. Nails stuck out of the floor, the ones that Hurley used to hammer back into the wood like overgrown weeds every day. One basket was still two inches too high, and still held upright by two radiators supporting its base. It was like the findings of a lost basketball civilization, a time and place undisturbed.

"They left it like you see," Walter said. "They took nothing."

They left the memories. They left the stories. And year after year, day after day, rich NBA players, famous collegians and fresh-faced Jersey City kids left it all on the floor in the Eagle.

Over there, that's the doorway where the late Norm Sloan, the University of Florida coach, stood for an hour without Hurley stopping over to greet him, eventually leaving the gymnasium without a word. Sloan had tried to recruit a St. Anthony player through a third party, bypassing Hurley, and Sloan would pay for it with a cold shoulder and a wasted trip to Jersey City. And in the far corner, beside the bingo stage, that's where Bob Hurley used to leave his toddler sons during practice, plopping Bobby and Danny down on a soft bed of winter jackets.

White Eagle was forever decaying, but the Hurleys and St. Anthony treated it with the protective dignity of a family heirloom. It was a badge of honor to have played ball there, a staple of street credibility spiriting through north Jersey and New York City and back down the Turnpike. "Our mystique was built around the idea that whatever odds were against us, whatever little we had, we would overcome it," says Carmine Charles, a 2001 graduate.

"What it taught us was that whatever you had, you took the best possible care of it," Hurley says. "If you had a three-room apartment, you made sure it was clean. You treated it with pride. If that was our little building, it was fine with us. We were a poor school, we had a dumpy little gym, and that was that."

White Eagle was sweltering in the summer and freezing in the winter. In a lot of ways, the chance to move to the charter school, complete with a pristine regulation floor and several side baskets, was progress. More kids could play at once, more stations were available to set up basket-to-basket drills in the gym. A new generation of St. Anthony players would be raised without ever setting foot in the Eagle, and maybe this was part blessing, part curse for the future of the Friars.

"White Eagle was part of their winning edge," the talent scout, Konchalski, says. "They were hungry. When the Eagle closed, I thought that was a loss for the program. The kids had to earn everything they got. If you made a bad play and hung your head, the court was so small that you probably missed the next two possessions. It did wonders for their focus. It was like jai alai in there.

"There was no sense of entitlement. One of the greatest cancers that afflicts today's athletes is that they're made to feel special; that the general rules of society don't apply to them. If you ever grew up playing in White Eagle, you could never feel a sense of entitlement. You felt you were lucky you had two baskets to play on."

On the final Friday afternoon in June 2003, the ending for St. Anthony and White Eagle, Bob Hurley invited his past and present players for the final hours with the old friend, serving up pizza and soda in a celebration of a lifetime of memories. Decades worth of ex-players and assistant coaches came to pay their respects.

Danny Hurley never made it to that Friday reception, because White Eagle represented something so solitarily defining in his life that he felt he had to go over to the Eagle alone. He brought a ball out of his car trunk, and as he bounced it, the memories of keeping up with his father and big brother, trying to make his reputation in the family's basketball business, flooded back to him.

"Here I was, thirty years old, and I was in there for an hour doing drills, playing shooting games with myself," he says. "I walked all around, even to the places where, when I was a little kid, I would be bored with basketball, I would go in and play—under the stage, places where you would crawl, where me and Bobby would get dirty.

"I told my mom that I probably spent more time in there than my bedroom. It was like an old friend that you could trust. Even in college, the Seton Hall gym would be open, but there would be better games at White Eagle. Local college players would go there instead of their schools. You knew you would get a better workout.

"It was pure basketball."

Out on the front steps of White Eagle, talking with the coach who would make sure his son got off to college, Brian Lee knew the purity of that truth until the hour of his death.

NOW, AS HURLEY studied his basketball team at the Boys Club before Thanksgiving, he doubted his seniors' connection to St. Anthony's past. They had grown up in White Eagle, but it was hard to know if its enduring will to overcome had rubbed off on them. Lamar Alston stopped over to tell Hurley that Marcus Williams had gone to get his driver's license that day and wouldn't be working out with his teammates.

"This is some senior year you guys are going to have," Hurley snapped. "Let's see: You can either go get your driver's license or you can try to get into college. Actually, I think all the coaches are here to see underclassmen today, so it probably isn't much of a problem for any of you seniors."

Lamar just stood before him, offering back a blank stare that suggested he was merely the messenger.

At the close of the open gym, Ben Gamble gathered the team in the middle of the floor. He wanted to get a word with them before they came back on Friday morning, before the long, hard and, as the assistant expected, contentious preseason started under Hurley. With the backdrop of all the seniors' problems these past years, even the past weeks and months, Gamble told them that going into the season, "You've got some hearts to win back over."

One heart, mostly.

On his way out of the gym, Bob Hurley wasn't nearly so poignant. He zipped his jacket, tugged on the collar, and promised, "The shit hits the fan on Friday."

CHAPTER 4

OUTSIDE THE WALL-LENGTH high windows, the barges and tugboats blink past through the darkness, the Manhattan skyline burning brightly above the shimmering surface of the Hudson River. Sometimes, Cindy and Sean McCurdy just stare out the fourteenth floor of the Avalon Towers and marvel, wondering how they ever dared to chase this basketball grail. How they have come to live high above Jersey City, between its restless streets and a mother's wish on the sparkling night stars.

Now, the takeout Chinese cartons sat on the kitchen counter, and Sean's sweaty basketball laundry lay in a basket in the hallway outside his bedroom. Sean sat on the couch of the two-bedroom apartment, his plate scraped clean of chicken and broccoli. His blond brush cut and steely blue eyes looked more Indiana farm boy than Jersey City hard-ass, but in part, his family's bloodlines and boldness made his basketball game a blend of these two divergent basketball worlds.

Her plan was playing out perfectly.

All over, they were discovering Sean McCurdy.

"And people are finding out that his mother knows something about basketball, too," Cindy said.

And with that, she roared in laughter. Now it seemed to her that paying the $30,000 annual rent on a Jersey City apartment and the mortgage on a Connecticut home on a golf course in Milford, the wear and tear of constantly commuting the two hours between the addresses, two lives, had been worth the trouble. Together, they had thrust themselves into a completely different world, where Sean found out that the kids here don't go to parties and hang out by kegs like the white boys where he came from, but instead stay on the alert to watch their backs. He found out fast that the Jersey City girls at St. Anthony didn't just stand around and gossip behind someone's back like the Catholic schoolgirls back in Fairfield County, because here they were far more willing to settle a score with an open-handed smack.

From his life of wealth and privilege on Connecticut's gold coast, Sean learned a lot in Jersey City, but most of all, he learned that when college coaches discovered the six-foot-one white kid playing for St. Anthony, *for Bob Hurley*, he got respect. Nobody had cared much about St. Joseph's High of Connecticut's Sean McCurdy on the sunbaked basketball courts of the Five-Star Basketball Camp in Pennsylvania. In the cutthroat climate of college basketball recruiting, where pedigree played so much of a part in perception, nobody wanted to miss out on courting the next tough, white guard out of St. Anthony.

"They think Sean is another Bobby," Bob Hurley says, arching his eyebrows to suggest that the only comparison that he had gathered so far was the color of his skin and the name across the front of his uniform.

Imagine that, her Sean—another Bobby Hurley. She reveled in a living room chair, her blond hair bouncing on her shoulders as she moved, her big brown eyes alive. She spoke loudly, her hands flailing in the air, punctuating her stories with uproarious laughter. Cindy McCurdy never had to announce her presence in the room.

"Sean likes the personal letters," Cindy said, pointing to the harvest of college correspondence on the dining room table. Notre Dame. Ohio State. West Virginia. Marquette. "Coaches have told us to our face, 'We're not evaluating you anymore. We're recruiting you.' They're telling him that he's not just a prospect, but they *want* him. Richmond told me the other day that they want him. I'm not trying to be mean or anything, but I think he's going to go much higher than Richmond, or Holy Cross. Places like that that are recruiting him.

"Not that most kids wouldn't jump for those kinds of scholarships, but still . . ."

In her mind, Sean wasn't most kids anymore. He was a rising star. She always knew he was special. "In his genes," she laughed.

"Hey, Sean—what did Marquette's letter say today? You're an Elite Eight player. And you're going to go to a school that's going to be in the Elite Eight [of the NCAA tournament]. When a head coach writes something like that, they are more than just a little interested in you."

Turning to a visitor, she exhaled and finally said: "Do you agree or disagree?"

Yes, Cindy McCurdy was relentless. She kept coming, and coming, and coming. Which was why she never flinched making what Hurley called "one of the most unusual moves of all time at St. Anthony."

If she manipulated the circumstances to get her son to St. Anthony, well, she had her reasons. The end justified the means. If she pushed Sean hard to uproot his life and move here, if she kept it from her ex-husband until the last minute, it needed to be done. If it cost Sean academically, socially, it seemed, she could live with it. Her oldest son, Mike, was a junior basketball player at Southern Connecticut State, a Division II program in New Haven. In her mind, he never should've had to play there. She was sure of that. He couldn't get a Division I scholarship offer out of Staples High School in Westport, where college recruiters came much more frequently for football, lacrosse and National Merit Scholars. The McCurdys spent $30,000 for Mike's postgraduate year at Cheshire Academy, but even that couldn't convince the Division I colleges of his talent.

"I don't think the coach at Cheshire ever even picked up a phone for Michael," Cindy said.

It wasn't like she hadn't tried herself. When Mike was still a high school underclassman, Cindy stopped by Cameron Indoor Stadium on a trip to Durham, North Carolina, and marched upstairs to Mike Krzyzewski's office to introduce her son. When she was told he wasn't there, she left a note to tell him to keep his eye on her son. Coach K wrote back, promising to do so.

"My son Mike idolized Bobby Hurley," she says. "Everything in his bedroom had to be Duke."

Years ago, she decided that there was no door that she wouldn't knock down for her youngest. To get Sean to Coach K, to be the next Bobby Hurley, maybe she had to take him to the man responsible for molding him, Bob Hurley.

"She had a sour taste in her mouth about Michael, and she wasn't going to let the same thing happen to Sean," her brother, Bill Shepherd, says. "On the flip side, almost every parent thinks their kid is good enough to play somewhere, and it's easy to blame this or that to say they should've gotten recruited higher. We all know that there aren't many secrets out there. If you can play, you can play. They usually find you."

The Shepherds. For Cindy McCurdy, it all started in her youth with the Shepherds. She was the youngest daughter of the first family of Indiana basketball, raised in round-ball royalty in the fever-pitch of Hoosier hysteria. Everyone knew the Shepherds in Indiana. In fact, no family had ever produced two winners of Indiana's most prestigious high school sports honor, "Mr. Basketball," like her brothers, Bill (1968) and Dave (1970). Together, the brothers scored 4,691 points for Carmel High. And together, they played high school ball for their father, Bill Sr., himself an inductee into the Indiana Hall of Fame.

"Cindy grew up with it," Bill says. "She hardly ever missed one of our games in high school, and even mine in college. This was before girls sports started to be popular, and our games were such a community event. Indiana basketball is like nothing else, and she was immersed in it."

Bill remains the top scorer in Butler University history, having averaged a cool twenty-four points per game for his career. He played three seasons with the Indiana Pacers in the old American Basketball Association, and spent several checking out prospects for Marty Blake, the NBA's scouting director. Dave Shepherd chose Indiana University, where he scored twenty-six points a game for the freshman team in 1971, only to have major issues with the ill-tempered new coach in 1972, earning the distinction as the first player to ever transfer out of Indiana during the Bob Knight era.

He finished his career at the University of Mississippi, where he was the team MVP in 1975, the same year a scrawny, six-foot-seven lefty, Bob McCurdy, had one of the most remarkable seasons in the country that year. Most basketball aficionados remember the two players who finished second and third, respectively, for the national scoring title that year—North Carolina State's David Thompson and Notre Dame's Adrian Dantley. Yet few remember the 32.9 points per game gunned by that year's scoring champion, the unconquerable shooter for the University of Richmond Spiders.

It was little wonder Cindy fell for him, a long-haired, cool New Yorker who had taken a job in Indianapolis at WFBQ-FM and WNDE-AM radio in ad sales in the late 1970s. He had hoped to give the NBA a shot, getting drafted in the eighth round by the Milwaukee Bucks, but a heel injury playing pickup ball a few months before training camp ended his career. On his first day in the real world, Cindy and Bob passed in the hallway, and before turning the corner, Cindy whipped around to get a second look—only to see he had done the same. Once they started seeing each other, she couldn't wait to introduce him to her family, a boyfriend who was a nice guy *and* scored more than her brothers did in college.

After dating for three years, they were married. Bob ended up a vice president for ClearChannel Communications in New York City, and the McCurdys raised two sons, Michael and Sean, and two daughters in the exclusive suburbs of Westport, Connecticut. The boys lived a privileged basketball life, sitting courtside at Madison Square Garden to see the Knicks, even traveling to Chicago to see Michael Jordan and the Bulls play in the NBA Finals.

Bob McCurdy drilled his sons thoroughly on the game, pushing them hard amid childhood surroundings that didn't lend themselves to developing dedicated basketball players. When they wanted to go to a party, they could count on him sending them into the yard to shoot a hundred jump shots. Sometimes they had to shoot over his six-foot-seven reach—often with him holding a paddle in the air, stretching to the sky with those long arms to simulate a shot-blocker.

He often dropped off his boys in the town's quaint downtown for long afternoons, leaving them money to grab a couple of slices at Westport Pizzeria between pickup games at the YMCA. One week, Sean and Michael kept moping home in a huff. Each night they had wanted to stay late and use the gymnasium for basketball, but a badminton net had been set up on the parquet floor, and the boys were shooed away.

After several straight nights of the boys returning home early from the Y, Bob started to wonder what was up.

"Why aren't you down there practicing?" he wondered.

"Two old losers keep throwing us out of the gym," Michael reported.

Finally, Bob McCurdy marched down to the Y to take care of the matter himself. Who the hell was this to keep tossing out his boys? They needed to get their shooting in, and after all, they paid membership dues, too. So the father arrived on the scene, and sure enough, there were the old men chasing that birdie baseline to baseline.

And just as he prepared to interrupt the game, he recognized one of the old losers swinging the racket.

It was Paul Newman.

With all the money the actor had donated to the Y, Newman had carte blanche to chase that birdie to his heart's content.

Basketball was a city game, and when white kids wanted to get better, wanted to make names for themselves, they left the comfort of the suburbs and strayed into the city. As the kids grew older, the parents took them into neighboring Bridgeport to sharpen their basketball talents. The McCurdys divorced when Sean was in the eighth grade, but they still took him to the Bronx to find the best competition. Sean played for the famed Riverside Church AAU program, and often he and his family were the only white faces in the gym.

Through it all, Cindy promised herself that there were no lengths she wouldn't go to get Sean noticed, to get him on his way to greatness. In the summers, this included traveling with him to basketball camps, sleeping in a nearby hotel room at night, and spending long, hot days in the courtside bleachers, following him game to game. Sean had met some St. Anthony players at a couple of the camps in August 2002 and ended at Five-Star Camp in Pennsylvania playing for a team coached by St. Anthony assistant coach Tony DiGiovanni. The McCurdys told DiGiovanni how they often traveled to the Bronx to play for Riverside, and knowing that, he extended an invitation for them to come down to White Eagle in Jersey City if Sean ever wanted a good run with the St. Anthony guys.

Upon returning to Connecticut, she wasted little time calling DiGiovanni and taking him up on the offer. She did her homework on Hurley, on the kinds of big-time colleges his players earned scholarships to, and of course, she knew all about Bobby.

When they visited, Cindy marveled over the talent in the gym, the aura of Hurley, and just like that, she really knew that this was the school for Sean. More to the point, she knew this was the basketball program for Sean. His high school in Connecticut, St. Joe's, had a well-respected coach, Vito Montelli, who was responsible for several championships and dozens of Division I basketball players through the years, but it paled in comparison to St. Anthony. Besides, she believed Sean should've been starting on the varsity as a freshman.

At St. Joseph's, in Trumbull, the arrival of her son as a freshman guard had cost the coach his athletic director's job of forty-two years. Montelli was reprimanded when the state's high school sports governing body declared it a violation for Sean, as an eighth-grader, to tag along to St. Joseph's workouts with his mother's boyfriend, Greg Bracey, who did strength and conditioning for the team. Apparently, someone within the school had reported it.

Anyway, Connecticut was a second-class basketball proving ground to Cindy McCurdy. Some years, the whole state produced as many good Division I recruits as St. Anthony had in one senior class. Still, classes would start soon at St. Joseph's and St. Anthony in the late summer of 2002, and she had to move fast.

As Cindy and Sean were leaving White Eagle after their visit, Hurley, impressed, told her, "Any time you want to stop down and play, feel free."

To his surprise, Cindy told him that she wanted to discuss her son transferring to St. Anthony. Did he think Sean was good enough to play there? Of course he did, but the family had to move to Jersey City for Hurley to agree, and that seemed far-fetched to him. He told them to take the drive back to Connecticut and think long and hard about making such a commitment.

Cindy didn't need to think about it, and she also had no intention of telling her ex-husband, Bob, of the arrangement. Not yet, anyway. Not until there was no turning back on getting Sean to St. Anthony.

"I didn't talk to Sean's dad, because I didn't want him to give me a hard time about it," Cindy says. "I just thought that if I could find a better opportunity for Sean, I was going to find a better opportunity for him."

Regardless, she first had to sell her son. "I was arguing the whole way home," Sean remembers. "I told her, 'I'm not coming down here. Are you kidding me? I'm happy where I am. I'm going to be first-team All-State. I'm going to be the leading scorer in Connecticut.

"On the next trip down there, I told her, 'I hope you know that the only reason I'm coming down here is to get a good run in.'"

Nevertheless, she wouldn't be deterred. In her heart, she believed Sean would thank her later.

"My mom was saying, 'I can't wait. We'll have so much fun here,'" Sean says. "Even the second time down there, the whole way home, I was saying, 'Mom, I hope you know that I'm not going to this school.'"

White Eagle was a moment-to-moment test of toughness. As an outsider, Sean was made to prove his worthiness to the St. Anthony players. They knocked him to the floor, only to see him hop back to his feet. The way Hurley figured, he wouldn't have dared come back a second time without a real resolve.

Nevertheless, Hurley was hesitant to take transfers, especially one as unprecedented as a privileged white kid moving into Jersey City. He was sensitive to the fact that the mission of St. Anthony was to serve the poor of the city. In the past, kids had come to play for him from surrounding cities and towns in New Jersey and, on a couple of rare occasions, even from New York City.

But in Hurley's mind, he knew that the rising junior class of Marcus, Beanie, Otis and Lamar was so unstable that he could lose one of them any day. What's more, they had been coasting everywhere—in class, on the court. If nothing else, Sean was a threat and they would have to respond to his work ethic, his desire, his passion for the game. He knew the buttons to push with city kids, and Hurley knew, one way or another, that they would have to deal with Sean McCurdy.

"You want kids to have bull's-eyes on their backs, so when they're just cruising along, somebody shoots the bull's-eyes and takes the job," Hurley said. "Most of them had just settled in. They were doing terrible academically and they weren't working hard on basketball. They wouldn't allow Obie [Nwadike] and Terrence [Roberts] to lead, and all of a sudden in the door in September came Sean. I can remember turning around to the kids and saying, 'Fellas, this is a breath of fresh air.'

"The kid could play and there was never going to be one time where I'd have to say anything to him. Once he started playing, they had to be blind not to see the things that he did on the court. But best of all, he was the same person every day."

There was something surreal about Sean dropping into Jersey City and St. Anthony, seemingly out of nowhere. Between Danny, and Melissa, their youngest daughter, the Hurleys had a baby boy, Sean, whom they lost ten days into his life. Now, it was almost like God dropped another Sean into their lives. When it came to determination and drive, there was no mistaking that there was a lot of Hurley in Sean McCurdy.

Soon, Cindy had two of the three people on board to make the transfer possible: Bob Hurley and Sean. She figured Sean's talent would take care of her with the coach, but she knew that she couldn't completely backdoor Sean's father on the move. The divorce decree didn't allow Sean to be moved over state lines without his permission.

As Vito Montelli scrambled to save Sean for St. Joseph's, he had the undying support of Bob McCurdy. Once Cindy told him of the plans, the father was livid. All this had happened while he was at a convention in Las Vegas, purposefully kept out of the loop.

"It all came down just a couple of days before school was supposed to start, and I was completely against it," he says. "It was one thing to make a decision to not see your son for a good part of the year, but another to have it thrust upon you in two, three days. There was no indication anything like this was going to happen. I didn't even know he was going down to Jersey City to play games. I really feared that the decision wasn't thought out as much as it should've been."

Bob had remarried and moved to Easton, Connecticut, with his new wife, Sydney Emerson. Sean had moved forty minutes away to Milford with his mother, and with him getting his driver's license soon, Bob figured that despite the distance, he would still have the chance to spend time with his son as he grew up. What's more, he feared Sean would wind up lonely and disillusioned at St. Anthony.

"I had never been to Jersey City and I just remembered a guy on my team in college from there telling so many stories about it," Bob McCurdy says. "I was concerned about some white kid showing up and what the reaction of the players would be. Would he fit in? Would he be able to function socially? How safe was the environment?"

Cindy recalls: "His father is the one who kept telling him, 'You are not going to New Jersey, you're not going to give up being one of the best players in Connecticut to go down to New Jersey and be a nobody and sit on the bench the whole year.'

"I said, 'Bob, I'm not taking my kid someplace he's going to sit on the bench. He's as good as any of those players right now. And my son is not going to be a nobody.

"That's why I called Bob last. Bob's thing was: He doesn't need to go to St. Anthony. He just got player of the week at camp. The college coaches know who he is now. Sean really wants to take this to the next level, I told him. You've got to take those kids to where they're going to be coached when they're young."

Bob McCurdy knew that Cindy was ready to take it to the "next level," but he wasn't so sure about Sean. Once the father talked a few times to Hurley on the telephone, many of his fears subsided. Yes, he was good enough to play at St. Anthony. And academically, it was solid enough for his own sons, Bobby and Danny, to prepare them to graduate from Duke and Seton Hall. Still, Bobby finished at the top of his class at St. Anthony and struggled academically at Duke. At its core, St. Anthony was still an institution mostly devoting its time and resources to catching up the kids who were behind, not challenging those with elite suburban school backgrounds and skills.

After talking to Hurley, Bob McCurdy felt better about St. Anthony, and much better about the coach. Still, this was crazy.

The three of them met at a McDonald's on the Merritt Parkway near Trumbull, Connecticut, between his ex-wife's home in Milford and his in Easton. School was starting in a matter of days.

"I wanted to see it in his eyes," Bob says. "I wanted to hear him tell me. If Sean had hedged one iota, I would've blocked it."

What choice did he have against the unstoppable Cindy McCurdy?

For the first three months of his sophomore year at St. Anthony, Cindy and Sean awoke at 5:15 every morning, drove two hours to Jersey City and, on the lucky days, caught a few minutes more of sleep in the school parking lot before homeroom. Sometimes, Cindy would use the bathrooms in school to freshen up, go about a day in Jersey City and drive him back to Connecticut after open gym in the evening, only to get up in the morning and do it all over again. The mother and son made the commute five days a week until moving into their Jersey City apartment in November 2002.

"Sure, it was a sacrifice," she remembers. "It's kind of like giving birth. It's painful while you're doing it, but you know it will be worth it in the end."

Whatever anyone else believed about her boy's talents, whatever they saw, she had big plans for her baby boy. He was special. It was in the genes.

CHAPTER 5

A LITTLE AFTER five o'clock on Friday morning, on the floor of a snug one-bedroom apartment in Manhattan's East Village, the alarm clock stirred a slumbering Darren Erman for the first day of basketball practice. He rubbed the sleep out of his eyes, rising to his feet from his bed—an inflatable air mattress jammed between the living room coffee table and couch.

As sure as the drunks in front of the tattoo parlor outside the fourth-floor window of his apartment on St. Mark's Place would get loud and belligerent overnight, the slight, bespectacled five-foot-seven assistant coach would wake up in the darkness, let the air out of the nozzle and fold the bed up with his blankets and set them on the black trunk in the corner.

He had bought that plastic trunk for twenty bucks at a Kmart in Chicago, over the summer, tossed his belongings inside, packed it into the backseat of his silver 2000 Honda Civic and started his drive east. Behind him, Erman, twenty-seven, had left his fifty-eighth floor office in the Sears Tower, a $175,000-a-year salary with the law firm of Latham & Watkins and a spacious apartment overlooking Lincoln Park.

He had always wanted to be a basketball coach, always wanted to touch lives, and he had felt so far from that in the skyline of Chicago. Once when his childhood idol growing up in Louisville, the Hall of Fame college coach, Denny Crum, suggested that the best way to get into the business was to find a high school job, Erman started to ask the college coaches he had met working summer basketball camps where he should turn. Who was the best out there? Where could he get the finest education? Almost always, it came back Bob Hurley and Jersey City.

He browsed the Internet, pulled up past newspaper stories on Hurley and St. Anthony, and instantly felt a pull to the school's mission of educating the kids of a decayed urban setting. He couldn't stand to close on one more corporate contract to make rich people even richer. He had been a middle-class kid, working his way through Emory University in Atlanta and Northwestern Law a year faster than everyone else, loading up on credit hours, fast-food restaurant jobs and student loans to spare his parents an expense.

Finally, one frustrating January afternoon in 2003, Erman called Hurley in his office. He told him his story, his background as a student assistant at Emory and his desire to come to St. Anthony and help the coach any way he needed. "You've got the bug, huh?" Hurley said over the phone, touched by the earnestness and enthusiasm he heard on the line.

"Yes sir, I do," Erman replied.

After they finished talking, Hurley hung up, never expecting to hear from him again. There was always some parent, or relative, calling him about moving their kid to Jersey City to play for St. Anthony. And there had even been these sorts of real-world dreamers insisting they would take some vow of poverty and come save the world with Hurley. He scribbled Erman's name on a yellow legal pad, but forgot it five minutes later. Probably just a lawyer having a bad day. He'll never call again.

Only, Erman kept calling Hurley, kept trying to convince him he was serious. Every week, it was like clockwork. The kid called. Again. And again. And again. "Hey, Coach," Erman would bubble, "I still want to do this."

Hurley invited him to take a trip to Jersey in mid-March of 2003, take a look around, meet with the Sisters and see how he felt about it. For Hurley, it was nice to have an assistant with a presence in the school. It was good for the players, and especially with Sister Alan touch and go, it gave Hurley a set of eyes and ears in the hallways and classrooms. What's more, Sister Felicia needed an environmental science teacher in the fall.

There was just one more thing.

"Have you ever played soccer?" she wondered.

"Two years in high school," he proudly declared.

"Great. You're our new soccer coach."

When Erman returned to Chicago and told his boss at Latham & Watkins that he would be leaving to teach and coach at St. Anthony, Jeff Moran stood speechless and stammering in his office. For the longest time, he had trouble getting a coherent word out. After the initial disbelief washed over the office, almost to a person, his colleagues told him, "I wish I had the guts to do what you did."

He was hired as the environmental science teacher for $24,000 a year, a job that gave him access to his ultimate motivation: his $500-a-year position as the assistant basketball coach. Only trouble was, they didn't have a soccer team. Or any soccer players. Between Erman's final class of the day and the open gyms at 4:30 P.M., in the fall, he would have to hustle to run soccer practices on the baseball field behind St. Anthony, rustling up kids in school with plans of beginning a varsity team in 2005.

In class, Erman learned environmental science right along with his students. He was the first teacher to arrive at St. Anthony in the morning, and the last to leave the neighborhood at night, after spending hours at the open gyms, picking Hurley's brain and taking pages and pages of notes in his binder. He drove to North Carolina to watch Mike Krzyzewski and Roy Williams run practices at Duke and North Carolina one weekend in the fall, and stole off to the University of Connecticut to take notes on Jim Calhoun.

As the sun was rising on Friday morning, Erman tossed that maroon St. Anthony gym bag over his shoulder and started his fifteen-minute walk to the Port Authority Trans-Hudson station—PATH—at Ninth Street, near Sixth Avenue. The train took him underneath the Hudson River and one stop into the Pavonia-Newport station, another fifteen-minute walk to St. Anthony High School and the charter school gym a block away.

He arrived a little after eight in the morning for the 9:00 practice, accomplishing his mission of beating everyone to the gym. He didn't just look young enough to be a kid on his first day of school, he felt like one. For everything he had given up, the chance to start a basketball season with Hurley still felt like a most one-sided trade.

"The only time that I miss practicing law is on payday," he would say.

HURLEY WAS SO wired for practice, he had been sitting since 7:45 A.M., in the parking lot of the Dunkin' Donuts a few blocks away from the gym, sipping coffee and reading the *Jersey Journal*. Near the entrance to the Holland Tunnel, the Black Friday commuters whizzed past Hurley, starting into Manhattan for a long day of Christmas shopping. He was just counting down the twenty-two days until December 20, when St. Anthony met The Peddie School to start its basketball season.

Chris Hurley had watched her husband pace the apartment late the previous night, unable to find a movie on television to distract himself. They had spent most of Thanksgiving Day at their Jersey Shore house in Belmar, a gift Bobby gave his parents upon signing his first NBA contract. Bob had been running the beach, trying to get his aching left knee back into shape for practice. He didn't just work his players hard in practice, but himself, too. Always moving, always teaching, always demonstrating, his players could expect days when he would get right into a scrimmage with them.

St. Anthony would start this weekend with 9:00 and 11:15 A.M. practices today, and again on Saturday, and one three-hour practice following a Hurley coaching clinic on Sunday afternoon. Because four of the five expected starters had missed so much gym time in the fall because of the suspensions, there wasn't a moment to waste. Less than a week after Peddie, St. Anthony traveled to the Torrey Pines National Prep Classic in San Diego, a tournament that included several of California's top teams. The best teams there would be well into the high school basketball season, each having already played more than ten games.

After finally pulling into the charter school parking lot at 8:20 A.M., Hurley found Erman and Ralph Fernandez, a sophomore guard from North Bergen, waiting for him. He wasn't surprised to see that Ralph had caught such an early bus to Jersey City. "You can tell a lot about the kids' lives in the order they come," Hurley said softly, watching Ralph disappear into the locker room with his black-and-white mesh St. Anthony practice clothes. Ralph's father had been in and out of prison and ultimately deported back to the Dominican Republic. His mother's problems had her son constantly shuttling between Miami and north Jersey, between living in her household and with godparents. Only one teammate had to travel farther to get to the gym that morning, and still, Ralph had beat them all to the start of the season.

If his players wanted to make a good impression on the first day, they would've walked into the gym a good thirty minutes before the nine o'clock start to practice. As everyone arrived, they would grab a practice top, get dressed in the locker room and begin stretching around the midcourt circle. A couple of players had the tops hanging out over the shorts.

"Tuck your shirts in," Hurley instructed them. "I don't want the refs to say you need to tuck your shirts in during the first scrimmage. I don't want someone else to have to help us with this information."

The rest of the coaching staff arrived, too. Ben Gamble, Tom Pushie and Dan McLaughlin.

Pushie noticed Otis Campbell sitting at the scorer's table, watching his teammates loosen up.

"Otis, what are you doing?"

"I can't practice. I've got an enlarged heart."

Pushie turned to Hurley. "Bob, do you know about this? Otis can't practice?"

"Of course I do," Hurley snapped.

Hurley turned to Otis, a sturdy, six-foot-two senior who emerged that summer as the best offensive player on the team. He had been the MVP of the AND 1 national tournament, and among the seniors, his grades and standardized test scores were good enough to allow him to be recruited for Division I. He had taken a trip to Central Connecticut State in the fall, where his old teammate, Obie Nwadike, was a freshman starter. Otis had been a shy, introverted kid for most of his time at St. Anthony, and Hurley believed it would be a benefit for him to go to a school where a familiar face could introduce him around and help him assimilate into campus life. Even so, Central had been recruiting him on the chance that his SAT scores would make a dramatic rise.

"Go get your stuff on, sit down and be the manager," Hurley snapped, pointing Otis to the mid-court table where he would operate the score-board clock.

Hurley turned back to Pushie, explaining that Otis had waited until the last minute on Wednesday to get his physical done at a public clinic. The doctor noticed the enlargement, which was fairly common among well-conditioned athletes. Usually, it was nothing, but Otis wouldn't be able to get it checked out until next week. And that meant he would miss the first several days of practice.

"If he had done this a month ago, like he should've, he could've seen a heart specialist and had plenty of time to get cleared for the first day of practice," Hurley grumbled. "But this is what happens when you have the maturity of a five-year-old."

It wouldn't be long before his teammates began to join him in trouble. A bed-headed Sean McCurdy burst through the door at 8:45, with a pan-icked look that came from barreling down Interstate 95 and across the George Washington Bridge, knowing he was running late for the first day of practice under Hurley. At 8:59, Barney Anderson, the six-foot-five ju-nior center, rushed through the doors and into the gym. The snarl curling on Hurley's lips in the middle of the floor told everyone that his two ju-niors would've better endeared themselves to Hurley by prank-calling his house all that previous night.

As the players surrounded Hurley on the court, his eyes burned into Sean and Barney's feet. Neither had slept home the previous night, and neither had gotten home in the morning to pick up his new practice sneakers. Reebok sent three shipments of shoes a season to St. Anthony, and to Hurley, showing up without them constituted an act of irresponsibility and ingratitude. Showing up late without them, well, you were testing his self-control.

Sean tried to explain himself. "Coach, I stayed in Connecticut last night."

Hurley didn't want to hear it.

"Think I give a shit?"

After taking a long look across his players, Hurley declared, "This is like basketball baby-sitting right now."

It was 9:10, the basketball season was officially ten minutes old, and everything else had been a warm-up act for the biggest drama of all. There was still no sign of Ahmad Mosby. Beanie was missing again. Gamble checked his cell phone a few times near the start of practice, but nothing. No call. After all the drama with Beanie, clearing every hurdle asked of him to get back on the team, back into Hurley's trust, back for a final chance to sidestep the streets that had swallowed up the Mosby men, Beanie had made it all the way back to the first day of a new season, all the way back to a clean slate. And nobody knew where he was.

Who finally did walk in the door was Ed Ford, known by everyone as "The Faa." He was one of the all-time Damon Runyon characters in Jersey City, mid-fifties, crew cut, a gut tumbling over his sweatpants. The way the heaps of smokeless tobacco were balled up in his right cheek, he looked like a cross between Don Zimmer and Popeye. He was a longtime baseball coach in the city and a respected Major League scout for several teams through the years, including the Cubs, Angels, White Sox and Braves. He was Hurley's stickball partner as a kid, the best man at Hurley's wedding, and now one of the coach's deputies in Recreation. The Faa didn't just live in a trailer behind the Rec offices at the Caven Point ball fields, but a trailer with six televisions.

The Faa was a nickname passed on to him by one of the great players out of Jersey City in the 1970s, Mike O'Koren, who would go on to the University of North Carolina and the NBA. Of all the opposites in the world, the Tar Heels legendary coach Dean Smith *loved* The Faa. They have been close for three decades. He knew Smith had decided to retire before almost anyone in Chapel Hill knew.

Ford wrote a colorful weekly column in the *Jersey Journal,* are referring to himself in the third person, "The Faa thinks this," and, "The Faa thinks that." After Sister Alan fired St. Anthony baseball coaches in consecutive years, it was in that space that he dubbed her "Sister Steinbrenner."

"Say hello to Mr. Ford," Hurley told his players.

"Hello, Mr. Ford," they yelled, never breaking stride in a defensive drill.

Nobody called him Mr. Ford, but respect was respect in Hurley's world. And he sure hadn't felt much in the gymnasium that morning.

"I was on my way to Wal-Mart, but I made it to the Pulaski Skyway and turned around," The Faa said quietly, sitting down in a courtside seat. "I did not want to miss this today. Selfishly, I want someone to screw up so I can hear him. It'll make my day."

Almost on cue, Hurley let loose about a drill that his upperclassmen just couldn't get right. Just then, the stressed-out sophomore, Ralph Fernandez, buzzed past The Faa's chair on the way to the bathroom to throw up.

As poor Ralph dry-heaved his way past and disappeared into the locker room, The Faa concluded, "This is definitely better than Wal-Mart."

There had been no oversight that left the practice sidelines bereft of Gatorade coolers, water bottles and a trainer to fuss over players' bumps and bruises. In the past, the team's trainer, eighty-two year-old Phil "Doc" Miller, tried to come to the basketball practices. He soon found that he wasn't welcome. After school sometimes, the players would go over to Doc's office at St. Peter's Prep to get ankles taped, but that was it. The whole mind-set of St. Anthony basketball hinged on mental toughness. At practices, you see collisions and crashes that would send opposing players screaming to the floor. The St. Anthony players simply bounce back to their feet and move along without a word.

After being told to take a five-minute break and get drinks of water from the fountain in the hallway, one of the kids started to ask a question, leaving the coach exasperated.

"What kind of question can you have?" he asked. "What could you possibly ask about going to get a drink? *What?* 'Where does the water go?' "

His exasperation wasn't as much with the kids in the gym on Friday morning as it was with the one missing. Ahmad Mosby. During the five-minute practice break, The Faa could see the hurt in his best friend's eyes. His mind was on Mosby. How could he just not show up today?

"Where is the kid?" The Faa asked Hurley.

"No idea," Hurley offered. "But this is going to turn into the elevation of Miles Beatty."

"Who is that?"

The best freshman in the state, Hurley told him. He was practicing over at the Armory, with the jayvee team. He was a superb talent, far more gifted than most of the seniors. Villanova and Rutgers had already started sending him mail—care of Coach Hurley, of course, just to be aboveboard.

Hurley had surprised everyone when he let Beanie back on the team the past spring, but everyone figured he had to be done now. And this was the hardest part for everyone, because they so genuinely liked him. And more than that, they understood the odds stacked against Beanie.

"I root so hard for that kid," Gamble would say.

FOR THE FIRST two days of practice, Hurley planned little cerebral instruction. He wanted hard, fast and emotional practices, where the ferocity would start to shape his team's persona and push leaders to the forefront.

Hurley's practices are planned to the minute, one drill leading into the next lesson, teaching and teaching and teaching. Everything has a distinct purpose. Hurley worked relentlessly on one of his team's traditional trademarks, the split-second switch from defense to offense and offense to defense. Because his players spent so much time working on the changeover, constantly chipping time away from what it took them to get back on defense and stop the offense's advancing ball, it would become rare to ever see them give up fast-break points. "When we're good—really good—no one runs on St. Anthony," Hurley says.

Conversely, the trapping St. Anthony man-to-man half-court defense—constantly pushing the ball's movement toward the sideline to create five-on-three defensive advantages—practiced turning steals and rebounds into fast breaks for themselves. It looked like a blur when Hurley blew that whistle in practice, and the five offensive and five defensive players speedily changed mind-sets, an instantaneous transformation that Bob Knight pounded into Hurley's head as the equivalent of football special teams. These were basketball special teams, the telltale time between offense and defense when being split seconds faster could be worth several points every game.

Hurley was forever building toward something, drilling fundamentals, a confluence of his practice ideas that he had picked up through clinics and conversations, through his own trial and error. There were those originated from his own imagination and needs, ones designed to teach the game his way, the St. Anthony way. There was UConn's fast-break drill, a perpetual cycle of three-on-two and two-on-one breaks where the ball never touched the floor with the dribble, just hard pass after pass. There was a rugged Michigan State rebounding drill, where a small St. Anthony lineup would need to stay adept at boxing out bigger opponents. And there was a simple passing drill, going back to Hurley's high school coach at St. Peter's Prep in 1963. When Hurley would want to work on a part of the game during the season, he was constantly digging through the boxes in his hallway closet, searching for the right drill for the right lesson. Sometimes, he would be standing in the shower and come up with his own.

Through it all, there was never a wasted moment, never a player standing idly by, gabbing with a teammate. There was a speed and urgency to his practices that shaped the mind-sets of the players, an understanding that Hurley held them accountable for every moment, every day in practice.

"I want my players always thinking, 'What else am I supposed to be doing to please him?'" he says. "I want them on edge that way. I want them to be thinking about what they need to be doing to stay accountable to me."

What Hurley had begun to instill in his team on that first day was poise—the constant theme in his teaching. And poise for a St. Anthony player was never reacting to a referee, an opponent, and most of all, a trying circumstance. St. Anthony players didn't argue with officials. They didn't get into trash-talking fits with opponents. And they never, ever made even the slightest tic toward Hurley. This lesson began on the practice floor, where he promised to turn something as seemingly innocuous as a slight sign of exasperation into a capital crime.

Qaysir Woods, a senior reserve, made a mistake in the fast-break drill that Hurley corrected and quickly seemed interested in moving beyond. It would've ended there. But Qaysir ever so subtly jabbed his head in response to Hurley's explanation of the proper technique, as though to suggest that his execution wasn't so off the mark.

Every day in high school practices across America, kids fire back at their coaches. They throw hands up in the air and wave dismissively at instructions. They roll their eyes. They exhale exaggerated sighs. They protest that some mistake was someone else's fault, that it was unfair that they were getting blamed for the misstep. Ultimately, they do so because they don't fear the consequences. Or they don't respect the coach. Or they think it's simply acceptable. At St. Anthony, consequences hang in the air like an anvil.

This wasn't somewhere else. This wasn't someone else's gymnasium, and those weren't someone else's twenty-one state championship banners hanging on the wall. This was Bob Hurley's gym, and Bob Hurley's standards, and now this was Bob Hurley rushing within a few feet of Qaysir Woods's face, screaming so gutturally that the floor would shake, hair would dance on necks and everyone would gulp back breath.

"THIS IS THE NEW FUCKING WORLD?" Hurley exploded.

Qaysir's back stiffened like a board, like a frightened pedestrian waiting to see whether that skidding car's brakes would stop in time, or run him over.

"YOU MADE THE MISTAKE AND YOU'RE GIVING ME THE TILTED HEAD? YOU GAVE ME THE TILTED FUCKIN' HEAD? ARE YOU SHITTING ME?

"WHO MADE THE MISTAKE? ME?"

Qaysir, a bony six-foot-three, had been on the junior varsity as a junior, his first season after transferring to St. Anthony from Plainfield High School, where he had been cut as a sophomore. As a senior, he wasn't expecting to play much for the varsity. Yet he had found out fast that the first and the last man on the St. Anthony High School team can expect to be rewarded with equal credit or condemnation, whatever they had earned.

Just past noon on Friday—an hour into the second practice session of the day—the Jersey City Boys Club's director, Gary Greenberg, strolled into the gym, wearing his cool sunglasses and those sharp Italian shoes. Of course, the seniors were his boys. They had grown up in the Club, stocked his trophy cases and became almost like sons to him. Without Greenberg's influence, in fact, there was a good chance that Marcus, Beanie, Otis and Lamar would've struggled to ever reach Hurley and St. Anthony. Through the years, he had fed dozens and dozens of his kids to St. Anthony, and kept a close relationship with Hurley and Sister Alan.

Figuring that the seniors had moved past the turmoil of the early fall, Greenberg had come to the first day of practice thinking that he would grab a chair, kick back and take in a little Bob Hurley Theater.

Moments after walking into the gym, his smile disappeared.

"No Beanie," Gamble said, walking past him.

"What?" Greenberg asked.

Hurley walked over to him on the sideline. "Four years of this bullshit, Gary," he said. "You can't make this stuff up."

Right away, Greenberg backed up out of the gym, reaching Beanie on his cell phone.

When Beanie answered, Greenberg blurted, "Where are you? I'll come get you now." But it was too late. As it turned out, Beanie had gone to a relative's house in Irvington, near Newark, for the holiday, and nobody would wake up Friday morning to bring him back to Jersey City. He had no ride. Beanie had feared it was too late to head down to practice when he finally arrived back in Jersey City at 11:30 that morning. Beanie insisted that he didn't have any of the coaches' phone numbers with him in Irvington and couldn't call them.

After hanging up, Greenberg slumped in a folding chair back in the gym. He had begged Hurley to give Beanie a second chance on the team. Everyone had. Gamble. Pushie. Sister Alan. Nobody wanted to lose him. Nobody wanted to see him cast aside. He was forever on the edge, forever teetering.

"It took months to get him back," Greenberg said. "This is the first practice and it's like everything you screwed up before today is erased. Today is like a new chapter."

Greenberg sounded resigned to the worst. "This could be it for Beanie, because it's compounded with him," he said, pointing over to a grim-faced Otis, who was now dutifully working the scoreboard clock.

After two sessions and four hours of practice, Hurley gathered the team in the middle of the floor. All things considered, it had been a productive day of work. They were picking things up fast, and the intensity and effort were never problems with this team. And all things considered, this had been the biggest disaster of a first day in his thirty-two seasons on the job. If Hurley harbored any illusions that this season wouldn't test him like few before it, they had been obliterated.

"What's going to happen is that the day after the basketball season ends, we're never going to see one of the seniors again," Hurley said. "Not one kid is ever going to come back, because not one kid has ever bought into what we do.

"After being in high school for three years, and having people repeatedly say that this is the worst class in school history—in terms of academics, athletic accomplishment, attitude—the only accomplishment that could give you even one moment of satisfaction is a state championship. And nothing short of that. Because nobody in the school can think of one good thing to say about you. You're all so mediocre.

"Now, the juniors, I would expect them to look up and say, 'Holy shit, this is not a very good group. Well, I've got to step up.' "

Hurley pointed to Sean and Barney, saying, "And what happens? They didn't even have their shoes. They can't even bring their stuff.

"You guys don't have any less than I did as a kid. I grew up on the playgrounds with one pair of sneakers. I had one pair from the beginning to the end of the season, and then I'd go outdoors for another six weeks with the same sneakers before I would buy another pair in April.

"Do you think you've accomplished something just because we give you St. Anthony uniforms? Bobby's senior year, 1989, was the first time we got anything from a sneaker company. And *those* players deserved shit. Guys get stuff here, and you think it's because of Lamar Alston's game, or Marcus Williams's game?

"Do you think that's why you got stuff? It has nothing to do with you as a player. None of you have done anything. None of you."

BEANIE WAS SPARED.

When he walked into practice late Saturday morning, Hurley glanced up, made eye contact with him and quickly turned away. This was standard protocol. As part of earning back the coach's trust, the kids had to earn it back with Hurley barely, if at all, even acknowledging their presence in practice.

"I've been here before with him," Beanie would say later.

Gamble had talked to Beanie later on Friday afternoon, listened to his side of the story and encouraged Hurley to let him back to practice Saturday. If he knew he was stranded in Irvington without a ride, he should've gotten up early and taken the bus to Jersey City, Gamble told him. Still, it came back to what it always came back to with Beanie: If they cut him loose, if he lost the chance for a basketball scholarship, he had nowhere left to turn.

As much as anything, this was one of those times when Gamble saved the backside of one of the players. Rest assured, Gamble knew how tough it was to play for Hurley because he had done it himself. Of course, it was much tougher in the old days. The rest of the past players suspected it, but Gamble was the only one in practice every day to see it was true. As hard as it was to imagine, Hurley had mellowed.

Gamble was a forty-year-old black man, six-foot and 200 pounds, wearing a mustache on his soft, round face. He had played on two state championship teams for St. Anthony in the early 1980s, before going to Walsh College in Ohio to play for a volatile young basketball coach who reminded him so much of Hurley. That was Bob Huggins, who would go on to fame at the University of Cincinnati. But after an injury midway through his freshman year, Gamble transferred back closer to home, finishing up at Pace University in New York.

Gamble now worked from six in the morning until two in the afternoon as a corrections officer at Northern State Prison, a medium-security facility next to Newark Airport. Every morning during the season, he called Hurley on his 9:30 break and they talked about the team. Neither feels comfortable until they do. There was a soft-spoken toughness to Gamble, an easygoing nature that the kids on the team found was best left unprovoked. No prisoner at Northern State had messed with him for ten years on the job, if for no other reason than there was a certain way Jersey City guys carried themselves. They don't have to tell you they'll kick your ass. You just know.

"Ben and I have a conversation and the same words come out," Hurley says. "We feel the same way about things. Both of us worked in law enforcement. He grew up here and knows how rough-and-tumble the streets are.

"He can point up at the championship banners and point out years that he played at the school, tell the kids things that happened when he was there. But one of the biggest things is that he's a married black man, a strong family man, and that's important for the kids to see."

Gamble had come out of these streets, understood the pressure of playing for Hurley, understood the heat the kids can take in the neighborhoods wearing those St. Anthony jackets. He had kids picking on him, too, insisting that he must think he's better than everybody else because he was a St. Anthony basketball player. He had left the program for several years in the 1990s, holding head coaching jobs at Hudson Catholic High School and County Prep in Jersey City, even trying life as a small-college assistant at Kean College.

Yet after a few years, Hurley told him that he missed him at St. Anthony. He could use him again with these kids. Nobody understood Hurley like Gamble. Nobody could decode his methods, his moods, his daily disposition like Gamble. When it came to basketball season, he could always break out the Hurley Road Map to make everybody understand where the coach was taking them. He could reason with Hurley when he was hardheaded on issues. He could talk Hurley into second chances for kids when no one else could. Without Gamble, Beanie probably would've been gone a long time ago.

Hurley couldn't have the kind of relationship Gamble had with his players now. After graduation, everything would change between Hurley and his players. There would be a closeness for life. Just not until they left, not until they made it out. "The kids here now have got to have that buffer, because I need to stay the hard-ass," Hurley says. "I don't have a problem being the hard-ass. But Ben can be the buffer. He can have a stronger relationship with the kids."

Beyond the sociological advantages of Gamble's presence, Hurley trusted him to scout opponents, to break down game tapes, and help him with game planning. During games, he listened to—even sought— Gamble's tactical advice more than any assistant who'd served under him in his three decades. As much as anything, Hurley trusted Gamble to know exactly what he would want when he couldn't be there. And nobody knew that unless he had spent so much of his life with him, as Gamble had. As Hurley advanced in age, he liked to say, "Ben allows me to just coach."

BACK AT PRACTICE Saturday, Beanie needed to count his blessings that Gamble was still with the team and still in his corner. Hurley nodded over to the neatly folded stack of black-and-white mesh practice jerseys and shorts, grumbling to Erman, "Get Mosby his stuff." A day earlier, Beanie was sitting in his family's apartment, fearing that he had blown it. "I kind of figured he would be done with me," Beanie said.

Once everyone had changed into their practice clothes, Hurley directed the team into the hallway outside the gymnasium. Everyone sat down, backs to the wall. Before Hurley could let his team back into practice, they needed to hear him out. He called it clearing the air, and he did it often. No one ever had to wonder what was on his mind.

Whatever everybody's demons and flaws, this was still St. Anthony basketball. There was still a standard that they had to reach, and Hurley would be damned if he was going to lower it for any team, in any season.

"Mosby is on his absolute last leg now," Hurley told them. Now, he turned toward Beanie. "But I'm not convinced you're going to be here the whole year. I think you're going to jerk us around like last year. Except that if I don't count on you all year, you're just jerking yourself."

The elevation of the star freshman, Miles Beatty, wouldn't happen now. Nor could Hurley call up the best sophomore in the school, David Bullock. Partly, this had spared Beanie, too. Miles had missed that morning's earlier practice with the jayvee, and Bullock still hadn't gotten his doctor's physical completed.

He turned to the seniors, and said, "But how can you say something to those young kids? You've got Mosby. You've got Otis Campbell. How could any of you talk to the younger guys?"

Which of them had ever held a summer job, Hurley asked the team. Who had even worked a day in his life? Hurley made Marcus stand up and tell the team what he told Hurley's brother, Brian, a Recreation employee, when Brian had gone to pick up Marcus the previous week for his part-time job working the sidelines at a youth football game.

"I didn't feel good," Marcus said. "I was tired."

Hurley shook his head, tapped his foot twice on the floor and looked up at his players again.

"So in school, where you guys are assholes—and you are—then every other kid in the school who sees you in a varsity uniform thinks it's acceptable to be an asshole, too."

In his mind, this was an old-school Greenville street fight, one where Hurley was determined to keep walking down the same side of the street, where he simply refused to believe that the trouble could be dealt with tomorrow. This wasn't just a fight for the 2003–2004 season, but for the future, too. This was bare-knuckles for the soul of St. Anthony basketball, and Hurley wouldn't let it go down without a blood brawl.

"So, starting today, we're going to go back to the way it was here . . . Not the way you all would want to make it."

If it was the last thing he ever did at St. Anthony, Hurley was going to get Robert Bullock—no relation to David—to remember the drills they did every day in practice. And maybe someday, he could get him to remember the plays in the games.

"John Wooden, the greatest basketball coach of all time, only coached the first seven players," Hurley stopped practice to tell the team. "If you weren't in the first seven, he didn't coach you. Meanwhile, this guy drives me crazy. Why do I let you do this to me, Robert? You're never going to get into a game. But I actually believe it's my job to coach everyone."

Sitting at the scorer's table, hunched over the scoreboard clock, Otis turned to the junior varsity coach, Damel Ling, and asked, "What school did John Wooden coach for?"

★   ★   ★

EARLY SATURDAY EVENING, the coach's wife slipped into the gym for the final minutes of practice, meeting Bob for an old-fashioned Hurley Saturday-night date. It was foggy and raining, and his knees were killing him. These were old times for them, rushing out the gymnasium doors for a harrowing, forty-five-minute drive through the storm to affluent Chatham.

Out in the land of circular driveways, they were waiting for Hurley, inside a tiny parish-center gymnasium behind Corpus Christi Catholic Church. Just two baskets on the far ends, and a narrow court. The father of a traveling suburban team of twelve-year-olds offered to donate $2,000 to St. Anthony High School if Hurley would come work his players for a practice. They were earnest enough kids, but they struggled with a few of the fundamentals of the game, like dribbling, passing, catching and shooting.

And still, here was Hurley on a rainy night, hobbling around on a gimpy knee, rounding up a donation for the Sisters in the school. "He coached those kids," his assistant coach, Dan McLaughlin, would marvel, "like they were the Knicks." Chris could tell how badly he ached when he actually went over to the sidelines and sat down for a minute. Hurley never did that at St. Anthony, but it was nearly 9:00 at night and he was hurting. He dipped his head, the sweat dripping onto the tiny gym's floor. Two grand the hard way for St. Anthony.

THE NEXT MORNING, Gamble and Pushie were sitting along the side wall, listening to Hurley talk to the forty-five or so coaches in the bleachers for the annual St. Anthony coach's clinic. He would give the money raised today to breast cancer research, a charity close to his heart because of the way his younger sister, Sheila, had been fighting it. Bobby was driving up from the Jersey Shore, to lecture. Under the basket, the players were dressed for practice, lined one by one against the back wall, waiting to be used as demonstrators.

"The streets are so much tougher now, but somehow, my guys are so much softer," Hurley told the coaches in the gymnasium. "The guys that used to play at St. Anthony, they would wipe the floor with these kids. These kids now, they're like shut-ins."

As his eyes reflexively took inventory of the players about fifteen minutes into practice, Pushie realized that there was no Lamar. Pushie had been an assistant coach and teacher in central Jersey for several years, before moving to north Jersey, so his wife could commute to Manhattan every day for work. He stayed home with his kids during the day, sacrificing his career for his wife. He had started to help Hurley at St. Anthony three years earlier, when these seniors were freshmen.

Hurley never missed much in his gymnasium, but it was possible he hadn't noticed. "And I'm sure not telling him right now," Pushie said.

Beanie was back, Lamar was gone. He had missed practice and never bothered to call with a reason. At the end of the clinic and practice, at the end of a long, strange weekend to start the season, Hurley let out a long sigh in the chill of the parking lot outside the gymnasium. "This is the way it's going to go during the season. It's going to be like a musical group: Marcus and the Underclassmen."

Once they started dispersing to their cars to leave, Gary Greenberg's steered into the parking lot, a serious look on the face of its beleaguered driver. How were his Boys Club guys doing that day? He was told that Lamar had disappeared again, that without a doctor's clearance, Otis had remained the manager, and that Shelton had finally made it to his first practice after spending two days grieving the death of a grandfather. And, of course, Beanie was holding on for dear life.

Hurley had to laugh, watching Greenberg tearing into the parking lot. "Look at this poor guy. In four years, he just wants one phone call that everything went OK. And he never gets it. When has someone been able to tell him, 'Gee, they're all doing well'? When has that ever happened?"

UNLIKE BEANIE, IT was no accident that Lamar had missed practice. No misunderstanding. Angry that Hurley had dropped him to the second team on Saturday, Gamble learned later, he used it as an excuse to blow off Sunday's practice. When Gamble called the house that night, Lamar wasn't around to come to the phone.

Lamar had told teammates after practice Saturday that he was angry that Hurley had demoted him. No one bought it. They always believed that his stepfather had pushed him to transfer to St. Anthony as a sophomore, leaving behind a starring role at Marist High School in Bayonne. Lamar always seemed to be looking for a way out at St. Anthony, and the seniors believed that's just what happened with him blowing off practice.

Anyway, Lamar quit the team. Before practice on Monday afternoon, the freshman coach, Dennis Quinn, considered the enigma that was Lamar Alston, and said, "The guys follow him in school, for whatever reason. In and out of basketball, he's got some kind of credibility with the rest of the kids."

More than his teammates, Lamar had money and car keys in his pocket. His stepfather, Joe Boccia, worked in a law firm over in Journal Square. Nevertheless, Sister Alan had grown suspicious of Lamar over time, suspecting he was a bad influence on his teammates. Whether that was true was hard to tell. They all seemed to have that effect on each other. But the coaches had found Lamar to be distant, aloof. Over the summer, he had played well enough at camps to spur the recruiting interest of some small Division I schools, including Canisius and Rider.

"It's a decision he'll regret as he gets older," Hurley said. "He had some schools interested in him."

The Friars would miss Lamar. With him, they had extraordinary depth and versatility. Without him, they were undoubtedly diminished. Still, one of his best friends, Marcus, would admit: "He's just got an attitude problem about basketball. Everyone wants him to do it, but he just does it because other people want him to do it. I think his stepfather is putting too much pressure on him."

"He's the one kid," Hurley said, "that I don't think any of us really felt like we ever got to know."

THE FRESH SHIPMENT of Reebok sneakers arrived at school on Wednesday, December 2, packed inside two boxes in the backseat of Erman's Honda Civic. He could barely fit them in there, given that most of his worldly possessions usually seemed to be stacked in there. Nevertheless, Reebok shipped sneakers twice in the preseason, and twice again in the regular season. They furnished the team with sweat suits and gave the coaches a modest clothing allowance to use with the company.

As the boxes of sneakers arrived in the gymnasium, Linoll Mercedes, the sophomore, considered for a moment the risks and rewards of his shiny new shoes. When the first sets of Reeboks had come in early September, Linoll had tucked the shoes under his arm and climbed on the light rail for the trip home to Bayonne. Before long, six thugs came up on him, one wielding a knife, and demanded the shoes. When one waved the blade in Linoll's face, he quickly passed over the shoes.

The maroon-and-gold Reebok sweat suits were tougher to take off the Friars, and Hurley had just one request for the Reebok rep who would soon send along the pants and matching sweatshirts.

Pockets, please.

He wasn't one of those high school coaches who wanted something in the pockets, just pockets.

"After practice, it's not like college where we're going up into our dorm rooms," Hurley explained. "We've all got bus fare, and we can't be walking around without pockets in our sweats. It's not like we need cars. We just need pockets for our sweatpants."

As it turned out, the irrepressible Robert Bullock needed more. He wore a size 12, but reported to the coaches that there was only a size 12½ set aside for him.

Hurley's face crinkled.

"Just put an extra pair of socks on, Bullock. My God, you just got a hundred-dollar pair of sneakers and you're worried about half a size?"

Hurley threw his hands up in the air, and walked away, saying to no one and everyone, "This is like aliens invading high school basketball."

CHAPTER 6

BEFORE EVERY PRACTICE and home game as St. Anthony coach, Bob Hurley had a routine of sweeping the basketball court. Between decompressing at the end of his day's work in probation, and later, Recreation, and transitioning his mind-set to the strategies and issues awaiting him in that gymnasium, the chance to be alone with his thoughts and his broom was a necessary and soothing catharsis.

He would march up and down the gymnasium floor with a determined gaze, lost in his own world. This was never the wisest time to disrupt him. As the charter school gym came to life at a little past 4:00 for St. Anthony's first preseason scrimmage with Hillside High School on December 9, Hurley was lowering his imaginary blinders and pushing the dust and debris and distractions to the wall's edge.

For the St. Anthony players, everyone was grateful for a chance to finally test themselves against the outside. No one was more curious than Hurley to see how they would respond, especially because Marcus Williams had gone home sick from school that afternoon and would miss the game.

Before the start of the scrimmage, Hurley laid out to Edem Akator the responsibilities of joining the team as a student manager. Edem lived in Newark and had to escape the crossfire of the city's gang war between the Bloods and Crips to make the trip into St. Anthony every day. He had grown up near Elijah Ingram, the McDonald's All-American guard now at St. John's University, and had gazed admiringly at the pride with which Elijah wore his Friars colors in the neighborhood. Now Edem sat on the St. Anthony bench, too, with a pencil in his hand and a spare squeezed over his ear, listening intently to Hurley's directives.

He would have to bring game tapes home with him and watch them to double-check the statistics that he kept live. He would have to come to practice every day, and do whatever was needed, from feeding players balls in drills, to manning the scoreboard clock in scrimmages. As long as they could count on him, he'd get his share of practice clothes and sneakers, just like the players.

Then, Hurley leaned closer, so only Edem could hear him. "I'll get you the last two years of college for free on a basketball manager's scholarship if you're the manager every day here," he said. "If you can get into Syracuse, I'll help you get a job working with the team there. If you want to become a coach someday, this is a very good way to go about it."

Back in the 1988–1989 season, the student manager of the Teaneck High School basketball team used to come with his friends to watch the great Bobby Hurley teams destroy opponents on the way to a 32-0 season and a national title. Actually, his friends came to watch Bobby. Lawrence Frank never took his eyes off Bob Hurley on the sideline. Fifteen years later, Frank would become the head coach of the New Jersey Nets, winning his first thirteen games in the NBA.

There were no bleachers behind the benches or main baskets at the charter school, just wooden seating for 150 fans rising fifteen rows from the floor across the way. There was a small scorer's table between the two benches, enough room for a public-address announcer, a visiting scorebook keeper, and Chris Hurley, who had been keeping the St. Anthony scorebook since her husband's first season in 1972–1973.

Chris had taken over the job one game after a student scorekeeper made a mistake in corresponding the names and uniform numbers in the official book, an error that caused a referee to award her husband's opponent eleven technical foul shots to start the game. As most might imagine, it didn't go over too well with him. From then on, the job was turned over to the person he most trusted in the world, his wife.

Hillside was long and athletic, a good New Jersey high school team with some size and strength. Because it was a scrimmage, and the coaches wanted to get as much work as possible into the afternoon, they would play five eight-minute high school quarter segments, or a game and a quarter.

St. Anthony scored twelve straight points to start the scrimmage and led 16–2 at the end of one quarter. They shared the ball. They took charges on defense. They held their own on the boards, despite the absence of Marcus and a significant size differential. After three quarters, St. Anthony had a twenty-five-point lead. In the fourth, they played even. By the fifth, Hillside had worn St. Anthony down and the Friars were playing ragged ball.

Late in the scrimmage, Barney Anderson and Hillside's best player, Hensley Charles, a chiseled, six-foot-seven, 225-pounder, squared off. It was precipitated when Barney did something that Hurley kept saying that Barney was too selfish to do well: set a screen. It was a clean play, but Charles was stunned that he got stood up straight by the contact. He stepped up into Barney's face and challenged him.

This was one of those moments when Hurley preached poise, where Barney, six-foot-five and almost able to look Charles in the eyes, needed to walk away and preserve the peace; where Barney had to control himself. He didn't. He pushed back.

At that point, Sean stepped between them, inspiring the hulking Hillside star to shove him, sending Sean backpedaling several steps. Sean let out a laugh, his way of telling Charles that he hadn't been intimidated.

Quickly, the coaches stepped onto the floor, gathering the two teams back to the benches. As high school basketball melees went, it was barely a hiccup. Escorting him back to the St. Anthony bench, Hurley had just one question for Barney.

"Are you out of your fucking mind?"

From then on, it was a rocky final period for the Friars. They missed Marcus desperately. He was the toughest kid on the team, always defending bigger frontline players and taking on the part of coach on the floor. He was a presence, constantly competing. The longer the game wore on, the more it seemed St. Anthony had lost its edge. Hurley became increasingly concerned because St. Anthony was always the best-conditioned team, always the toughest mentally and always the strongest finishers. If there were ever teams that relished the chance to play all day long, they were his. Because they did play all day long. It didn't matter to him that St. Anthony outscored Hillside by more than twenty points in the scrimmage, because Hillside had pushed St. Anthony around in the final minutes, cashing in on a physical dominance that made it clear that *they* would've been the ones glad to stay and play longer.

As the starters were getting outplayed and outhustled in the final minutes, Linoll Mercedes, Robert Bullock, Ralph Fernandez and junior Eric Centeno were laughing it up on the far end of the bench. It looked like even A-student, two-parent Centeno had been getting his initiation into the knuckleheads. From his seat next to Hurley, Pushie kept glancing over at them in the final seconds, finally standing as time expired, pointing a finger and yelling, "You guys are a bunch of assholes."

Hurley turned toward Pushie, wondering what precipitated his outburst.

"They were laughing, Coach," Pushie said. "They were fooling around the whole end of the game."

Quickly, Hurley walked through the line of Hillside coaches and players, shaking hands, wishing them well on the season, and never paused as he made the sharp right into the locker room. In the coach's mind, the final events of the afternoon had been symptoms of a far bigger issue. So much was on his mind, marching into that locker room, so much coming to a crescendo. Hurley had instituted an after-school study hall that past Friday, only to find out that Linoll, Robert and Ralph had gotten up in the middle to head to the McDonald's next door in the Newport Mall.

Marcus had commanded them, "Hey, you can't leave," but they didn't listen and kept moving out the door. Just as they walked down the front steps of the school and were turning right down the sidewalk toward the parking garage that separated the corner of the school and mall, Gamble pulled around the corner in his car coming to St. Anthony to check on the study hall. The three teammates didn't see him, and kept walking merrily on their way. Hurley had ended up punishing them Sunday, forcing them to be managers for most of the practice. "They super-sized their lunch and downsized their careers," Hurley had told his assistants. "All the honor roll kids, Sean and Ahmad Nivins, were in there doing their homework, and the knuckleheads were walking down the street."

What had frightened him most for the state of St. Anthony basketball wasn't that they skipped out of study hall for a burger and fries, but, as Hurley said, "They walked out like Marcus didn't exist."

The locker room inside the charter school was cramped, the kids packed into the middle, sitting shoulder to shoulder on the benches and the floor. Hurley sat on a chair on the shower tiles, hunched forward, rubbing his eyes as his players and assistants finished trudging into the room. He began to talk, his voice calm and even.

"This to me is the lowest we've reached," he began.

"It starts with a very important player not playing today, the most competitive kid in school, Marcus Williams. Do you know how great you made him look today? Him not being here greatly enhanced what we think of him, especially when we look at the rest of you.

"The issues never change with the senior class. This is just a group who mopes through their lives. Very simply, the guys who were on the floor today, that was not good enough to do very well this year. We played well for two quarters, won the third by a point, lost the fourth by one, and then in the fifth quarter, which is about conditioning and character, we got our asses handed to us."

Hurley took a long look around the room, his eyes stopping on the end-of-the bench underclassmen now lined up just a few feet from him. He kept talking, his words still even and measured.

"And while that's going on, this asshole over here, and these two kids are doing what, Tommy?"

Hurley didn't let Pushie answer.

"Laughing," Hurley said, spitting the word out like a sip of spoiled milk.

"Sitting there laughing.

"Sitting there *fucking* laughing."

He let the words hang in the air, just to make everybody understand what an utterly contemptible offense this had been to him.

His eyes stopped on Robert Bullock, the pudgy kid with the deer-in-the-headlights gaze. "How about the nerve of this asshole?" Hurley said. He edged forward in his chair, stopping short of Bullock's thick face and pursed lips.

Hurley still hadn't raised his voice. Somehow, this made his delivery more haunting. Now, there were just inches between him and Robert.

"I'd love a piece of your fucking ass—and anybody else you want to bring right now, you little *motherfucker*. This is important to me. . . ."

Bullock stared back, motionless. Hurley finally screamed. It sounded like something between rage and desperation.

"THIS IS IMPORTANT TO ME!

"You don't play one minute. You have no impact whatsoever in what we do here. Nothing. You should be lucky there's a fucking uniform for you.

"And what are you doing? You're playing games?"

He turned to the rest of the team again.

"They're laughing at you," he told them. "They're fuckin' laughing at you."

Behind Hurley, his assistant coaches stood in a row: Gamble, Pushie, Erman and McLaughlin. They stood in the showers, arms folded, like stone-faced centurions.

"Our jayvee and freshman teams sat there in the stands, clapped when there was an opportunity today, but like everybody else, sat stunned for the last couple quarters because they found out something that we already knew.

"That we're not good enough. We don't work hard enough. It's not important enough to us."

He called out a senior now, Shelton Gibbs, who started the game, with Marcus out. Several months ago, Shelton had moved when his parents purchased a house in Hillside, to get him and his younger sister out of Jersey City.

"I can guarantee you," Hurley said, "that Shelton never goes to any places the kids on that Hillside team play.

"Do you know any of those kids, Shelton?"

"No," he said.

"When did you move there?

"April."

"Does that tell you all you need to know?

"You're the new kid on the street, and in a matter of moments after moving to a place, you should know where all the rec gyms are, where the playgrounds are—unless of course, you never play. And you look today like someone who never plays."

After another long disdainful run of his eyes around the room, Hurley finally said: "Your problem is going to be this: If the seniors here are fuck-ups, the underclassmen are going to become wise guys. And we already have an insurrection here. We have a jailbreak.

"We've got kids sitting on the bench laughing at the guys on the floor. And we've got guys on the floor who young players have so little respect for, that when they try to act like something is important to them, they don't listen. What's happened here is that we've had so much of this stuff, so many problems with the seniors, that the seniors can't lead. And there's no question that the juniors have been completely affected by it.

"Unfortunately, when you wear this uniform, people want to try and see if they can hang with you. And right now, this is such a poor relation to any of the teams we've had, any of the teams that were going to be good. Because those teams had character. And you are all so lacking in character.

"Listen, I'm staying awhile. This is what I do. Because if I leave right now, you lazy shits, guess what happens? The school closes. What I'm trying to do is bite my tongue, not take a job at the college or pro level, where I could make a shitload of money and travel a bit. I'm trying to do this, because a) I like high school basketball, and b) I think it would be sad if the school closes. But when you watch all of this, what would make you want to keep this place open?

"This kid is getting a Catholic school education?" he said, pointing to Robert Bullock.

"And that loser over there?"

Linoll just stared back blankly at Hurley. They all did.

"If Barney and that kid had a fight, what would've happened? We would've had to put Barney back together again. That kid would've kicked his ass. You know, it would be something else if we had tough sons of bitches who we just had to hold back out there."

With that one, Ahmad Nivins let out a muffled giggle, and Hurley, who had a significant loss of hearing in his left ear, knew he heard something, but wasn't sure what it was. Nivins, the earnest but playful six-foot-nine transfer, was fighting the urge to just lose it. It was like laughing in church on Sunday. You know you're not supposed to, but it only makes you want to do it even more. In his mind, he berated himself. Unlike the rest of the team, he had never seen Hurley this way. He had no idea. Back at Hudson County Prep, basketball was more like an after-school club, something closer in intensity to stamp collecting than life with his new coach at St. Anthony.

Ahmad let out a silent sigh of relief when Hurley started up again, realizing he had spared himself an unpleasant experience.

"Hopefully we can straighten out the basketball problems with the basketball players, and the baby-sitting shit with the others," Hurley said. "Because this is St. Anthony, and people all over the country talk about this school. Not because of freakin' Linoll Mercedes. Nobody knows who he is. Or will ever know. Or Robert Bullock." The sarcasm kept coming. "There are a lot of newspaper stories on him, a lot of people talking about a kid who comes to practice every day and knows basically nothing that we do.

"You're horseshit students. You have disorganized home lives. And you're going to come in here and be a great player? It doesn't happen, fellas. I'm sure study hall should be interesting tomorrow because you probably won't be too into studying, huh? Ah, you really don't need it anyway. You're all such good students.

"So, keep cranking away. Laugh at your teammates. Hang out. Do all the stuff you do and still somehow expect to be successful at the end. Still expect that you're going to win here, because somebody else won in the past."

THE MIRACLE OF ST. ANTHONY

And with that, Hurley stalked out of the locker room, leaving the seniors to consider that they were a long way from the season that began in eleven days on December 20 with the first game, a longer way from the state championship that they needed for redemption.

HURLEY HAD PLANNED to leave practice to his assistants that next day, but he stayed up late after the Hillside scrimmage, thinking, and decided that there was no use scouting Peddie, a prep school in Hightstown, when in his heart he felt he wasn't reaching his players. They needed him today in practice.

As far as understanding everything Hurley was instituting basketball-wise, he actually felt they had made good progress in the preseason. That was part of the reason that he knew he could afford to stand on the practice court for fifty minutes on that Wednesday afternoon with his players surrounding him as he delivered the best of Bob Hurley, the motivator. If he broke them down with anger yesterday, he would pick them back up with inspiration today.

He started by pointing at the state championship banners, the twenty-three titles and the fact that nobody here had ever taken a shot that meant anything, that they'll never be able to walk around Jersey City and enter into conversation with players of past championship seasons. Hurley worked the players, asking them to tell him the goals that they had for the season, for life. Everything they described was too vague for Hurley, too broad.

The balls would stay locked in the steel bin for most of the next hour. Bob Hurley had a story to tell. Maybe the greatest story ever told in Jersey City.

They were going to hear about the St. Anthony standard for dedication and determination, the story of squeezing the last drop of potential out of a young man's body, about how a five-foot-four, 110-pound eighth-grader who told his teacher and classmates what he wanted to be when the subject of goals came up one day, told them point by point, laid it all out for everyone. And they had laughed at him. They laughed when he said he was going to break David Rivers's assists record at St. Anthony, when he said he was going to earn a big-time basketball scholarship to college and when he said that he would someday play point guard for the Boston Celtics. They had laughed him all the way out of school that day, all the way down to the projects, where he went back to work on his game.

Yes, the balls would stay locked in the steel bin for now. The St.

Anthony Friars were going to hear the legend of Bobby Hurley. Three quarters of an hour later, they were still sitting mesmerized at mid-court, and the balls hadn't come out of the bin since the Hillside scrimmage.

"I have a road map. If you follow it, you'll be successful. A lot of you older guys here, you've gotten off it and you're lost.

"But if you haven't reached your potential, it's not too late right now."

There was one thing that the coach swore for sure: If Bobby walked into this team as a freshman that moment, he would've gone after someone.

"There would've been a problem here," Hurley said. "Bobby would've told somebody, 'You're messing with my dream.'

"That's why you have Linoll and Ralph the way they are now, because they don't see guys here who are driven to be successful. They see guys moping through life. And none of you are good enough in anything— you're not smart enough, you're not rich enough, and you're sure as hell not talented enough."

Hurley jabbed his finger to the basketball court beneath his feet and finally said, "This here is a ticket for a lot of people.

"And how do we treat it?

"We treat it like shit."

CHAPTER 7

EVEN THROUGH THE fog of fading, blinking eyes, Chris Hurley knew she had started racing the passage of time on her nightstand alarm clock. This had gone on too long now, a past problem with a rapid heartbeat returning with a vengeance. What had begun as a mild palpation in the morning, when her husband left for work, had taken a traumatic turn, pounding faster and faster until she had been so sapped of strength that she couldn't crawl across the bed to dial 911 on the telephone.

She lay praying her husband would walk through the high-rise apartment door, pleading privately, "Please, Bob . . . Please." It was past noon on December 18 when he had arrived to pick her up for the doctor's appointment they had made in the morning, just to find his wife's limp body sprawled in bed. He scooped her into his arms and rushed to the elevator.

While he had gone upstairs to the eighteenth floor to get her, The Faa waited unsuspectingly with the Recreation van, using the few free minutes to clean out weeks of accumulated wrappers and newspapers from the seats and floor.

Suddenly, Hurley came charging out the front door, Chris, white as a sheet, crumpled in his arms. They laid her flat on the second row of seats and sped away to Bayonne Hospital.

They made it in time for the doctor to give her a shot that slowed down her heart from 160 beats per minute to 110.

"I'm dying," Chris said to the doctor, the breath rushing out of her.

No, the doctor assured her, it just felt that way with the heart slowing down. "Just keep taking deep breaths," he said.

After finishing teaching his history classes at St. Benedict's Prep in Newark, Danny Hurley snapped shut his cell phone after his sister's call and rushed to Bayonne Hospital. He found his father sitting vigil by the only girl he had ever dated, the wires stretching from the machines to her heart. The kids had never seen Bob Hurley so vulnerable, but this was their mother, this had been a close call, and they had seldom seen such fear flush on their father's face.

Danny could tell that his father had been crying and, without a word, walked over and hugged him. So much went unspoken among the Hurley men, so much understood in strong silence. It wasn't long until the three kids reached the hospital: Danny, Bobby and Melissa. Outside of the summer and holidays, it was so rare for everyone to be together.

Bobby, thirty-two, lived in Colts Neck, on the Jersey Shore, and he had planned to drive up the Turnpike that day to scout the Knicks game at Madison Square Garden, in his new job with the Philadelphia 76ers. After four years as an assistant coach at Rutgers, Danny, thirty, had been the coach for three seasons at St. Benedict's, where he had introduced a perennial soccer and fencing power into the world of big-time high school basketball. Melissa, twenty-four, was a schoolteacher in Jersey City and lived with her parents in the waterfront high-rise.

Bob called his wife "Red," because of her carrot-colored short hair. She was a Polish girl, Christine Ledzion, out of Sacred Heart Parish, a kindergarten teacher at Public School No. 6 in Jersey City. They met at a party near St. Paul's grammar school in Greenville, started dating when he was a freshman at St. Peter's College and she was still a high school senior. Neither had ever had a steady before, nor would they ever again. On one of the first dates they ever had, Hurley took her to watch him coach his younger brother's team at St. Paul's Parish. They would get married after college, move into the back apartment of his parents' house on Linden Avenue, and start a life together.

Chris had lived a basketball life with Bob, following him to camps and clinics and basketball games the whole way. She spent her summer vacationing at the camps he ran in the Pocono Mountains of Pennsylvania, upstate New York and Rhode Island. She spent a lot of nights sitting in the bleachers of Jersey City summer basketball leagues, and sitting in the sweatbox of White Eagle, watching Bob work Bobby and Danny to the bone.

They did everything, and went everywhere together. Now grandparents in their mid-fifties, they were like love-sick teenagers. Beside her bed in Bayonne Hospital, the prospect of a world without his Christine was too terrible to imagine.

"I learned the importance of the relationship with your spouse from what I saw with my dad," Hurley says. "If he wasn't working, he was in the house. Every consideration went to the family."

Basketball consumed him 365 days a year, but it was what they did together. This was the family business. The coach's father had taught him that when work was over, there was no stopping for a drink, no nights playing cards with the boys. The lessons that his father passed down deeply shaped the life he and his wife had together, the life they wanted for their children.

An ever-present worn, faded basketball under his arm, his scuffed canvas Chuck Taylors on his feet, a teenaged Bob Hurley every so often slipped unnoticed into the back row of the Municipal Court on Montgomery Street in the early 1960s. He rested his chin on the wooden chair backs and fixed his eyes on his father, beside the judge's bench. Bob Hurley Sr. was a beat cop out of the seventh precinct with an uncanny acumen for city statutes, the only police officer in the state of New Jersey to be appointed a court clerk. From the back of the room, the oldest of his four children—three boys and a girl—watched Robert Patrick Hurley Sr. running courtroom traffic, navigating everyone, from the judges to the attorneys to defendants brought before the court.

As a young man, Bob Sr. had dreams of practicing law and playing professional baseball. Before leaving for World War II, he had been a semipro pitcher and began work on his undergraduate degree. After making it home, he had to abandon both dreams and go to work. His first job was a pressman for the *Hoboken Observer*. When the paper closed, he worked on the docks in Elizabeth, before passing his entrance exam for the Jersey City police force. He would work for forty years in different jobs on the force, building a reputation that would distance itself from Jersey City's dark past.

If Boss Hague's twisted police state had been the prism in which Bob Hurley Sr. witnessed the cop's role in the community, he wouldn't let it define his own value system. He believed the police had a responsibility to reach down to people with a helping hand, not a raised one. When Officer Hurley came around the corner, he didn't want to inspire fear, but respect. And compassion. "All Bob ever wanted to be was someone just like his father," Chris says. "He wanted to stay in the city and help."

Bob Sr., married Eleanor O'Brien in 1945, and they had Robert Patrick Jr. in 1947. Next came Sheila in 1950, Brian in '52 and Tim in '56. He never had a chance to go back to school to finish his undergraduate work—never mind chase a law degree. Ultimately, his true calling on the force came assigned to the courthouse.

When Bob Sr. worked his second job, nights, driving a high-low at a freezer near the Holland Tunnel, he was still on call at the courthouse. If someone had been arrested, they still needed him to write out search warrants. There was no such thing as an off-duty cop in those days, especially in the Hurley household.

If help was needed, they sought out Bob Sr. Even the squirrelly guys in the neighborhood knew that if they found themselves in lockup, they could count on him stopping by the cell with a cup of coffee, a pack of cigarettes, or just a reassuring word. Every arrest in the city had to come through him at the municipal court for arraignment, so little made it past his watch. Often, he talked judges into lowering bail for those incarcerated, especially when Bob Sr. knew it was someone worth cutting some slack.

"Even the hoboes in the neighborhood would be marching to the rectory at St. Paul's, for the soup kitchen there, and you'd find my father along the way, helping them out with something," Brian Hurley says.

What stayed with Bob Jr. was his father's relentless devotion to service. For most of the son's later life in Jersey City, there was rarely a day that passed when someone didn't stop and tell him of something his father had done to touch him years ago.

An agreeable, reserved man, Bob Sr. had three indulgences: Notre Dame football, Joe Namath, and his unfiltered Chesterfields. They would have grilled cheese or tuna sandwiches on Friday nights, and a formal meal on Saturdays in the house. The fate of the roast beef and turkey for the weekend dinners rested with the final score of the Fighting Irish game. If they lost, they could count on bulky, uneven cuts of meat on the serving plate. "He'd cut big chunks out of the thing," Brian says. "It didn't matter if it was roast beef or a turkey, you could see him take his frustrations out on it."

For Eleanor Hurley, it was a most modest flaw in her husband. What mattered most to her was that the family stayed together. As a young girl, she had lost her own mother, which led to the scattering of Eleanor and her four siblings to different homes. Eleanor and one sister lived with an aunt, and another sister and two brothers lived with the father. It wasn't until she was older that her father was able to raise the five children together. Eleanor Hurley worked two part-time jobs, in the evenings and weekends, to help pay the tuition for the boys to attend private high school.

She worked at Bambergers, a big department store in Newark, until

Bob started high school. After that, she worked part-time as a nurse at the Roosevelt Stadium ice skating rink in Jersey City. For wintertime skating, it cost fifty cents for the kids to store their shoes behind the main desk, and fifty cents for a hot chocolate and donut at the food stand. She hated to see the kids have to make that choice with two quarters in their pockets. When Eleanor was on the clock, her boss would get all riled up to find fifteen or twenty pairs of children's dirty sneakers and shoes stashed in her office.

"Meanwhile, that place was going broke," Brian says, "but all the kids were eating donuts and drinking hot chocolate. That's just the way the old neighborhood worked."

The old neighborhood would always be Greenville for the oldest boy. Greenville was where Hurley learned to shoot a jump shot watching George Blaney and Mike Rooney on the playgrounds. Greenville was where he coached his first basketball team, the grammar school boys at St. Paul's, who included his younger brother, Brian. After playing freshman basketball for St. Peter's College in 1966, George Newcombe, a fireman, could no longer coach St. Paul's, and asked Brian to check with his brother, Bob, and see if it interested him. A lot of winter days, when the gym was being used, they shoveled the snow off the outdoor courts at St. Paul's and practiced in dungarees and sneakers. "The balls wouldn't even bounce, it was so cold," Brian remembers. "We didn't know how to win. Really, we didn't know how to play. He taught us. And he made us city champs."

After school, Greenville was where you declared yourself as one of two kinds of guys: Either you wore dress shoes outside the candy store and tried to meet girls, or you wore canvas Chuck Taylors and headed for the park to play ball. Once, Greenville was where a kid believed that the worst that could happen to him walking its streets was squaring off in a fistfight. In those days, for boys on the brink of manhood, Greenville played the part of a protective apron.

One August night in 1966, an eighteen-year-old Hurley left Chris's house on Wegman Parkway, planning to cross over Jackson Avenue on his way home. A squad car pulled over, the cop telling him to climb into the backseat. The Newark race riots had spilled over into the streets of Jersey City, and that was no night for an Irish kid to be walking back to Greenville.

"In a lot of ways, the times had no impact on me," Hurley says now. "I was playing basketball. The whole Snyder High School team at that time was becoming primarily black, and they were all the kids I played with in Audubon Park and in the No. 40 School. It was a time of unrest—a lot of drugs, a lot of experimentation, political unrest, and racial turmoil. I missed it all. I was still walking up and down the street going to gyms.

"For me, I knew I had to be ready to fight on the street, but that was my revelation about what was going on in the world beyond Greenville."

Bob Hurley had grown up largely unaware of the sordid state of race relations in Newark, let alone Cordele, Georgia, out of where an abusive stepfather and the Ku Klux Klan's evil shadow chased Bill Denmark and his family to Linden Avenue in Greenville. It was midnight in Georgia when Bill's mother stirred her three children and told them to gather their belongings, pack it all into the car and never look back. When Bill's stepfather sobered up that next day, his wife and her children were long gone from little Cordele, a segregated town about fifteen miles north of Albany, Georgia.

In the mid-1950s, the Klan guaranteed the blood of blacks who were found crossing the train tracks running through the middle of town. "We wouldn't dare get caught on the white side of town," Denmark says. Cordele had been the last gasp of the Confederacy, the town where the state's war governor hid in a farmhouse to sidestep the fury of Sherman's March to the Sea. These days, the Chamber of Commerce declared Cordele "The Watermelon Capital of the World," but Bill Denmark's Cordele resembled nothing so sweet and innocent.

The Denmarks moved into a family friend's house on Linden Avenue, a neighborhood where second-generation Italians and Irish predominated in the two- and three-family structures.

Ten years old, and a promising athlete, young Bill mustered the courage to wander toward the youthful voices on Linden. Before long, the most competitive kid on the block had sniffed the talent out. They were choosing teams for a pickup basketball game, when the strangest thing happened to Denmark: With his first pick, Bob Hurley passed on his brothers, Brian and Tim, and picked him. Before long, nobody would let them play on the same team. Whatever the game—basketball, box-ball, stickball—they were designated the two captains, charged with choosing the players and balancing out the sides.

"When I got here from Georgia, it was a new world," Denmark says. "I had never played with white kids in my life—had never even been around white people in my life—and here was this totally white neighborhood where it wasn't about black or white. It was about sport. There was no segregation on this block, except for those who could hit the ball and those who couldn't. When Bob chose a team, it wasn't on the basis of color, but on ability. His whole intensity was about winning."

Through the years, Denmark kept a soft spot for Hurley's two younger brothers, Brian and Tim. Something was always festering within Bob, manifesting itself in a fury that left him with little patience for his siblings' failures and missteps. For the rest of his life, Bob Hurley never found use for those who didn't care about winning like he did, who refused to pay the price necessary to do it. "His brothers would rather play with me than with him, that's for sure," Denmark says. "If they struck out on my side, I wouldn't throw the ball at them. I used to get mad at Bob. I wished he had more compassion for his brothers."

Then and now, winning consumed him. As much as anything, that bonded them. They would go everywhere together, even if it meant that Denmark's black friends teased him for his relationships with the white kids on Linden.

They would smuggle grapes and apples out of old man Palumbo's orchards, drop a nickel on the counter of the Bergen Bakery for a cookie, and play in the brush on Society Hill. Denmark never did tell Hurley the story of his life before Jersey City when they were kids, but it was something he thought a lot about later in life, especially when he brought his own grandchildren back there. Bill Denmark always told the kids about a time and a place in his life that grew with fondness through the years, that maybe it was the best thing that ever happened to him.

"Bob Hurley will always be a friend of mine, because he could've turned those people against me on Linden Avenue," he says. "A lot of those kids would've flipped against me. He had that power. He was the best athlete. He had the power to make that a racist situation, but it was never about that with him. Bob was always about one thing: winning."

THAT WEDNESDAY AFTERNOON, while Hurley was with his family at Bayonne Hospital, Gamble told the players that they would scrimmage Manchester and Englewood high schools in a three-way game—two teams on, one off per quarter—without Hurley there.

"Mrs. Hurley has taken ill," Gamble said.

Hearing the news, Marcus walked down to the supply closet, pulled out the broom and started sweeping the court. He grew up in the Greenville section of Jersey City, the toughest, most competitive kid in his neighborhood the way Hurley had been in his Greenville neighborhood. They just came out of different times, different circumstances. In the history of St. Anthony basketball, there were few kids who confounded Hurley more, whom the coach saw so much of himself in, and yet felt like he hadn't reached beyond basketball.

Even so, this was to be one of those quiet moments when Marcus tried to be the leader, the man, that Bob Hurley wanted him to be.

THIRTY FEET AWAY from the basketball courts at the Curries Woods housing projects in Greenville, between the swings and seesaws, a young black woman closed her eyes, took a long drag from her joint, and held the smoke in her lungs before exhaling.

The smoke carried in the breeze, blowing past her baby cooing in a carriage. Marcus Williams never noticed her, nor the two men she passed the pot to when she was done. All alone on the court, Marcus was concentrating. He balanced a basketball on the palm of his hand, his upper arm bent parallel with the ground. This was the way Hurley taught him to practice his shooting form, starting five feet from the basket, shooting it with one arm to exaggerate the proper form. And then work your way back.

Maybe it was a little late, but Marcus was trying to make up for lost time, trying to take the teachings of Hurley to heart. In a lot of ways for the coach, Marcus had been one of the greatest enigmas that had ever come through St. Anthony. There were times that Marcus was everything that Hurley ever wanted out of one of his basketball players, and times Marcus was everything that he didn't want. "He could've been so much better," Hurley says. "I know that he knows it, and he knows that I know it." For Hurley to feel like he was failing to get the most out of a player—the most out of a young man—was always the biggest coaching bane for him.

There was just an unspoken nobility about Marcus, an announcement of pure presence—as much about his deep, sullen eyes, as those thick biceps. "Put Marcus on the street corner, and pound for pound, he's the toughest kid in Greenville," Gary Greenberg says. The Boys Club director's favorite memory of Marcus was of him standing outside of a van in the Bronx, challenging an entire gang of New York kids giving grief to his teammates. The Boys Club team had gone to the Bronx, won a basketball game, and someone wanted to start something with the Jersey City team for the audacity. Marcus Williams invited the whole lot of them to start with him, and see if they could even make it to his teammates.

They took one look at him, and decided to beat it.

Among the top seniors—Beanie, Otis and Lamar—Marcus was the player who never flinched in the face of Hurley's hellacious coaching style. Otis and Lamar came close to quitting as sophomores and juniors, and Beanie would leave the team. "If your mind ain't right, he'll get in your head," Otis says. "I know he's got in my head a lot of times."

Marcus had the toughest shell. To him, Hurley's relentless testing of his players' will was almost a game. He relished it. Deep down, he reveled in Hurley pushing him. Deep down, he was desperate for the challenge. "Marcus walked over everyone else in his life," Greenberg says. "His teachers at school. He's been running his own house for a while now. I'm not sure his mother really gets in his face on anything. But Coach Hurley always showed him the line, and he craved that."

He was a chiseled six-foot-two, 190 pounds, a promising quarterback and pitcher in his younger days. For two hours a day, in practice, he was the smartest, toughest and most disciplined kid in the St. Anthony gymnasium. He didn't just remember where he needed to be on the floor, but where every one of his teammates needed to be, too. He knew every play, from every position. From top to bottom, he committed scouting reports to memory. He could defend much bigger and stronger players using the angles on the floor, coupled with a natural tenacity that overcame his lack of significant height. He had a real sense of anticipation, always getting steals and deflections largely because he could see a play developing before anyone else.

Four years earlier, Marcus Williams was going to be the next great St. Anthony player. He was a freshman starting on the varsity Tournament of Champions, certain to be the next Jersey City star to climb into the rarefied air of St. Anthony's five first-round NBA Draft picks: Bobby Hurley, David Rivers, Terry Dehere, Rod Rhodes and Roshown McLeod. Historically, starting as a freshman at St. Anthony had been a ticket to stardom. Before he arrived at St. Anthony, Marcus was something of a cult figure in New Jersey high school basketball lore.

Those legs had such spring, such life. As a kid, Marcus leaped so high into the air that they thought he would catch himself on a star and hang there. He had a mythical reputation on the Boys Club AAU circuit, where, Otis swears, "You could throw the ball up over the rim, he would go get it and slam it. He would dunk on bigger people. We threw him lobs on inbounds plays in the eighth grade.

"But," he adds, "he was hungrier then."

One high school scouting service wrote that as a freshman, Marcus was *"the cream of the crop for the class of 2004. The kid has a combination of basket-ball skills that you don't normally see in freshmen. Many 14-year-old AAU bas-ketball teams would stop in awe as Marcus dunked in layup lines. Marcus plays above the rim, and not just in layups! Just ask a few of the kids he dunked on about that!"*

Over the rest of his school career, something changed. The drive inside Marcus dulled; partly because there was no one pushing him at home, and partly because it just seemed he moved past high school before he was done. He had an older girlfriend, Shameka, who was an upperclass-man at St. Peter's College. The coaches said he was seventeen going on twenty-three. Sometimes, there just didn't seem to be much kid left in Marcus.

"Kids can get into two worlds," Hurley would say. "The world of gangs, hanging out with the guys, or settling into a relationship with a woman where they start acting like adults. He was living like he was grown up with a college girlfriend, and he lost some of the hungriness to just be playing ball all the time."

Those were Hurley's words when he knew just part of the story of his life, and Marcus made sure the complete truth stayed with him. There was something else that Marcus couldn't tell Hurley. He just couldn't. But he didn't live basketball like he had as a kid. Once, he spent every waking hour working on shots, playing pickup ball and keeping those legs strong. Now, away from Hurley and St. Anthony, Marcus seemed to do just enough to get by. He was probably on his way to an All-State senior year, but that wouldn't do justice to what Marcus could've been.

"I never listened enough to coach," he says now. "When I was a fresh-man, I had a lot of success real fast and I'd be going into New York to play AAU basketball, but I was never really working on my game. I don't shoot the way I should have been shooting."

By his junior year, Marcus struggled to dunk with no one between him and the basket, a far cry from the old days when he could do it in his sleep.

Gathering his ball and carrying it to the bottom row of the metal bleachers, Marcus sat down and nodded into the distance. "The hustlers watched out for me here," he said. "They didn't want to see me in nothing bad. I think they would've beat me up."

Before the city tore down six of the seven high-rise apartments in the past few years, Curries Woods had been a playground for dealers and thugs. It used to seem like there was a shooting, a stabbing, a beat-down every night. Pushers filled the halls, strung-out hookers servicing johns in the shadowy corners.

"At one time, Curries Woods was the most prolific site for criminal activity," Hudson County prosecutor Ed DeFazio says. "Notorious. I don't think the stories about Curries Woods can be exaggerated. It was a disaster. Every year, there were just so many drugs, so much violence, so many homicides out of there."

Back in the mid-eighties, St. Anthony basketball and baseball star Willie Banks, a hard-throwing right-hander who would be the first-round pick of the Minnesota Twins, was struggling to get back into one of the high-rises at night, when a gang of older thugs, smacking him around and teasing him, insisted that his St. Anthony jacket must have made him think he was something special. Bobby Hurley had gone with him once into the high-rises, and never again. "Worse than anything you could ever imagine," Bobby says.

When Bob Hurley found out what was happening to Willie on the way home, he decided to give him a ride himself. By the doorway, the same crew was waiting for them. Hurley walked up, and told them to spread the word in Curries Woods that anybody who wanted to give Willie Banks a hard time would need to give Bob Hurley a hard time. Beyond that, they could expect Hurley, the probation officer, to start checking the court dockets for outstanding warrants. Hurley stood a little longer in the doorway, stared them down and left Banks to hustle upstairs into his apartment.

They never bothered Banks again.

"There are still nights when I get off the bus and walk home, when I think to myself that I could be dead before I get to the door," Marcus says. He was sitting on the metal stands next to the basketball court now, looking out at the projects. "I just think that someone could start shooting. I still get off that bus and think that this is the day someone is going to get me. That I won't get home."

The city left one high-rise standing, renovating it so ninety-one senior citizens could live there. The buildings used to be lined up, thirteen floors high, seven in a row. After a $32 million revitalization grant, the housing authority constructed 238 town-home rentals. Marcus was the man of the house now. He lived with his mother and twelve-year-old sister in a two-floor rental. His father was never in his life, and his older brother, Kenyatta, left in July for the start of a prison sentence at the Hudson County Jail in Kearny.

Kenyatta had gone down in a wild car chase through Jersey City, which began a few feet away in the parking lot of Curries Woods that past summer.

When police came to arrest him on several outstanding warrants, just to find him driving into the projects as they were driving out, he sped away with his girlfriend and infant in the car, leading the police into Bayonne and back to Jersey City, where he stopped the car in an alley and made a run for it. Kenyatta jumped through a basement window and hid in a closet until the cops cuffed him.

"We haven't really talked," Marcus said, shrugging. "Right now, I'm worried about watching out for my mother and sister. I don't ask my mother for anything. I just want to help my sister more where I can."

Marcus acted unaffected by his brother's incarceration, as though it was a fact of life, a rite of passage for a black male in Jersey City. He passed no judgment on it, showed no regret. This was just Jersey City, and this was just Curries Woods. They played ball, or they did time.

"What you gonna do?" Marcus asked. "My brother is locked up."

"What you gonna do?"

He was a struggling student, his grade point average beginning his senior year below a 2.0 on a 4.0 scale. He had no chance to pick up his grades to become eligible for a Division I scholarship.

"Marcus is one of those Jersey City public school kids who had nobody helping him, who fell so far behind that he couldn't catch up," Sister Alan says. "He learned how to cover it. He can fool teachers. Some teachers test him orally because he can handle it. When I tested him for his learning disability, I told him, 'I'm not doing this to put a mark on you. But if you get classified, you can have un-timed testing. You can go to college with a special program.' He was OK when I explained it to him."

The college recruiting letters still trickled in for him, impersonal correspondences from big-time schools that never deleted his name out of those underclassmen databases. He knew the letters were inconsequential. If schools were serious, they wrote personal, handwritten notes. Under his bed, he had several boxes of recruiting letters. When he was younger, he tore them open right away. Then, they represented the possibilities for him. As a senior, they became something else altogether: a reminder of what could've been, of the opportunities he let slip away.

Now the letters stayed snug in the envelopes, unopened and useless to him.

"Ain't no point in reading them anymore," Marcus said.

Even with his modest development, Marcus still had the talent for a Division I scholarship. For now, though, he didn't spend too much time thinking about leaving Jersey City, about what junior college in the middle

THE MIRACLE OF ST. ANTHONY

of nowhere he'd end up at next year. He had won state championships as a freshman and sophomore, a younger player caddying for the upperclassmen. He celebrated with them, but nobody ever sees Marcus wearing those state championship jackets.

As a senior, this was the title that he had to get with his boys, the Boys Club gang of Otis and Beanie, Lamar and Shelton. The worst class in St. Anthony history, Hurley told them over and over, but Marcus had too much pride to let him say that forever. Everyone else in the class had crumbled at one time or another to Hurley, but Marcus Williams never had. He didn't just want the Parochial B classification state title, and the Tournament of Champions, but, beginning to end, he wanted the most imperfect senior class to author the perfect season.

"We can go unbeaten," Marcus said. "That's my goal: an unbeaten season."

There had been three undefeated seasons for Hurley: 1974, 1989 and 1996. Those teams all had All-Americans. They all had superstars. Marcus Williams still believed he had time to become that player for St. Anthony. For him, this was a run for his St. Anthony legacy, the chance to be remembered as something beyond the player that he wasn't, but the one that was: the ultimate winner for Hurley.

CHRIS HURLEY STAYED overnight at the hospital, but returned home on Thursday morning, and had an appointment to see a heart specialist in Manhattan.

After Hurley walked into practice the next day, Marcus met him at the folding chair, where the coach arrived every day, set down his practice plans, baseball cap and car keys. He handed Hurley a get-well card that he had the team sign. Hurley, looking genuinely touched, softened up for a moment and extended his hand to Marcus. The thoughtfulness clearly moved him and, given his history with this senior class, surprised him. For some St. Anthony players through the years, Mrs. Hurley showed far more interest in their personal and basketball lives than did their own mothers. As tough as Hurley could be, they figured he couldn't be all that bad if he had married her.

It would be Hurley's most patient practice of the preseason.

THE START TO the season was just twenty-four hours away, on December 20, and the time-honored tradition of St. Anthony High School was the preseason pep rally. The students spilled out of the front doors of St. Anthony, freed ninety minutes early on a Friday afternoon for the block-long walk down Manila Avenue to the Golden Door Charter School gym.

"I'm not really a pep rally kind of guy," Hurley said, by his car outside the school, and laughed. Even Hurley had to admit that it would defeat the purpose of generating enthusiasm for the season if someone handed him a microphone at the pep rally, and one by one, he told the student body what he *really* thought of his team. Just a week earlier, Hurley had done exactly that at a winter sports kickoff banquet in the school auditorium. "Be nice," his wife warned him as he left the dinner table for the microphone, but that would prove impossible once Hurley began the player introductions with sophomores Linoll and Ralph. "Take a good look at them," he said, "because their butts are probably going to get sent down to jayvee pretty soon." Exasperated, Chris Hurley bowed her head over dessert.

Beyond his own task of tearing his team down in the preseason and building it back up again, Hurley wanted the kids to have something for themselves. To have some fun. They had worked hard in the preseason, as hard as anyone in the state, he was sure, and they deserved a chance to get cheered.

As the students started filing into the gym, Lamar Alston, wearing an army fatigue jacket, clomped along in his bulky work boots. His ex-teammates were lined up in chairs, side by side at center court. Marcus encouraged Lamar to come sit with the team. It was an idea Lamar eagerly embraced. For thirty seconds or so, Lamar grabbed a seat, sitting between Marcus and Otis, the old Boys Club gang back together again. Sister Felicia was standing a few feet away, manning the microphone for the rally, and as soon as she saw the scene she could imagine the horror of Hurley's reaction. She quickly shooed Lamar into the bleachers with the rest of the student body.

The students packed the bleachers, pounding their feet and swaying from side to side. Once Sister Felicia introduced the team, the players climbed out of the folding chairs, preened through a tunnel of cheerleaders and grabbed basketballs. They were about to delight in giving their classmates something of a show. The students in the stands didn't want merely dunks from the team, they wanted dazzling dunks. Meanwhile, Lamar worked his way down to the floor, standing to the side and staring blankly at his old teammates.

After the rally, the players had two and a half hours until practice, the final preparation for the season-opener against Peddie. Lamar stood in the charter school parking lot, a girl waiting on him a few feet away. Recently, Lamar had gone to Ben Gamble to tell him what the coaches figured he eventually would, that he regretted quitting the team. He wanted a second chance to be part of his final high school season.

"By not being around it now, I realize how much I miss it," Lamar said in his soft, even voice. "Before all of this, I was playing basketball so much, I didn't realize how much I loved it."

It sure sounded good, but many inside the program had been unsure of the true reasons Lamar played the game: Was it out of love for the game, or an obligation to his stepfather, or just a way to be near his friends on the team?

Even so, Lamar looked longingly on his old teammates at the rally. And outside the gym, Lamar told the story of what had been bothering him most—not Hurley pulling him off the starting team in that second day of practice in late November, but about the biological father, who had left Lamar's life when he was just an infant and finally coming back into it just a few months earlier. Only, Lamar lamented, to walk out again.

Ernest Ford had moved back to Jersey City after spending most of his son's eighteen years away. Still, Lamar said, he seemed to show little interest in reconciling, and the rejection riddled Lamar with angst. "He won't have anything to do with me," Lamar said. "I try to call him at my grandmother's but he won't come to the phone.

"That's hard, man. Your own father doesn't want anything to do with you . . . I mean, why would it be like that?"

Everyone constantly referenced Joe Boccia as Lamar's stepfather, but it was probably an unfair label for considering he had legally adopted Lamar and raised him with his mother since he was nine months old. There were stories some family members recalled for Lamar, hazy recollections of confrontations when Ford left Lamar's mother's life and Boccia arrived in it.

"It still haunts him right now," Boccia says. "My wife talks to him about it, but back in the time, his birth-father and I had some very serious fights. I wound up having to hurt the guy. He had been trying to intimidate me and it got physical. He backed away from me and left me alone. But it's always been in Lamar's mind that I tried to kill him. His [birth-father's] family made me out to be the bad guy."

When Lamar disappeared for several days in September, Hurley was frustrated to hear Boccia promise him that Lamar wouldn't miss any more open gyms. This wasn't about open gym, Hurley told him. This was about getting your son's life in order. Hurley told him, "You don't know where he's been for the last few days, and you need to get him into counseling."

When the two talked recently, Gamble told Lamar to keep his grades up, and keep working out. They would talk again when the team returned from the California trip.

For now, the players were running off together to kill a few hours until practice, leaving Lamar back in the charter school parking lot, wondering what was next for him. "I've been trying to deal with those issues," Lamar said. "I'm trying to get my head right . . . If I don't play basketball again, I'm worried about my future.

"What am I going to do next year?"

BEFORE THE START of practice, News 12 New Jersey television reporter Bryan DeNovellis stopped by the gym to conduct interviews for a preview of the state's preseason number-one-ranked Friars. For three years, Marcus watched Hurley choose the senior stars to be team spokesmen, and finally, it was his turn. But he didn't look thrilled to see Hurley sending Sean to talk with him. The truth was, Marcus had never been thrilled with Sean McCurdy in the gymnasium at St. Anthony. "It just seems like he showed up here, and too much was handed to him," Marcus says. "It seemed like he didn't have to work for nothing here."

For Marcus and most of the seniors, the evidence was in the way that Sean was chosen as the starting shooting guard as a sophomore transfer, over the junior Otis. For Hurley, the elevation of Sean was part his talent, and part a presence that the coach knew could scare Otis and his classmates straight. Instead of fighting to protect his turf, Otis used Hurley's screaming and Sean beating him out as a reason to leave the team. Otis would eventually be allowed back before the start of last season, but as Shelton Gibbs said, "To all of us, it looked like Sean was just given a starting job. But Marcus was always the maddest about the whole thing with Sean coming here. Otis was his boy and Marcus was always going to look out for him."

Marcus seemed a little unsure of himself on air, carefully trying to choose his words. It was never easy when that red light blinked on the camera, and questions kept coming. But Marcus did fine, even revealing his thoughts on a possible unbeaten season. When Marcus was done and off camera, DeNovellis asked about the schools recruiting him. Marcus mumbled something inaudible, and the reporter asked again. He seemed more curious than interested in gathering the news. Mostly, he was just trying to be friendly.

"Just some junior colleges," Marcus said, as though he had wished he could tell the man something else.

When it was his turn, Sean smiled into the camera and said, "All of those preseason rankings don't mean anything. We haven't proven anything to Coach Hurley." Sean often said that he wanted everyone to know him, that he loved how St. Anthony could bring his face to the masses. News 12 New Jersey, huh? Well, this was a start.

As the cameraman unhooked the microphone from Sean's tank top, he eagerly asked, "When is this going to be on? When can I see this?"

This was the kind of stuff that Marcus hated. He resented like hell that Sean had come rolling into Jersey City thinking he could take all this adulation for himself.

Once DeNovellis finished filming some practice and left, Hurley walked across the middle of the floor and talked out loud to his team. "I'm going on a San Diego radio station at seven o'clock tonight, because we're supposed to be a team that can win the tournament. I'm supposed to tell them how good we're playing. Either I'm going to tell them the truth, or lie my ass off and help them sell some tickets for the tournament."

In the hours before the opening tip to the season, Hurley found little reassurance in Sean forgetting where he was supposed to be in a couple of offensive sets—nor with Barney just returning to practice after a dental problem that had left his jaw wired shut. Hurley would have to bring Barney off the bench for the Peddie game because he had missed too much practice in the past week. It left Linoll to start at center in his first varsity game.

"The baby crap on the bench has hopefully been taken care of," Hurley warned the team. "It's a privilege to wear this uniform. This has been the most successful high school team in the state of New Jersey for a very long time. People all over the country are looking at the USA Today poll and saying, 'Oh, St. Anthony is in it again.'"

Before Gamble gave them the scouting report on Peddie, Hurley, forever focusing on the most minute of details, had them rehearse checking into the game from the bench. He taught the reserves to stand and count down loudly the final ten seconds of every quarter when St. Anthony had the ball. That way, the players on the floor didn't have to search for the game clock.

Eventually tiring of Ralph, Robert Bullock and Qaysir Woods butchering his practice at the far end of the floor, Hurley instructed them to come watch the regulars run through plays on the opposite basket.

"Just sit down here," Hurley ordered. "If we didn't have our first game tomorrow, I would go over to one of the classrooms in the charter school, get some construction paper, some scissors, markers, and we could make some Christmas decorations together.

"And then I could stick 'em up your asses."

Even the kids had to fight back laughter over that one.

In the Peddie scouting report, there was one name that Hurley harped on: a senior guard, Will Monica, who had the Ivy League schools recruiting him. Marcus had him, and the rule was simple: He would stay with Monica the whole game, never leaving him to help a teammate on his man. Peddie had a seven-foot center, but six-foot-five Monica was the man.

"I know Monica's had fifty-nine in the last two games for them," Hurley had said on the way out of the gym, "and if we don't have Marcus on him the whole game, he might get fifty-nine in one game."

St. Anthony had once beaten Lower Merion High School's Kobe Bryant with two Friars starters suspended for missing a practice in a snow-storm, had held the national high school player of the year Tim Thomas of Paterson Catholic to nine points, but in Hurley's mind, Monica was the most dangerous player on the planet: the one between St. Anthony and the first victory of the season.

EARLY THE NEXT afternoon, on Saturday, the bus waited outside the school. Gamble had been inside the main office, talking to Sister Felicia about Lamar. She was telling the story about Lamar at the rally, which didn't exactly boost his reinstatement chances. Back on Bluebird bus No. 5404, Gamble sat in the front row of the maroon leather seats, with Darren Erman across the aisle. Hurley never took the team bus, always drove ahead, with his wife. He was so tense on game days, he didn't want it rubbing off on his players.

Once they arrived at Caldwell College, they marched across the floor and down a hallway to the locker room. Gamble pulled off his 2002 St. Anthony state championship jacket and looked for someone to give it to, for safekeeping in a locker. "Who's going to be the good luck charm this year?" he asked.

Before anyone could answer, Gamble passed the coat to Marcus.

Chris Hurley looked pale and drawn, in the bleachers. She had missed just three games through the years—all losses, she noted—and as Melissa would say, rolling her eyes, "She would've come here if she had those IVs in her arms." Before long, Chris assumed her seat at the scorer's table, reading glasses perched on the bridge of her nose.

Once warm-ups were complete, Hurley gathered his players in the locker room. The first five trips down the floor were scripted. He went through them again. Greg Bracey, the conditioning coach and boyfriend of Cindy McCurdy, slipped a rubber glove onto his hand and massaged the muscle on Sean's tender hamstring. Everyone locked on Hurley.

"We've worked very hard, and this is what we have to do now," Hurley said, holding his right hand in the air. "Five fingers becoming one."

He closed his fist.

"Five guys becoming one.

"We may not get the tap. They may get the first possession of the game. But that's the only thing they're going to get. We're St. Anthony. They don't score forty against us today."

The entire team and assistant coaches crowded into the center of the locker room, hands raised together in the air, Hurley in the middle of it all.

"Hail Mary, full of grace," he began, a prayer that they would repeat before and after every game. At the end, Hurley said, "Lady of Victory pray for us, St. Anthony pray for us."

And then everybody picked it up, louder. "One-two-three, HARD WORK!"

The St. Anthony High School Friars rushed out the door, down the corridor and into the basketball season.

The Peddie School had two players of consequence: the six-foot-five Monica, and a lumbering seven-foot, 270-pound senior, Danko Barisic. After the kind of preseason Linoll had, it was the ultimate irony that he would make the first move of the season for St. Anthony, jumping center with Barisic.

The ball went up and Hurley was wrong. Somehow, St. Anthony came down with the tap. Peddie would get nothing on this day. As planned, they passed the ball to Linoll on the first trip down. He missed a jump hook over the seven-footer, but Marcus crashed the boards and laid the ball back into the basket. Marcus had delivered the first blow toward his dream of a perfect season.

St. Anthony set up its three-quarters court pressure. Sean stole a pass and drove to the basket for a layup, but the ball rolled off the rim. Moments later, the seven-foot center tried to drive the ball down the baseline, but the smallest man on the floor, five-foot-seven Derrick Mercer, stood his ground. The giant plowed him over, allowing Derrick to take the first charge of the season, the hard way.

Soon, the St. Anthony ball-control superiority and defensive pressure turned into an avalanche of Peddie turnovers and Friars baskets. It was 9–2 when Peddie called its first timeout. Marcus and Otis hit back-to-back three-pointers to make it 21–5 at the end of the first quarter, and it just kept coming. Marcus threaded a perfect pass to Shelton for a slicing layup and Barney dunked, and it was 33–8 when Peddie walked warily back out from a timeout. They were dragging. The court looked like the last place in the world that they wanted to be.

Soon, Beanie dove into the St. Anthony bench to save a loose ball, crashing into little-used senior Justin Lewis. As he raced back into the play, Beanie had a big smile on his face. His expression said what his words didn't dare: This was fun. He swished a three-pointer with two and a half minutes left in the half, then another, thirty-five seconds later, and another with a little over a minute left until halftime. After Sean hit a three just before the half, it was 52–13 as St. Anthony ran into the locker room.

Hurley feared they could be sluggish to start the season, because he was a coach, and coaches always fear the worst. But they had been terrific, and Hurley struggled to find fault with much at the half.

"Now all we have to do is get rid of the unforced errors," Hurley said. "But we don't need to do anything to embarrass them."

After the 89–36 victory, a performance in which St. Anthony scored on a surreal thirteen three-point shots and played the bench the entire fourth quarter, Hurley would tell the kids they would have Sunday off to do Christmas shopping. The Friars wouldn't play another game for six days, until they arrived in California.

"We looked a little bit like a team today," Hurley told them. "We have a chance to be pretty good.

"But we have a lot of work to do."

CHAPTER 8

BOB MCCURDY'S GRAYING hair flopped in the warm Southern California breeze, an ease and confidence to him that seemed much more West Coast than East Coast. All these years later, at a fit six-foot-seven, he still had the look of the big man on campus.

Beyond the luggage conveyer belt at Long Beach Airport, he waited outside the rental car trailer for Hertz to deliver his van. He wore small, rounded glasses, a golf shirt, and an easy disposition. He had his second family in tow: his wife, Sydney Emerson, and her three college-aged children.

The weather was gorgeous, one of those classic Southern California days, just the kind that New Yorkers fresh out of the blustery winter were glad to wrap around themselves. The family hadn't come 3,000 miles for sun; they had come to watch Sean play in the tournament down in San Diego that night. After a coast-to-coast flight, it was still just ten in the morning out here, and they were preparing for a lunch date with a wise old man in Encino whom McCurdy wanted his step-kids to meet, the way his own children, Meagan, Mike, Ashley and Sean had done several times in the past. The man was John Wooden.

One of the trip's lures for his college-aged stepchildren was the promise of several days at a beachfront hotel. The team was staying inland at the Doubletree in Mission Valley, closer to the gymnasium than the glistening Pacific Ocean. There always seemed to be distance between Bob and his youngest son now.

During the season, there were never free days for them to spend together. Sean's trips home to Connecticut were rare because St. Anthony almost never had a day off. "And when he does," Bob McCurdy would say, "he wants to hang with his friends. And I don't want to get in the way of that."

Even after he signed off on it during their meeting at McDonald's, Bob McCurdy had never been completely convinced that sending Sean to live in Jersey City was the right thing.

"I still don't know if it's a good idea," he says. "I mean, Sean is playing for the John Wooden of high school coaches in Bob Hurley. Being around him every day is the best reason for this. It's not that. But there are just some things you miss out on as a family, the time at the breakfast table with him, the spontaneous stuff between a father and son."

His youngest was growing up, and he was missing it. It broke his heart. And it wasn't just a father's influence that he feared was missing in Sean's life, but his mother's, too.

For more than a year, Cindy had been commuting back and forth to Connecticut for her business, leaving Sean at the apartment under Melissa Hurley's watch for most of his sophomore year, and as a junior now, staying many nights with Darren Erman. There were too many times that Bob was saying good night to his son on the telephone, unsure just how lonely, how distant, his son felt from his family.

"That's a big concern of mine," he says. "Darren is wonderful, but Sean needs parents. I try to keep on top of that. But the agreement was that there would be a parent with him at all times. That's what we agreed to when he moved down there.

"I didn't sign up for this.

"But look, I see the upside in pursuing his dream. Basketball has always been a very important part of his life. I give him a lot of credit for taking this risk and going after what his heart needed to pursue. I'm proud of his conviction to chase this. In my mind, he's going to a boarding school. He was taken out of my life far sooner than I ever hoped, and that's how I'm justifying it in my mind at this point.

"When I get him on the phone I just tell him: Let's keep it to a one-'yo'-per-sentence limit."

He wished Sean could've been with them that afternoon on the ride to Encino, but he had met his father's old friend several times over the years. Bob considered himself pals with John Wooden. Around the time of his graduation from Richmond in 1975, he wrote the legendary UCLA coach for advice on becoming a high school teacher and coach. Wooden wrote him back. McCurdy passed on the education career, but wound up with a friendship that blossomed over time.

An audience with John Wooden remained something straight out of the heavens. Walk through Wooden's front door and you enter a world where modesty overrides hubris, where an old teacher celebrates a life of lessons learned, far more than celebrating himself and those ten national championships at UCLA. Wooden was still a remarkable man, still sharp, lucid and in complete step with the time. Though he was frail at ninety-three, walking slowly and surely with his cane, he still traveled the country giving speeches and making appearances. He had just finished some publicity for a new children's book he had written. An audience with Wooden remained something straight out of the heavens.

His books on Abraham Lincoln sat next to the doorway, a small library devoted to his favorite historical figure. Next to them, there was the Presidential Medal of Freedom awarded him just that spring in Washington, with the pictures of George W. Bush presenting it at the White House. Inside his study, there were his two Hall of Fame plaques. He was the first man in history to reach the Naismith Memorial Basketball Hall of Fame as a player and a coach. There were autographed photos of New York Yankees manager Joe Torre with Wooden ("To the best of the best," Torre inscribed).

To suggest to Wooden what most sensible sports minds consider fact—that he was history's greatest basketball coach—invited a disapproving grimace, an understanding that he wasn't interested in contributing to such a consensus. Wooden rose to his feet and instructed a visitor to walk with him to a mantle, saying softly, "I want to show you something."

He grabbed a small wooden box, flipped back the lid and cupped a bronzed medallion in his hands. It was an award the Big Ten delivered to him as a Purdue graduating senior in 1932, representative of the top student-athlete in the conference.

"It's my most prized accomplishment," Wooden said, "because only I was responsible for it. All the coaching awards, I had just a small part in them. Those belonged to my players. This, though, I was responsible for earning."

Mitch Kupchak, the general manager of the Los Angeles Lakers and a childhood friend of Bob McCurdy's on Long Island, would join in on visits to Wooden, listening to the old coach spin stories for hours. McCurdy would always have a plane to catch back East, always be rushing out the door, and Kupchak would invariably ask him, "How can you walk out on John Wooden?"

It was never easy. In the living room, McCurdy turned the talk to Sean and his college recruitment.

"Texas Tech has started to send Sean some mail," he said. "But it's the one place in America where I would absolutely not let him go."

Wooden had a long-standing frost with Bob Knight, often critical of Knight's penchant for volatility and even physical aggression toward his players.

"Like I've always said, I would never want a loved one to play for Bob Knight," Wooden said.

Over lunch, at Wooden's favorite neighborhood restaurant, the subject of Pistol Pete Maravich was raised with the old coach. He had to laugh, saying, "Someone once told me he would be the first million-dollar-a-year player, and I said he would never win a championship. We were both right."

Putting down his sandwich, McCurdy turned to Wooden and made a small confession. "You probably wouldn't have liked me very much as a player."

Bob McCurdy was a pocket Pistol for the University of Richmond, where he finished his college career in historic fashion in 1975. He had been recruited to the University of Virginia out of high school in Deer Park, New York. Before freshmen were allowed to participate on the varsity, he was a spectacular show in the Atlantic Coast Conference freshman games. "I had thirty points on [North Carolina's] Bobby Jones, and forty on [Maryland's] Tom McMillan. I averaged thirty-eight that year." But a coaching change at Virginia lost the man responsible for recruiting him to campus, and at the end of his sophomore season, he transferred for the final two years of his eligibility. He scored twenty-four points per game for Richmond in the 1973–1974 season, but he was just getting loose.

As a senior, McCurdy scored those 32.9 points a game for the national scoring title. In one game against Appalachian State, he scored fifty-five points. Richmond finished 11–17 for the season, but Bob McCurdy made a name for himself.

"Looking back now, it was a remarkable feat," said Kevin Eastman, who was Richmond's point guard and works now as a Boston Celtics assistant coach. "He had virtually no quickness. He didn't really have dribbling skills. He couldn't jump that high. He couldn't run real fast. He was a prime example of how will and enthusiasm and effort allowed him to rise to another level.

"But the same characteristics that allowed him to be successful caused some friction on the team, too: total belief in self, supreme confidence on the edge of cockiness."

Eastman used to marvel at the single-minded nature of his teammate. He would be walking with McCurdy on campus and see him keep going past the professor on his way to teach the class that McCurdy was cutting. "He'd say, 'Hey, Doc,' and keep walking on his way to the gym," Eastman said. "Guys like him could do that and still be successful in the classroom. I just remember him laying in bed, prone on his back, and shooting the ball up in the air over and over, working on his follow-through and touch.

"He worked harder than anybody else on the team, but he was very focused on one skill, and that was shooting. I'm not sure I saw him in a defensive stance all year, and the one or two assists that he got were mistakes. But he knew what he was good at, and he practiced to be good at it. He was the best pure shooter in the country that year."

Like Wooden, Bob Hurley wouldn't have loved Bob McCurdy's game, but he would've wanted his passion for playing. And he had found it with Sean. Hurley was relentless on teaching Sean to be a complete player—a passer, a defender, a thinking man's guard—but his instincts were born of the genes of his father and his uncles in Indiana. The sweet stroke and the tunnel-vision ethic to be a drop-dead shooter were passed on to Sean, along with, perhaps, a family gene that often equated stats and scoring with success. That wouldn't have worked with the UCLA dynasty, and it sure wouldn't work with the St. Anthony's, either.

BOB HURLEY HAD found himself sitting on a South Carolina beach in 1984, next to an older, black high school coach from inner-city Memphis. They were together for a national tournament, and all the Jersey City and Memphis high school players were running back and forth in the warm sand, playing touch football.

Hurley turned to the man and said, "Coach, look down at the game now. Do you have any idea why the two of us are sitting here?"

The old man just laughed a sad, resigned laugh.

"You're from the North," he said, amazed that Hurley didn't understand.

The six other teams in the tournament were staying near the gymnasium downtown, enjoying the conveniences of a modern hotel with a big-screen television to watch college games at night. "And here we were at a Holiday Inn off the strip, where they were doing construction," Hurley says. "During the week one of the St. Anthony kids fell into a construction hole and had to go to the hospital."

His suspicions started weeks before the tournament, when a tournament official called Hurley seeking the "makeup" of his St. Anthony team.

"Well," Hurley told the man. "We have five seniors, and four juniors and . . ."

"No," the voice on the phone corrected him, "the *racial* makeup."

It was too late to back out of the tournament, so Hurley just figured he'd really piss them off and win it.

"That was 1984," Hurley says, "and I have bad-mouthed that tournament every opportunity for twenty years."

Hurley didn't win their damn tournament, but he did go down in the championship game, shattering his clipboard against a wall with a fling all the way from mid-court.

San Diego was different. Hurley loved this tournament. The warm weather, the beaches, the top teams in the West—it was perfect. The kids were able to see a part of the country few of them would otherwise get a chance to visit, and Hurley would get an opportunity to test his team in a tournament atmosphere with four games in five nights.

The *San Diego Union-Tribune* declared in its morning paper, "St. Anthony returns, giving the tournament instant credibility."

Nevertheless, this was a tough test, especially considering that most of the teams from California, and the talented team from South Florida, Flanagan High School, had played more than ten games each already. Winning the tournament wouldn't be easy. St. Anthony had now moved up to third in the *USA Today* poll, and everybody wanted a shot at them. The defending champion from nearby Oceanside, El Camino High School, and powerful Dominguez of Los Angeles, were waiting on the far side of the bracket for a possible championship game meeting.

This was St. Anthony's sixth trip here, and it had won twenty-three of twenty-four games, including four championships (1990, 1993, 1997 and 1998). A year earlier, after it lost its first game ever in the tournament opening round, St. Anthony won the consolation bracket, but "It wasn't much fun of a trip after that," Marcus says. "Coach didn't like the consolation games too much."

There had been holiday tournaments where Hurley had his players lifting weights in the hotel fitness room at 5:30 A.M., before flying home. There had been a tournament in Baltimore, where they had to be packed, in the buses and on the road before dawn, because 10:00 A.M. was the only practice time that Hurley could secure in a gym back in Jersey City. Once, on a flight home, the team trainer, Doc Miller, walked over to Hurley's seat on the plane, and said, "I talked to the pilots, but they said, 'No.' "

"No to what?" Hurley wondered.

"They won't let you set up baskets on the plane's wings."

The tournament sponsors picked up most of the traveling expenses for St. Anthony, so the school's financial straits weren't a deterrent. Hurley didn't want the players to have to fly out on Christmas Day night, but part of him used these opportunities to toughen his team's mettle. They met at 4:15 A.M. on December 26 at the Astor Bar near the Armory to drive in cars over to Newark International Airport. They flew in on a 6:30 A.M. flight, tried to nap for an hour or two when they arrived, grabbed an early dinner and drove to Torrey Pines High School for the opening-round game.

Torrey Pines was an affluent suburban high school, and St. Anthony had use of a spacious locker room. The players had a cubicle of lockers to dress at and go over the scouting report with Gamble until Hurley came to give the team its final instructions before the first-round game with San Diego High School. Sean dribbled a ball back and forth in the hallway, off alone, yelling to his teammates that they needed to play together.

Across the locker room, Marcus winced and shook his head.

"We do everything as a team," he said to no one in particular. "And he's doing his own shit."

"Let's go, guys!" Sean yelled out. "Let's play together!"

"So don't shoot so much," Marcus sniffed.

Once again, Sean couldn't hear him. And nobody in the locker room acknowledged it. Everyone was still tired. Linoll sat on a bench and yawned. Beanie had those droopy eyes and he was one of the few kids who had been able to sleep on the plane.

Outside the locker room, a San Diego State University assistant coach was approaching Hurley and introducing himself. "I've admired your program from afar," he said, shaking Hurley's hand.

Once inside the locker room, Hurley prepared his team. Yes, everyone was tired. He was, too. This was part of the reason he wanted to play on the first night out there. Where he could do it, he wanted to instill his own adversity into the long season's journey. He knew this was hard. It was supposed to be hard.

"It's been a long day," Hurley said. "A character day. Everyone's been up since 4:15. Nobody got any sleep."

He paused, running his eyes across his players.

"And nobody gives a shit."

Fighting through the fatigue, with little resistance against a freewheeling San Diego High School team, St. Anthony won, 58–37. Sean finished

with seventeen points, but tired Friars legs made for a poor overall shooting performance. Nevertheless, the Friars' suffocating defense made the
trip. "Defense is like your conservative savings," Hurley would say. "You
know what you're going to get. Offense is like the stock market."

At the end of the game, Hurley simply told the team, "Get back to the
hotel and get to sleep. Anybody who is a pain in the ass in the room tonight, I'll bring you right to the airport."

The next morning, they were on the outdoor courts on the gorgeous,
hilly campus of the University of San Diego for a practice to prepare for
the second-round game against unbeaten Bishop O'Dowd of Oakland. It
was sunny and seventy degrees on December 27, inspiring everyone to
wipe the sleep from their eyes and come alive. If the climate was unfamiliar to Jersey City kids, the cracked concrete court with peeling green paint
on the sidewall boards had a decidedly homey feel. The steel backboards
had rims with worn nets.

Phil Miller shaded his eyes in the warm morning sun. They called him
"Doc." He would turn eighty-three on New Year's Eve, a birthday celebrated most of the past twenty years traveling home with St. Anthony
from a holiday tournament. He was smart-mouthed and quick-witted, a
man who had lived his life as an ironworker by day and a big-time college
and professional basketball referee by night.

Once, St. John's coach Lou Carnesecca had teased Doc before tip-off
about how red and weathered his face looked. "Louie, why don't you
come work with me thirty stories up on the bridge tomorrow," Doc asked,
"and see what happens to *your* face?"

Hundreds of feet in the air, Doc had driven rivets into steel beams on
the Tappan Zee, Throgs Neck and Kingston-Rhinecliff bridges. He had
helped build hangars for Pan-Am airlines, and the Nabisco plant over on
Route 208 in northern New Jersey. After finishing his day job in the winter, he would come home, down a martini and pack his whistle into his bag
for a ballgame that night.

He used to have a hell of a time with a hotheaded young coach at West
Point in the late 1960s and early '70s. When Bob Knight would try to
intimidate Doc, he used to tell him, "I'm not some teacher, I'm an ironworker, and I didn't come here to listen to your shit. Now, sit your ass
down or you're going to the locker room." Miller figures that he had to be
the only official in history to have called technical fouls on Bob Knight
and Bob Hurley.

He liked working Hurley's sideline much more than he did Hurley working him from it. Doc was never sure how Hurley felt about him until that game in Atlantic City a decade earlier, when a St. Anthony player caught a cut over his eye. "We've got some real good doctors here to take care of him," a tournament staff member told Hurley.

"No, no," Hurley said. "I've got a real pro working for me."

"Doc will stitch him up right."

On the outdoor college court, Doc paused to take in the scene as Hurley, who wore a Jersey City Recreation T-shirt and a baseball cap, worked up a good sweat growling to his players in the mid-morning sun. "Watching him here, you'd think you're back home," Doc said. "But I'll tell you, his hard-nosed tactics are so good for today."

Across all his years, throughout the pages of his personal scrapbook of characters, everything ran a distant second to taping up the St. Anthony kids in the shadow of a coach who kept him coming back again and again.

After his years as an ironworker, Doc caught on with the Atlanta Braves and Montreal Expos in front-office jobs. He worked as a trainer for the Pittsburgh Steelers. He stayed a close friend of Joe Namath, working his football camp every summer in Connecticut. Still, he lived for the basketball season at St. Anthony, his time with Hurley and the kids. It broke his heart that over the past summer, he had to miss out on working the coach's basketball camp in the woods of the Poconos. "Prostate cancer," Doc explained. "But I beat that son of a bitch, too.

"I was the first one to tape young Bobby when he was a freshman in '85," Doc said. "Then they asked me to go to Raleigh with them on a trip. And that was it. I was hooked. Bob is like wine. He just gets better. He's right there with Knight, with Red Holzman, the best coaches I've ever seen. People want to compare Bob to Knight, but he's really like Red in the way that he teaches the game, the way he sees things that nobody else sees. These kids don't even know the knowledge they're getting."

After a late morning at the hotel, Chris and Melissa Hurley arrived at the courts figuring that they would catch the end of a light, hour-long walk-through. But practice had gone well past an hour now, with Hurley cherishing the chance to have his team's undivided attention far from the distractions of life in Jersey City.

"Why were we rushing over here again?" Melissa asked.

"You know your father," Chris said.

"Yeah, I know my father—if he says an hour, it'll be an hour and a half."

Melissa sighed. She didn't even want to consider the hours of lost

beach time she had endured through the years watching her father's basketball practices on these trips.

"St. Anthony, so big, so tough . . . Let's see how tough they really are,"
Pete Morales muttered, just loud enough for Melissa's boyfriend, Joe Stein,
to hear the Bishop O'Dowd of Oakland coach as he slowly walked past an
empty Friars bench during warm-ups.

The coach wasn't alone on the O'Dowd side with his unimpressed
view of St. Anthony. Bob McCurdy and Ben Gamble heard their fans talking the same way in the stands, all of them judging St. Anthony's sluggish
performance at the end of a long travel day and their relatively unimposing
height and individual talent as reasons to believe they had more than a
fighting chance to beat the Friars. At number three in the *USA Today* poll,
they wore the lofty ranking like a bull's-eye into the Torrey Pines gymnasium that night.

But St. Anthony had seen an untold number of out-of-state teams
come into games through the years with comparable confidence to
O'Dowd. "The other teams see us in the hotel lobby and we don't look
like much," Gamble says. "But once the ball goes up, you won't be able to
get us off your guys."

And what would happen was that the St. Anthony trapping pressure
would wear teams down early, and eventually lead to waves of turnovers
later. They were like piranha in a fish tank, always able to target the
unsteady, inexperienced guards most susceptible to crumbling under the
pressure.

"You can sniff them out," Otis says.

Even the good, experienced guards eventually wore down. And so it
would be once more that night.

At the end of the first quarter against O'Dowd, Hurley asked his players a question: "What's setting in over there?"

Everybody knew this answer.

"Fatigue," they yelled together.

It was 33–20 at halftime, and the Friars were relentless to start the third
quarter. They had their legs back, and that promised doom for O'Dowd.
Several times, O'Dowd's guards were helpless to escape the St. Anthony
traps in the backcourt, failing to cross the mid-court line within the allot-
ted ten seconds. Otis pressured the ball, and forced an O'Dowd guard to
stumble into the backcourt for another violation. Beanie made a steal and

passed to Marcus for a layup. Another Marcus steal and another layup, and it was 40–22. St. Anthony was everywhere on the court. Out West, they just didn't see defense like this.

It turned into the Otis and Marcus Show the rest of the way, the two seniors completely controlling the game. This was classic Marcus, but Otis had transformed himself that day. In the past, he had been something of a one-dimensional player, just concerned with his scoring, but the years under Hurley had finally taken root. He was defending like a demon, passing the ball beautifully, constantly creating opportunities for his teammates and himself. Otis finished with a career-high twenty-four points and Marcus had a quintessential all-around line of fourteen points, eleven rebounds, seven steals and six assists in the 68–42 victory. Beanie had played a fabulous game, too, pressuring the ball with Derrick Mercer to make it impossible for O'Dowd to run a deliberate offense. They could've easily held an unbeaten O'Dowd under forty points, but the bench cast that Hurley had come to call "The Bombardiers"—Ralph Fernandez, Robert Bullock, Qaysir Woods and Linoll Mercedes—had given up a few easy baskets.

Still, Hurley could see something happening. O'Dowd had been an unbeaten team, one that would go on to win twenty-six games that season, and St. Anthony had obliterated them. For Hurley, this had been victory number 799 as St. Anthony coach. The Friars would try for his milestone eight hundredth in the semifinals in two days, against Flanagan of Pembroke Pines, Florida, which was unbeaten in twelve games and started two juniors over six-foot-six who many of the top college programs in the South were recruiting.

"This is why people coach," Hurley told his players in the locker room after the victory. "I'm looking at people changing now. I'm looking at people starting to become leaders, good all-around players."

As the St. Anthony players watched the late tournament game in the bleachers before returning to the hotel, Beanie had a satisfied look on his face. "After all the stuff that's happened, we're starting to step up the way coach wants us to," he said.

The next day, Sunday, the twenty-eighth of December, the practice was at seven in the morning, because there was a full docket for the kids: indoor soccer, a golf driving range and a barbeque.

During a playful hour of soccer, Hurley stood on the sideline and called Gary Greenberg at the Boys Club to report on the seniors' progress. For once, Hurley had nothing but good tidings for his wayward crew.

"Marcus and Otis are playing unbelievably," he told him. "Otis was walking up and down the hall in the hotel this morning getting the kids out of their rooms and started. It's like the light went on with him. It took a long time, but the light went on."

That Sunday, Hurley had tickets for the Oakland Raiders-San Diego Chargers game at 1:00 at Qualcomm Stadium, a trolley ride from the Doubletree Hotel. For a lot of the kids, it was the first pro sporting event they had seen in person. It was a typical Raiders crowd, thousands of silver-and-black bikers and other Neanderthals rolling into town for the game. It didn't so much resemble a football crowd as it did the old Monday and Friday parade of humanity into Hurley's probation office in Jersey City.

Back at the hotel Sunday night, Marcus had Hurley's eight-hundredth career victory on his mind. If St. Anthony beat Flanagan of Florida, they had planned to hold a small celebration in the Doubletree after the game on Monday night. Marcus decided to write a speech for Hurley. He spent most of his Sunday night on the seventh floor working on it. He ran some lines past his roommate on the trip, Otis, and kept reworking it. As Otis dozed in bed, Marcus stayed at his desk, lamp lit, pen scratching into paper.

AWAY FROM JERSEY City, there was no chorus of gunfire in public housing to stir the players from sleep, no apartment heat turned down to save money in the dead of winter, no going to bed on an empty stomach.

Hurley once brought a team to South Jersey for a tournament, where they stayed in the homes of players on opposing teams.

"One kid came back to school," Ray Page, a St. Anthony teacher, said, "and said to me, 'Man, they were rich.' I asked him why he thought that. He told me, 'Well, they had milk *and* orange juice at the breakfast table.'"

San Diego was a far different world for most of the players, far more controlled, and it made beating Hurley in a tournament atmosphere an even tougher task. He could scout the opponents himself, use the mornings to runs his team through detailed walk-throughs and, most of all, keep a twenty-four-hour watch on his players.

After a practice at the University of San Diego gym on Monday, everyone piled into cars for a late-morning visit to the beach. The caravan pulled down to Belmont Park, where the players took off for the arcade and the signs for dollar Big Macs at the McDonald's. They were just told to stay away from the small roller coaster and carousels. "I'm not going to deal with motion sickness," Hurley told them. "Go to the arcade and go crazy."

The coaches and Chris Hurley sat on a wall along the boardwalk, watching waves crash on the beach. Hurley wore a nylon maroon St. Anthony sweat suit, feeling good about the progress the team had made in a short time. He was feeling nostalgic about the opportunity to win his eight-hundredth game, remembering back to his first victory as St. Anthony coach in 1972. "West New York High School," he recalled. "Frank Grasso was the coach. And he got thrown out of the game."

For his eight-hundredth victory to come before his one-hundredth loss was beyond his wildest dreams. He had won almost nine out of every ten games he had coached at St. Anthony, and that included seasons where, because of the gym situation, St. Anthony had fewer than five true home games. Hurley felt like he could keep coaching another ten years, and maybe chase 1,000 career victories. "I just want to be able to keep doing it the way that I'm doing it," he said.

In the distance, Ahmad Nivins was running on the beach with Greg Bracey, the conditioning coach who made the trip with Cindy McCurdy. The coaches had to find things to keep Ahmad working hard on because there were fewer chances to work him into practices during the tournament. They were so far down the shoreline, they had literally run out of view. "I still can't see Ahmad," Hurley said, squinting into the distance. "I hope he's back by the time he's eligible."

Because of his transfer, state rules mandated that Ahmad wouldn't become eligible until thirty days after the start of the season, on January 19, against St. Joseph's of Metuchen.

Hurley couldn't stop talking about Otis, about how far he had come as a player and a person. He had been so shy and introverted as an eighth-grader that Gary Greenberg used to tease Otis that Hurley was holding on the telephone line, wanting to talk to him, only to see Otis run right out of his office.

Erman was inviting Otis to take a closer look at a dead eel in the sand. As Otis sheepishly hovered over the lifeless corpse, Pushie tossed another dead eel at Otis's feet, testing the limits of his vertical leap.

"That's the most explosive move I've seen Otis make all year," Erman laughed.

Marcus wanted that eight-hundredth victory badly for his coach, and it showed in the beginning of the tournament semifinal game against unbeaten Pembroke Pines. In contrast to his usually pragmatic approach on offense, Marcus forced shots to the rim. Early in the game, he was shooting three-pointers and jamming passes where they didn't belong. He was trying too hard. Otis was off, too, and without the two best players on the team clicking, St. Anthony was losing by a point at the end of the first quarter. Finally, Sean took over near the end of the half, turning a 29–25 lead into 36–27 with seven straight points over the final ninety seconds.

In the locker room, Hurley was confounded by Marcus. It never occurred to him that Marcus would be trying too hard because he wanted to get his coach number 800. "Marcus taking three threes in the first half?" Hurley asked out loud. "If you're a good player, what do you try to do?" he asked. Then he answered. "Fill up every category."

Early in the third, Derrick controlled the ball on a three-on-one St. Anthony break, leaving a pass behind him for a trailing Marcus to finish. With the score still fairly tight at 38–29, Marcus could've done the safe thing and just laid the ball softly off the backboard for two points. He didn't. He tried to dunk it. The ball clanked embarrassingly off the back rim, high into the air. Hurley shot a disgusted glance over at Gamble, suggesting, "What the hell ever happened to that kid?"

St. Anthony pulled away in the third, and early in the fourth, Hurley turned to the delay game on offense. Without a shot clock, the Friars could spread out on the floor, play catch, and when the defense inevitably came to force the action, attack the basket. When Flanagan did, St. Anthony's guards made them pay. Derrick dribbled into the lane, passing to Barney cutting to the rim for a dunk and a nineteen-point lead with four and a half minutes left in the game.

Behind the bench, a smattering of St. Anthony fans stood and stayed cheering as the final buzzer sounded. The public-address announcer declared that the 65–43 victory was the eight-hundredth of Bob Hurley's career, and Gamble, who had been a player under Hurley when he won his two-hundredth game in 1981, reached out his hand to congratulate his coach.

But Hurley wasn't listening to the announcer, and he wasn't looking at his assistant's gesture, and he sure wasn't thinking about that standing ovation. All he did was march across that floor to sophomore Ralph Fernandez, asking him why after Flanagan scored a basket in the final seconds it was the little point guard, instead of a big man, passing the ball inbounds.

As the cheers washed over Hurley, he just stood there, oblivious, waiting for Ralph to give him an answer.

Finally, Hurley did raise his hand to thank the 2,000 fans. He had been coming to the Torrey Pines tournament for so long that the San Diego fans felt like they knew his program well. Melissa handed Ahmad Nivins a placard reading "800 wins," which she had made at the hotel. Poor Ahmad. There he was in his St. Anthony golf shirt and his khakis, so proud to be a part of the program—even though he was still weeks from his debut. When Hurley finally saw Ahmad parading with that sign around the floor, looking like an oversized ring girl between rounds of a boxing card, Hurley snapped, "Put that down," and told him to get moving toward the locker room.

Hurley hadn't liked the last few minutes of the game, when the "Bombardiers" struggled to run the plays. To make matters worse, Linoll had mumbled something under his breath after Hurley yelled at him in the morning shootaround—and he wasn't finished letting Linoll have it for that. With the blowout victories, the bench was getting a lot of time in the fourth quarter, and Hurley sensed that they were losing the motivation to work hard.

"What's the restaurant we're going to eat in right now?" Hurley asked out loud in the locker room. "The Red Robin? Maybe I'll just go over there like Linoll and Qaysir, throw my feet up in the air and say, 'I didn't play, but I don't care.'

"You know what Qaysir is worried about? 'Is there another snack coming today?'"

Where that inference had been inspired was during pregame dinner at the Hometown Buffet, where Qaysir had raised Chris Hurley's ire by stacking desserts sky-high on his plastic tray.

"I know Bullock is thinking about food. And Linoll, too. 'Are we going to get a chance to eat again?' Well, I think we are, fellas.

"Don't worry, you're going to get another meal.

"You know, I worry about this stuff. I do. At the Raiders game yesterday, I was like a mother hen. There are some guys that I'm worried that I've got to protect, worried that I'm going to have to jack somebody who's starting something with them. I could never relax and enjoy the game.

"Linoll was standing up, and there were gangbangers in the back ready to call his ass out. And when they did, I would've had to handle it. I'll go in with some of the other guys here, but Linoll, you're not the one that I want to go in with.

"You're in a rough world," he told them. "You've got to be mentally tough. Just don't say that I'm the craziest person that you've ever met. Just tell them that I'm one of the most demanding people that you ever came across in your life."

So much for savoring his eight-hundredth.

That would come back at the Doubletree, where there was a cake and sandwiches in a conference room off the lobby. As his teammates plowed into stacks of subs, Marcus read over his speech at a table. He worried how the words would come out. He had never done any kind of public speaking.

"Only I knew how important the game was to coach," Marcus said in a quiet moment at his table. "The rest of the team, they just know that coach don't want to lose."

And then he laughed.

"I never shot so many three-pointers in my life."

Yes, Marcus had known him best. In a lot of ways, he was trying to make up for what he never became in Hurley's eyes, on and off the court. Outside of Greenberg at the Boys Club, Hurley was the only man whom Marcus had ever truly been able to count on. Because he had been a part of two championship teams in his freshman and sophomore seasons, he knew better than his teammates about the shared satisfaction between the coach and the team when they finally reached the finish line together. He knew the way Hurley counted on his best senior to lead the way, and wanted desperately to be that player for him.

When it was his turn, Marcus un-crumpled his speech, smoothing it on the podium. The words didn't come easily to him. Part of it was nerves, part of it expressing his feelings about Hurley; and part of it his learning disability that made it hard for him to fluidly read what was on the page.

The words tumbled sluggishly out of his mouth.

"It's a pleasure and an honor to be a four-year varsity starter under one of the best coaches in America," he started, clearing his throat a few times, flattening out the paper again. "Coach Hurley has helped me become a better player on the court and a better person off the court. Before I came to St. Anthony's, Coach saw something in me that I didn't. He has helped me become a leader and has given me a better understanding of the game and life."

Marcus stopped there, breathing out slowly. He lifted his eyes from the speech for a moment, just to see if people were still listening to him. The room had fallen silent. Hurley sat to the right of the podium, beside Chris.

They listened to Marcus struggling, and all wished they could help him somehow.

"Coach Hurley has made me into the player that I am today by never allowing me to take a day off and always pushing me to get better. I just wanted everyone here to know how proud I am to be a part of this program." Finally, his voice cracked, his mouth trembled and the words stopped coming. Marcus bowed his head and bit his lip. Around the room, his teammates watched motionless.

The toughest kid in Greenville was fighting hard now, trying to tell the toughest man he had ever met what he meant to him. What it meant to be a four-year starter. What it meant getting a shot to get out of Curries Woods. What it meant to earn Hurley's trust as the leader.

Finally, Marcus gathered himself. "I just want everyone to know how proud I am to be a part of this program and a part of Coach Hurley's eight-hundredth win. I also plan to be a part of Coach Hurley's twenty-second state title."

As everyone in the room rose to applaud, Marcus walked past Hurley's table to sit with his teammates. Hurley ran his hand over Marcus's head, slapped him on his shoulder.

"The one thing that all my players through the years have understood," Hurley would say a few moments later to the room, "is that there are a select few people who can manage to be pushed in a society now where all around you, kids don't work as hard as they should.

"Tomorrow night is going to be spectacular for us. This is going to be something for you all to put in your memory bank. I've had so many opportunities to be a part of special games that the school has played, but you've got one here. The building is going to be jumping. El Camino is undefeated.

"We know we're just a bunch of people who work hard, who have some good tradition."

EL CAMINO OF Oceanside was 13–0 and rated near the top of all the polls in the state of California. They reached the finals by beating powerful Dominguez High of Compton in the semis. The best player was University of San Diego–bound six-foot-eight forward Gyno Pomare, and in the middle they had six-foot-eleven Craig Austin, who had signed with Arizona State. The guards were excellent, including a sharpshooting senior, James Daniels, who would go to Brown University. Another rugged senior,

Justin Armstrong, was six-foot-four, 190 pounds, and destined for Columbia University. Four Division I recruits in the starting lineup, and to a man, they were bigger at every position on the floor.

"We're going to be a defensive clinic," Hurley promised the players in the pregame locker room. "They're not going to get momentum. I haven't been calling timeouts to let you play through tough situations, but I will tonight. Listen, every big game is won with defense. In baseball, it's pitching. In football, it's stopping the run."

Outside, Chris Hurley studied the nearly seven-foot El Camino center, Austin, walk past in warm-ups and marveled, "Wow, how big are they?"

SOMEHOW, BARNEY BEAT Austin for the tip, and as usual, the predesigned play in the locker room for the opening possession resulted in Marcus scoring on a layup. Still, it wasn't long until Marcus picked up two fouls, sending him to the bench just four minutes into the game.

The St. Anthony depth was a real aid now, allowing fresh bodies to stay on the floor when a fourth game in five nights, a tough travel itinerary, promised wear and tear.

The El Camino players were tugging on shorts, the universal basketball body language for tired. "Look at them already," Hurley yelled to his players on the bench. "Where do they have their hands already?"

The Friars did a fine job, even with Marcus on the bench for an eight-minute stretch, what with Hurley protecting him with his two fouls. Hurley inserted Marcus back into the game halfway through the second quarter, and within a minute, he picked up his third foul on a delicate contact. The two free throws gave El Camino a 23–19 lead.

"This is why teams don't like to travel," Hurley barked at the officials. "The best player comes in for one possession and he gets called for a touch foul."

It was a three-man crew, and Doc worked them from his seat at the end of the bench. "Look at the young one out there," he hollered. "He's got diarrhea. He's scared shitless."

With his third foul, Marcus would go to the bench for the rest of the half, spelling deep trouble for St. Anthony. It wasn't just the size and skill of El Camino that they needed to offset, but a stirred hometown crowd. It was a loud, intense, 2,500 fans packed into Torrey Pines gym, most of them pulling hard for El Camino.

With all things considered, the 25–25 halftime score would be something St. Anthony would gladly take on the way to the locker room. Before leaving the floor, Hurley intercepted the officials about the call on Marcus for his third foul. Mildly protesting for a few moments, he started back toward the staircase leading up to the locker room when someone lured him back.

"Get off the floor, ya' bum!"

Right away, Hurley whipped around and stomped straight for the mid-court section of the bleachers where he thought he had heard the voice. Tom Pushie had stayed back to walk with Hurley and quickly thrust himself between the coach and the front row of the bleachers. He wouldn't be the first assistant coach in St. Anthony history charged with holding Hurley back from a lunge into the stands.

Hurley lived by his code: If you're not allowed to yell at him while walking past him in the shopping mall, you don't have the right to do it during a basketball game.

"Wherever you do it," Hurley promises, "it won't go unchallenged."

In the corner of the gymnasium, a tall, dignified man, John Olive, the boys' basketball coach at Torrey Pines, was watching. He would have to think back fifteen years, when he was visiting the Hurley household as a Villanova assistant coach under Rollie Massimino, and hope that this was a gentler Hurley walking toward the stands. If nothing else, whoever had heckled him couldn't have possibly raised Hurley's ire any more than Massimino did.

Massimino, an increasingly pompous, self-absorbed figure in the years after Villanova's NCAA championship season in 1985, had kept an appointment to visit Hurley's house in the fall of 1988 to recruit Jerry Walker.

As Massimino's top assistant and son, Tommy, finished a presentation to Walker in Hurley's living room, he asked, "Do you have any questions?"

"Yes, I do," Walker said.

He pointed to Rollie, who was sitting on the couch with his hands on his head. "If he's so interested in me," Walker wondered, "why did you do all the talking?"

Massimino straightened in his seat, clearly taken aback.

"That's a pretty good question," Hurley said. They had grown tired of listening to the Villanova coaches list all the other recruits they had as higher priorities over Walker, finding it all distasteful and disrespectful. If they wanted Arron Bain so badly, they should just go get him and stop wasting Walker and Hurley's time.

Rollie told Walker to watch his mouth, and Hurley stood up, declaring, "This visit is over." Next thing everyone knew, Rollie muttered something else and Hurley stepped toward him, promising to pound Massimino senseless unless he dragged his ass out—and fast. Nobody came into Hurley's home and insulted him. Nobody. Soon, Massimino's assistants were dragging him out the front door

"I will kick your ass right out the front door," Hurley barked, and by then, Danny Hurley had felt so uncomfortable in the living room with the tension between his father and Massimino, he retreated to the staircase and watched from there. Eventually, he called up to his older brother. "Hey, Bobby, come down here. I think Dad's gonna fight Rollie."

That never happened, but Hurley did chase Massimino, down the stairs, out the door and onto Ferncliff Road. Hurley encouraged the assistants to let Rollie loose, but wisely, they stuffed him into the car and sped away.

And if they peeked back in the rearview mirror, they could still see Bob Hurley standing in the middle of the street, shaking his fist in the air.

All this time later, Olive prayed there wouldn't be a Hurley moment 3,000 miles away in California. This wasn't Hurley's house anymore, but Olive's gym at Torrey Pines. To Hurley, everything was a test of his manhood. He cupped his right hand to his ear, turned his head sideways, and narrowed his eyebrows. He dared someone to say it again. Anyone. Come on down and take your best shot at the old coach. Come on down and get yourself a good old-fashioned Jersey City ass-kicking.

"Why don't I hear anything now?" he barked.

When no one responded, Hurley turned back toward the locker room, just to hear that same voice wait until he was halfway up the stairs, and yell back to him, "Get off the court, ya' bum! You're getting every call!" And without looking back, without breaking stride, Hurley flung his left hand into the air.

For a fleeting second, Melissa, knowing her father all too well, feared that he could be delivering the one-finger salute.

But Hurley gave him a thumbs-up and kept moving to rejoin his team. When he found Gamble and Erman waiting for him at the entrance to the locker room, he said, "This kind of atmosphere has gotten all of my senses going." They both looked at Pushie, who was trailing Hurley into the locker room. His look suggested, *Don't ask.*

As they had consistently done before, St. Anthony took control in the third quarter. The backcourt pressure and traps inspired turnover after turnover—nine of the seventeen that El Camino committed for the game would come in that one quarter. They negated El Camino's size with speed and conditioning. Barney did a monumental job on the boards, blocking out Austin and Pomare to snag rebounds and score inside. It should've been far-fetched that St. Anthony could contend with the size, but the precision and speed with which St. Anthony sent double-teams disrupted El Camino's timing. More than that, Derrick and Beanie hounded the bigger guards so relentlessly, sliding step for step with them, belly to butts, that El Camino was running its offense close to mid-court.

Otis buried open shots, and Sean finally started to get his bearings in the game. Hurley had been right. They would put on a clinic. When Marcus picked up his fourth foul with a little over two minutes left in the third quarter, Hurley had no choice but to sit him. Suddenly, this had turned into the ultimate acid test for his St. Anthony teammates: Could they hold on with him on the bench?

Still, Pomare, the gliding six-foot-seven El Camino star, began getting loose in the fourth quarter. With Marcus on the bench, he felt unshackled. Sean hit a three-pointer from the corner to make it 49–41, but Pomare kept coming and coming. He hit a soft jumper, and tipped his own miss back into the basket to make it 49–43 with five and a half minutes left. Marcus reentered the game with 4:16 left, and amazingly, St. Anthony had a 52–45 lead. Somehow, they had held on without him.

Still, Pomare wouldn't go away. He kept dropping those soft jumpers over the defense, finishing with twenty points and seventeen rebounds.

Finally, Marcus was fouled with forty-two seconds left, sending him to the free-throw line with St. Anthony clinging to a 55–53 lead.

"Did I foul you?" the El Camino guard, Daniels, asked, walking past Marcus to take his position for the two shots.

"Yeah, you did," Marcus said, his eyes following Daniels all the way, his hands coolly caressing the ball at the line.

And with the 2,500 people standing, pounding the bleachers, Marcus bent his knees, locked his elbow and, stone-faced, swished the two free throws.

Over on the near sideline, the sweat poured down Hurley's face. He was beet-red, trying to will this last minute to be over, trying to get his guys to hold on. He wore that maroon sweater-vest in the cold of Jersey City, and the warmth of Southern California. It didn't matter. With twenty-five seconds left, and St. Anthony leading 57–53, Otis, trying desperately to keep the ball out of Pomare's hands, was whistled for a foul away from the ball. Pomare made one of the two free throws. Moments later, Otis was sent to the line with a chance to close out El Camino with twenty seconds left.

"Put 'em away, O!" Hurley yelled, crashing his hands together hard like cymbals.

Otis nodded. All he needed was to make one of the two shots.

He didn't come close. El Camino grabbed the second miss, calling time-out to set up a play for a final three-pointer that could force overtime.

As Hurley grabbed his clipboard to diagram the final defensive stand in the huddle, his eyes followed Otis all the way to the bench. He wasn't so much displeased with him for missing the two free throws as for the way he missed them.

"You can't do that, son," Hurley told him. "You front-rimmed both. You gotta be back rim on both shots because you feel *strong*."

In the huddle, Hurley described the way they needed to protect the three-point line, assigning Beanie, Derrick and Sean to contest every pass and give El Camino no chance for a good look at a game-tying three-pointer. Hurley was now sopping wet, the glistening droplets of sweat dangling off his chin.

Before they broke the huddle, Hurley screamed one final thought over the pounding bleachers and shrieking voices in the steamy gym.

"WE'LL FINISH IT WITH OUR DEFENSE, FELLAS! IT'S APPROPRIATE!"

All three St. Anthony guards overplayed the three-point line. Beanie blanketed Armstrong and Sean smothered Daniels, who finally forced up a shot. It grazed the side of the rim, bouncing harmlessly away as the final buzzer sounded.

The Friars sprinted up the stairs and into the locker room, a stray fist or two pumping into the air, but it was hardly much of a euphoric celebration scene. St. Anthony didn't win its championships in December, but in March. Still, the kids were high-fiving and laughing when Hurley walked in to meet them.

They had beaten a terrific team, in an emotionally charged environment, and they had done it the St. Anthony way: playing harder, tougher, and smarter. This had been one of those games when the weight-training in the parking lot behind the charter school gym back in Jersey City had made a difference, because without the strength to go with their speed, they wouldn't have been able to hold off El Camino. Otis had finished with nineteen points and been named the tournament MVP. Marcus and

Sean were also named to the All-Tournament team. But in the locker room, Hurley declared that the job Barney had done with thirteen points and eight rebounds against that towering front line should've earned him a trophy, too.

"We beat three straight unbeaten teams, and a team tonight maybe as talented as anybody we'll play all year," Hurley said. "We ought to be proud of this."

El Camino would go on to finish the season 31-3, and its coach, Ray Johnson, would be chosen the California state high school coach of the year. At the end of the year, someone asked him what was the highlight of his season and he said, "That I was Bob Hurley's eight hundred and first victory, not his eight-hundredth." But thinking back, he admitted, "It was an honor to be on the floor with him."

In his hotel room later, Hurley was sitting on the edge of his bed, the championship trophy on the floor next to his feet and George Costanza high jinks blasting on the television. His players were wandering in and out of the room, grabbing steaming Burger King burgers to bring back to their rooms. Hurley sipped on a can of Sprite and downed a double cheese burger.

"This tastes like prime rib," Hurley said, laughing between chews. "You want to know the glory of high school basketball? We won a championship and we end up driving around our rental cars [afterward] to find a gas station to fill the tanks, because we're getting up at 4:30 in the morning to fly home."

So, Hurley had his trophy, a Sprite, and another double cheeseburger awaiting in the bottom of the bag. He was 27-1 in his seven trips West to this tournament. This time, Hurley felt like St. Anthony stole one. "A little later in our season, maybe two weeks from now, I thought we could win this game," Hurley would confess. "I wasn't so sure we were ready to do that tonight."

It was past midnight when the kids stopped running in and out of his room for seconds and thirds on the fast-food, when his assistants had cleared out, and once again, it was just Bob, Chris, and another championship trophy beside the bed. In the glory of high school basketball, 4:30 in the morning came fast, but the old coach never got tired of these late nights far from home, when the legend of St. Anthony basketball grew with one more last-second defensive stand, one more improbable victory, one more championship against the longest of odds.

CHAPTER 9

THE CLASSROOM PROJECTOR flashed a photo of a tourist on the observation deck of World Trade Center Tower 1, smiling for a snapshot and seemingly unable to see the 757 jet roaring toward the tower. The picture had circulated on the Internet, a twenty-first-century urban legend of a man mere moments from impact on September 11, 2001.

Ray Page posed the question for discussion: Could this be a genuine picture?

The books had been closed for the final fifteen minutes of third-period French 1 class in room 204, but Page had taught long enough at St. Anthony to know that his lessons could never be confined to something as limited as a foreign-language textbook. He could no better use his classroom to teach just French than Bob Hurley could use his gymnasium to teach just basketball.

For many of the students, these classes were the one chance for someone to mold the analytical part of the mind, to mold values and character, to raise a voice over the static and slumber of the neighborhoods and projects from which they come. To teach in urban America, it was simply the charge of educators to fortify students the best they could for a world where the kids were always coming from behind, always making up for lost time.

Needing to learn to think for themselves, to unravel mysteries and discover truths, some of Page's most productive days in class were when the textbooks closed and the minds opened. He spoke with a booming but encouraging voice, a burly six-foot-three ex–Marist Order brother with a bushy, graying beard and slightly unkempt hair. Images of Albert Einstein splashed on the necktie flopping over his belly. The crucifix centered over the projector, the oblique walls tightly surrounding the class.

The composition of the class was entirely black and Hispanic, mirroring St. Anthony, which was more than 90 percent minority. The students largely agreed that the picture could've been legitimate, until Page reminded them that the man in the photo wore a winter parka and ski cap. And the attacks of September 11 had been on a warm, late-summer morning. Also, the first building hit was Tower 2, which didn't have the observation deck. And the way everything incinerated in the explosions and the building's collapse, there was little chance a camera and its film could've survived unscathed for developing. The class concentrated harder on the picture, digging deeper for its flaws.

"You never want to let the analytical part of the brain stop," Page said.

His first time around at St. Anthony, he was Brother Ray, a Marist Order clergyman assigned to the school from 1983 to 1995. Beginning as an English teacher, Page moved on to physics and ultimately tried his hand at French. After five years away, Page returned again in 2000. Brother Ray had left the priesthood between stays at St. Anthony, with a stop at Marist High School in Bayonne.

The second time around, Page found the St. Anthony students' stories of home life more horrifying, and just as disturbing, the incoming students' increased lack of preparation for high school-level work. On a weekend retreat with the kids, shortly after returning to St. Anthony a second time, he listened to a sobbing girl tell the story of her father trying to choke her older brother for messing with his classic record collection. She broke down in tears, wondering how a father could want to kill his own son.

"Even five years earlier," Page says, "you weren't hearing the intensity of strife that we were hearing now."

The kids were poorer, their home lives more dysfunctional, and the urgency for St. Anthony to be a safe haven had never been so profound.

"The solution is still the same," he says. "The Hindu proverb says even if a room has been in darkness for a hundred years, when you flick the light on, the darkness still goes away. I think the solution is still here."

As a younger educator, Page never would've interrupted his classroom curriculum to tangent into a cultural reference such as the purported 9/11 photo. But more than ever, the kids needed it. Page, who is white, subscribed to sociologist W.E.B. DuBois' belief that a black American had to learn to exist in two worlds: the black and the white. To teach at St. Anthony was a balance between honoring the world the kids live in, and preparing them for another that appeared to them largely inaccessible.

"I think a lot of our kids are absolutely brilliant, but they don't have the cultural references that other kids their own age have," he continues. "Even in French class, we went over the months of the year. In a quiz, I asked them to tell me a month of the year that was in spring. There were three kids who didn't know what spring was—didn't know if it came before the winter, or after. It was a cultural reference that they just didn't have.

"We had a girl here who graduated a couple years ago—brilliant, absolutely brilliant. You ask her to compare Macbeth and Oedipus Rex as tragic heroes, and she'd run circles around the topic. She got herself an academic scholarship to Swarthmore. In classes there, everything is fine. In her dorm room, the girls are talking about whether the skiing is better in Gstaad or Aspen. Well, she doesn't have that kind of cultural reference. For her, it's a real difficult kind of cultural adjustment.

"So one of the things that I do here is to constantly put in these kind of thinking things, puzzles, general kinds of knowledge. What I hope is that they can carry them in their heads so that if they encounter a situation where there are a few cultural references that they don't understand, they have some cultural references that they can make."

In his senior English class, Page spends a good deal of time on the Hindu epic the *Mahabharata*. That way, if the students ever find themselves in some unfamiliar intellectual situations beyond the walls of St. Anthony, beyond the neighborhoods of Jersey City, Page says, "They can say, 'There's this Hindu epic,' and they can feel part of the discussion."

St. Anthony students are in a constant race against time, the teachers trying to undo years of neglect in the understaffed and under-budgeted public school system. They have so much ground to make up to get their students out of St. Anthony and into college with a fighting chance. In the lower grades, they load up on the reading, writing and math, bombarding them with fundamentals and basics.

"Let's say I've got a kid in the ninth grade with a fourth- or a fifth-grade reading level," Page says. "I always think that if he's gone through eight years of school, and his reading level is, say, fourth grade and a half, even if I can double that over the course of four years, and get him to advance a year (academically) every year, by the time he finishes his senior year he is still only going to have a ninth-grade reading level.

"That is the problem. There is an urgency about that. The unfortunate thing is that the students don't understand the urgency of that until their senior year."

The mean teaching salary at St. Anthony is $29,801, well below the New Jersey state average for teachers of $53,281. Yet, the trustees had raised salaries by several thousand dollars in some cases in the past year. Despite the school's financial plight, one trustee, Mike Slater, said, "We had to be able to keep the good teachers we had, and also attract other quality ones." Just one clergy member taught in the school, basically because the archdiocese no longer assigned them to St. Anthony. Sister Appolonia wore an electric-blue habit, a Nigerian nun with an incredibly diverse double-dip of undergraduate and graduate degrees—a bachelor of arts at the Pontifical School in Rome and a master's at St. Peter's College in Jersey City. The rest were lay teachers, struggling to balance a modest check with a devotion to teaching where they're most needed.

"For so long, Catholic schools were used to having the religious do all the teaching," Sister Alan says. "The salaries were so low. Technically, tuition was $300 or $400. You didn't have to meet the large school budget. But the biggest problem today will be, 'Can Catholic schools survive health-care costs?'

"There are no easy answers because you can't blame teachers for wanting reasonable salaries and health-care benefits. But it's really hard to meet them."

For Page, something he called the "ethos" of St. Anthony drew him back. At Marist High School, the principal talked of enacting "zero tolerance" policies, something he rejected. "That's war talk," he says, "and I'm not at war with my students." To him, St. Anthony was at its best when teaching was a cooperative process, a give-and-take that demanded a sobering self-examination of his methods back in his early days there.

He was given a second chance at St. Anthony. And for that, Page was forever grateful. Not by the administration, nor by Sister Felicia and Sister Alan, but by the students. He had been like so many well-intentioned, idealistic teachers walking in the door of an inner-city high school. "When I entered here, on a subconscious level, I came in with the idea that, 'Here I am, great teacher coming to this poor inner-city school to help you young children,'" he remembers. "That was in my mind. And the children didn't respond to that. And who would? It was so condescending. The greatest gift that I've gotten in my twenty-six years of teaching is the second chance that the kids gave me at St. Anthony."

His first five years of teaching had come at Bishop Carroll, a rural Catholic school in Evansburg, Pennsylvania, where Page delivered a one-man classroom production. He developed a loud persona about himself, constantly wielding a swagger stick in the air, smacking it against his desk to punctuate points for dramatic effect.

At Bishop Carroll, the students loved it. "They had never seen a crazed persona before and it was entertaining to them," he says. "And they would learn very, very well from that."

When Page brought the shtick with him to St. Anthony, he quickly discovered that it was jarring to the students—even downright menacing. "What I didn't realize was that these kids had seen crazy people, and the crazy people were out to hurt them in their own neighborhood. In Evansburg, there weren't any crazy people around. They knew that it was kind of this persona and act that I was creating."

In his first year of teaching English at St. Anthony in 1983, it became clear to him one day. There was a scene in *Julius Caesar* where Brutus was deciding whether to join the conspiracy, and made an analogy of Caesar climbing a ladder and reaching a point where he was only looking up, and not looking down at the common people anymore. Page wanted to act out the metaphor, and climbed on his desk yelling, "He's up here now and he's starting to look up, and he's climbing even higher. . . ."

Shouting even louder on top of his desk, and looking down on the class, the fearful expressions of backpedaling students told him everything that he needed to know about teaching in the suburbs versus the inner city.

"It never occurred to me that the jarring nature of the experience is really going to conflict with their ability to understand the metaphor. Ultimately, there are students who, within the structure of what we have here, I can't reach. And that's all been very jarring to me. A school that works well is a sacred community, and I like to think there's a healing power in a sacred community. Kids come in here damaged. And I like to think there's a healing power to somehow make it through that wound.

"When a number of freshmen come here—I call it a preemptive strike—they come with an assumption that everyone is against them. And in order to prevent any arrows being shot at them, they're going to shoot an arrow at you first. Because they're convinced that if they don't, you will do it to them first. So they want to preempt you from doing that. Especially those coming in in bad academic shape, because they've been made fun of, they come in primed for the preemptive approach.

"I hope that after three or four weeks, sometimes even months, they learn that you don't have to be defensive here. If you make a mistake reading, nobody is going to get on you. Well, one especially volatile kid came in, believing everyone was out to get him. I would sit down and say that I needed to speak to him, and he'd immediately say, 'I didn't do anything . . . what am I doing wrong?' When I spoke with his mother, she told me that at night, he was banging on her bedroom door screaming, 'I'm going to kill you.' "

They found out that the freshman boy had a deep drug problem already, and found a clinic in Pennsylvania to send him to. He never did return to St. Anthony.

For the kids staying the course on Eighth Street, they will continue to teach them the best they can, as long as the doors stay open to allow them.

But what if the money dried up, if St. Anthony closed, if there was nowhere else these families could send their kids for an affordable parochial school education?

"There are certain kids who are resilient, who would succeed wherever they were," Page says. "But for a lot of our kids the idea of aiming to go to college is very counterculture to the kinds of neighborhoods they live in. Not to the parents, because they're willing to spend the money to send them here. But it is to the influences around them, where they live.

"Sure, some kids would be resilient enough to be able to do it, but I don't think that's the case for a majority of our kids. For a majority, that resilience and those kinds of dreams would go by the wayside."

THREE DAYS AFTER the Torrey Pines tournament organizers had honored Hurley with a brief ceremony in San Diego, the St. Anthony Friars were back on the floor for their home opener, a Friday night game against Life Center Academy at the charter school gym. Familiar Jersey City faces wandered into the gym, an assortment of old-guard St. Anthony supporters filing past the coach during the junior varsity game. They were happy that the team had come back undefeated from California, and curious to see how the kids had come along in the early season.

As Hurley watched the jayvee play from a row of chairs set up in the corner of the gymnasium, his wife reminded him that Sister Felicia had planned a brief pregame ceremony to honor his eight-hundredth victory.

"We're really milking the eight-hundred win thing a lot, aren't we?" Hurley said. "I'll be at eight-forty, and we'll still be having ceremonies for eight-hundred."

"Well, get ready," his wife warned. "They're doing another one Sunday for you at St. Peter's."

"What?"

"Well, Sister Alan wanted to be there for one. . . ."

For several weeks, chemotherapy had been pounding Sister Alan. A catheter pump installed in her kidney had grown infected, leaving her too weak to make it to the game that Friday night. It had caused her to miss the San Diego trip, and angered her even more that she couldn't get over to the gym to welcome the team back. Still, she was tired and weak and knew that trying would just set her back again. She had targeted the game in two days against Christian Brothers Academy at St. Peter's College to be her home opener.

Gamble assigned three of the seniors, Marcus, Beanie and Shelton, to march a banner commemorating the eight-hundred victories to center court for a brief, pregame ceremony before Life Center. However, he had a different assignment for Otis.

"You're going to present roses to Mrs. Hurley," he instructed.

Gamble remembered Otis telling him that his goal for his senior season was to take his turn in the St. Anthony tradition of presenting his mother with flowers on senior night. In all the years that Otis had played basketball since childhood, through freshman, jayvee and varsity basketball, Earleen Campbell had never seen one of his games. "She don't know how good I am," he would say.

Still, Otis was hopeful she would finally make it for the senior-night ceremony in March.

"I want to give Otis a little practice for it," Gamble said.

Behind the St. Anthony bench, Gary Greenberg beamed. The daily updates on the seniors from California had invigorated him. It has been such a long, troubling journey with them, maybe they were finally getting it. When things were going well for the seniors, he always felt better about bringing the next generation of St. Anthony kids over. And Hurley always loved to see the eighth-grader who was with Greenberg this night, Travon Woodall, who was carrying with him the clipboard passed out in November at the St. Anthony coaching clinic.

"I write down every word I hear Coach Hurley say," Travon proudly declared.

Travon Woodall had big eyes, and a soft, friendly face. He was considered the best eighth-grade guard in northern New Jersey, a kid so talented that he played in the high school All-Star game at Hurley's summer camp in the Poconos back in August. He lived in Paterson, about fifteen miles away, but dreamed of playing for St. Anthony and Hurley. There was a family friend who had volunteered to drive him to Jersey City every day. Hurley was thrilled at the possibility of coaching him, because when that kind of talent was married with that kind of dedication, it spawned a chance for greatness.

"Look," Greenberg would say, pointing down to Travon's diagrams of Hurley's offensive plays. "He writes down every word." And with that, Travon lifted up the clipboard, thick with pages and pages of notes.

All of Greenberg's Boys Club kids were starting to see the light. Really, there weren't three players more essential to the St. Anthony season than the three seniors—Marcus, Beanie and Otis. Especially Otis. As a sophomore, Hurley wanted to bring Otis up to the varsity to practice and dress for the state tournament. Hurley did this with the young players to give them a glimpse of the way upperclassmen handled themselves, the way they committed and worked toward a state championship.

For a lot of the jayvee players, it was the first taste of day-to-day dealing with Hurley's intensity on the practice floor. Otis never made it to the varsity that year. He had spread glue on a teacher's pet rock in hopes she would lay her hand across it before it dried. Unfortunately for his state tournament practice hopes, it worked. She needed hot water to pry the rock loose, a prank that earned Otis a laugh in class and a suspension from school.

"What it really got him," Hurley believes, "was out of the pressure and responsibility of having to come up to varsity. It was easier to just be a screwup and stay away."

Otis had come a long way from that tonight, presenting those roses to Mrs. Hurley with a hug and a big, beautiful smile. He had become downright effervescent, a transformation that manifested itself on the basketball floor, too. Central Connecticut and Quinnipiac College were still recruiting him hard, believing that Otis had a fighting chance to get his core grades and SAT scores improved enough during his senior year to be eligible for a full scholarship next fall.

One day at practice, he had asked, "Do you think it would be better if I qualified and went to Central now, or just went to JUCO with the rest of the guys?" There was a part of Otis that needed the courage to overcome the fear of achieving beyond Marcus and Beanie, of separating himself from a group of friends who had done everything together through the years.

In so many ways in his life, Otis had shown the resolve to change, to grow, and he had come back to Jersey City with that MVP award from San Diego looking like he was on his way to a first-team all-state season. Ever since Notre Dame coach Mike Brey, one of the Duke assistants during Bobby's college days, had sent Hurley a scoring system that gave points for the little things—deflections, steals, taking charges—Otis had consistently delivered the best statistics on the team. Before then, he had been a one-dimensional player, never asking much more of himself than getting shots to the rim.

Bursting with breakthroughs, it felt fitting that he embarked on one more in the opening moments of the game on Friday night. On the first trip down the floor, Otis stepped across Life Center's three-point arc, intercepted a pass and had a clear run to the basket. With the packed gym rising with his every step down the floor, with the murmurs growing with each dribble to the rim, just one thought crossed his mind: timing his take-off, leaping, rising over the rim and polishing off his first high school dunk. He had been waiting for this moment, and nothing could stop him. Otis Campbell had come of age as a high school basketball star, and the rite of passage of a hard, rim-rattling dunk belonged to him.

And as Otis picked up his dribble, made that one final hard push off with his left foot to propel his body into the air, up and over the rim, the sensation of floating through the air was suddenly short-circuited.

Something gave.

Something snapped.

All he could do was gather himself in the air and drop the ball over the rim for a layup. As he landed, a pain pulsated through his left foot. He limped back and forth on two more trips down the floor. But he knew.

From the bench, only Erman noticed Otis favoring that left leg with a limp.

Erman nudged Pushie. "I think Otis is hurt."

The elder assistant shrugged Erman off, only to have him persist. Erman said it louder, trying to get Hurley's attention.

"Otis is hurt!" he yelled.

Finally, Hurley could see him limping, too.

In the tradition of a hardened St. Anthony player, Otis had refused to ask out of the game. He wouldn't let Hurley see him hurting. A year earlier, Sean broke his kneecap in the final scrimmage of the preseason, in so much pain that he was crying when he reached the bench. It was Otis, who had originally quit in response to Sean's arrival, who had thrown his arm around him on the bench that day, even wiping the tears from his teammate's cheek.

After the next stoppage, Doc Miller helped Otis through a door behind the bench and into the St. Anthony training room—the kitchen for the concession stand. As the school's office secretary and game-night concessionaire, Toni Bollhardt, walked to the back of the kitchen to mine pretzels from hot ovens, she kept warning Otis to be careful he didn't burn himself leaning against the searing steel stoves. Doc struggled to get Otis balanced on a cart. His Reeboks unlaced, his right leg extended out toward a countertop, Otis's toes dodged a canister of dill relish, another of ketchup.

"It's hurting," Otis said, his head wobbling backward. "Doc, it hurts!"

THEY WOULD KEEP trying to call Otis's mother, but she wasn't home. Otis didn't know where she was, or where they could reach her. But he was eighteen, so they could take him to the emergency room without parental permission. Erman left the bench, and along with The Faa, loaded Otis into a backseat of his rickety Jersey City Recreation van and sped away.

As they waited for the results of the X-rays at St. Francis Hospital, The Faa stood a few feet away, watching a college football bowl game on television.

"Who do I put as the emergency contact?" Erman asked Otis.

"Your mother, right?"

"Put yourself," Otis said.

Otis propped his foot on a chair, genuinely fearing that a bone was broken and his basketball season was over.

"All these guys talk about wanting to play in the NBA, or go to Europe," Otis said to Erman. "I just want a college scholarship, an education. I just want to get a degree in business, and a get job like you used to have."

Erman laughed. "Like I used to have?"

Erman was a curiosity to the kids, mysterious for having given up so much money and prestige to come crashing into their world. It was hard for the kids to see that Hurley could've been making a million dollars a year in college basketball somewhere, because he had never gone and done it. They knew Erman's story, and wondered why anyone would choose to give up what he did to come to Jersey City, when it seemed so many of them were trying to get out, and get what he had.

"I'm just using basketball to earn a degree," Otis says. "I just want to support my family in Jersey City. I don't care how hard I have to work. After Coach Hurley, I can do anything. I just want to be able to provide for my family."

Otis had grown up on one of the worst drug-trafficking blocks in Jersey City, out on Armstrong Avenue, where his boyhood buddies, called Little Bit, Fidge and Packy, used to sidestep the pushers and junkies to play ball in the courtyard. The police had come and rounded up a gang of Bloods a few blocks over, on Wegman. "Twenty-five years to life, all of them," Otis says. "It was so crazy. Shootings. Drugs everywhere. But it's calmed down a lot, though."

Why?

"Everybody's locked up—or they just can't do it anymore."

His father, Otis Sr., lived in the South, and worked as a trucker. His mother, Earleen, had moved him and Otis's older brother out of Armstrong a year earlier, to an apartment in a blue house on Emory Street, next door to the parking lot for the No. 17 school. It was safer there, but Otis missed the action on Armstrong. The community. He missed the people sitting on the porches, missed the pork fried rice and chicken wings at the Chinese takeout on the corner of Armstrong and Martin Luther King. Still, it had changed so much. Everybody was gone. Some of his friends just went to Snyder High School, dropped out and ended up in prison. Some graduated, but are still hanging out on the street corners.

"They're all struggling now," Otis says. "Some are just getting out of jail. Some are struggling to find a job. But they're struggling. I hear Coach Hurley tell the stories about the ones that don't get out, and that stays with me. Because I'm not going to be one of them."

THE NURSE TOLD him that they wouldn't know for sure until seeing a foot specialist on Monday morning, but it looked like a cracked bone in the side of his foot. Probably six weeks out of the lineup, which would get him back just before the state tournament. They put Otis in a walking cast and discharged him.

When The Faa, Erman and Otis arrived back at the gymnasium, the Hurleys were still in the gym. Even without Otis, St. Anthony had won easily over Life Center, 81–56.

Hurley instructed Otis to get home, get his foot iced and elevated on a pillow and stay away from practice the next day. Maybe they could come get him for the game on Sunday against Christian Brothers Academy, but he wanted to keep the swelling down before his exam on Monday. Otis leaned his crutches against the van, hopping on one leg as he tried to climb into the second row of seats. From there, Otis couldn't see the tear welling in his coach's eye between the gym lobby and the glass doors, between Hurley's thoughts about who Otis Campbell had been and who he had become.

"Ah, we can hold the fort down without him," Hurley said, zipping up his coat for a mean winter night outside. "I mean, I've been doing this a million years. But it was just something to see him finally manage to figure it all out, an introverted kid who tried to get outside of his personality and become someone who got everybody else going."

The van pulled out of the parking lot, steering Otis back home.

They still hadn't gotten his mother on the phone.

"This is a part of sports," Hurley said. "You deal with these things. But here was a kid who had just started to see the light, to get it, and the season goes out for him like that. . . . I'm old. I've done this a million times, but a kid like that. . . ."

He didn't finish his thought. There was no need.

The Friars were 6-0, but Otis was done for several weeks, and his best basketball of the season had been played. His chance for a Division I scholarship straight out of St. Anthony had all but vanished. It wouldn't be long before his most persistent suitor, Central Connecticut, backed off.

CHAPTER 10

ON HIS DRIVE to St. Peter's College for a 1:30 Sunday game against Christian Brothers Academy, Ben Gamble had a 10:00 appointment at Lamar Alston's house.

When Gamble walked into the living room, there was no sign of Lamar. His father called upstairs to him, rustling him out of bed. The coaching staff had reached out to Lamar, offering him one more chance to get back on the team, and here came a slumbering Lamar out of his bedroom, rubbing the sleep out of his eyes. Gamble didn't like that he wasn't downstairs waiting for him to arrive. He didn't like the answers to his questions, didn't like his body language, didn't like the fact that Lamar couldn't tell him the reasons he wanted to play again.

"This should've been like a job interview for him," Gamble would say later. "I mean, let's face it: Right now, I'm the only one who could get him back on this team. Tommy and me, anyway. But I'm the one who is going to have to stick my neck out. Because if he comes back and it blows up again, I'll have to hear it from coach."

Before the California trip, Gamble had told Lamar and his father that he would revisit Lamar's possible return to the team that next Monday, January 5. All of them sitting down to talk ended up happening a day sooner. The issue had come up again at practice on Saturday morning, and Hurley left it to Gamble and, partly Pushie, to make a recommendation.

"As far as I'm concerned," Hurley had told them, "this is my team right here."

A team that without Otis was down to just one substitute—Shelton Gibbs—whom Hurley trusted to insert into a tough game like C.B.A. Beanie had moved into the starting lineup, but Hurley had little faith in the sophomores Bombardiers, Ralph and Linoll. And it was still two weeks until Ahmad Nivins would become eligible.

From a purely basketball standpoint, the team could use Lamar. But this was far from a basketball decision. They had to believe that they could trust him again, that he wouldn't go running after the first obstacle tumbled in his way.

LAMAR AND HIS father, Joe Boccia, watched the C.B.A. game from the wooden bleachers of the Yanitelli Center. It was a triple-header of Jersey's top Catholic school programs, including St. Benedict's, Seton Hall Prep and St. Pat's, a good 3,000 fans with the gate receipts going to a scholarship fund to be shared among the six schools playing.

Hurley had called Sister Alan on Saturday night and told her in no uncertain terms: No more ceremonies for eight hundred victories. He had had it. He was just glad she was here. Normalcy meant everything to Hurley, and that meant Sister Alan sitting by his side with Sister Felicia behind the bench. Still, she'd have to live without another ceremony for eight hundred. She gladly agreed.

This wasn't one of C.B.A.'s most talented teams, but they were extremely well-coached, employing the patient Princeton University passing offense, an elaborate web of handoffs, cuts and screens, forever waiting for the backdoor opening for an easy layup. St. Anthony and Christian Brothers had a history of epic New Jersey high school basketball games, and for three quarters, this had the makings of another. St. Anthony had only one day of practice without Otis, and Hurley wasn't interested in style points. This was about surviving. He scaled back the Friars full-court pressure, knowing that he just didn't have the reservoir of bodies to sustain it. To start the fourth quarter, they were clinging to a 35–34 lead. C.B.A. had controlled the tempo of the game, miring St. Anthony in a sluggish, half-court game that benefited the Jersey Shore school because of its lack of athleticism.

As much as anyone, Sean had struggled. He had turned the ball over and forced several bad shots. These were both becoming increasing problems for him. A Georgia Tech assistant coach watched closely in the stands, diligently taking notes on Sean.

Before the start of the fourth quarter, Hurley yelled in the huddle, "This is when the seniors need to make plays."

This had been when they feared Beanie could crack. With Otis and

Lamar gone, the pressure belonged to Beanie to deliver, and God only knew how he'd react to it.

The answer was mesmerizing. It started with a mid-court trap on the Christian Brothers point guard, Chris White, a five-foot-ten senior, when Beanie stole the ball along the left sideline, then tap-danced for several feet to stay inbounds. Once Beanie regained his balance and control of the ball, there was a defender waiting for him at the basket. Streaking from the left side, he ducked beneath the rim, hanging in the air to absorb the contact, and reached up and under for the basket and the foul.

After the free throw, it was 40–34 with just under five minutes left in the game. As C.B.A. tried to bring the ball across mid-court again, there was Beanie in perfect defensive position: low to the floor, palms up. When the point guard, White, gave him just a brief peek at the ball, Beanie swung upward in an instant with his right hand, popping the ball into the air. White knocked it out-of-bounds and lost possession to St. Anthony again.

White had turned just that: ghostly white. Beanie hadn't just stripped him of the ball, but embarrassed him again.

After the St. Anthony delay offense worked another minute off the clock, a turnover gave the ball back to Christian Brothers with a little over three minutes left. Once again, it was Beanie and White meeting at mid-court, where the Christian Brothers guard was so spooked over another trap closing his way that he lost his composure and dribbled the ball backward across the mid-court line for a violation. Moments later, Sean buried a three-pointer from the corner, stretching the lead to 43–34. C.B.A. then made a three-pointer with nineteen seconds left to cut it to 45–41, but a sure sign of Beanie's suddenly unconquerable confidence was his eagerness to catch the inbounds pass so he could shoot the two free throws when Christian Brothers went for the intentional foul. He would swish both with 13.5 seconds left, capping a 47–41 victory.

Downstairs from the gymnasium, in the St. Anthony locker room, Hurley would tell the team, "We willed this one. It's going to be this way for a while, playing just six guys until Ahmad Nivins gets eligible in two weeks. This was one that we had to grind out."

In his mind, there wasn't much help on the way in the near-term. Certainly not from Lamar Alston, who lingered in the corridor upstairs. The Italian father and the black son stood in the doorway as the St. Anthony coaches and players sat in the bleachers, catching the start of the Seton Hall Prep-St. Pat's game. Lamar hadn't dared cross Hurley's path yet. They still hadn't spoken.

About his meeting with Gamble that morning, Lamar said, "I don't think it went as well as it could've. I didn't tell Coach Gamble what he wanted to hear, but I told him my feelings. They really don't know how much I miss it."

As his son's words trailed off, Boccia spoke up. "He's a little shy in expressing his true feelings. He's always been a keep-it-inside kind of kid. But I think the time off gave him an opportunity to refocus. Coach's main objective is to get kids to be able to handle life's challenges. He said if you've got problems away from the court, you've got to take care of those things." Boccia insisted that the Division I schools that had started to recruit Lamar over the summer, like Rider and Canisius, were still courting him.

"Not quite," Rider assistant coach Tom Dempsey would say. "The father is still calling us." There was no way Rider would keep recruiting a St. Anthony player who Hurley had thrown off the team, especially when they really wanted junior Barney Anderson next year. To get a chance for a basketball scholarship, Lamar still had to win over Hurley. Wherever he wanted to go beyond St. Anthony High School, beyond Jersey City, only one man had the clout to get him there.

And as the release of Tuesday's *USA Today* said, that man coached the nation's number-two-rated high school basketball team—with or without Lamar Alston.

AFTER OPENING THE steel doors and stepping into the narrow foyer of St. Anthony High School, Josh Moore hesitated before pressing the button to be buzzed into the building. It had been a long, long time and he could still turn back. He just couldn't *go* back anymore.

The Los Angeles Clippers had checked into the Hyatt on the Jersey City waterfront a day earlier, and Moore had been moved to take the half-hour walk to the school. It had been dusk, late Sunday afternoon, and he just stood on the Eighth Street sidewalk and stared. Everything rushed back to him. Still seeing himself contorting his seven-foot body to fit into the classroom desks, still seeing the pretty girls smiling back in the narrow corridors, still seeing Sister Felicia shooting him that nasty glare for tardiness that made him feel like he was going straight to hell, it all rushed over him Sunday.

In the gathering darkness and whipping winds, mostly Josh Moore heard the voice of Bob Hurley.

And now, it was Monday afternoon, January 5, and Moore had come the final few feet to the school's entrance. Maybe this wasn't such a good idea. Maybe they wouldn't remember him. Maybe he should've stayed back at the hotel, playing video games, until the team bus left for the game against the Nets in the Meadowlands. After six years, maybe Josh Moore should just turn and walk away. Again.

For all the stories of past St. Anthony basketball players looking back with such satisfaction over staying the course, here was Moore on Monday in his Clippers sweatshirt and sweatpants, pursing his lips and shaking his head side to side in regret and saying, "Leaving here, leaving Coach, it's the biggest mistake I ever made in my life."

The buzzer sounded, the doors unlocked and Josh Moore stepped back into St. Anthony High School. It felt like someone had thrown a warm blanket over him.

THE CLIPPERS SHARED the downtown Los Angeles Staples Center with the Lakers, the disparate fortunes of the two franchises easily embodied in the two team's seven-foot-two centers, both born in Newark, both owners of size 22 sneakers: Shaquille O'Neal and Josh Moore. Ever since Moore had been a seven-foot freshman at St. Anthony, Shaq had been sending him his hand-me-down clothes and shoes, dressing the young man from his hometown who had been delivered by the same doctor, in the same hospital.

He still had the innocent eyes of a kid who had never mentally grown into his 330-pound body. The Clippers had stashed him on the injured reserve list to start the season, believing Moore to be the personification of the basketball term, "project." His sheer immensity and youth got him a first-year, non-guaranteed NBA minimum contract of $366,931, but his staying power depended on his dedication to developing day to day. The self-discipline to stay committed without getting activated, without playing in games, was the toughest test for him. Since St. Anthony, he hadn't stayed with much of anything. Once he quit on Hurley, the path of least resistance had become his preferred choice.

From his sixth- to seventh-grade year in Newark, Moore grew nine inches to six-foot-nine. By his freshman year at St. Anthony, he had reached seven feet. The growth spurt had been a product of a tumor in his pituitary gland, lodged at the base of his brain. It wasn't until he had started experiencing sharp headaches and blurred vision in his first year at St. Anthony that doctors diagnosed the problem. He would undergo a sensitive ten-hour surgery at Newark's University Hospital in the summer of 1996, a successful procedure that had him back inside Hurley's gymnasium in the fall.

He remembered the way they had been there for him, Coach Hurley, and his wife, his teachers and his teammates, and even now he doesn't understand how he could've let the illumination of life's fragility fade so quickly from in his mind. From a lawyer to summer-league coaches to hangers-on spilling out of the concrete crevices, an army of influences had a hand in turning him from one of the nation's top college prospects into a cautionary tale.

The flesh-peddlers had gotten it into Moore's mind that Hurley was holding him back, and he began to fulfill fewer and fewer of his obligations at St. Anthony. Finally, Hurley threw him off the team halfway through his junior season in 1998, telling Moore he needed to get his act together and lose that sense of entitlement that had arisen with the growing entourage of sycophants.

He never made it back for his senior year, telling a reporter about transferring out of St. Anthony, "From my perspective, I just look at it as another step in my development."

From St. Anthony, it was off to St. Thomas More Prep in Oakdale, Connecticut, and then the dubious and now-defunct Christopher Robin Academy in New York, where jocks were miraculously gaining academic credits despite little recollection of the subjects, teachers, or curriculum.

He would sign a letter of intent with Rutgers, but never make it to campus. And then it was on to UCLA. Long Beach City College. Compton College. After playing parts of two seasons at the University of Michigan, he was thrown out of school in January 2002 for floundering academically. After entering the 2002 NBA Draft, where he went un-chosen, Moore spent his first season of pro ball with the Zhejiang Horses of the Chinese professional league. Twenty-six games in, lost, lonely and a long way from home, he packed his bags and moved back to California.

The more Moore drifted from St. Anthony and Hurley, the more he came to long for those days, for the school and the Sisters and the coach whom he eventually realized were the last people who ever truly cared about him.

"When I was in St. Anthony, I had a coach and style and system that I knew really well, that I believed in," Moore says. "After I left St. Anthony, it was really hard for me to find something that I believed in, or somebody who I could follow, somebody who was a leader like Coach Hurley. It was kind of hard to accept anything less from a coach."

Over the summer of 2003, his agent had secured him a workout with the Clippers. Moore had never been through an NBA workout, had no idea what to expect, or how to prepare. He picked up the telephone and called his old coach, the one he had walked out on five years earlier.

Hurley talked him through it.

"Coach Hurley always told you what you needed to hear, all the time," Moore says. "He never told you what you wanted to hear, not one time. He was always up front. When I bounced around, I was looking for someone to be like that. You don't get that anywhere else. Coach Hurley is one of the top five coaches on any level, and I can say that, now that I'm finally in the NBA. I should've realized it back then.

"But there was a lot I should've realized then. I had Sister Alan and Sister Felicia, they were like a family. They kind of watched over me. If you were slacking off, they got on you. When you leave that kind of community, where you know they care about you, it's hard to adjust to money-driven places, where everyone has an agenda.

"That's what I'm struggling to adjust to now. I don't think I've ever gotten over leaving St. Anthony like I did, and I don't know if I ever will."

Josh Moore cautiously walked through the doors, up the stairs and turned right at the statue of St. Anthony holding that little boy in the palm of his hand. Suddenly, he appeared in the doorway to the principal's office. Would they remember Josh Moore? Would they want to see him? In a chair across from Sister Felicia, Sister Alan was visiting with her. Sister Alan leaped up at seeing him, and before she knew it, Josh Moore had lifted her off her feet into a long, tight hug that he wished he had never let go of.

The three of them sat down together and talked about what happened to him, and how life had gone and how the Sisters always did have a soft spot for him. He had come to them a little boy lost in a man's body, a prankster who had won over their hearts after he survived that risky brain operation. There was still such a vulnerability to him, a desire to rewind the clock and climb back into the protective womb of St. Anthony High School.

"I'm really glad you're doing something good with basketball," Sister Alan said. "Maybe you had your bumps in the road early, and now you're going to be all right."

He smiled and nodded. "I was talking to my mother last night. I was telling her that I would've been graduating college this year. Instead, I'm graduating the school of hard knocks."

Sister Felicia asked Moore if he was happy.

"Give me a couple more years, and maybe I can say that I'm really happy. Maybe I can come back and donate a whole bunch of money."

As they got up to walk downstairs to the cafeteria, Sister Alan looked up and told him, "I was always on your case. You look wonderful. You put on some weight that you needed. How tall are you now?"

"Seven-two."

She laughed, craning her neck as they walked down the stairs. "You weren't that much shorter when you were a freshman."

There was an awkward silence for a moment, Moore starting to say something and then stopping himself. As they walked into the cafeteria, the kids' heads turned. They always do with Moore. He wasn't looking at them, but trying to get the words out to Sister Alan.

"I rebounded and I still love you," he said. "I want to get as many kisses from you as I can. I don't know when I'm going to come back to New Jersey next."

He bent down, kissed her on the cheek and hugged her again.

It wasn't unusual to have old students stopping by the school, just to give her one of those hugs, just to tell her what she had meant to them. They knew she was sick, and they knew they would regret never taking the time to tell her. She never got tired of hearing it. Her eyes teared up.

He tried to lighten the moment, running his eyes over the bustling cafeteria. "I'm looking at all these kids now and they look like the same faces. The white dude with the big ears reminds me of the white dude with the big ears we had."

Soon, they walked back upstairs and said good-bye. Outside the school, he slid his hands into his sweatpants pockets and started walking. "What Sister Alan said, that really touched me," he said, squinting into the sun. "I was one of the guys who left that really touched her. Now that she's battling that cancer, I give her as many kisses as I can. I don't know how long she's going to be around."

He turned left into the chain-link-fence entrance to the parking lot, hoping to catch a ride back to the Hyatt, back to another lonely day on the road. All those years back, Moore had been so anxious to leave Hurley and the Sisters behind, to boldly break out into a big, basketball world that seemed to be opening its arms to him. He was twenty-three years old and felt like an old man. With whatever he did take out of St. Anthony, he was holding tight the best he could these days. If only he could go back and try it again.

"I really wish I could tell people that I was an alum of St. Anthony," Josh Moore said.

CHAPTER 11

TWENTY-FOUR HOURS AFTER *USA Today* had elevated St. Anthony to its number-two national ranking, Hurley still didn't presume to know where the Friars belonged in the poll, especially now with the injury to Otis. What he did know was that his teams always improved over the course of the season, and this one in particular defended well enough to keep them in any game, anywhere. Perhaps even against mighty Oak Hill Academy, the barnstorming number-one-ranked team out of the blue mountains of rural Virginia.

At the moment, Oak Hill was globe-trotting through Spain, playing against junior national European teams. They weren't just unbeaten on the season, but unchallenged. Across the ocean at the St. Anthony practice on January 7, Hurley manufactured a moment of disgust to deliver his own dose of perspective on the new ranking.

"That *USA Today* that came out, that says you're the number-two team in the country?

"Get a copy, go home and wipe your ass with it!"

It was the ultimate contrast to have Oak Hill, largely a collection of blue-chip mercenaries from across the country, and St. Anthony, largely a neighborhood team of childhood buddies from the streets of Jersey City, ranked first and second in the nation. Oak Hill and St. Anthony—the new school and old school of high school basketball dynasties—had gone back and forth in the national rankings for years. The 2003–2004 season would come to be one more study in how championship high school basketball had become transformed into big business across the nation, and how it had stayed largely unaffected in Hurley's world within Jersey City.

There was a burgeoning new world order in high school basketball, where sneaker companies, national AAU teams, boarding schools and agent-funded sports academies had been propped up as the new gods of the game.

However the elite found their way to Mouth of Wilson, Virginia, they came like never before for the 2003–2004 season. Oak Hill had the biggest high school free-agent harvest in the country, bringing four of rivalshoops.com's top-50-ranked prospects to the campus for their senior seasons. The best of the star-filled cast was Josh Smith, a six-foot-nine forward from Powder Springs, Georgia, who would eventually turn his back on a commitment to Indiana University to make the leap straight into the first-round NBA draft selection of his hometown Atlanta Hawks.

From Oak Hill to the pros wouldn't be that immense of a leap in basketball lifestyle for Smith, considering that his high school team would play just one less game than the NCAA champion Connecticut Huskies, a total of thirty-eight. Oak Hill took its all-star show on the road for two-thirds of its schedule, jetting to tournaments in Europe, Hawaii, California and New Jersey. They had a modest 400-seat gymnasium on campus, although the president of the school lamented that they probably could afford a sparkling new facility if the eighteen alumni who had reached the NBA banded together to write checks. Considering the fact that graduates Carmelo Anthony, Jerry Stackhouse and Rod Strickland spent just one season on campus, it shouldn't have been too surprising that they didn't feel an excessive loyalty to their alma mater.

The sooner Hurley disposed of any discussion of Oak Hill, the better for his players. In past seasons, he knew he had teams mature enough to handle what came with the lofty national rankings. They had leaders with fuller bodies of high school achievement, kids able to keep the rankings in perspective, and consider them for what they were: an arbitrary opinion. This team was far too fragile, far too susceptible to letting the hype overwhelm them. Hurley knew there were people telling his players that they must be superstars to be part of such an elevated national ranking. For that flawed line of thinking alone, he had to be a stronger, more persuasive voice than those surrounding the kids.

"The information they get from everybody else in the city is brutal," he says. "The thinking goes, 'If you're the best player on St. Anthony's and that's the number-two team in the country, you can probably go right to the NBA.' That's the dumb information that you get on street corners."

To his players, Hurley named five teams in the state that he believed were better than them that day, including New Jersey's second-ranked team, Seton Hall Prep. St. Anthony wouldn't be truly tested again until

they would play Prep on January 17, and that was still two games—
Lawrence and Pleasantville—and eleven days away.

The trimmings of national prominence had seeped into the gym that
afternoon with the arrival of the sharp maroon sweat suits that sponsor
Reebok had sent the team. For some reason, passing them out blanketed
Hurley with guilt. He knew they needed the clothes, knew it made the
kids look like a team, but that old-school part of the coach never wanted
them to feel entitled to it. Around Jersey City, he knew the prestige and
pride with which the players wore the St. Anthony gear, and he knew it
was important that they believed that maroon and gold separated them
from the colors of the gangbangers. It made them feel special.

In an ideal Hurley world, the sweatsuits' arrival would've inspired a
tremendous practice, would've convinced Marcus to end his post-
California malaise and make up for the loss of his best friend, Otis, with a
week of impassioned practices. Hurley had them running the UConn fast-
break drills, the ball never touching the floor. Day after day, they practiced
snatching that ball out of the basket or off the rim, filling the lanes, threading the passes and finishing the breaks in a flash. Over and over, Hurley
taught running so it became an instinctive, second-nature discipline.

He wanted them constantly attacking the rim with the ball, and lately,
too many of his players were tiptoeing to the basket. He wanted them
leaping in the air off one foot and inviting contact—not slowing to jump
stops under the basket, or meekly pump-faking the ball a time or two so
bigger defenders could block them.

To that end, Hurley brainstormed a drill where the offensive player
started in the corner, dribbling hard and exploding into the air for a dunk
or layup at the apex of his leap. The defender closed on him from an angle,
trying to block the shot. When some of his players were shying from the
contact, still pussyfooting into the air, Hurley shared a thought with them.

"I've been doing this for over thirty years, and I'm happy that some of
you are being recruited, but those are all 'program' scholarships," he said.
"That's when people are recruiting our school because of players in the
past. Don't kid yourself right now. I'm trying to find a five-man team of
dangerous players. And it's not here."

He was talking to the juniors, mainly the two most highly recruited
prospects, Sean McCurdy and Ahmad Nivins.

Otis sat on the sidelines, his crutches leaning against the wall. He
would have surgery in a few days, to have a small pin placed in his foot, one
that the doctor expected would strengthen his foot when he returned in

four to six weeks. This would lessen the chance for a reinjury. "I wish Lamar was still playing," Otis would say. "They could use him, with me out now. Everybody wishes he was back."

Gamble had talked to Lamar a second time since that disastrous Sunday morning visit and was feeling better about offering a recommendation to Hurley to allow him back. At that time, the last thing that Hurley wanted to do was insert more senior attitude into the team, especially as he watched Marcus, once the most competitive player in practice, suddenly start playing slower than Marcus warp speed. In nearly every other gymnasium in the country, the way Marcus was playing, the way they were all playing, would've been more than acceptable. It would've been celebrated. Last season, one New Jersey high school coach approached Gamble and Pushie at the PrimeTime Shootout in Trenton and told them, "I wish I could get my team to play as hard for one possession as you get your guys to play every possession of every game."

The standard was different here, higher, an expectation of performance that the kids found nowhere else in their lives. With the release of the national ranking and the long lull before St. Anthony faced the stiff test of Seton Hall Prep, it was inevitable that Hurley would find displeasure with whatever happened in the gymnasium. He would let no one dare feel comfortable.

Hurley finally tossed the team out with fifty minutes left in practice—before they could even go over the scouting report for the road game at Lawrence High School the next day. Screaming at them all the way into the locker room, Hurley snapped, "That's OK, fellas. You all got your nice new sweatsuits today, didn't you?"

As the final players disappeared into the safety of the locker room, Hurley screamed, "You pieces of shit, get out of here!"

He knew he couldn't let up, because he knew they couldn't police themselves. What worried him most was that they were out of his around-the-clock watch in California and back in Jersey City, where the streets were still such a lure. Mostly, Marcus worried him.

When he left practice, where was he going? What was he doing?

Marcus still hadn't told him and had no plans to do so. He had protected one of the best-kept secrets in St. Anthony basketball history, and that wasn't easy to do. It was still tough to get much past Hurley, because he had eyes everywhere in Jersey City. But in the old days, they were his own eyes and own feet out there as a probation officer.

When Hurley still lived on Ferncliff Road in Greenville, still worked the streets for probation, no one escaped his watch. As long as he had coached, fear had always been a great motivating factor for his players. Fear of repercussions; fear of failing; fear of disappointing him.

Years earlier, Hurley would navigate the streets from the wheel of his van, searching for straying St. Anthony players on ever-expanding lists of forbidden Jersey City street corners.

"The big, brown van was his only flaw," Jerry Walker says. "If he would've taken someone else's car, he would've caught a lot more of us."

Walker remembered the trouble he had been constantly getting into his junior season in 1988, remembered standing on Pacific Avenue when a spotter did his duty and identified Hurley in the distance. Walker panicked anyway. Leaping over a row of bushes, he crashed into a yard and lay by a statue of the Virgin Mary. As any good Catholic schoolboy would do, he prayed to the Mother of God to spare him the mother of all beatings.

"It was like South Central L.A., and I was hiding from a drive-by shooter," Walker says. "I was laying there in these bushes, praying, 'Oh God . . . I know he's seen me . . . Oh God . . . ' I'm just about crapping my pants in there."

After Hurley passed in the van, Walker wouldn't move. He just lay on his back, imploring his friends, "Just tell me when he gets to the traffic light. Tell me what he does there."

Two blocks down, when Hurley reached the light, he turned around and started working his way back down Pacific Avenue. Walker scrambled to his feet, jumped over a hedge and sprinted for his house.

Where kids grow up fearing nothing, Hurley makes himself a cloud of consequences constantly hovering above them. A week later, two of Walker's friends stopped over at the house. It was past curfew, he told them. He couldn't go out with them. Still, they persisted.

Walker made it as far as the doorway.

"I was literally too scared to walk out that door," he remembers. "Too scared of the consequences of facing that man."

He had had a feeling his friends had something bad in mind, a suspicion confirmed when word hit the streets the next morning. They had been busted for stealing a car. They would end up in Jamesburg, the juvenile detention center, as Walker went to practice and breathed a sigh of relief.

Years later, Walker still shakes his head and laughs over the memory. He now runs the Team Walker Foundation in Jersey City, on Communipaw Avenue, in the heart of crumbled and crime-ridden Jersey City. After seven seasons of playing pro ball in Europe, then returning to Seton Hall to complete his degree, Walker had come back home to watch over the kids of his old neighborhood, the way his coach had watched over him.

And all these years later, Jerry Walker still freezes when he sees his old coach coming toward him.

As THE BUS rolled down the Turnpike for Lawrenceville—home of Lawrence High School—early in the evening on Thursday, Ben Gamble, sitting in the front, his black knit cap pulled tightly down to his brow, was telling the story of the greatest motivational speech he had ever heard Bob Hurley deliver to a St. Anthony basketball team.

"Two words," Gamble remembered. That's all it had been. Two words.

In his junior year, 1980, St. Anthony was playing like garbage against Plainfield High School. A big, tough kid, Kenny Fields, was killing them, dunk after dunk, a sure sign to the coach of St. Anthony's softness. How could they let him just do that? Down sixteen points at halftime, St. Anthony fought back to force overtime, before losing the game.

When Hurley arrived at White Eagle the next day, he told the team to toss the basketballs back into the bin.

Take the foam mats down from the wall and lay them on the floor, he instructed. Get on your knees, Hurley told two players. Lock hands. And then, just using upper-body strength—the kind that St. Anthony presumably lacked while Fields did chin-ups on the rim—they had to wrestle until one of the two had been pinned.

The memory still so vivid, the pain still pulsating, Gamble dropped to his knees in the aisle of the school bus, showing how his old teammates had him locked up. Behind Gamble, the St. Anthony players hardly noticed him. They were dozing with earphones on, or staring out windows watching the scenery blur past them.

"Fights were breaking out like crazy," Gamble remembered. "Coach Hurley would let you go at it with the other guy, and once it was done, he'd say, 'OK, it's not over. You've still got to pin him.'"

It turned into the most hellacious two and a half hours of Gamble's St. Anthony career. Each player had to square off, one by one, and go down the line with his teammates. After the first man, he moved to the second. And the third. And all the way down the lineup. When the wrestling was done, they got up and ran suicides. The balls never left the bin. His players would limp home that day with scratches and cuts, bruises and aching bones. Had this happened in the suburbs, the kids probably would've gone home, told their parents all about it, and had Hurley's job.

In Jersey City, a St. Anthony parent responded that they probably deserved it. St. Anthony parents trusted Hurley so implicitly, they gave him complete freedom to coach his way. No one second-guessed him, no one took him to task for his methods. They knew how St. Anthony players turned out, and knew how non–St. Anthony players turned out in Jersey City. And they trusted the track record.

One season later, St. Anthony traveled to Las Vegas for a Christmas tournament. They were playing Valley High School of Las Vegas, led by All-American Freddie Banks, a future UNLV star, and were down sixteen points at the half. Gamble remembers trudging into the locker room, thinking, 'Oh, man, Coach is going to go nuts. He's going to jump all over us.' "

As calm as could be, Hurley walked into the room.

Two words.

"Plainfield, fellas."

And walked out.

Plainfield?

Plainfield!

"We ran out the door of that locker room and just kicked their asses in the second half," Gamble said. "That's all we needed to hear. Nobody wanted to go through that again. The greatest motivational speech I ever heard him give.

"Plainfield, fellas."

As they pulled into the Lawrence High School lot at 6:30, running late for a 7:00 tip, fans were waiting two lines deep outside the school's front doors. Wearing his Stetson Miller hat, Doc leaned forward on the bus and said, "Everywhere we go, we pack them in. But we never get a percentage of the gate."

They had come to see St. Anthony, but when Hurley talked about "putting on a show for people," it had nothing to do with flashy passes and reverse dunks. A St. Anthony basketball show was one of tenacious defense, selfless passing and team play. It was performing to the level of his program's historic standards, not the talent of the opposition. They had to rush through warm-ups that night after a late arrival, but Hurley had enough time in the pregame locker room to give the team a reason to perform against Lawrence, when clearly the overmatched opponent wouldn't suffice.

"I've had unbelievable players throwing up before games that we were going to win by forty points because they had such basketball pride," he told them. "When they would come out here for a game in Mercer County, they would want people to walk away saying, 'Damn, that player is good.'

"When you're warming up, you're warming up representing St. Anthony High School. They didn't schedule this game for what's going on now, but because of decades of being dominant in our state. People are coming here to see what we look like."

Sean McCurdy would throw up in the locker room at halftime, but after the 64–34 victory, Hurley had no bouquets to pass out. St. Anthony had superior talent, and as much as anything, that was the reason they had won the game. As Hurley shook the Lawrence coach's hand, he made sure to tell him how impressed he had been with his team's half-court offense. He always tried to pay an opposing coach a compliment, especially those who otherwise wouldn't expect it from him.

In Lawrenceville, the basketball fans would walk out marveling over the discipline and desire of the nation's new number-two team. But this wasn't about their standards. Hurley saw slippage. Beanie was reprimanded for yelling at Sean on the floor ("This isn't a halfway house, this is my basketball team," Hurley reminded him). Off the bench, Shelton Gibbs brought little inspiration.

Most of all, Hurley was disappointed in Marcus. With Otis out, Marcus had regressed. He had been invisible. His commitment to lead every day was fading in and out. Without tough games to motivate him, without a challenge, Hurley knew Marcus's tendency was to drift. He needed Marcus to challenge himself—and, by extension, his teammates every day. They could half-ass a victory over Lawrence, but the only way St. Anthony could make it to the finish line with a championship season would be by playing above itself, and nobody did that better than Marcus.

"How many points did Marcus have?" Hurley asked the manager, Edem.

"Two," Edem said, without even needing to check the stats on his clipboard.

In the clean, well-lit locker room, Hurley ruefully shook his head and leaned closer to his players.

"Instead of me watching one of those reality shows, I watch how teenagers practice every day," he said. "And I watch how they come to games. Once, there was a man named Nostradamus, who predicted the way things were going to go. I'm *your* Nostradamus. I can watch you and predict what's going to happen one week from now, two weeks from now, all the way to the rest of the season.

"And to get this team's attention, something's got to happen again: a suspension, a dismissal, some form of punishment. Because you are all so lacking in the ability to come and work every day."

Hurley was standing now, jabbing a finger in the faces of his Friars.

"You want to win a state championship?

"You want to win a state championship?" he asked again, the disbelief dripping in his delivery.

"I'm good, but not *that* good. Not good enough to carry you and you and you."

He pointed to the three seniors, Marcus, Beanie and Shelton.

After they left the locker room, Gamble and Pushie told Erman to encourage Miles Beatty, the wunderkind freshman, to get his act together in the classroom, especially if he wanted to be considered for a promotion to varsity. In Erman's environmental science class, Miles had missed three assignments in the past two weeks.

Earlier in the day, it had been decided that they would bring Lamar back on the team. He would start practice on Sunday, with six days to prepare for the Seton Hall Prep game. Even then, Hurley probably wouldn't let him dress for it. In fact, Lamar had to understand that Hurley would largely ignore him for the first week or two, and there would be no telling when he'd actually let him back into games.

And yet with Otis out, there was no kidding themselves. They needed him. More than that though, Lamar Alston needed them.

"THE EIGHTEEN-YEAR-OLD SENIORS who want to mess with us here, who will keep us from winning a state championship, I want to take them into the locker room, close the door and straighten this thing out," Hurley was saying before practice on Friday, inspiring Miles's eyebrows to rise, if just a fraction of an inch.

With one day between the Lawrence and Pleasantville games, Miles was having a quick indoctrination into varsity basketball, the Hurley way. He sat on the outer edge of the mid-court circle with his new teammates, understanding that he was a long way from the pressure-free world of jayvee.

He was considered the most talented freshman player in the state, a six-foot-two point guard with a thick, strong body that belied his years. He lived in Guttenberg, a small town six miles west of Jersey City, on the Hudson and Bergen County lines. North Bergen was the next town over, where he had met and made fast friends with sophomore Ralph Fernandez. They took the public bus to school together every morning.

He was light brown-skinned, with wavy black hair, and had worn No. 5 on the junior varsity, for his favorite player, New Jersey Nets star Jason Kidd. All around northern New Jersey, there was a generation of young guards influenced by Kidd's pass-first, shoot-second style of play. Yet no young player came closer to pulling off the Kidd persona on the floor than Miles, who had uncanny peripheral vision and a high, arcing jump shot.

A creative and spectacular passer, delivering the kind of no-look dishes as a freshman that St. Anthony hadn't seen since the days of Friars alumni Bobby Hurley, David Rivers and Kenny Wilson—the all-time assists leaders at Duke, Notre Dame and Villanova, respectively—Miles had a chance to be one of the best players in the country by his senior year. He had come to the right place to be groomed. No one in the history of high school basketball had sent more top guards into college basketball.

Late in his first practice, Miles beat his man on the dribble to the baseline, burning past him to the rim for a basket. Hurley's eyes lit up. This was the way a Jersey City guard was supposed to play, and this wasn't even a Jersey City kid. Hurley loved to give his point guard freedom to be aggressive, to create, to make plays happen. This had been just the kind of instinctive move that had been missing with his veteran guards, the kind that Derrick and Sean struggled to make.

"Miles, be careful now," Hurley warned. "You've got a little more energy than they're used to seeing here. You're going to make people a little uncomfortable. We don't have guys here thinking about going to the basket and scoring."

Miles just gave him that blank freshman stare, clearly trying to calculate his coach's tone and respond to it in the right way.

Hurley laughed. "I'm being sarcastic, Miles." The kid *was* a threat to everyone in the gym, and Hurley loved it. He needed it.

For the Saturday afternoon game against Pleasantville, it felt like the old days: no heat in the gymnasium. Only this was the modern charter school where they were frantically working to get it running again, not the Armory, where, years earlier, St. Anthony had played games with tanks and military jeeps parked at the far end of the floor. During those days, the lack of heat had been merely part of the St. Anthony basketball mystique.

Because St. Anthony couldn't afford the gym rental *and* the heat, they would turn on the blowers for the game, so the visiting team believed the heat was on its way. "They would be thinking, 'Oh, it's probably still warming up,'" Sister Alan says. "But the game would end and it would still be blowing cold."

Nobody minded on this day, because there was a buzz about Miles wearing a varsity uniform. Fans had watched him in the junior-varsity games, where along with two freshman teammates, Kaihrique Irick and Donald Johnson, they were steamrolling teams.

Miles was partly a product of the Playaz, an Adidas-sponsored summer team that crisscrossed the country on a circuit. The program brought out all the worst in basketball. The shoe company poured six-figure financing into the traveling teams, empowering Playaz director Jimmy Salmon to gain access to extraordinary high school and grade school talent in the Northeast corridor. For the superstar player, life on the Playaz was guaranteed to secure three things: national exposure, closets full of free gear and bad basketball habits. As a grade school star, Miles traveled to tournaments throughout the country, on the fifteen-and-under Playaz team, living out the American adolescent basketball dream: always a green light to shoot, and always a pristine pair of Adidas for his feet.

"This is the first wave of AAU kids coming into St. Anthony, young kids who are used to getting things and getting their asses kissed," St. Anthony junior-varsity coach Damel Ling says. "This happens younger and younger with players now, and they come with a whole sense of entitlement. I've tried, but it won't be me who disciplines Miles at St. Anthony. It will have to come from Coach Hurley. Miles has trouble listening, and trouble focusing on what you tell him. That's from AAU ball. They just play. They're not expected to think.

"It's almost like Coach will need to deprogram him."

This had been a major reason that Willie Irick Sr. had sent his youngest son, Kaihrique, to St. Anthony. His oldest, Willie Jr. was a freshman at Vincennes Junior College in Indiana, a stop on his way to Division I basketball because of academic shortcomings at Teaneck High School. Willie Sr. hadn't been able to convince his ex-wife, Betty, to let Willie enroll at St. Anthony, and believed his son paid a price for it.

"Kaihrique thinks the world owes him something over basketball already, and he needs to be deflated," Willie Sr. says. "I played for Coach Hurley [in the late 1970s], and I know this is still the best place in basketball to come to get deflated."

Betty was similarly steadfast in refusing to allow their youngest, Kaihrique, to play for Hurley, until a fateful January 2003. After another in a series of loud, drag-out arguments, Betty Irick's roommate, Rosalinda Molina, told her that their relationship was over. To try to stop Molina from driving off, Irick heaved herself on the hood of Molina's moving Ford Taurus. As Kaihrique watched in horror, Molina didn't stop. She pressed the gas pedal and carried Betty Irick some fifty yards until she was thrown through the air, crashing to the pavement. Someone called 911, and Molina and Kaihrique waited by his mother's side for the ambulance to arrive. Two days later, Betty Irick died at Hackensack University Medical Center.

This was a crucial time in Kaihrique's life. Willie Sr. had grown wary of his son playing for Riverside Church, a controversial AAU powerhouse in Manhattan, whose founder and benefactor, Ernie Lorch, had been accused of molesting a past player. New York City AAU basketball was the ultimate cesspool, where side deals between college coaches and middlemen were as common as chain-link nets on the city playgrounds. It was a culture that warped young men's value systems, creating a belief that they deserved constant rewards for basketball to be worth the time.

"They're giving out spending money and sneakers, and in my mind I'm asking, 'What are *you* getting?'" Willie Sr. says. "That's what I don't like. They try to keep everybody else blind to what's going on. [Lorch] came to Hackensack when my wife died. As a matter of fact, he put $2,000 down on her casket.

"The kids walk in the gym and say, 'I need a new pair of sneakers.' Boom, there it is. Kaihrique and Willie got fifteen pairs of sneakers under my bed, ones they don't even want. After a while, you wonder what these people want from your kids. What's the payoff down the road? A lot of the college coaches start coming around and say, 'Steer the kid my way,' and you could end up with people doing deals under the table."

KAIHRIQUE WOULD SPEND his entire freshman season on junior varsity, constantly testing Damel Ling and the assistant jayvee coach, Todd Dagosta, with his immaturity, while Miles made the leap to varsity.

There he was now, sitting in the locker room before the Pleasantville game, taking deep breaths, trying to gather his nerves. On this team, Marcus wore No. 5, so Miles was given 21. Four years ago, Marcus had been the freshman everyone believed was destined for national attention. He had never made it there.

Now, Marcus was just a senior trying to stay off Hurley's shit list. After all these years, Marcus had something to prove against Pleasantville, just like Miles. Hurley had screamed Marcus off the practice floor a few days earlier, insisting, "Something's up with you. Something's up. . . ."

The last thing Hurley told the team before they left the locker room for the chilly court was, "We'll bring Miles in today and see if he can help us."

As the team dribbled out onto the court, an age-old St. Anthony basketball battle stirred near the scorer's table. Chris Hurley tilted the portable boom box into the microphone, an outdated music-mix tape greeting the players in the layup line. The salsa song "I Like It Like That" blared, prompting Melissa Hurley to roll her eyes.

"Mom," she said flatly, "the music is an embarrassment."

"Why?" Chris asked, sincerely befuddled over her daughter's protest.

Of course, it could've been worse. Only in recent seasons did her husband stop having them play "Who Let the Dogs Out." For the longest time, St. Anthony players lobbied Gamble to talk to Hurley about it. He sympathized with the objections, but learned long ago to never sweat the small stuff with the coach. Sorry, boys, Gamble shrugged, but that wasn't worth the fight.

Otis sat at the end of the bench, his crutches leaning against a chair. He was still trying to do what he could to contribute to the team, which meant calling up Marcus that morning and challenging him. "He's going to do great today, you watch," Otis promised.

From the opening tip, Marcus would waste no time reestablishing himself as the core of the Friars. Popping out at the left corner of the free throw line, Marcus swished a fifteen-foot jump shot. Next, he grabbed an offensive rebound and laid it back into the basket. But he was at his best for St. Anthony on the defensive end, stealing the ball on successive trips for layups in the first quarter.

He played expressionless. No bounds of joy, no fist pumps. Marcus played like some ten-year NBA veteran, punching the clock for one more night on the job.

"I told you he'd be back," Otis said at halftime.

For the game, Marcus finished with twenty-one points, eight rebounds, seven steals, three assists and two blocks—and that was despite sitting out the fourth quarter of the 74–42 victory.

But afterward, the buzz was about Miles's eight points, six rebounds, and five assists. In the third quarter, Miles made his first shot—a three-pointer. Moments later, he had dribbled his way into the lane, bringing defenders to him before sending a gorgeous no-look pass through a sea of arms to a cutting Marcus for a layup.

The rest of the game, Marcus counseled Miles in quiet moments on the floor, instructing him on where to be, and how to play. Outside of the coaching staff, no one had the St. Anthony system down colder than this senior. From beginning to end, this was Marcus at his best. With Miles proving himself, Hurley had extended his bench rotation. They could go deeper and, Hurley hoped, inspire the rest of the guards "to stop being so robotic," an affliction that had especially touched Derrick and Sean.

"Until Otis is ready to go, we should be able to hang in there. If we get through two more games, we've got the big guy here," he said, pointing to Ahmad Nivins in the locker room. "But I liked what I saw out of Miles today.

"There was more enthusiasm out there. More electricity."

Everyone clapped. Sean and Ralph slapped Miles on the back. He smiled sheepishly, his varsity debut going better than he could've imagined. Hurley looked over to his jayvee coach leaning in the locker room and laughed. "I want to thank Damel for getting Miles ready for us.

"Now say good-bye to him, Damel."

Everyone roared with laughter.

Minutes later outside, Miles hugged his father, and his girlfriend, Naeemma Ricketts, set down her video camera to give him a kiss on the cheek. Normally, Hurley would've been mortified that his freshman had a steady, but this was different. She was a junior, at the top of her class academically and the star of the St. Anthony girls team. In the off season, she regularly played pickup with the boys—and more than held her own. Nobody teased a teammate when Naeemma scored on him. Because she did it to everybody. She was a player.

"I hear a lot of superstar players say he's too tough to play for," Miles said of Hurley. "But this was the chance I wanted. Coach told me that he wants me to take some chances, to stir things up a little."

He tossed his bag over his shoulder, bundled his jacket and left the gym stirring in his wake.

"He's one of those guys like Kenny Wilson and David Rivers and Bobby, where everyone else had to have their hands ready because you could get hurt out there," Hurley said, watching Miles go. "All of a sudden—bang—here comes a blind pass.

"Someone just left here saying, 'He's the next Magic Johnson of high school basketball. He's another Bobby Hurley.' "

Hurley shook his head and laughed.

"There's me who doesn't want to bring a freshman up, and someone else saying, 'We've got Magic. We've got Bobby Hurley.' "

Around here, do yourself a favor: Don't compare a freshman to Bobby Hurley.

Magic, maybe. Just not Bobby. Not in Jersey City.

CHAPTER 12

BOBBY HURLEY WAS born on June 28, 1971, blessed with his father's competitive fire and lungs and legs that would be conditioned to run forever. He tagged along everywhere—practices at White Eagle, playgrounds, summer basketball camps and clinics. Anywhere there was a bouncing ball, there were Bob and Bobby, often with a younger Danny in tow.

As far back as anyone could remember, Bobby could do anything with a ball. Anything at all. He could spin it on his finger, and whiz it through his legs and do the "spider dribble," where the ball would roll down the back of one arm, over his back and neck, and then across the other side of his body.

When Bobby was barely strong enough to hoist the ball to the rim, he would run up and down the floor at the Eagle in shooting drills with the St. Anthony team. He would come dribbling his ball onto the Pershing Field courts during halftime of summer-league games, as well as the winter during halftime of St. Anthony games in Jersey City. Once, the Friars were playing for the county championship at St. Peter's College when Bobby was seven years old. The gym was sold out, with thousands of people packed into the Yanitelli Center, and throughout halftime, the St. Anthony players exchanged puzzled looks in the locker room. Upstairs, they could hear the thunderous ovations that grew longer and louder.

"What the hell is going on up there?" Ben Gamble, then a St. Anthony senior, wondered to himself.

Arriving back on the floor, the players could still hear the people buzzing over little, scrawny Bobby, who had grabbed a ball and put on a dazzling performance. The next day in the *Jersey Journal,* below the headline that reported St. Anthony winning the county title, there was a subhead: LITTLE BOBBY JR. PUTS ON A HALFTIME SHOW.

Tom Konchalski, the metropolitan New York high school talent evaluator, had been coming to Jersey City for years to scout St. Anthony players and had often seen Bobby's solo performances at halftime, but he remembers, "I had never seen Bobby play until the summer before his eighth-grade year. He was down at the Villanova camp with Danny, playing in a gym off campus, across the street from the school. There were no scoreboards. No clocks visible. I was just watching him and couldn't believe how good he was: how quick and aggressive he was with the ball. Of all the stereotypes of little white guards—supposed to be slow, half-court players—he defied all that."

At the end of the game, when the horn sounded and Bobby's team had lost by one point, "Bobby was inconsolable," Konchalski says. The rest of the kids were already moving on to the next thing, wondering when they could pick up those ice cream sundaes before bed, and Bobby was a basket case. Konchalski walked over and tried to cheer him up. "Bobby," he said, "you were terrific."

It didn't matter. He didn't move. He just sat there, crying his eyes out.

"It was amazing how important this camp game was for him to win," Konchalski marvels.

He was so small, so slight, that it was hard to imagine the possibilities ahead of him. Because of his size, his father knew that Bobby would have to work much harder than everyone else to earn a basketball scholarship. "Beyond that, how would you have possibly projected anything else for him?" Bob says now.

Just like a young Tiger Woods, Bobby wrote out his athletic goals and taped them over his bed. He wasn't chasing Jack Nicklaus's eighteen major golf championships. Instead, Bobby hung his objectives: the St. Anthony assist record, a Division I scholarship, and playing point guard for the Celtics.

Growing up together in the blue-collar row houses in the Country Village development of Greenville, one of his best friends, Darren Savino, a future St. Anthony teammate and, later, a big-time college assistant coach, would inevitably knock on the door at 64 Ferncliff and invite Bobby to play stickball or touch football, or maybe take a dip in someone's above-ground pool. Bobby wouldn't need to say a word.

In the doorway, Savino could see the answer in his eyes. It told him, *Come on, you know I've got to go with my dad.*

"That was just a fact of my life," Bobby says now. "That was just the sacrifice. I didn't do much of what normal kids were doing growing up."

Day after day, the normal kids would watch him dribble his ball through Greenville on his way to meet another classmate, Terry Dehere, on the edge of the Booker T. Washington housing projects. Terry would be his escort into a world where nobody who looked like Bobby Hurley played ball like him. He was fast and fearless, defying his stature and, as Konchalski noticed back in the eighth grade, defying the stereotypes of what a white guard was supposed to be—a suburban, driveway-bred jump-shooter. Bobby made the case that basketball strengths and skills didn't have to be about products of race, but rather environment. Bobby Hurley was a city kid, and he played a city game.

Most of all, Bobby Hurley was molded into a product of his father's drive. Once he reached St. Anthony and got promoted to the varsity halfway through his freshman season, Bob went far out of his way to prove that there would be no suggestion of favoritism toward his son.

When something wasn't going right in practice, it was Bobby's fault. When the team was flat, distracted, tired, whatever—it was Bobby's fault. Sometimes, Bob would throw Bobby out of practice at White Eagle, because he wanted him to understand that if he was going to be the coach's son at St. Anthony, and have the ball in his hands while playing with black friends and teammates from the projects, then Bobby would learn to live like they did. After getting tossed, Bobby would have to figure out how to take the public bus home from practice, or run, because most of his teammates did it every day.

"Bob was throwing Bobby out once, just when Chris walked into practice," The Faa remembers. "Bob warned her, 'If you drive him home tonight, you better all clear out of the house.' And the day that he booted Bobby out in a snowstorm as a sophomore, that's when Bobby got completely accepted by his teammates."

One night in the summer of '88, a plan had been hatched in the sympathetic minds of Jerry Walker's neighborhood gang, the Puma Boys, a gang in the loosest sense of the word because most of their activity centered on admiring one another's Puma sneakers. The Puma Boys had been discussing Bobby, wondering if that little white boy ever had a night of fun in his life. All they had ever seen was Coach Hurley and Bobby sweating under the summer sun at the Baby Rucker and Country Village playgrounds, the father drilling his son over and over, working on Bobby's game until everyone had come to believe that the Hurleys never slept, never ate, and never stopped chasing something that nobody but them could see.

"We're going to do something for your boy Bobby," a Puma Boy named Heartbeat Wilson declared to Walker. "Go get Bobby and we gonna have a party for him."

In season or out, for St. Anthony basketball players—never mind the Hurley boys themselves—parties were forbidden. From the possibilities of drinking and drugs, violence and meeting girls that the coach believed could ultimately lead to distracting relationships and, worse, devastating pregnancies, the cons forever outweighed the pros in his mind. Besides, the way the St. Anthony players worked year-round, part of Hurley's objective was making sure they were too exhausted at day's end to do anything but go home and sleep.

Nevertheless, the Puma Boys laid out boom boxes, invited some ladies and told everyone to get over to the No. 22 Elementary School park on Van Horne Street. With Bobby's parents usually asleep by 10:00, Walker stopped the car on the block behind Ferncliff an hour later, and waited for Bobby to crawl out his window, leap the backyard fence and dart out of the neighbor's bushes into a waiting car at 11:00. It worked to perfection.

Everyone had a good time that night in the park, dancing to the music under the stars. For everyone there, it was the first time they had ever seen Bobby in a park without a basketball yo-yoing from his fingertips. At two in the morning, they drove Bobby back home, dropping him off on the street behind his house and sending him scurrying back through the bushes, over the fence and back through his bedroom window.

"And that was the only time Bobby ever got out," Walker said. "When you look back, Bobby made the total sacrifice in his life to be successful in basketball. I don't care what nobody else says—I don't care what Michael Jordan says, or Larry Bird says, I'm telling you: ain't nobody ever worked like Bobby Hurley worked. His father drilled him from sun up 'til sun down. That boy couldn't do nothing else."

By Bobby's senior season, St. Anthony would be ranked number one in the nation, on the way to a perfect 32-0 season and soon to be considered the best pure high school basketball team in history. They routinely beat outstanding high school teams by thirty points. That season, everyone admitted that the toughest opponent they had all season was Bob Hurley, fighting to keep complacency out of his gymnasium.

But it was Bobby who made everything go. After watching everything Bobby had to endure for four years, his teammates were tremendously protective of him. If any of them resented him as the coach's son at the beginning of high school, it didn't last long. The kids he grew up with—Jerry, Terry Dehere and Mark Harris—loved Bobby, because he was one of them. To be jealous of Bobby on any level would've meant that they might be willing to trade places with the coach's son, and there wasn't one of them who wanted that job.

Near the end of a White Eagle practice in his senior year, Bob was riding Bobby to follow through on his free throws. Bobby protested on some slight level. Shooting across the gym, Jerry, Terry and Mark kept a wary eye, feeling the tension rising with every developing degree of defiance from Bobby. After another free throw, Bobby still didn't do what had been asked of him.

"We were saying to ourselves, 'Please, Bobby, follow through with your fuckin' free throws and let's get out of here,'" Harris says. "But his father was pushing his buttons, and Bobby made some kind of hiss, and Coach Hurley just lost it."

Hurley exploded, Bobby bolted out of the building and started running into the night. His three teammates, Harris remembered, considered the possibility of jumping Coach Hurley in a statement of solidarity for Bobby, but that plan of action didn't gather much momentum. A few months earlier, they had been on a trip to Hawaii for a tournament and on the way to dinner had walked out the front door of the hotel. With his team behind him, Bob Hurley had turned a corner in Honolulu only to have a member of an island gang of twenty or so members, trying to impress his buddies, purposely brush up hard against Hurley on his way past him.

"Yo . . . Yo . . . Yo!" Hurley had cautioned, stopping in the street, and starting to rub that wristwatch the way he always did when it was go-time.

Hurley offered the four toughest guys in the gang the chance to take him on, suggesting that Jerry Walker, six-foot-six and 225 pounds, would take four. The gang could feel free to start with Hurley right there in the street, right there on their turf. They had tried to embarrass him around his family and players; that wouldn't stand on the shore of the Hudson River in Jersey City, and it wouldn't stand halfway across the Pacific Ocean.

The Hawaiian gang declined the invitation, waved off Hurley that everything was cool and kept going down the street.

No, the seniors wouldn't be making a move on Hurley. Hell, Walker thought Hurley was going to kick Rollie Massimino's ass that night in the home visit, and Massimino had just won the national championship. What would stop him from pounding them senseless?

Still, that night it wouldn't be long before Hurley tossed everyone out of the gym, ending practice early by chasing them all down the steps of

White Eagle and into the cold night. Right away, the three seniors and the freshman star, Rod Rhodes, went on a frantic search for Bobby. Nearly three miles away, they found him running under a bridge.

"You go chase him," Mark Harris ordered the freshman. "We ain't getting out of this car."

When Rod caught him, Bobby was declaring that he was done at St. Anthony, that they would read all about this in the newspaper the next day. Jerry and Mark, holding Bobby now, told him to stop talking crazy, to calm down. They were going to take him back to Jerry's house, but Bobby broke away and started running again.

"That practice was long and shitty," Walker remembers, "and I was too tired to go running after him."

Bobby never did go to the papers. He didn't keep running. He would find his way home, and go back to practice the next day.

As St. Anthony finished off that national championship season, closing out with the first-ever Tournament of Champions title at the Meadowlands Arena, Bob Hurley sent Danny, then a sophomore, into the game to replace Bobby and allow him leave to a final ovation. As Danny congratulated Bobby on the way off the floor, leaving behind a 115-5 career record on his way to Duke that fall, the big brother laughed, "He's your problem now."

Bobby Hurley would take his father's name beyond the borders of New Jersey high school basketball lore and deliver it to the biggest basketball stages in the nation. His first act as a Duke freshman was to call his father and find out what number he had worn at St. Peter's College. That was how he came to wear No. 11 for the Blue Devils.

Eventually, Bobby became the living, breathing embodiment of his father's genius, his tenacity, his love for basketball. Until Bobby, Bob Hurley was seen as another successful high school basketball coach. Bobby changed everything. As much as anyone, Bobby lent so much of the charm and romance to the St. Anthony story. For the coach and the school with no gymnasium and no money, Bobby was the ultimate personification of his father and his high school's mission of doing more with less.

America watched the six-foot, 155-pound coach's son turn the prestigious Atlantic Coast Conference and the National Collegiate Athletic Association tournament into his own private playground. His big shots, peerless passing and unending nerve earned him a part of three Final Fours, two NCAA national titles, a Final Four most outstanding player award and the all-time collegiate assist record of 1,076. Bobby holds the career NCAA tournament records for three-pointers (43) and assists (145).

Bob Ryan of the *Boston Globe* wrote of him, "He looks like a 1940s kid and he plays like one from the '50s."

After performing for a college all-star team that scrimmaged behind closed doors against the 1992 original U.S. Olympic Dream Team—including several days of out-playing Utah Jazz great John Stockton—Bobby, the rising Duke senior, earned effusive praise from Michael Jordan, Larry Bird and Magic Johnson. He was going to be a star in the NBA. Not a player, they agreed. But a star.

This was the Bobby Hurley that everybody remembered, the puny Jersey City kid who stayed forever young, forever flying down the floor and throwing no-look passes to Duke teammates Grant Hill and Christian Laettner. This was the Bobby Hurley who would be voted onto the all-time NCAA Final Four team in 2004, elected to a starting five that included Kareem Abdul-Jabbar and Isiah Thomas. This was the Bobby Hurley who everyone remembered so fondly for what he became in basketball—everyone, it seemed, except for Bobby Hurley himself.

When he entered high school, his parents never expected the big-time recruiters, but at the end of his junior year, there was Mike Krzyzewski and Dean Smith and Jim Boeheim in Jersey City. And before his senior year at Duke, Krzyzewski called Bob and Chris Hurley, telling them that they needed to plan a trip down to Durham to sit down and discuss choosing an agent.

They had never expected the possibility of a professional career. They had never dreamed of that seventh overall selection in the 1993 draft, the $16.5 million guaranteed contract with the Sacramento Kings.

Looking back, no one had. And once it happened, no one ever expected the fairy tale to end like it did.

Except Bobby himself.

"I was kind of always waiting for the other shoe to drop on my life," Bobby says.

It was December 12, 1993, an hour or so after the nineteenth game of his NBA career for the Kings. He had started slowly, sharing minutes with Spud Webb in the backcourt, and losing more games in the first month of his pro career than he had in nearly four years at Duke. He had left Arco Arena on the outskirts of Sacramento alone in his Toyota 4Runner, passed an overpass at the intersection of Del Paso and El Centro roads. Just then, the driver of a 1970 Buick station wagon, his lights turned off, sped through a red light, crashing into Bobby's 4Runner.

Another driver on the dark stretch of road, Mike Batham, stopped and rushed over to the 4Runner. He couldn't find a driver. Without his seat belt buckled, Bobby had been tossed some seventy-five feet into a drainage ditch. Before Batham could see Bobby, he heard him mumbling in the shallow water. Hurley was on his hands and knees, in a foot and a half of water, trying to turn and look toward Batham. At that point, Bobby slipped and fell face first into the water, and would've drowned without Batham, an engineer, lifting him out. A couple in the next car stopped and called 911 on a cell phone.

Soon, Mike Peplowski, a rookie teammate with the Kings, drove to the scene and rushed down into the ditch. Only then did he realize it was Bobby. Suffering from a detached trachea, two collapsed lungs and multiple rib fractures, Bobby kept asking Peplowski if he was going to die. Peplowski kept telling him no, all the while running his fingers over the rosary beads in his pocket and praying for Bobby.

"I knew that whatever was going on at that scene, death was present," Peplowski said to Mark Kreidler of the *Sacramento Bee*. "It was very present."

A trigger of miraculous events that kept Bobby Hurley alive that night unfolded, beginning with what happened at the scene of the accident, and continuing at the UC Davis Medical Center. There, his doctor quickly diagnosed that the trachea and left lung had been torn apart and needed to be reconnected. Dr. Russell Sawyer knew that right away, largely in part because he had just completed reading a chapter in a book on it. The author of the book, Dr. William Blaisdell, happened to be one of the surgeons on staff at UC Davis that night. Together, they worked furiously to save Bobby.

The doctors later declared it a miracle that Bobby had survived the trip to the hospital and emergency surgery—"coroner's statistics" they called his chart of injuries. He never should've made it alive to the emergency room, and then never should've made it out of the operating room. In fact, they had to revive Bobby on the table. After all that, the doctors prayed he would just be able to walk and breathe and live a normal life again.

But play ball? Pro ball?

That possibility seemed resoundingly remote, maybe much more so than the odds that Bobby had already beat to become an NBA lottery pick.

As much as his beleaguered body struggled to regenerate itself after the accident, his fractured psyche turned into his most formidable foe. For the longest time, the mere act of driving was transformed into a traumatic experience for Bobby. If someone honked a horn, it often caused him to pull to the side of the road, his heart beating, his breath short, and the demons dancing again. After weeks at his bedside in northern California, Bob and Chris Hurley finally returned to Jersey City with him, where Bobby vowed a comeback to the NBA and began a rigorous rehabilitation.

After missing most of a month with his St. Anthony team, Bob Hurley was diagnosed with pneumonia, a product of sheer stress and exhaustion.

By February 1994, all Bobby could do was walk for five minutes on a treadmill before tiring to a stop. In March, he picked up a ball and tried to shoot it. All he could do was push it meekly in the direction of the basket. By May, he ran a mile in twelve minutes. One step, and then another. And another. All of it faster than anyone could've imagined just weeks before.

He tried a comeback to the court too quickly seven months later, that June, in the Jersey Shore Summer League. To no one's surprise, Bobby was still sluggish, his body still working its way back from the trauma. He was a shell of his old self. For the first time, Bobby reached out for his father to help him. He wanted Bob to take him back into White Eagle. After Krzyzewski and the national titles and the NBA millions, he wanted his father to take over again. Bobby wanted Bob to fix him.

"That was a time I probably needed him more than any other in my life," Bobby says. "I gave him carte blanche to do whatever he needed to get my game back. We connected in a way that we never had. It was different than when I was growing up, because this time I wanted him to do it."

For two straight weeks in late June, they worked for hours and hours in the ninety-degree heat. For intervals of ten straight minutes, Bobby would dribble full speed down the floor, coming up shooting every time. "My left arm was so damaged that it wasn't reacting or moving," Bobby says. "Him getting me in the gym, doing all the stuff again with the dribbling stimulated my motion again. He brought my game back."

Within weeks, Bobby made his way back to the summer pro league in Utah. Within months, he was back in the NBA with the Kings.

Bobby tried to recapture his old quickness, his brashness, his swagger, but the truth was unmistakable. His body had betrayed him, even if his spirit never would. As his father says, "He was diminished as an athlete."

Maybe Bobby Hurley should've considered his greatest victory just getting back to the NBA for parts of three more seasons with the Kings and Vancouver Grizzlies. He lived to marry his wife, Leslie, and have three children.

After blowing out his knee in a Jersey Shore Summer League game in 2000, ending his final comeback at twenty-nine years old, a foray into the thoroughbred horse business tided him over. But the years between his release with the Grizzlies and taking the scouting job with Philadelphia had done little to dull the disappointment over what he never became in the pros.

"If my career didn't take a certain path, it would be easy now," Bobby says now. "Maybe coaching will heal me a little bit, but when your career went like mine did, where I had built up all these expectations, put in so much work, and then just everything falls apart—it was tough. And it still is. I'm not saying I was on the way to being an All-Star, or a Hall of Fame career, but I know there could still be a job in that league for me. The way it ended, it's never really going to resolve itself for me."

What he did resolve was how hard his father pushed him, and how it shaped him later in life. Like so many of his teammates, Bobby appreciated his father much more once he didn't see him every day in the gymnasium.

"What I became was because of my father," Bobby says. "Would it have been even close to possible without him? Not with my body, not with my God-given ability. Without him, me and Danny would've been the backcourt at Jersey City State. Yeah, maybe I was blessed to be able to run a little, but I didn't have any physical skills. It happened for me because he pushed me nonstop, and it happened because I was willing to handle that. Everyone isn't made to handle as much as my dad gave me.

"He was harder on me than anybody else. And at the time, I couldn't understand. I resented him. When you're so young, you don't know why someone would push you so much—even push you when you felt like you had been pushed beyond your limits."

Sometimes, Bob Hurley digs out his son's old Duke game tapes buried in boxes, the marker scribbled on the side strip telling the date and the Blue Devils' opponent. It inspires him to remember a time and a talent that the father never forgot. He makes sure to pass his discoveries on to Bobby, insisting that the fearless Blue Devils' No. 11 is someone his son should see for himself.

Everyone close to Bobby Hurley wants him to remember the greatness of his glory days. They want him to remember sitting on top of the world at Duke and St. Anthony High School, rather than sitting on the bench with a broken-down body in the pros. All the sacrifice, all the devotion, they figured that he deserved to be honored with the sweetest memories of his marvelous talent. They deserved to burn brightest in his own mind, his own heart. He owed himself that.

"Bobby never realized how good he was," Chris Hurley says. "That was the problem from the beginning. His father would tell him after a

Final Four, 'You should sit back and think about what you just accomplished.' And he couldn't do that well."

The birth of Bobby's first son, Robert Trey Hurley, over the summer of 2003 made his father believe that Bobby would eventually find the rewind button on those old game tapes, on a remarkable basketball life. On the greatest story ever told in Jersey City.

"Bobby's son is going to be the way he goes back through these things and remembers," Bob Hurley says. "It's important that he does."

TEN YEARS LATER, the Bobby Hurley with the teenaged shaved sides and ghostly complexion is gone, replaced with the gray specks scattered in his cropped haircut, a V-neck sweater and a T-shirt. Sitting courtside at the Meadowlands Arena in East Rutherford for the Nets and Memphis Grizzlies in early December 2003, the rookie scout was scribbling his observations in a notebook, reaching occasionally to sip the Mountain Dew in his cup.

For the first time since retiring from the NBA, in 1999, Bobby Hurley had a job in basketball again. He had been hired as a scout for the Philadelphia 76ers. The general manager, Billy King, a Duke alumnus, was sending him out to pro, college and even high school games to uncover and evaluate ballplayers. More and more, Bobby had felt himself pulled toward the family business, the inevitable move into coaching. He had interviewed for the head job at Columbia University in the spring, but he knew he wouldn't land a Division I coaching position until he had been an assistant. For now, scouting had him back in the gymnasium with a purpose. It felt like it had been a long time.

"I think he's going to coach," his father says. "He's going to coach," his mother promises.

They all believed that it was just a matter of time.

"As much as I like watching the players," Bobby said, nodding over to Hubie Brown on the Memphis Grizzlies' sideline, "this is one of the coaches that you want to watch all night long." It had been a long time, a long struggle of healing his body and mind. A long time of trying to get back to basketball, trying to find out where in the game he belonged. "I don't know where my niche is yet, and I'm not sure how I'm going to get there," he said. "I've just come back to basketball because this is what I know the best. I want to see if scouting is something that's going to inspire me to want to do something more again."

To quench his competitive fire, the horse racing business had appealed to Bobby these past few years. He had plunked down $1 million for a young thoroughbred, Songandaprayer, and raced the colt to the Kentucky Derby. When he called his wife to tell her of his investment, she hung up on him. He was grooming his own horses at DevilEleven Stables in Pennsylvania, near his Jersey Shore home, but ultimately, basketball still had his heart. He just needed time. And healing.

Out on the floor, Jason Kidd of the Nets made a gorgeous pass on the break, and still Bobby couldn't see Kidd without remembering the final game of his college career, the NCAA tournament loss to the hotshot freshman and his University of California Bears. All those magical March memories in his life—several of which had unfolded in this northern New Jersey arena—and yet he found himself remembering back to his final college game in the Sweet 16 of the 1993 NCAAs, when Duke had been down twenty points and come back—largely on the strength of Hurley's seven three-pointers—to take a one-point lead in the game.

"I had a wide-open three that could've put us up four, and it still haunts me," Bobby said, swishing the ice in his cup of soda. "I can still see it."

The end of that college game turned out to be the end of innocence for Bobby Hurley, the end of the fairy tale. The tenth anniversary of the night that changed everything would be upon him in a little over a week, on December 12, and there had been a time in his life when approaching the anniversary was like a death march back into a state of despair and depression. As the Nets game ended, several fathers and sons crowded down to the barrier between the lower stands and press row, trying to get Bobby to sign some programs. They called his name, and he still seemed so uncomfortable with it. Every day, someone reminded him of his playing days and every day it left a pit in his stomach.

"I'm lucky to be alive," Bobby says. "I know I'm lucky. I do. It's just . . . It's just hard for people to understand, who didn't grow up with the game like I did to understand the regret. I know it sounds strange to some people, I know that. But it's just something that I've had to learn to live with."

Even years later, it was still Bobby's nature to regret what couldn't be as a basketball player beyond that fateful night, instead of what he amazingly had been: He lived to be a husband, a father, and still, a son and a brother. The way he was raised to never be satisfied, to never stop pushing, maybe it was unavoidable that he would always feel that way.

In the end, maybe he learned his lessons too well. Through it all, Bobby Hurley forever remained his old man's boy.

CHAPTER 13

THE RADIATORS CRACKLED, spitting heat into the idling yellow bus outside St. Anthony on January 17. The cheerleaders sang softly to themselves, lost in the rhythms of portable compact disc players. Behind the windows of the school bus, the Friars wore hooded sweatshirts under North Face parkas. Outside, that Saturday, the wind whipped, the fresh covering of snow blowing past the furrowed brow of an increasingly impatient Ben Gamble.

Where was Barney Anderson?

This was one of the days when everyone was grateful that Hurley wouldn't take the bus. He had driven down to his Jersey Shore house after practice Friday, and would meet the team at the Asbury Park Convention Center. Twenty-five minutes after the bus was supposed to leave, Barney finally came huffing and puffing to the front door. If there was ever a game they couldn't afford to leave without him, Seton Hall Prep was it.

Lamar had returned to practice that week, and now sat in the back of the bus with Marcus. Before they boarded, Lamar had asked where Marcus had been a night earlier. Lamar had tried to call him and get him downtown, over to a party that was flooded with girls. This was the kind of influence that the coaches feared with Lamar, and it would ultimately make his return to the team a short one. Unless he kept it from the coaching staff.

Hurley ignored Lamar for the first week of practice, refusing to let him dress for the Seton Hall Prep game. Hurley wanted to see if he was willing to commit himself again, and despite how well he had practiced, nobody knew for sure when he would use him again.

"I told Lamar, 'If you come in and do what you're supposed to do, you can win his heart back,'" Gamble said. "Right now, I think Beanie has won his heart back. He was mad at Otis for a while, and Otis won his heart back. It can happen. You just have to be willing to put the time in to do it."

With Ahmad Nivins finally eligible to play on Monday night against St. Joseph's of Metuchen, with Lamar settling back into the team, with Miles dazzling in practices, the Friars were gathering momentum again. Even so, Seton Hall Prep, ranked second in the state, presented the Friars with the toughest test since El Camino in California.

Because of Barney, they were running late for the game. Gamble turned to the back of the bus, still five minutes from the Asbury Park Convention Center, and told the players to start stretching. It was 1:30 when they pulled up out front, with the tip-off at 2:00. Chris Hurley had called Gamble's cell phone twice in the final minutes of the trip on behalf of her uneasy husband, wondering where they were.

The Convention Center, situated on the shore of the Atlantic Ocean, was constructed in 1920 by the same designers responsible for Grand Central Station in New York City. Before hitting the big time, Bruce Springsteen had honed his act there on summer days. This was an odd venue for basketball, especially considering that the winds gusting through the doors almost made it as cold inside the building as outside of it. They were playing as part of a triple-header called the Battle on the Boardwalk, a set of games including several major Jersey teams on this Saturday afternoon.

Gamble didn't blame Barney for the team's tardiness, because the last thing the team needed was Barney catching grief from Hurley before this game. They needed him too badly. No Friar was more crucial to beating Seton Hall Prep. After all, he had been assigned to stop Brandon Costner, the broad-shouldered, fluid six-foot-eight, 220-pound star for Seton Hall Prep, who was considered one of the top thirty juniors in the nation.

Before the game, the Friars were led upstairs into a cramped locker room where they practically had to dress standing on top of each other. This was the biggest game of the season so far in the state, with the two traditional powers and state's two most respected coaches, Hurley and Bob Farrell. Hurley had the highest respect for Farrell, but hadn't lost to Prep since the 1990–1991 season. Farrell had sent numerous players into the college game, but was the antithesis of Hurley's disposition: Mild, nonconfrontational, and his team reflected his personality. The St. Anthony freshman coach, Dennis Quinn, had played for Farrell at Prep, and couldn't ever remember a time Farrell had raised his voice there. "Two coaches couldn't be more different, except for that they're both the best in the state," Quinn says.

Prep had won nine of ten games—the one loss coming in a holiday tournament in South Carolina. For the state tournament, Seton Hall Prep, with a larger student body, would play in the Parochial A pool. St. Anthony played in Parochial B. Each was the favorite to win those titles and advance to the Tournament of Champions as the top seeds. Privately, they expected to meet again in March in the 20,000-seat Meadowlands Arena for the final game.

"They're a good high school team, but they don't have guys who we can't defend," Hurley told his players before the game. "Costner is going to be hard work for Barney. But it's our job to put pressure on other players so they don't get easy looks during the game. They're not instinctive players, so the thing is, we don't want to be sitting in the half-court all the time, like against C.B.A where everyone in the stands is clapping while they're running plays.

"They run a nice system. But when we trapped the guards last summer, their system went to shit."

From the start, the team executed Hurley's plan perfectly: St. Anthony pressured the Prep ballhandlers into indecision and mistakes, never allowing them clear avenues of vision to feed Costner the ball close to the basket. After Barney and Marcus pushed on him, refusing to give an inch, Costner retreated outside and seemed content to loft jump shots. And Barney beat Costner down the floor for easy baskets, too. With a 34–26 halftime lead, St. Anthony had to walk behind the bench, across an elevated stage, through a curtain and up a flight of stairs to return to the dressing room. Once they reached the top of the stairs, they found the locker room door was locked shut. And nobody had a key. Hurley jiggled the handle, but it was stuck. Nothing.

Tournament officials scrambled, but they couldn't find one. The clock was ticking on halftime. It was cold and dark in the hallway, and they were practically on top of each other. Part of Hurley wanted to go off, but it served no purpose.

"I could knock that sucker down," Hurley declared.

"I wouldn't do that, Coach," one building official recommended.

"Well," Hurley told him, "this is not exactly the optimum situation for a halftime speech."

He didn't need to give them a speech. And he sure didn't need to be angry. As St. Anthony had learned long ago under Hurley, they made do. Nobody grumbled. Nobody acted put-out. Hurley stood in the dim hallway, scribbling on his clipboard at the top of the staircase. Above him, wires hung down. His players gathered around him, wrapping around in a huddle that extended down several steps.

Across the way, Seton Hall Preparatory School nestled comfortably in its dressing room. A part of Hurley reveled in it. One more slight for St. Anthony, one more time they had to do it the hard way. Where someone else found distraction, Hurley found a source of motivation.

It turned out to be a wonderful game, in a terrific high school basketball environment. Even after it tightened to 49–46 with five minutes, forty seconds left, largely because of the Friars' struggles at the freethrow line, Hurley still had the presence of mind to step outside the moment and yell, over the din, "This crowd is great, Ben, huh?"

Seton Hall Prep would cut it to three points in the fourth quarter on three occasions, including one when Miles blanked out on the scouting report and let himself get beat backdoor for a layup. This wasn't Pleasantville, where his natural talent could take over. Prep was exacting in its offensive execution, and the instant a St. Anthony player was daydreaming, he would get embarrassed. Miles looked lost out there, and Hurley substituted him quickly. This was the first sign that varsity wouldn't just be a breeze for Miles, that maybe he was still too young to absorb the mental demands of playing in these high-level state games.

After the freshman mistake, Marcus wouldn't let Prep get any closer. He had a remarkable tenacity for staying with rebounds on the backboard, able to jump that second, third, and even fourth time if necessary to keep a ball alive and ultimately bring it down. He would out-will his man, every time. This was one of those times. Marcus and Costner were fighting for a rebound in the air, and despite giving up six inches to the Prep center, Marcus's third try finally tipped the ball to Barney with 4:40 left in the game. Costner was too exhausted to leap again, leaving Barney to lay the ball into the basket for a five-point lead.

Inside the final two minutes, Sean had a chance to push the game out of reach with two free throws. Doc did his best to try to lighten the moment for Sean.

"Hey, how'd my tape job work on you today?"

Sean looked back quizzically, refusing to believe he had heard him right in such a pressure moment of the game.

Doc yelled louder. "How'd my tape job do?"

Sean just rolled his eyes and shook his head.

He swished the two free throws, his thirteenth and fourteenth points of the game, and St. Anthony held on 58–52. Marcus had fifteen points, and Barney fourteen. Together, they had held Costner to fourteen—well below his season average.

Hurley headed to his favorite Shore burger joint with his family, the players flirted with the cheerleaders in the back of the bus as St. Anthony rumbled back to Jersey City on the Parkway, leaving distance between them and the rest of the teams in the state. Lamar would be available soon and Ahmad Nivins became eligible on Monday. The Friars were getting everybody together now, getting bigger, getting stronger, and on the bus ride back, Ben Gamble said softly, "We're going to be tough to beat."

Before practice the next morning, Hurley would gather his players together at center court before practice. There was no more kidding them that there were five teams better in the state.

"All the television stations and all the papers in the state are validating us today," Hurley said, holding up the headline in the Sunday *Star-Ledger*. "Let's see how mature we are to handle that."

The paper had a photo of Marcus rising in the air, his hand pressed firmly against the ball as it left Costner's hand. A gorgeous, clean block, six-foot-two on six-foot-eight, a metaphor for St. Anthony on the whole state.

DRIVING NORTH ON the FDR Drive, hugging the road between Manhattan's East Side and the East River, Chris Hurley made a call from her cell phone to room 1631 at the Sloan-Kettering Cancer Center. It was Monday morning, Presidents' Day, and the Hurleys were on the way to visit Sister Alan. Chris expected to hear her beleaguered voice, weary of several fresh rounds of chemotherapy and the infection that had sent her back into the hospital. And what may have been even tougher for the Philly girl to overcome, the Eagles had lost again in the NFC Championship game.

Margie Calabrese answered the telephone in the room, but Chris could hear Sister Alan in the background. She could hear her a mile away.

"It's not a cocktail party!" she was screaming.

From the passenger seat of the Camry, Chris hadn't the slightest idea what Sister Alan was raging over. But the fact that she was fighting couldn't be all bad.

"I'm going to an awards dinner!" Sister Alan yelled louder.

One way or another, Sister Alan was determined to get there.

Sister Alan had wanted out of the hospital for Wednesday night's $100-a-plate benefit dinner for the Jersey City Boys Club, where Bob Hurley and she were scheduled to be honored for longtime service to the city's children. When the doctor had suggested that maybe it wasn't the best idea to be discharged on Wednesday just for her "cocktail party," Sister Alan had snapped.

She was going, and that was that.

When the Hurleys arrived, Sister Felicia and Margie were sitting together near the windowsill. Arrangements of flowers brightened the antiseptic hospital room, otherwise made gloomier by the clouds hovering over the skyline outside her window. Sister Alan wore black-and-gray-checkered pajamas, her eyes tired and puffy, looking like she had just gone fifteen rounds with the doctors here.

"I'm doing terrible today," she said as they walked in the room.

As Chris sat down on the edge of her bed, Sister Alan propped herself up. She looked exasperated, like she wanted to cry.

Sister Felicia had to fight Sister Alan to get her checked into the hospital. Now it was a struggle to get her to stay. The nurse stopped by the room to give her a vitamin shot, jabbing a needle into her left arm. Sitting on the edge of the bed, Sister Alan's stubby legs dangled over the side.

As the needle pricked her arm, she never stopped talking. These damn doctors didn't know her, nor did the endless parade of interns sent to the room. Her cancer physician, Dr. Fong, had watched over her case like a guardian angel. "He's a protector for me," she said. But he couldn't be there all the time, and the whole damn thing felt so impersonal.

From a bedside stand, she picked up the *Parade* magazine out of Sunday's *Daily News* and reread a passage she had read out loud for one of the doctors earlier that morning. "Patients aren't diseases," Sister Alan said, lifting her eyes as though she was surveying a classroom. "They're people."

She had been fighting with the doctors and nurses most of the morning, refusing to simply surrender to tests upon tests without the doctors taking the time to talk to her. "I have cancer, but there is nothing wrong with my mind," she reminded a doctor.

With that, Sister Alan listened to herself and started to laugh. They all did. Truth be told, Bob Hurley probably never would've stayed at St. Anthony all these years without Sister Alan. She had replaced Tony Nocera as the athletic director in 1980, at a time when Hurley and the old school administrator had been at odds. Gamble was on the St. Anthony team in those days, and he remembered one flare-up in particular that had him believing that Hurley was going to take the job over at Marist High School in Bayonne. With Sister Alan and Hurley, though, everything was different.

Most of all, she had his back. And he had hers. When he was thrown out of a game in Elizabeth three years earlier, she stood by a sight-way in the bleachers, giving him a play-by-play in a back hallway and serving as a go-between the rest of the game with his assistant coaches.

"We just naturally got along well," she says. "We're the same kind of people. It was funny: There was a priest in charge years ago, Father Walter. He said to me, whispering 'I heard Bob Hurley is looking for another job.'

"I said, 'Well, did you ask him?'

" 'Noooo,' " he said. 'I wouldn't do that.' "

So, she did. She never saw a reason to pussyfoot around Hurley. He appreciated the directness. If Hurley had ever needed her uninterrupted presence in school every day, it would've been these past two years, for the benefit of this senior class. As tough as Sister Alan was, she was still a soft hand to balance Hurley with the players.

So many times she had called Hurley at his probation desk, told him of something happening in a kid's home life, or at school, that would serve as a forewarning to lay off him in practice. So many times, she talked players out of deciding that it was just too tough to play for him, that it would never be worth it in the end.

"She has a way of softening up things," Hurley says. "My reaction to every problem that occurs is a penalty. She would take so many of the things and handle them, a lot of times without me ever knowing. She would take the kid who I was ready to dismiss, get him to come back and apologize and do something to get him off the hook. You know me. I just explode. But the last couple of years, it's just not been the same without her around as much. It's especially evident with this group of seniors, because they needed much more help."

When St. Anthony's baseball coach had been hassling him about also playing basketball in 1986, Willie Banks told Sister Alan he wanted a meeting with her and the coach. Banks wanted her to play along with something, too. Once all together, he would threaten the coach with a transfer to Snyder High School unless he was allowed to play basketball for Hurley, too.

"I'll never transfer," he said, "but don't tell him that, Sister, OK?"

The baseball coach worried that Banks could injure the arm that powered his ninety-five-miles-per-hour fastball, to which his unblinking pitcher countered, "I could get shot every day I walk out of my door in Curries Woods, and I'm going to worry about getting hurt in basketball?"

Sister Alan went along with Banks's bluff, Hurley spared that golden right arm, and Banks signed for a $175,000 bonus as the third overall pick of the Minnesota Twins in the 1987 amateur draft.

She loved basketball and had a soft spot for the kids willing to endure four years of Bob Hurley. In the end, he could always count on her to be there for them. After graduation in 1995, St. Anthony guard Ned Felton took a job in an electronics store. He had a standing scholarship offer at James Madison University in Virginia, but hadn't reached the minimum score of 800 on the SAT. The NCAA enacted a rule that allowed an athlete to keep taking the test until the start of the spring semester and still be allowed to become eligible for that season.

In early January, Felton passed the test. James Madison was struggling badly, thin at the guard position, and legendary coach Lefty Driesell told him to get to the campus right away. He would have one day to practice, and they would throw him into a game right away. Unfortunately, he had no one to take him to the Newark train station. He tossed his belongings into trash bags and climbed into Sister's Alan's car, and she raced him over to catch his train.

After one day of practice, he made his college debut against William & Mary. Within a week, he attended his first class. Within two games, he had a sixteen-point, five-rebound, and five-assist performance in a victory over George Mason. Within four years, he had earned his degree.

On the sixteenth floor of Sloan-Kettering on Monday, the Hurleys and the Sisters had been going well over an hour and a half, remembering old St. Anthony stories and turning Sister Alan hysterical with the memories. They remembered how years ago, shortly after she had been made athletic director in the old-boy Hudson County Athletic Association, the rival athletic directors scheduled the first meeting at a dive bar in Bayonne, confident that a nun wouldn't dare come to it. She not only came to the bar, she pounded her fist on it when she felt like they were trying to pull something over on St. Anthony. They remembered when the Sisters' veils and habits kept them out of jail in Tijuana on one of those San Diego tournament trips years ago, right after Margie had run a red light and the Mexican police pulled them out of the car.

"The chaplain stopped up today," Sister Alan said. "He was a Dominican priest, from Providence. He asked us, 'Where are you Sisters from?' and we told him where.

"He said, '*The* St. Anthony?' "

Her eyes sparkled telling the story.

Two days later, Sister Alan made it to that awards dinner, delivering a stirring speech on caring for the children of Jersey City and St. Anthony that brought a cheering room to its feet.

ABOUT AN HOUR before the game that night, the St. Joseph's of Metuchen coach, Marc Taylor, stopped over to see Margie Calabrese at the ticket table in the lobby of the charter school.

"What kind of a crowd do you usually get here?"

"Usually pretty good," Margie said.

"Well, you're going to get a lot of people here to see our big guy."

Had Sister Alan been sitting there, she would've undoubtedly told him that the story of the night wouldn't be St. Joe's six-foot-eleven transfer Andrew Bynum making his debut, but St. Anthony's six-foot-nine transfer, Ahmad Nivins. He had come a long way in a short time.

Seven months earlier, Ahmad stood shivering in a doorway to a summer-league game, preparing to come running onto the floor for warm-ups with his teammates. Gamble struck a curious glance at Ahmad, who had his arms crossed and hands massaging the goose bumps on his biceps.

"What is wrong with you?" Gamble asked.

"Coach," Ahmad moaned, "I'm cold."

It wasn't exactly the intimidating presence that the coaches wanted to see in a towering high school center. "You're the biggest kid in the gym, and you've got to act like it," Gamble told him. "Now toughen up."

It wouldn't be easy. Ahmad was a well-mannered, agreeable kid, and St. Anthony basketball and Hurley was a bold new world for him. He wasn't out of the projects. He wasn't a street kid. He was an excellent student, the son of college-educated parents, and he had never taken basketball more seriously than he had other sports. Truthfully, he had never taken basketball seriously at all.

He had been a baseball player for The Faa on the Jersey City Cobras, but he kept growing and basketball soon stole his interest. As a freshman at County Prep, his classmates had laughed at his gangly, uncoordinated presence on the floor. At his old school, practices were easy, the games played in pressure-free environments that pushed him little. His father, Larry, had played basketball at Lincoln High School and Slippery Rock University in Pennsylvania, and knew where his son had to go to develop as a player.

Because he had played mostly baseball, Ahmad had been uncorrupted

by the sleazy summer basketball culture. Most kids with his size and athleticism in the area would've been convinced the world owed them
something, but there had been no one giving him free sneakers, free trips
and a free pass on responsibility. He came to Hurley and St. Anthony an
unspoiled specimen, one that the college coaches had started to find
before he ever played his first varsity game for the Friars.

Ahmad was raw, but the college recruiters knew that getting coached
for the first time in his life—and by Hurley—made his potential immense.

Whenever recruiters wrote to him, Ahmad would log on to the Internet with his father at night, and read up on the academic programs, study
a campus map, and ask all the pertinent questions that most basketball-
obsessed prospects pushed past. This refreshing attitude would be tested by
his close friendship with Sean.

For Ahmad, there was a moderately corruptive element to hanging
with the McCurdys, because Sean and Cindy were not particularly interested in the academic reputation and majors that the schools that recruited
Sean offered. They seemed determined to choose a basketball factory, and
one day when Sister Alan heard Sean suggesting to Ahmad in school that
he planned to sign with the biggest school that recruited him, she snapped,
"That's about the dumbest thing I've ever heard."

She quickly told Ahmad to disregard that kind of nonsense. Of course,
she couldn't always be there. Sean encouraged Ahmad to think that bigger
was better. When Princeton had called Michael McNutt, the guidance counselor, to check on his 4.0 GPA transcript, Sean was unmoved. "I didn't come
to St. Anthony for that," he said of an Ivy League education. "This is about
basketball." They hung out a lot together, because as much as Ahmad was a
Jersey City kid, he had little in common with the seniors. He didn't grow up
in the projects, and he didn't have a history of playing ball with them.

Martelli had scouted Ahmad on his campus during the AND 1 Championships last summer in Philadelphia, and he worked hard to make his
recruiting inroads before the rest of college basketball discovered him.
After two years of tutelage under Hurley, most college coaches believed, it
wouldn't be long before his rawness would be refined into a major college
talent. His height and athleticism promised to translate into production.
Privately, Hurley and Sister Alan believed St. Joseph's was perfect for
Ahmad, too, a smaller campus environment that gave him a chance to play
big-time basketball.

Hurley loved his innocence. Every day was a discovery for him in the
gymnasium; every lesson brought an epiphany.

"I've never played in front of so many people in my life," Ahmad said that night, peering outside the locker room before the opening tip.

He would quickly shake out the jitters. Within moments of checking into the game, Sean made a steal and dribbled to the rim for a layup. His layup teetered on the rim, and overzealous Ahmad, trailing the play, leaped into the air and slammed it back through the basket. He should've left it alone, but he couldn't help himself. The referee called offensive interference, waving the two points off. His teammates on the bench had a good laugh.

Hurley now had the front line that he had been imagining since the summer: Ahmad, Barney and Marcus. They could match up with bigger teams without losing the athleticism to fast-break and run the floor. Ahmad finished the game with four dunks and a gorgeous baseline jump shot over the taller Bynum. He even blocked one of Bynum's shots.

After St. Anthony's 67–34 victory, Hurley was thrilled for Ahmad. He had so little game experience, so few reference points, and Ahmad himself needed to understand that he would no longer be the kid anyone laughed at on the floor. The Rutgers, Richmond and University of Massachusetts coaches scouting the game left impressed.

Margie had told Hurley the story of the St. Joe's coach's purported boast before the game, and he was only too glad to share it with his players in the locker room later.

"He said the place would be packed tonight to see his six-eleven kid," Hurley told the team. "Yes, because of him, that's why everybody came to see a St. Anthony game. But we want to zip our lips and be nice to them, because we want their asses next year when this kid is a senior and the guy is talking about him being a McDonald's All-American center.

"I don't care what this kid is next year. We're going to keep working and getting better, because we have the formula right here.

"*We* have the formula."

FINALLY, THE PHONE rang in room 1631 of Sloan-Kettering on Monday night.

Ahmad Nivins had been terrific in his Friars debut, and *the* St. Anthony had won, Margie reported.

Finally, Sister Alan could close her eyes and go to sleep.

CHAPTER 14

It was 10:30 on Friday, the last day of mid-term exams at St. Anthony, when Darren Erman finally found Miles Beatty. He was downstairs in the cafeteria. First thing that morning, Hurley had called Erman with a message to deliver to his freshman guard: Life can change fast at St. Anthony.

"Don't be mad now," Erman told him. "Keep your head up."

Miles didn't like the sound of where this was headed.

"You're to go to jayvee practice today."

Hadn't Hurley just told the jayvee coach to give Miles's uniform away to someone else? Didn't they just cheer him in the locker room after the Pleasantville game? All those questions flashed through his mind, the confusion and anger tumbling into his face. The trouble with Miles was simple: He couldn't concentrate in practice. For him, he had always played AAU ball—the equivalent of basketball junk food. He had been used to playing a video game, and Hurley's practices were more like reading a book.

For those two hours in practice, it took incredible discipline to stay sharp the whole time. And when Miles's mind wandered on the sideline a day earlier, he missed Hurley telling him to replace a teammate on the floor.

"Get in there, Miles," he yelled.

Miles was daydreaming. He didn't move. Hurley didn't tell him a second time.

"Get out of here," Hurley snapped, and threw him out of practice.

It had happened in the Seton Hall Prep game with that backdoor cut too. More than that, Hurley feared that it was just a matter of time before the seniors' dysfunction had a trickle-down effect on him. For now, Miles was being told to shuttle between jayvee and varsity. He would balance the two worlds, but this was a step backward that Miles believed he had moved past.

Erman's instincts were right. Miles was livid. As the two of them stood beside a lunch table, a classmate wandered over to Miles and started to tease him.

"What's wrong, man?" the kid asked, playfully jabbing at Miles. In no mood for it, Miles pushed him back. Hard. The kid staggered backward and Miles stayed on him.

"Why don't you take your jacket off and let's go!" Miles barked at him.

Miles was one of those kids who had never been told "no" in his young basketball life. When he wanted something, there was somebody there to hand it over. He had a closet full of sneakers. He had taken trips around the country. Hell, he could've made a call that afternoon, told Jimmy Salmon of the famed Playaz program that he wanted out of St. Anthony, and there would've been a line of high school coaches from New York City and Jersey working deals to get him into school. He was impatient, and the fact that he had to wait his turn was a shock to his system. But he was also a student of the game, an inquisitive kid who deep down understood that Hurley and St. Anthony was best for him. Talent had always carried him, always been his excuse when he had goofed off, when he didn't listen to coaches, when he knew that whatever he did, someone had to play him.

Erman grabbed the other kid by the arm and led him out of the lunch-room. Then he came back to talk to Miles more. He had become an important connection for Hurley in the school, someone with his finger on the pulse of his players. He could see potential problems and deal with them. Because he was young, just twenty-seven, the kids confided in him. They trusted him. They knew he wouldn't run back to Hurley with stuff, but would help them. He was a full-time teacher and a part-time coach, psychologist, counselor and friend.

From then on, Erman told Miles, the coaches would tell him when he would practice with the varsity or the jayvee. He would play in the jayvee games and still dress for the varsity. He was expected to dress for the varsity game against Linden on Sunday.

"You have to pay attention more," Erman told him. "You have to work harder in the drills. Right now, you're not getting as much playing time. It makes sense to go down and play more on jayvee."

Miles had stopped listening to him. He was staring into the distance, his mind somewhere else. He was so talented, sometimes it was easy to forget:

He was only fourteen, just a freshman. And despite his status as an anointed young AAU star, despite those frequent-flier miles to summer tournaments across America, those once-worn Adidas stacked in his closet, he was still a St. Anthony freshman. Here, Miles Beatty still had to pay his dues.

IT WAS PAST midnight on Saturday when a telephone call woke Shelton Gibbs Sr. and his wife, Elyse, in Hillside. There had been a shooting in the doorway to a pool hall on Kennedy Boulevard, across from St. Peter's College. Matthew Givens, a nephew and senior at St. Anthony, had been shot in the wrist and the thigh and rushed to the hospital.

Givens should've been home sleeping like his cousin, Shelton Jr., who was getting his rest for a Sunday afternoon game against Linden High School at St. Benedict's Prep in Newark. Shelton and Matthew had gone to Sacred Heart grammar school, where they were stars on the team. They had played on those Boys Club state championship teams, with Matthew the leading scorer over Otis and Beanie in some big games against New York City teams. He used to be one of them, all the way through the unprecedented AAU state championship run, through freshman and junior-varsity basketball at St. Anthony. But after junior year, he stopped playing ball and started hanging out. He told everyone: No way did he want to spend his senior year listening to Bob Hurley yell at him.

"He was on the streets a lot more than he would've been with basketball," Shelton said.

Says Otis: "[Matthew] couldn't handle the discipline with Coach Hurley. He would've been the guy to say something back when Coach called him out. That probably wouldn't have worked. I like him, but if you stay out there in the streets long enough, something is going to happen."

Something did finally happen to Matthew Givens that Saturday night.

Shelton had stayed the course. He was never going to be a star of the senior class, but he had the most going for him: devoted parents, good grades and a clear compass in his life. He hadn't been a kid out there looking for trouble, but the streets of Jersey City didn't discriminate. Sometimes, they had a way of finding you.

"That's all I could think of when we got the call," Elyse would say later. "What happened with Shelton."

Five years earlier, it hadn't been the phone stirring Shelton Sr. and Elyse. It was the rat-a-tat of gunfire on an otherwise quiet Jersey City street.

Warner Avenue had always been good to the Gibbs family. They had lived there for fourteen years, and never felt unsafe. But one night, while Shelton was on his way home from an eighth-grade basketball game, a masked man appeared out of the shadows, telling him to hand over his new coat. Before he had the chance, Shelton could feel the cool steel of a gun barrel against the side of his face.

Shelton was just a kid, and who knows what goes through a kid's mind? All Shelton knew was that he didn't want to give up his new coat. So he swung his right hand up, grabbed the gun and threw it. And he started to run. And when the robber picked the gun up off the ground, Shelton was flying. He could see his house. The front door. If he could only get to his father, he thought. He wanted to scream, but nothing came out. And then, the gun fired. The bullet whizzed past him. Shelton kept flying.

And another shot.

Shelton never turned back. He kept moving.

Upstairs in the house, his father leaped to his feet, and looked out the window. He could see his boy running down Warner, busting it for the door. "Oh my God!" he screamed. By the time Shelton Sr. leaped down the staircase, his boy was frantically trying to rip that locked door off its hinges and get inside.

Shelton Sr. swung open the door, ushered him inside and yelled.

"SON, ARE YOU HIT?"

Shelton was hunched over and breathless.

"ARE YOU HIT?"

"No, Dad," Shelton gasped. "No."

After the police finally left the house, after his mother and father held Shelton tight for a long, long time, Shelton Sr. told him, "I don't care what happens. Give them what they want and put it in God's hands."

"But Dad," Shelton pleaded, "it was my new coat. I didn't want to give it up."

"Son, we can get you a new coat. We can't get you a new life."

They told him that he had been through a lot that night, that maybe he should take the next day off from school.

"Know what he tells me?" Shelton Sr. would say years later. "'Nah, Dad, I got a test tomorrow.' So, he went in his room and studied."

That night, the parents made a decision: They had to move out of Jersey City. This was home, and there was so much that they loved about it. Still, they kept saving for a down payment on a new house. Three years later, they would pack up Shelton and his younger sister and brother and move out to Hillside, about ten miles west in Union County.

"If we didn't have any kids, if it was just us, we would stay in Jersey City," Shelton Sr. says. "But we've got to try and give the kids a safer atmosphere. It's not guaranteed you're going to be safe; you're not guaranteed anywhere. But the chances are better out of the city."

Shelton Sr. had worked in probation and was a longtime colleague of Hurley's in the department. He had been a fabulous player for St. Peter's College, scoring 1,688 career points for the Peacocks before being selected in the fourth round of the 1985 Continental Basketball Association Draft. He had been an assistant basketball coach years earlier at Snyder High School, where most of the students came out of the poorest parts of the Greenville and Lafayette sections of Jersey City. "Like social work," he called the experience.

Snyder was a high school of low retention, armed guards and constant violence, a place where, in the past couple of years, students had shoot-outs outside the school on lunch breaks, where a thirteen-year-old freshman football player was sodomized with a broomstick. Before every period, the students milling in the hallways when the bell rang were rounded up like stray cattle and herded into a downstairs holding tank. At the sound of the bell, classroom doors were locked shut.

When the Gibbses arrived at St. Benedict's Prep for the Brian Doherty Classic Sunday, a benefit game honoring the memory of a close friend of the Hurley family and a major St. Anthony benefactor, Shelton Sr. told Hurley that his son had been awake late into the night awaiting word on his cousin. Hurley would see what he could get out of Shelton in the game, but wouldn't push him.

The gymnasium crawled with college recruiters. For Sean McCurdy, it was like a candy store. Pittsburgh. Georgia. Marquette. Seton Hall. Rutgers.

"Marquette is here to see you and me," Sean breathlessly told Ahmad Nivins in the pregame locker room.

Nobody could pick those college coaches out of the stands like Sean. He had an eye for them. Ahmad smiled faintly, but marching through those 900 fans packed into the St. Benedict's gym on the way to the locker room, his stomach churned. He had been used to playing his County Prep basketball games with parents and the school custodian watching on folding chairs. This was another world for him.

Before St. Anthony played its game, Hurley studied one of the state's most explosive teams, Bloomfield Tech, from the bottom row of bleachers.

As the Tech coach Nick Mariniello called out an offensive set named "One-Again," the young coach could see Hurley's eyes fixed on him. When the play was run perfectly, finishing with Tech's all-state guard, Courtney Nelson, scoring on a backdoor layup, Mariniello peered back toward Hurley out of the corner of his eye. Ever so slightly, Hurley nodded, as though to tell him that he was impressed.

"It made me feel really good," Mariniello said later.

Bloomfield Tech was one of the most talented teams in the state, and Mariniello was a talented thirty-seven-year-old, with slicked-back Pat Riley hair and the sharpest wardrobe in the gymnasium. Tech had played St. Anthony the toughest in the Friars' unbeaten summer, fighting back from a twenty-point deficit in a tournament game to actually take a lead before losing. "As a young assistant coach at Marist High, I was always in awe of the St. Anthony mystique, the Bob Hurley mystique," he would say.

Now he had to convince his team that if they overcame a few tough early-season losses, they still had a chance to meet St. Anthony in March. Every day, Mariniello told his team they were preparing for St. Anthony in the Tournament of Champions.

As much as Hurley would've loved to look down the road at possible tournament opponents, he knew St. Anthony had come to a critical juncture in its season. Despite a great deal of trepidation about letting Lamar back on the team, Hurley had decided to allow him to finally dress for that afternoon's game against a solid Linden team. Lamar had practiced for two weeks, largely without a word from Hurley.

To a man, the senior starters were thrilled to have Lamar back. There was even a small victory scored for the senior class when, because no one had brought a uniform for Lamar to wear, Hurley had Miles give him his No. 21 jersey.

"Whatever Coach wants from me," Lamar said softly in the locker room before the game, "I'm going to try to do. I just want to fit in again."

As Lamar tucked his uniform into his shorts on the way up the stairs into the gymnasium for pregame warm-ups, Marcus stepped alongside him. They caught each other's eyes for a moment before breaking into smiles.

"Crazy, yo," Marcus said, shaking his old friend's hand.

Danny Hurley would coach the third game of the afternoon in his home gym. With his father's team leading 15–4 to start the game, he would walk behind the Friars bench and say with a sly grin, "When you're running an event, you always want St. Anthony winning. You wish them all the best."

This was his way of saying that on a demanding day of hosting all these teams, and worrying about his own game, the last thing that he needed was an unhappy Bob Hurley in his gymnasium. For that, there was still time. With the Friars winning 28–18 midway through the second quarter, Hurley looked down the bench and sent Lamar into the game.

Behind the bench, Otis stood leaning against the wall. His foot was making progress, his return date for practice possibly within seven days. "He's going to be a little bit rusty," Otis said. Lamar kneeled at the scorer's table, waiting to get into the game.

"I hope he does good. We need him."

As the buzzer sounded and the official waved Lamar into the game, Otis yelled out, "Let's go, L."

His teammates knew that they had to offer support, because there was none forthcoming from Hurley. It wasn't long before Lamar found himself on the baseline, his dribble gone and two Linden players smothering him. He had let himself get trapped, and the best thing he could do was split the defenders, and try to find an open teammate. But he panicked and tossed a wobbly shot toward the rim that missed everything. It was a terrible start.

The biggest disaster of the day would be a mortified Ahmad Nivins. He shot two air balls in the game, but much worse to Hurley, gave up defensively on plays and let people score on him. The level of intensity needed was new to him. All that confidence from his debut had drained out of him, and he looked like that frightened, self-conscious kid at County Prep that his freshman classmates had teased for behaving so clumsily on the court. As Ahmad came out of the game after a disastrous few minutes, Hurley barked at him, "College coaches, big-time crowd, where's your damn energy?"

Sean later regretted telling him about all those college coaches in the stands. "Bad idea," he decided. "Ahmad wasn't ready to hear that."

When Hurley took Marcus out late in the fourth quarter, he leaned into him on the bench, and said, "Same thing—weekend game and you don't have anything. Look at that lazy-ass shit from you out there."

No one could convince Hurley that Marcus wasn't running late nights in Greenville. Marcus just said, "That's not it at all. He doesn't know. He just doesn't know."

The final score would be 67–51, but Hurley seethed over so many soft performances on his side. As the players and coaches shook hands, something was stirring under one of the baskets. All the college recruiters sitting close by were mesmerized by the scene of Cindy McCurdy bickering nose to nose with a Linden fan. "Get your hands off me, lady!" the middle-aged black man screamed, insisting he was a police officer and he didn't have to take another word from her.

Cindy had come to the defense of Melissa Hurley, whom some of the Linden cheerleaders mistakenly believed had said something or other about them during the game. Witnesses in the stands said it came from someone behind Melissa, but once the girls started on the coach's daughter, Cindy couldn't sit it out. It wasn't long before people had separated Cindy and the opposing fan, and led them to opposite sides of the gym.

Downstairs, the Friars gathered in a sweltering locker room. No air, no ventilation, and the heat seemingly at full throttle. It was almost like Hurley had flipped a switch in the room.

"I don't coach well with things on my mind," Hurley said, turning toward Lamar, "so let's clear the air."

Finally, Hurley had something to say to Lamar Alston.

"We dressed a kid lucky to have a uniform. No kid has ever returned to one of our teams like this. I've never done this before. Only because of you two am I doing this," he said, pointing to Gamble and Pushie. "And I'm not sure I should be doing this now.

"As soon as Alston got in, he should've been convincing everybody that he wanted to be part of what we're doing right now. What were we when we gave him his two minutes today? What was our record coming in? Eleven and oh.

"If Oak Hill had lost last night, we would be the number-one team in the country today."

Suddenly, a cell phone started singing a song in one of the lockers, a ding-a-ling-ling programmed into the ringer. In the middle of a Hurley rant, it suddenly didn't sound so snappy. It was Barney's. Frantically, he searched for the phone in a coat pocket. Every eye in the locker room turned to him, praying that Barney would please, please, shut it off. Rest assured, there was a time when Hurley would've reached into the pocket himself and smashed the phone against the wall. He had mellowed, of course. This was mellow.

In mid-speech, Hurley simply said, "That thing better get off fast." And then he went right back to laying into the seniors.

Next, it was Marcus's turn: "You're not even college material right now. You've become a role player on a good high school team again. We can't run shit for you on offense."

"And the ninth-grader?" Hurley said, whirling around to Miles sitting under the chalkboard, legs stretched straight out on the floor. Just two weeks earlier, he was the toast of the winning locker room. Now, he didn't even have a name. He was just "the ninth-grader."

"Back to jayvee every day," Hurley commanded. "The house needs to be cleaned. Something happened to you up here. A freshman around seniors, it just isn't working."

Outside the locker room, on the staircase leading back to the gym, Hurley was working over his assistant coaches on Lamar. "You know what this Alston thing has done already? It's destroyed the chemistry. Do you know who's sensitive to this whole thing? Shelton Gibbs.

"There has to be a valid reason for doing this."

Shelton stood the most to lose with Lamar's return, his minutes promising to dwindle as Lamar's eventually rose. Shelton had a terrific knack for getting his hands on loose balls, deflecting passes—all the subtle, scrappy things that coaches loved players to bring off the bench. Yet, Lamar was a far more polished offensive player and someone who could lock down a man one-on-one. At best, Hurley hoped he could work some contacts and get Shelton a scholarship in Division II basketball. If Lamar got his act together, he had the talent to play Division I ball.

In the postgame spread in a conference room upstairs at St. Benedict's, Sister Alan watched the players pile chicken wings and pizza onto their plates. Almost four weeks had passed since she had seen the team play. She called Barney out of the food line, and told him, "You've really improved. I can't believe how tough you've gotten out there."

His eyes brightened. "I've been lifting weights, Sister."

Now, she nodded over at Ahmad, saying, "He's the one we have to toughen now." He smiled weakly and dug back into his plate of food. She wore her maroon 2001 state championship jacket, the sleeves extending far beyond the end of her hands. She had missed the games, missed these times with the team. She was now out of the hospital four days since the infection subsided, and she could get back to school.

Hurley and his assistants slumped on couches in the back of the room, talking quietly amongst themselves. The topic was still Lamar. At the core of the conflict for Hurley was bringing a dysfunctional senior back into a team where it could lead to disruption. He was a kid that none of the coaches felt like they could get a handle on, kind of a recluse who never bubbled with enthusiasm, never made it seem like basketball was anything but a chore. They just knew there would be a game in the state tournament when his ability to defend someone and make a jump shot would benefit the team. Gamble and Pushie sold Hurley on that one quarter in that one state tournament game in March when Lamar Alston's minutes could be the difference between winning and losing.

Sister Alan worked her way into the conversation, offering the input that she couldn't give them from the hospital bed. "You are crazy," she whispered, wagging her finger in the air. "He is bad news. He's going to bring someone down."

Once, she had liked Lamar. She always thought he was a bright kid, full of possibilities, but she believed he had changed. And she wasn't willing to sacrifice the rest of the senior class to spare him this year. She worried about his influence, and nobody could convince her otherwise. Shaking her head, she walked away saying simply of the coaching staff, "These poor bastards are going to get it."

As far as the team was concerned, they were thrilled to have Lamar back. For Shelton, maybe it was a different story. He wouldn't say it, but he knew that Lamar would squeeze into his playing time. But he had gone home with his parents to Hillside, leaving the rest of the team, the Jersey City kids, rumbling through the streets of Newark on the bus. The cheerleaders packed the front, the players in back. The driver started blasting some smooth R&B music, and soon, everyone was singing. The Friars were 12-0, and rolling past the gutted-out buildings and boarded-up storefronts. In the back, Otis Campbell stood on his injured foot, using a fist as a microphone. His teammates urged him on, and the cheerleaders swayed to the music.

Doc Miller, a Sinatra man all the way, sighed.

"I'm riding with the Sisters next time."

THE NEXT THREE days of practice should've been used to stay sharp with two easy games at the end of the week: Morris Catholic on Thursday, and Monmouth Regional at St. John's University on Saturday. After that, it was February and the schedule grew progressively tougher with the state tournament on the horizon. Quietly, there started to be talk about the possibility of an unbeaten season, but it sure didn't come from Hurley. That kind of talk was about the last thing these kids could handle. In February, they would face bigger, stronger teams—Niagara Falls, Our Savior of New

American and the game everyone had circled on the schedule, St. Raymond's of New York City, the jewel of the New York City Catholic League.

That was a long way away. If nothing else, this was a good week to get Lamar sharper. Otis could start running late in the week and perhaps return to practice by the weekend. As much as anything, they needed to start taking complete shape as a team. They needed everybody for the stretch run. There were just under four weeks left in the regular season, and this team was finding its stride.

Yes, this should've been an easy week, and probably would've been if Marcus and Barney hadn't blown off a midterm exam on Friday. Gamble had been made aware on Saturday that they had missed the tests, and told them they had better retake them on Monday. After the weekend, Marcus came to school to retake the test, but insisted that his mother didn't have the $10 fine he needed to pay to sit for the makeup. "I just figured that I would take the exam on Tuesday," he would say.

And Barney? He never showed. To compound matters, some of the seniors came late to school on Tuesday morning. Sister Felicia called Gamble, leaving him to tell Hurley.

Of course, Hurley exploded.

When everyone arrived at practice Tuesday afternoon, Hurley slammed the locker-room door shut and thundered into the team for twenty minutes—hitting all the familiar themes of irresponsibility, immaturity and imminent life failure. It wasn't a coincidence that Marcus had scored six points against Linden, and two points against Lawrence. "He's sloppy in his life now and it carries over," Hurley said.

He suspended Marcus and Barney for the Morris Catholic game on Thursday night, and considered the possibility of sitting them on Saturday, too. More than ever, Hurley was convinced he had made a wise move sending Miles back down to junior varsity. That way, there was far less of a chance of these seniors contaminating him.

Among them, there was a sense that they were going to junior college anyway, and because those were open admissions, all they needed to do was graduate. Barney was a different story. At six-foot-five and a low Division I prospect, he was stuck somewhere between the complete academic disaster of the senior class and the honor roll juniors, Ahmad, Derrick and Sean.

Gamble called Barney Anderson Sr., a construction worker, to touch base with him. He was shocked to hear his son had missed an exam on Monday, especially considering that Barney told him he had completed his finals and didn't need to go to school. From there, it just got worse for Barney. Gamble shared with his father some of the excuses that Barney gave the coaches over the previous summer for missing games and team activities. Barney had told them that he needed to help his father on-site for some construction jobs.

"He's never worked a day of construction in his life," the father informed Gamble.

Barney Sr. thanked his son's coach for the information, and promised to deal with Barney himself.

"We caught him in a whole bunch of lies," Gamble said.

Once practice started on Tuesday, Hurley wasted little time sharing Barney's story with his team. "There's only one story in life for which you'll have every answer: the truth. If you live an exemplary life, and do what you're supposed to do, you walk down the block and you don't worry if someone is tapping you on the shoulder asking a question.

"The only thing worse than not being alive at all is being a person who doesn't tell the truth."

For the next two days, no one could do anything right in the coach's eyes. He had been reminded again that he had to stay on them all the time. He could never let up. Outside his gymnasium, he wasn't sure that he ever had a team where fewer people in their lives held them accountable for anything they did.

That Wednesday, school had been canceled because of the ten inches of snow blanketing Jersey City. Hurley could tell his players had just vegetated for hours before trudging over to the gym by how limp the practice felt to him. With twenty minutes left in practice, Hurley had had it. He couldn't leave things unsaid. Something was on his mind, and it wouldn't be long before everyone knew about it.

Hurley had waited for Marcus to ease back, if just for a moment.

Waited all day.

And when he broke the silence in a scrimmage, Hurley used it to climb all over the team. But Marcus knew Hurley was talking to him.

"How do you think you get yourself things in life?" Hurley barked, standing in the middle of the floor. "You go out and you *earn* it. Unless, of course, you're just going to get that welfare check. Unless you're just going to have some woman and children. Unless you're just going to go get that check on the first of the month, and take half that money and walk out the door. If that's the way you want to live, then walk down the street and never look at anybody. Because you'll never be able to look anybody in the eye, because you'll have never earned anything.

"This is supposed to be preparation for a game tomorrow, and what are we doing here? We're lecturing the inmates."

The thirty-year probation officer looked to the corrections officer.

"Ben, don't you feel like you're having the same conversations at work every day?" Hurley asked. "I used to leave work in probation every day, and it was a relief to come to practice. Because there were young people with potential.

"This is turning into Snyder High School, except that I'm not allowing it," he said, pointing an accusatory finger at his team. "It's not going to happen here."

Hurley stopped now and turned to Marcus. This was one of those days when he just wanted to smack him, when he wondered whether he had ever reached Marcus at all. In his mind, Barney wouldn't have felt so empowered to pull off the scam had the seniors not created such a leadership vacuum. And that began with Marcus.

Ultimately, Marcus wasn't sure how much he had going for him in life, but he knew whatever he was—whatever he would be—his four years as a St. Anthony starter separated him. In a lot of ways, Marcus was as tough as his coach. For that reason, it was almost as if Hurley asked himself: What would wound me the most? What would shake me to the core?

The answer was unmistakable: tell Marcus that he didn't belong here, that he wasn't a St. Anthony guy, that he was just one more knucklehead out of Greenville. This was his way of telling Marcus to take that speech he gave in California, take those two state championship jackets hanging in his closet, take it all and toss it.

"The next thing that happens that sets me off—where does Marcus Williams go?" Hurley barked.

"Gone!

' "GONE!"

His shirt off, Marcus was standing under the basket, his muscled torso drenched with sweat. He was staring straight back, the two of them going eye to eye as the coach stalked toward him.

"Know what you can do, Williams? You can get to Snyder, get eligible for the state tournament in thirty days and join the *Greenville guys*. OK, Williams?

"Because then what everyone said would happen to you will happen:

You'll have gone right back into the city. You know, we always used to get a kick out of putting kids into college here, out of having guys who were different than everybody else they grew up with.

"But with you, Williams, you might be the one dragging down your whole neighborhood now."

After practice, the players trudged out of the locker room and into the cold night. Outside, the snow still flickered in the icy air. Every step they took disturbed the peaceful coating of white in the parking lot. Hurley had grown so disillusioned with the broken homes and city that they were going home to these nights. His flushed face and exhausted eyes were palpable. Hurley felt like he was losing the fight. He felt like this season was turning into a failure, because whatever the record and the rankings, something was slipping away here. Something was dying in his arms.

"They don't get it," Hurley said wearily to his coaching staff. "Every day is a new adventure. I mean, James Wright, who graduated with Bobby in '89, lived right off Arlington Avenue. They had to condemn his house. His family was living in a motel down on Tonnelle Avenue until they got back into an apartment. He worked cleaning bathrooms in bars before school to get money to live on. He got a scholarship to Wilkes University. He got married. And now, he has better than what he had. Because he worked at it. And he never gave up."

Out in the middle of the basketball floor, in the middle of a long basketball season, Bob Hurley shook his head and sighed.

"James Wright," he said softly. "He had *values*."

As MARCUS AND Barney were reduced to spectators at the end of the bench with Otis for the 74–32 victory over Morris Catholic on Thursday night, a glum Sister Alan sat at the scorer's table, insisting that none of these suspensions would've been necessary had she been in school last Friday.

"I would've seen them and gotten them to take the test when they were supposed to," she said.

SOMEWHERE, SOMETIME, MARCUS Williams had to make a stand. He kept telling himself. School was out for the weekend, practice still two hours away, and he knew he had to make a stand. Here he was, on Friday afternoon, reflecting inside room 109 of St. Anthony and feeling stranded somewhere between a free-wheeling kid and a man with real obligations now. He kept telling himself he had to grow up, had to stop the sliding. He had to be accountable.

"I gotta be a man," Marcus said. "I gotta live up to my responsibilities. What Coach did was right. There had to be a punishment."

Still, Marcus's secret weighed on him. Every time Hurley unleashed his wrath on him, there was a voice in the back of Marcus's mind, fearful that this would be the time that it would all come out of his coach's mouth, that his secret was no secret at all, that Hurley knew the truth. Even the day before, when Hurley started in about cashing welfare checks and dropping off child support money, that sinking feeling stirred within Marcus. He knew Hurley's heightened level of outrage with him, and thought maybe it was on the way.

Someone must've told him. After all, it seemed like a stranger couldn't take the shortcut past the school on the way to the Holland Tunnel without Hurley knowing about it.

If Hurley knew the truth, that Marcus had a son, he never let on. Whatever happened with Hurley happened, Marcus decided. If Hurley ever did confront him with the question, he would tell him the story.

"I been with Coach Hurley four years out of my life, and a little bit of me says to myself that he's like a father figure," Marcus was saying now. "He talks about things that nobody ever talks to me about, that you ain't never gonna hear on the street, that's for sure. But by me telling him about this, I just don't know what type of reaction he's going to have.

"For right now I'll just keep it to myself."

Two and a half years earlier, Lamar had been playing with his baby boy in a park when Gamble happened to show up. Lamar had spent his freshman year at Marist High School in Bayonne, and had just finished the process of transferring over to St. Anthony, where his stepfather, Boccia, had wanted him all along under Hurley. When the mother of the boy yelled over to Lamar, "Go get your son," who had started to wander away, Gamble looked surprised.

"Go get who?" he asked Lamar. "That's your son?"

From that moment on, they always looked differently at him at St. Anthony, Lamar said. It wouldn't be long afterward that Hurley raised the issue of fathering children at a young age, and Lamar never forgot the way the eyes of his coaches and teammates flashed his way during the lecture. He never forgot the way, in his mind, they judged him so harshly.

"I look back on that one day, and I know that was a falling point for me at St. Anthony," Lamar says. "I fell in a lot of people's eyes after that, especially Hurley's. Nobody ever treated me the same again."

Marcus didn't forget it, either. For him, those thoughts—along with the times Hurley had talked to them about fighting to end generations of dependence in their own families—left a lasting impression. "All that told me that I need to keep that secret to myself," he says.

No, Marcus couldn't tell Hurley about Marcus Jr. He couldn't tell him about his eight-month-old son, about the baby he shared with Shameka, his college-student girlfriend. The pregnancy and birth had been the best-kept secret in St. Anthony High School for a year, but slowly, surely, the word seemed to be seeping out. Somehow, Cindy McCurdy knew. She must have told Greg Bracey, Marcus figured, because Doc had been teasing him about it. All that conspired to make Marcus concerned that his worst fears could be realized: that Hurley knew; that he thought the worst of him; that he had lost respect in his eyes.

In Marcus's mind, his most important priority was ending the cycle of fatherless children in his own family, an inner resolve that his own son would not grow up without a father in his life, the way Marcus had. "My father figure was my brother, but he's locked up now," Marcus says. "But I'm always going to be there for my son. No matter what goes on in his life. I know that he's got to have a father. It's been hard for me to just be raised by my mother, and I don't want all that pressure to be on his mother."

The baby lived with Shameka and her parents in Jersey City, and she kept encouraging Marcus to hold tight to his college dreams. She kept telling him that getting an education, getting his degree, was the best way to secure his son's future. Marcus even talked to her about bringing the baby to school with him, about trying to become a family at one of the schools recruiting him. Pensacola Junior College sounded good to him, and maybe they could find a way to make it work.

"She said she would think about it," he would say.

Whatever happened, Marcus knew he needed to get away from Jersey City for college. These streets were wearing him down, exhausting him. Hurley wanted Marcus, Otis and Beanie to go to Pensacola together. "All the coaches be talking about Otis and me coming to the same school together, but I don't want to be fighting for the same spot with him in college," he says. "At some point, we got to break away from each other.

"We got to break away from all this Jersey City life."

★ ★ ★

ON THE SNOWY, bitterly cold campus of St. John's University in Queens, New York, a sweet Siren calling the Friars out of the winter frost and toward the warm embrace of basketball excess. The image of LeBron James, the radiant face of the NBA's biggest young star, was splashed on the back of a long, sleek bus in the parking lot.

As the Friars emptied out of their own yellow school bus outside Alumni Hall, they could see the wide-eyed teenagers drifting in and out of the sleek, sexy touring machine pushing promotional products. Inside, kids ogled over the freshest new lines of LeBron sneakers and gear. The music thumped on surround-sound speakers, the rap lyrics blistering through the frigid air.

"Check it out before the game!" a Nike rep yelled to the Friars. Some of the players stopped for a moment, like kids getting tempted by a stranger promising candy in his car.

"Come on," the rep said, motioning to Sean.

"We've got to play right now," Sean told him.

"The game won't start without you," the man countered.

Sean shook his head, threw his bag back over his shoulder and trudged toward the entrance to the gymnasium.

The past two seasons, Monmouth Regional had given St. Anthony trouble, but it wouldn't matter that Marcus and Barney, suspended for Thursday's victory over Morris Catholic, wouldn't start the game against them. Monmouth didn't score a basket until the second quarter, cutting the St. Anthony lead to 20–2. It would be an easy victory, 71–31, in the Tom Crotty Memorial Classic.

It seemed strange that St. Anthony had to cross into New York to play a New Jersey team, but New Jersey had a rule for state-tournament quali- fication that 75 percent of your victories had to be against Jersey schools. It limited the out-of-state teams they could play in the season. It made little sense, but the only way to get St. Anthony onto the docket in the long afternoon of New York and New Jersey high school games at St. John's was by allowing them to move one of their home games with a Jersey opponent to the classic.

After the game, tournament officials needed someone on the victori- ous St. Anthony team to pick up a small team trophy at mid-court.

"They're asking for a team captain," Hurley said to the bench. Every- one looked up and down the bench. Marcus was the leader, but Hurley had

refused to choose an official captain out of this group. Marcus had the status, but after his week, the only way Hurley would've let Marcus touch a
St. Anthony trophy that day would've been upside his head.

"Ahmad Mosby," Hurley finally called. "Go get it."

That act alone was a message to Beanie that Hurley had been pleased
with his progress. Asked about it later, Beanie gave his usual unimpressed
shrug. "That don't mean nothing," he would say, but given the history
with Hurley—the cold war that raged between them—it meant a lot to
Beanie.

After the coaches and players left the postgame locker room, St. John's
sophomore Elijah Ingram, the All-American high school guard from the
St. Anthony Class of 2002, walked into Alumni Hall, returning to campus
from the Red Storm's victory over UCLA that afternoon at Madison
Square Garden. Elijah had scored twenty-one points, the best game of
what had become a lost season for St. John's and himself.

Throughout much of Elijah's year-and-a-half career at St. John's, Hurley cringed when he watched him play on television. He couldn't believe
all the mechanical problems and bad habits that had crept into his game,
the kind of things a good coach corrects and controls every day in practice.
Once, Hurley had gone to watch one of his ex-stars, Georgetown's
Anthony Perry, play Rutgers in Piscataway. Danny Hurley was on the
Rutgers coaching staff and could see his father growing frustrated with
watching Perry in warm-ups. Bob Hurley could see the thumb of Perry's
guide hand getting in the way of the shot, and had to tell him. Soon, Hurley had worked his way down to the floor, trying to get Perry's attention,
and Danny knew exactly what was happening.

"Don't do it," he yelled across the court. "Don't do it, Dad!"

He *had* to do it. Perry was one of his guys, a guard he had sent to
Georgetown to play for John Thompson, only to have him end up playing
for his overmatched successor, Craig Esherick. Perry had his best shooting
game in weeks, scoring fifteen points before his steal in the final seconds
preserved a narrow Georgetown victory.

"You had to do it, didn't you?" Danny asked his father later.

In Hurley's mind, it was unthinkable that coaches could get paid so
much in the Big East and be so completely clueless. St. John's coach Mike
Jarvis had been fired mid-year, and the Red Storm was getting blown out
of most of their games. Elijah and his parents had stayed in constant contact with Hurley throughout the season, with Hurley urging him to keep
his grades up, maintain his own standards amidst the chaos and make it to

the end of the school year. At that point, Hurley promised to help him find a new school to transfer to.

"Who do you play next?" Hurley asked.

"At Pittsburgh, on Wednesday," Elijah told him.

Before leaving, Chris Hurley gave Elijah a kiss and told him to take care of himself.

"I love you," she said.

CHAPTER 15

As soon as the words had left his mouth, Bob Hurley wanted them back. It was just before the home game against The Hun School of Princeton and Hurley was running through a play that St. Anthony used against the 3-2 zone, where two guards played on the perimeter and the third ran back and forth on the baseline as the big man screens. "Sean, I want you running the baseline tonight, because there's a coach here to see Ahmad Mosby."

Hurley glanced over at Ahmad. "I want him to see you handle the ball."

There's a coach here to see Ahmad Mosby. Damn it, that was all Beanie needed to hear. The Pensacola Junior College assistant coach, Terrance Harris, had come on a recruiting trip this February 4th night, and in his enthusiasm to sell the college's coach on Beanie's talent, Hurley dismissed for a moment the fragility of his senior's psyche. Beanie was worried about enough in the world, without needing to attach that kind of pressure to this performance.

Harris had driven up for an open gym at the Armory, a day when the coach became enamored of Marcus and Otis, but left needing to see more of Beanie. Hurley had gone to Pensacola to speak at a coach's clinic in the fall, and came away impressed with a junior college program that conducted itself like a four-year school's.

Hurley had checked out the academic tutoring, the majors and even took a tour of the dormitories. Pensacola was a destination where head coach Paul Swanson's beliefs aligned with Hurley's own. He had pushed Pensacola hard to his seniors, telling them they would make a visit there in the spring.

A live wire of electricity coursed through the charter school gymna-

sium that night, a packed house thanks largely to the two buses of students
and fans that came up from Princeton to support The Hun School. Around
St. Anthony, everyone remembered the racially condescending overtones
of the Hun's chants a year earlier in Princeton. They remembered when
Hun officials stuck them in an open locker-room area where the school's
football players and wrestlers merrily marched through, interrupting St.
Anthony's pregame preparations. What Hurley really remembered was a
student getting into it with Melissa, ultimately inspiring her father to invite
the kid to take the drive up to Jersey City for the return game next season.

"Twenty-seven thousand dollars a year to go to school there and no
locker rooms for us?" Hurley told his players before they dribbled out for
warm-ups. "They were rude hosts."

Essentially, they all wanted to drill these prep-school elitists.

It wouldn't be that easy. The Hun had upgraded its roster this season
with fifth-year high school postgraduates looking to improve academically
before moving on to college, and already having beaten the immensely talented number-one prep school in the state, Lawrenceville. From the start,
the Huns charged the Friars. They had St. Anthony down 7–2, with the
Friars dazed and back on their heels. As St. Anthony scrambled to get back
its bearings, the Hun students chanted, "This is our house!" Before long, it
felt like Huns *had* taken over the gym. The Friars weren't just getting outplayed on their home court, but screamed out of it, too. And no one liked
hearing the preppies getting obnoxious and giddy with themselves in Jersey City, but the Friars had done nothing to discourage them. The Friars
were down 18–17 at the end of the first quarter, the most points the team
had allowed in a quarter all season.

They needed something. Marcus couldn't score. Barney's concentration was missing. And Beanie was thinking too much. That was clear. He
was pressing, and he had never pressed up until then this season. He had
missed several wide-open shots, which he hadn't done all year. He was
stripped of the ball in the backcourt, allowing a quick Hun point guard,
Mingus Murray, a Derrick Mercer clone from Los Angeles, to lay the ball
into the net.

Meanwhile, the Hun fans were shouting down the St. Anthony students. They were getting cockier, surer of themselves in Jersey City, and
soon serenaded Sean with Eminem lyrics, singing the words to the white
rapper's song, "The Real Slim Shady." To these children of privilege, it
seemed, any white kid on an all-black-and-Hispanic team must have had
the audacity to believe he was black, too.

It didn't matter to Sean. To him, this was the highest form of flattery. He wanted people to notice him. And whatever they yelled, nothing would disrupt Sean this night. For the first time as a Friar, he was unstoppable. For all the reasons Cindy and Sean long wanted, he was suddenly the player nobody dared take their eyes off of. Something had happened. Something had clicked. He stopped thinking, and he just played. There was a sudden swagger to his step, scoring ten straight points to end the first quarter on twisting layups and three-pointers. On one ferocious drive to the rim, Sean rose over his defender and released a perfectly arced swish for two more.

In the bottom row of the bleachers, Cindy looked like she was witnessing a religious revival, rising to her feet and throwing her arms in the air with every glorious moment. This was the game of Sean's life and his team needed it badly. Scoring was always balanced for the Friars, but not this night. Not with Sean in that zone all scorers live to experience.

As the final seconds ticked down until halftime, Sean would miss a breakaway layup, but Hurley couldn't say a word to him. Sean had saved St. Anthony. He started them on the way to a crushing 62–44 victory, finishing with twenty-seven points—twenty of which came in that telltale first half, when St. Anthony needed to fight off that initial Hun wave.

It was another good test passed. St. Anthony was now 15-0.

Outside the locker room, the Pensacola assistant, Harris, marveled at the St. Anthony defense. After allowing an eighteen-point Hun first quarter, it had tightened up, holding the Hun to just twenty-six points the rest of the game.

"That's Division I college defense," Harris said. "There's not a high school team in the country that I've ever seen defend like them."

He was downright delirious over the possibility of signing into his program three winning, tested players. Beanie had struggled, but Harris would take Hurley at his word for his talent. Even the way he had spottered offensively tonight, the assistant could tell Beanie was a hellacious defender.

In the mill of family and friends in the postgame scene on the floor, Harris stayed to talk to Marcus, Otis and Beanie about Pensacola. "You're going to have crowds of 1,500 to 2,000 fans every night there," he promised.

Before leaving, Harris turned to Beanie.

"Do you want to go away to college?"

"Yeah," Beanie said. "Yeah, I do."

At that point, only Ramapo College was seriously recruiting him, a Division III school about forty minutes from Jersey City in Mahwah. They had sent a coach to almost every St. Anthony game, despite the fact that Beanie seemed not to reciprocate their interest.

"They're Division III, so I would have to pay there," Beanie would say. "And it's just too close to home."

At P.J. Ryan's, the restaurant and pub a few blocks from St. Anthony that the Hurleys retired to after each game for dinner and a glass of wine, the coach was in a terrific mood. Sean walked into the restaurant, arriving to eat ahead of his mother and Greg Bracey.

"What are you doing here?" Hurley asked. "Best game of your high school career and you're going out to celebrate?"

Sean smiled sheepishly. It was an awkward spot for Sean, out in a social situation with the coach and his family when, back in the locker room, Hurley had told the team to go home and get some rest.

Actually, this was one of those times when it was good for a player to see Hurley in a softer setting, where his game face was gone and his guard was down. Like most of the team, Sean had stayed at the coach's Jersey Shore house in the summer for camps. And like the rest of them, he marveled how a persona that seemed so bigger than life could be "just a regular family man, watching games on TV."

During dinner, Hurley leaned down the table to Cindy McCurdy. "North Carolina called today about Sean," he told her. "There's something to put away in your back pocket."

WHEN BEN GAMBLE and Bob Hurley talked on the telephone every morning, the discussion moved free and easy from the team to game plans, to college basketball and the Knicks. Whatever was happening, they touched on it all in those few minutes.

With the news that had flooded the metropolitan New York airwaves late in the afternoon and evening on Thursday, spilling into salacious headlines in the Friday morning papers, what was *happening* had been the unfolding of a nightmare for the St. Anthony family. Gamble knew Hurley too well to want to make that call Friday morning and ask him about Elijah Ingram.

"Coach," Gamble began that morning, because he still had never in his life called him Bob, "I guess you're getting a lot of calls today, huh?"

"I'm not talking about it with anyone," Hurley said, clearly a cue to

Gamble to move on and start talking about a tough weekend of games, Saturday night at 15–3 Raritan and Sunday against powerful 15-1 Niagara Falls in the PrimeTime Shootout in Trenton.

Sometimes, this was how Hurley dealt with something so troubling, so beyond his capacity to compute: by not dealing with it at all. To him, the details were too disturbing, too devastating. Too unthinkable. Yet, there was no hiding from them: Elijah Ingram and two of his St. John's teammates, Grady Reynolds and Abraham Keita, had been questioned by police after an accusation of rape had been leveled against them. In the hours after St. John's lost at the University of Pittsburgh Wednesday night, the players had sneaked out of the team hotel past curfew, picked up a down-and-out flight attendant at something called Club Erotica and brought her back with an understanding that they would pay her $600 for sex.

Initially, the woman told police that, after arriving back at the hotel, the players simply raped her. That story fell apart when it was discovered that she was simply angry that, after fulfilling her end of the bargain, she found out the players only had $6 among them. What ultimately spared Elijah and his teammates from criminal charges was his video cell phone, which had recorded her threatening the bogus claim unless they paid in full. That part of the story didn't come out until late Friday, so the first twenty-four hours of the scandal centered on the sexual-assault allegations.

Elijah had always been one of Hurley's favorite kids. He had a historic career at St. Anthony, winning two Tournament of Champions titles and earning his way onto the McDonald's All-American team. His father still loved stopping at the St. Anthony open gyms in the fall to watch the next generation of Friars play and discuss his son's college career with Hurley. Now, Elijah Ingram was the scourge of New York sports. This story was everywhere, its sensationalistic details insatiable for the tabloid culture of the New York media market.

Elijah's involvement stunned everyone. When Sister Felicia heard the initial nameless radio reports of a police investigation Thursday afternoon, she thought, "Please don't let it be Elijah."

Watching television later, Sister Alan saw Elijah's picture pop up on the screen. She wanted to cry. He wouldn't get to transfer out of St. John's at season's end, but instead would be made to withdraw to spare himself from expulsion. Among the three players, the St. John's president, the Rev.

Donald Harrington, said, only Elijah had expressed deep remorse over the incident.

After St. Anthony's practice on Thursday—just hours after he had heard the news involving his ex-player—Hurley had rushed out with Chris for Manhattan, where they had tickets for a Broadway play. At the theater, Hurley bordered on catatonic, occasionally nudging Chris to leave early. She made him stay. He sat there mortified, staring blankly into the distance.

At St. Anthony the next day, the phones were ringing like crazy, newspeople searching for the Sisters to provide some insight into Elijah. "Who are we supposed to be, the sex police?" Sister Felicia laughed in a light moment. Really, what could they say? He had been a wonderful kid at St. Anthony, and he had done something profoundly stupid in college. Once the rape charges were dismissed, the severity of the transgression lessened in the minds of almost everyone. It was bad, but it sure wasn't the end of the world.

Nevertheless, Hurley had a much tougher time reconciling what he considered to be an unthinkable moral breakdown. He was inconsolable. His wife called Sister Alan Friday in school.

"Please talk to Bob," she asked.

In a lot of ways, the tough persona of the street-smart ex-probation officer and basketball coach masked a social innocence. He had dated only one girl in his life, and had married her, and the thought of bringing a woman back to a hotel room to pay for sex was beyond his capacity to comprehend.

He felt like someone had punched him in the stomach. Maybe worse, he felt like St. Anthony's reputation had been dragged through the gutter. He had stopped answering the telephone in his office that Friday. When people approached him over the weekend, he felt himself tensing up. He knew they would probably bring up Elijah, and he wouldn't talk about it. He couldn't talk about it.

In a private moment two days later, Hurley's eyes grew glassy. "When kids get involved in these things—I mean, when things become unlike fistfights—I'm not good with that. My life was on a street corner in Jersey City. Fighting, two-hand touch football—those are things I know. I don't know this world.

"It's very, very awkward for me."

He bit his lip, shook his head and that was it.

Bob Hurley was done talking about Elijah Ingram.

★ ★ ★

THE LINES OF parents and eighth-graders snaked from the first-floor corridor, down the short flight of stairs and swung around to the long, wooden
tables in the small St. Anthony auditorium. For months, St. Anthony had
been sending out an admissions officer, Donnie Fritz, to the Jersey City
elementary schools, with the message that this was still the little school
fighting its way out of tough times.

This was Saturday morning, the seventh of February—registration day
for next year's freshman class. Sister Felicia greeted families at the entrance
of the school, passing out St. Anthony T-shirts and pens to the kids arriving to make commitments to enroll. Sister Alan passed out financial aid
and scholarship forms. Margie Calabrese collected the $200 deposits for
the class of 2009.

The Hurleys stopped over too, with Bob thumbing through a copy of
Basketball Times.

"The first ten people who signed up, only one had any money," Sister
Alan said. "The rest were as poor as church mice."

She shrugged and laughed. After all, this was St. Anthony. Poverty had
only worsened in the city. It was a catch-22 for St. Anthony: There was a
greater calling for affordable Catholic-school education, but it left the
school needing to raise more money for scholarships and financial aid,
never mind just operating costs. St. Anthony needed eighty to eighty-five
students to secure a solid freshman class for 2004–2005; they only had
fifty-seven on Saturday, with six or seven more planning to register on
Monday. Out of the students paying the deposit at this registration, some
would never enroll in September. The school year would start and the
family would still be short the money to pay the $3,350 tuition, the level
they'd been able to hold it at for three consecutive years.

There was a time when St. Anthony's business plan was simply this:
"Pray and hope." When financial guru Tom Breen took over as the president of the St. Anthony trustees in 2003, he pushed an aggressive agenda
of targeting new revenue streams for the school. As opposed to the biggest
city in the state, Newark, where foundations played an immense part in
funding the inner-city parochial high schools, nothing comparable existed
in Jersey City.

They had been creative with fund-raisers, turning the $100,000
Bobby Hurley Golf Tournament in 2002 into a $200,000 net in 2003.
They had a 3-on-3 Corporate Basketball Challenge scheduled in the

spring, with which they believed they could raise another $100,000. Still, St. Anthony needed a broader base of supporters to finance the future. They needed corporate support. They needed volunteers to mentor. They needed to rehabilitate and modernize the physical plant of the decrepit, ninety-year-old structure. They needed a scholarship endowment. They needed to transform themselves from a mom-and-pop operation, praying for the generosity of friends and strangers, to an efficient fund-raising machine.

For fund-raising, Hurley had always been the ace in the hole. He passed along thousands of dollars he earned every year conducting clinics, but trustees and administrators couldn't count how many times he came to a luncheon or a meeting with prospective donors, where so much of the formal presentation went by the wayside when it was usurped by Hurley regaling them with basketball lore and St. Anthony kids overcoming long odds. In so many instances, people fell over themselves to write out checks.

It wasn't hard to quantify the impact that Hurley and his basketball program had on the school, other than to say that St. Anthony would probably last about as long without Hurley, as, say, the earth would without the sun. For overall enrollment, as much as half the male student body, almost sixty this year, came to St. Anthony with the dream of playing basketball. Hurley tried never to cut kids out of his freshman and junior varsity programs, because it often led them to dropping out of St. Anthony, or even dropping out of school altogether.

Back in November, Hurley had given a pep talk to the baseball, soccer and girls basketball coaches, telling them how to get out in the community and sell those sports programs as a way to boost enrollment.

"Ultimately, this affects the future of the school," Hurley told them. "This school was at a huge intersection last year, the light was yellow and nobody knew what was going to happen. Now we're in the intersection, but we're not through yet. We were disturbed by the number of kids that ultimately came to school this year. We thought we were going to have another twenty or so."

At that meeting, Sister Alan had laid out the ground rules for recruiting kids to play on the teams. "The good thing about being in Jersey City is that a lot of the kids are poorer and are not going to be registered at a Catholic high school in February. Those kids are fair game. But if the kid has registered for another high school, don't touch him. He's off-limits. We'll have the state association down our throats."

At a fall open house for eighth-graders, a group of girls approached Sister Alan and asked about the state of the St. Anthony softball program.

"It stinks," she said. "But this year, we're going to be better. We have a girl who can do the windmill pitch, and if you join us, you'll have a great chance to start right away."

At the registration on Saturday, there was a copy of that morning's *Asbury Park Press* laying on the table, opened to a story about the anticipation of Raritan High School in Hazlet of having St. Anthony travel to its burg for a showdown. They were the best team on the Shore, with two young, talented Division I prospects. They were calling it the biggest basketball game in Raritan history.

Earlier in the week, Sister Alan had talked to the Raritan athletic director. "They put the tickets on sale at 2:00," she said, "and were sold out at 3:30."

As THE TEAM bus rolled down the Parkway, Beanie huddled in the back with his cell phone, listening to his sister give him the play-by-play of the Oak Hill–Cardinal Dougherty of Philadelphia game in Trenton being televised on the YES Network. Hurley rarely raised the issue of the number-two national ranking, but everybody knew: If Oak Hill lost a game, St. Anthony was poised to move to number one, and staying the course on an unbeaten season could give the team the national championship. That would give St. Anthony its third in school history. There were three days of games at the PrimeTime, so after Oak Hill won the late game Friday night, it had to turn around and play a 4:30 game on Saturday against nationally ranked Cardinal Dougherty.

With the caliber of teams left on Oak Hill's schedule, Dougherty was probably the best chance they had to lose a game the rest of the way. And when Beanie's sister told him the score—Oak Hill down fifteen at the half—word spread quickly through the bus.

Somehow, St. Anthony could be playing for a chance to move into the number-one ranking in the national poll this weekend.

Once they arrived at Raritan and walked through a tunnel of taunting fans outside the front doors of the school, they found out the final score. Oak Hill had made a frantic comeback on Dougherty and stole the game in the late moments of the fourth quarter. The neighborhood team from Jersey City was still running second to the all-stars out of Oak Hill.

About an hour before the game at Raritan, Cindy McCurdy sat on the top row of the bleachers, talking about the world of possibilities unfolding for Sean. This year, her oldest brother, Bill Shepherd, had taken over as coach for Muncie Central High School outside of Indianapolis. Fifty years ago, Muncie Central had been the opponent for tiny Milan High School in the 1954 Indiana high school basketball championship game that would serve as the climactic conflict in one of Hollywood's great sports movies, *Hoosiers*. This month, the ESPN Classic network planned a fiftieth-anniversary rematch of the game on February 22 in the Muncie Central Field House, where a sold-out gym of 6,500 promised to revel in the Hoosier basketball heritage.

Things were happening for Sean back in Indiana, she said. The stars were aligning for him. Bill had suggested to the Indiana University coaching staff that they start recruiting Sean. He told them about his nephew's Hoosier roots, how Cindy had grown up in Carmel with two Mr. Basketball winners for brothers, how he was a tough kid with a good shooting touch. This would've perked Indiana's interest alone, but when they found out he played for St. Anthony, Indiana assistant Dusty May moved quickly to contact Hurley. In recent years, Indiana had cast its recruiting lot with too many AAU players long on talent but short on the concepts of fundamentals and team play. The idea of a kid from a championship high school program had great appeal to the Hoosiers coaching staff. Indiana wanted to see his game tapes immediately.

His uncle had more immediate plans for a Hoosier homecoming for Sean, and pitched his sister on them. Why wait until college to bring that Shepherd flesh and blood back home, he said. For Sean's senior year, why not move him out to Indiana to play under his uncle at Muncie Central?

This started the wheels spinning in Cindy's mind again. Once Bill started selling her on the possibility of getting Sean in the running for that Shepherd family heirloom—the Mr. Basketball award—she couldn't help but get swept up. Imagine what they would be saying back in her hometown of Carmel if her son moved back as a big high school basketball star whom the Indiana Hoosiers were desperately recruiting?

Bill promised to build his whole team around Sean, something that she had come to understand would never happen at St. Anthony. Hurley had delivered added dimensions and overwhelming credibility to Sean's rising stock, but going back to Indiana for his final season could be a triumphant homecoming.

"I'm going to call his dad," Bill had promised Cindy. "If Bob says he can transfer out here, will you let him?"

"It's not about me," Cindy demurred. "And it's not about his dad. It's about Sean."

Of course, none of this was just about Sean. After all, Cindy would have to uproot and move them again. Up in those bleachers at Raritan, in the rarefied air of Sean's twenty-seven points against Hun, she repeated the wonderful words her brother had told her son. "If you come out here," Bill Shepherd said to Sean, "you can shoot until your arm falls off."

Now there was a coach talking about how best to utilize Sean. The possibilities of the move were intriguing, to say the least. Whatever road Cindy believed she needed to take for the greater glory of the McCurdy basketball name, she was willing to travel it.

WHEN SHE HAD wanted to get her son to St. Anthony, she had coaxed and cajoled Sean and Bob into seeing it her way. If need be, she could try again. That was for another day, though. Before the game with Raritan, she had prepared herself for an important day at the arena in Trenton tomorrow, where she said that Ohio State was sending an assistant to scout Sean.

"And I don't think they're coming to see anyone but Sean," she was sure to point out.

The St. Anthony players were on the floor loosening up when a high school girl in the Friars rooting section at Raritan said, "I don't see Sean out there."

"He and Derrick are probably getting taped in the locker room," Cindy said. "Sean is a little more noticeable when he's not out there. It wouldn't have to do with the color of his skin, would it?"

And with that, she started laughing hysterically. The girl nodded. It was a good point.

In the end, Cindy would have to be grateful that the recruiters stayed away from Raritan on Saturday night. After his best performance of the season, Sean had his worst, scoring five points and doing little to distinguish himself on the floor. The scouting report on Sean was out: Pressure him with the ball, and he'd turn it over. His ball handling had to get better.

It turned out to be Barney Anderson's night in the 73–55 victory, the six-foot-five junior scoring twenty-three points on a perfect 11-for-11 shooting against six-foot-eight Qa'rraan Calhoun, one of the best under-classman forwards in the state. Hurley had purposely scheduled the Raritan game back-to-back with the PrimeTime Shootout as a way of forcing his team to go from one quality opponent to the next. This way they would have to absorb the scouting reports on the fly, just like they would have to do in the state tournament. Additionally, they would have to fight through some fatigue late in the Niagara Falls game tomorrow.

Before the Friars boarded the bus back to Jersey City Saturday night, Hurley told them, "There are going to be twenty NBA scouts there tomorrow. But don't worry, it's nothing any of you have to worry about."

ON SUNDAY, MARCUS Williams propped his feet up on the row of chairs before him, sitting in Section 119 of the Sovereign Bank Arena in Trenton, about an hour south of Jersey City. As he thumbed through the game program, listing the dozens of elite high school basketball teams in this three-day event, he came upon a page honoring the 2003 PrimeTime Shootout appearance of the greatest draw in the event's history: LeBron James.

James had sold out the building, turning a respected national high school basketball festival where basketball junkies and college recruiters traditionally congregated into something of a rock concert, a standing-room-only euphoria to witness the boy wonder in his first game back from an Ohio state high school association suspension.

It had been an unforgettable performance, fifty-two points with ESPN covering his comeback as though it were Michael Jordan returning from the baseball bush leagues. Marcus, Lamar and Derrick were arguing over the authenticity of James's scoring explosion that night. Marcus insisted that James had been basket-hanging most of the game, getting his points on easy breakaway shots. Lamar and Derrick told him he was nuts.

"So why didn't LeBron get fifty against Carmelo Anthony when they played?" Marcus asked.

A few rows down from the players in the end-zone seats, those wheels were turning in Cindy again. She had a question of her own: What were the chances of scoring a press pass to spare her a most unfavorable seating location? She needed to get downstairs to the choice courtside seats, explaining, "There are a lot of college coaches here to see Sean today, and they'll want to talk to me."

Somehow she eventually talked her way down to the arena floor, but the college coaches stayed away. As they understood, it would be a violation of NCAA rules for them to speak with the mother of an underclassman prospect at a game.

Most of the twenty or so NBA scouts who had filled the 9,000-seat arena for Oak Hill's games on Friday and Saturday night were gone. Many had come to see point guard Sebastian Telfair of Lincoln High in Brooklyn meet six-foot-eleven Dwight Howard of Southeast Christian in Atlanta. Most scouts believed Howard had a chance to be the number-one pick in that spring's NBA Draft, but Telfair had become one of the high school basketball season's most intriguing stories. Never had a guard so small—he was five-foot-eleven—made the leap straight from high school to the NBA, but it appeared he would be the first to give it a shot. At Louisville, Rick Pitino was rapidly losing hope that his top recruit would ever step foot on campus.

The mere mention of Telfair still made Ben Gamble melancholy. He couldn't get the St. Anthony loss to Telfair and Lincoln in the 2003 PrimeTime out of his mind. It had been here at Sovereign Arena, where after the death of his mother, Eleanor, Hurley had missed his first St. Anthony game since Bobby's car accident nearly a decade earlier. He had left Gamble to coach them.

Gamble still played the final minutes of the game over again, when a late lead slipped away in a 65–61 loss to Lincoln. "I think about what I could've done differently," Gamble said, beating himself up one more time. "You never want to let Coach down, and that's how I felt after that game."

"It was like your dad giving you the keys to the Mercedes and you just wanted to bring it home safe," Pushie said.

For Gamble, there was a profound sense of responsibility. Of course, he was much harder on himself than his mentor ever was. Hurley watched the game on the YES Network and told Gamble later, "There was nothing you could've done about it. You put the kids in the right position and they just didn't perform."

For Gamble, the year-old loss lingered only as long as he wrote out the scouting report for Niagara Falls on the locker-room chalkboard. And then it left his mind. They had enough to worry about that day with once-beaten Niagara Falls, who had only lost to Rufus King of Milwaukee when King was ranked fifth in the USA Today poll. Niagara was an immense team, with a six-foot-eleven, 275-pound center, Franklin Jones, in the middle. They were centered on two six-foot-four forwards with thick arms and muscled legs—Paul and Robert Harris.

With legs still a little wobbly from the Raritan game Saturday night, Hurley hoped his players would find the burst of energy needed to grind Niagara down with constant ball pressure, using the long arena court to tire them and negate the huge size differential with speed and quickness.

St. Anthony rushed out to a nine-point lead twice in the first half, but they struggled with getting shots over the long reach of the Niagara Falls players. Even with its offense reduced to basically firing up three-pointers and crashing the boards to gobble up the misses, Niagara Falls still fought back to tie St. Anthony, 21–21.

Near the end of the third quarter, as they had done throughout the season, the St. Anthony defensive pressure kept causing Niagara Falls' bigger, lumbering players to turn the ball over. The self-assured swagger of Niagara Falls seemed to dissolve in a tidal wave of panicked passes, traveling violations and giveaways. Niagara Falls would turn the ball over twenty-four times in the game.

Beanie made two fabulous plays in the final seconds of the third quarter and the first few of the fourth to turn the game St. Anthony's way for good. His drive to the basket and teardrop floater over the nearly seven-foot center fell through with four seconds left in the third. From there, Beanie made a gorgeous, twisting up-and-under move for a reverse layup to start the fourth, pushing the lead to ten points. Niagara Falls would go nine minutes without a field goal during this time, scraping together just a couple of free throws. Beanie had the biggest part in putting them away.

The 59–46 victory took its toll. Afterward, Beanie was a mess, his jersey and shorts splattered with blood dripping off a cut finger. All Doc Miller needed to do was bandage that up, but Marcus appeared to have a bigger problem. After he had tumbled on defense in the second quarter, his left hand smacked against the floor, leaving his middle finger swollen and throbbing. He played the rest of the game, but now had a bag of ice nudged against it.

Each team had an MVP chosen for the game. As Niagara Falls' Paul Harris jogged out to mid-court to accept his team's, Hurley quickly turned to his bench and said, "Someone is going to be on TV in a minute. Let's make sure all of our shirts are tucked in."

The MVP was Sean, with fifteen points. Most of those had come late in the game, on a fourth-quarter parade to the free-throw line when the victory seemed already secure for St. Anthony.

As Sean hustled to the floor to accept his trophy, Hurley whirled back to the bench.

"Ahmad Mosby should've been the MVP," he said.

His eyes found Beanie sitting on the bench, that forlorn look on his droopy face. "I know a hell of a lot more about basketball than the people who picked that, OK?" he told him. "You were the MVP today."

Two years earlier, Hurley had taken matters into his own hands at the Shoot-out. Obie Nwadike had been selected MVP, but Hurley believed that his teammate Terrence Roberts had earned it. When Hurley extended his hand after the game, Obie thought his coach was congratulating him on a job well done. Reaching back to shake his hand, Obie realized he had it all wrong. "The trophy, please." Obie handed it over, and Hurley, final arbiter of all basketball matters, passed it to Terrence.

"Sean could've gone a long way in that locker room by giving that trophy up to Beanie," Erman said. "He could've won some favor in there.

"Right now, he could use it."

CHAPTER 16

EVERY FEW MINUTES, there was someone else calling the powerful sports voice of WFAN 660 AM radio in New York City, selling the candidacy of Bob Hurley as the next basketball coach at St. John's University. It was 4:24 P.M., on Monday, February 9, and a caller from Lodi, New Jersey, was checking into the "Mike and the Mad Dog" drive-time radio program to deliver an impassioned case for Hurley to save St. John's. Just imagine, the caller said: the chance to coach at Madison Square Garden, to be the man responsible for resurrecting the tarnished gem of New York City college basketball. How could he refuse?

Across the river, inside the charter school gymnasium, where his assistants were going over the final touches on the Our Savior of New American scouting report, the would-be St. John's coach could be found pushing a yellow bucket of soapy water across the court, occasionally dropping down to scrub away the sticky remnants of tape left behind from the grade-school phys. ed. classes held earlier that day.

As the players sat on the floor against the wall waiting for the scouting report, Hurley grabbed a chair and plopped down, with Gamble and staff standing to the side. Usually, Gamble started talking, describing the individual tendencies of the opponent. This time, everyone just sat and listened to Hurley talk about Tuesday night's game.

"How good are they?" he asked. "For the first time in our school's history, an NBA team asked for credentials.

"And," Hurley added, straightening out his face and flattening his voice, "they're not coming to see any of us.

"They're coming to see Palacios."

Juan Diego Tello Palacios was the best uncommitted college prospect in the East now, a six-foot-eight, 260-pound forward whom Gamble compared to a "younger, more athletic Karl Malone." Rick Pitino described him as a young Jamal Mashburn. Either way, St. Anthony had no one like him. He had averaged more than twenty-five points a game over the past ten games or so, obliterating double- and triple-teams along the way. A native of Medellin, Colombia, Palacios had been the cornerstone of this traveling basketball show. Our Savior of New American was a one-room schoolhouse on Long Island founded by the Rev. Ron Stelzer, a preacher who doubled as the basketball coach.

"Palacios gets everybody's attention—college coaches coming to see him from all over the country, NBA people coming to see him," Hurley told his players. "And he also gets the attention of the other team."

Hurley surprised everyone by giving Barney, instead of Marcus, the job of stopping Palacios. They would collapse several people on him at different times, but Hurley wanted to give Barney's fragile confidence a boost with such a show of belief. They were in the middle of a four-game-in-six-day stretch, especially taxing for a team that exerted so much energy on defense. Hurley would take it easy on the Friars' legs this afternoon in practice.

Otis had been practicing for several days, and the doctor had cleared him to make his return against Our Savior. Still, they would have to work him back slowly. He had gained a few pounds during his month off, and Hurley figured it would probably take all the way until the state tournament to get him back into real shape.

The Friars' spotty outside shooting against Niagara Falls worried him, too. For all the shooting drills Hurley had accumulated over the years, all the camps and clinics and creativity that stocked a memory bank like few else's in the profession, Hurley reached all the way back to the playgrounds of Jersey City to stir his team's touch. They would play "Around the World," the old schoolyard game of jump-shooting risk and reward.

The reality of high school basketball had changed dramatically, with NBA scouts flocking to monitor prospects like Palacios. But for Hurley, "Around the World" wasn't the name of a scouting service that procured Central American teens like Palacios—just a little game that Hurley dragged out of the mothballs to shake his team out of a shooting malaise.

Before long, Hurley couldn't help himself. He grabbed a ball from Sean and started to show the kids how it was done. His players still marveled at his touch, especially when he hadn't warmed up. "How about my roll?" Hurley marveled, bouncing one ball into the net and moving to the next spot, where he bounced in another. And another. Sometimes, Hurley just trusted his instincts to be the best remedy for his team.

"Around the World," Hurley declared to no one in particular. "The best way to get out of a slump."

On his way out of practice that Tuesday, Barney held the lone object of college affection that had come for him, a recruiting letter from Liberty University. Where that was, he had no idea. But this was St. Anthony, and there was always a chance for a ballplayer to prove himself. One of those games was coming for him, a chance for Hurley to someday tell the story of the night when the NBA finally came to St. Anthony, only to find that Jerry Falwell's recruiting target, Barney Anderson, shut down Rick Pitino's, the great Juan Diego Tello Palacios.

AFTER WORK THE next day, Bob Hurley stopped home to change clothes for the game. He was pulling his maroon sweater-vest over his long-sleeve white shirt, when his wife told him that Bobby had called that afternoon.

"Oh yeah?" he responded. "Good."

"He said you're a brilliant coach, Bob," she continued. "He said that this was something that you were born to do."

"Uh-huh," Hurley answered, slowly, trying to figure out where this was going.

"Bobby says whoever you have, you're going to be able to coach them."

"What's the bottom line here, Red?" Hurley finally asked.

"Bobby thinks you ought to take the St. John's job."

Once again, Bobby and Danny were engaged in a familiar old dance for the brothers, conferencing on calls and trying to think of a way to finally convince their father to take a college job. They had willing accomplices in Chris and Melissa, too. The family wanted to see him get his due on a bigger stage. Bobby had played for Krzyzewski, the best college coach in the country, and believed his father to be every inch the equal of Duke's legend. He wanted his father to feel what it was like to take a team to the NCAA tournament, even a Final Four.

"We'll get you the players," Bobby would promise him. "Just sit on the bench and coach. Danny and I will organize everything else."

Through the years, Hurley had turned down dozens of college offers and feelers. Lately, athletic directors had stopped calling. He was fifty-six years old, and everyone has gotten the idea that he was never leaving St. Anthony. Through the years, they had tried. How they had tried to get him to leave. Whatever his own ambitions, he always knew the consequences of leaving St. Anthony.

Yet his family believed that it was unfair for Bob to think that his own agenda had to be forever shackled to St. Anthony's survival. They admired him deeply for it, but told him that it wouldn't be selfish to chase something else in life, to show the world that his acumen transcended to the next level. People had a hard time understanding why Hurley never left high school basketball, especially those who assumed he subscribed to the commonly held value system within the business: that a bigger stage and a bigger paycheck meant *better*.

Fordham University's athletic director, Frank McLaughlin, was a Hudson County kid who had grown up playing ball against Hurley in high school and kept a close watch through the years on the fiercest competitor he had ever met. McLaughlin had to hire a new basketball coach in 1987, so he drove down to Jersey City for a St. Anthony game. He sat high in the bleachers, watching Hurley work, waiting for his old friend once the gym emptied out. He didn't need to interview him. He had come to offer him the head coaching job. He imagined Hurley mining top talent out of metropolitan New York and New Jersey for the Jesuit school in the Bronx, turning Fordham back into an Eastern power.

The gesture was flattering to Hurley. After all, he was human. It meant a lot to him that someone thought he could make that kind of leap into college basketball. McLaughlin never forgot how genuinely touched Hurley looked when he said "Thank you" for the offer. He rejected Fordham on the spot, understanding he never needed to leave St. Anthony to know high school basketball was his calling.

"There was a sense that I was showing a tremendous amount of respect and admiration for him by coming over," McLaughlin remembers. "I just think he has a mission there. I'm not sure there's anybody else in the coaching profession who I admire as much as I do him."

What had changed by 1987 was that Bobby was a sophomore at St. Anthony, and Danny was in the eighth-grade. As hard as the sons pushed their father to take a college job later in life, they were a lot of the reason why he stayed, especially during his one, true crisis of conscience about his college coaching ambitions. Notre Dame assistant coach Pete Gillen had been hired as Xavier University's head coach in the spring of 1985, and he offered Hurley his top assistant's job.

"It's time," Gillen had told him. "You know that."

For a brief time, he wondered if maybe it was. Bob and Chris flew to Cincinnati, toured the neighborhoods and visited the high school, Moeller, where in 1980 the football coach, Gerry Faust, had made the historic leap to head coach at Notre Dame. Hurley tried to imagine his sons playing high school basketball at Moeller, while he was off recruiting someone else's kids to Xavier. The thought made him uneasy, but nevertheless, he felt like perhaps he should take the job. The Hurleys returned home, brought the boys into the kitchen and laid it out for them. Bobby broke down in tears.

"Who's going to coach me?" he asked.

His own boys were like every other kid in Jersey City. They dreamed of playing basketball for Bob Hurley at St. Anthony.

Bob looked at Chris, Chris looked at Bob.

And that was that.

"In the back of my mind, I never thought we were going," Chris says. "The boys had been watching Bob for years, and they wanted to play for him. And Bob wanted to coach them. For as long as St. Anthony is going to stay open, Bob is going to be there."

Danny says, "He says the same thing every time: 'I've got a great group of eighth graders coming into the school.' I can set my watch to it. Listen, he's never going to go. He means too much to the school, to the city. He's never going. But the day he's gone from St. Anthony, it's over. Regardless of whether Bobby or myself wanted to go there and try to replicate that, we couldn't. He's different. He grew up in a different time, and he's a different man."

Through the years, the calls kept coming. Eddie Donovan, the old Knicks general manager, had gone back as an administrator to his alma mater, St. Bonaventure, to revive the basketball program. He tried to hire Hurley. Hurley's alma mater, St. Peter's College in Jersey City, offered several times, too. The most all-out family pressure came in 1998, when Monmouth, a small Division I school on the Jersey Shore, had an opening. Melissa was entering her freshman year at the university. Danny was miserable as an assistant at Rutgers. Bobby was out of basketball. The family had the house down on the Shore. They worked Hurley relentlessly, until he finally put a stop to it.

"I can understand all your points, but it makes sense for everybody but me," he told them. "Who's got to make the decision? Me. And I don't want to do this. So will you all stop?"

Well, it was starting again. Hurley escaped Chris's cornering in the apartment, only to make it over to the gymnasium Tuesday and find the inquisition starting anew. The Our Savior of New American's vans were lost, delaying the junior varsity and varsity games. Bob McCurdy had just arrived from his office in Manhattan, resplendent in his long winter coat and suit. He stopped to say hello to Hurley on his way to the bleachers.

"I'm driving today," McCurdy told him, "and someone calls up on the radio and says, 'I know who should take the St. John's job,' and I'm thinking to myself, 'Don't say Bob Hurley . . . Don't say his name.'

"He says, 'Bob Hurley.' "

One of his assistants, Dan McLaughlin, arrived, declaring, "Hey, Bob, someone told me that you turned down the St. John's job today."

Hurley just shook his head and rolled his eyes.

The pregame conversation would turn into one more referendum on his future, everyone talking around him like he wasn't there. Melissa compiled an assistant coaching staff. McLaughlin, a genius businessman who built and sold a multimillion-dollar company, figured out financial terms of a contract that Hurley could share with St. Anthony to keep the school alive.

But Hurley had a game to coach. He had gotten out of bed twice late Monday night to write himself notes on defending Palacios, on getting Otis back into the flow. Nothing on angling for the St. John's job.

"Listen, all I want to do is roust these guys, go have a burger after the game and get home in time for *Seinfeld*," Hurley said.

"I love college basketball, but I belong here."

As they kept talking, kept waiting for Our Savior to arrive, nobody seemed to notice him slip away.

"Where's Bob?" Chris finally asked.

McLaughlin looked over and nodded to the solitary figure marching up and down the basketball floor.

"Sweeping," he said.

THIRTY MINUTES LATER, Our Savior had arrived, and the mother of one of America's most shamed college athletes walked into the gymnasium and started straight for her son's old high school coach, who was sitting in the corner. Hurley could see Camay Ingram walking right to him.

She started to hug him, holding on tight. She didn't let go. She just held on.

Hurley welled up, and pulling back, looked her in the eye and assured her, "We're going to get him going in the right direction."

Elijah had called Hurley on Monday night, the hardest eleven digits he had ever dialed in his life. "I just worried about what he thought of me," Elijah said later. "I wanted to tell him my side of the story. After my family, I wanted to get to Coach Hurley."

Hurley told him to come on down for the game against Our Savior and bring his folks with him, too. He faced a disciplinary hearing at St. John's, where they would ultimately give him the chance to withdraw from school, rather than be expelled. He couldn't think of a place in the world where he wanted more to be invited, where he wanted to still be welcome, than here at St. Anthony's.

Shortly after his parents arrived, Elijah entered the charter school. Sister Alan greeted him in the lobby, hugging him and confessing she really didn't know the right thing to say to him. That's all right, he said. Neither did he, except that he was sorry. She knew it would be tough for him to show his face in public, but she wanted to make it easier. And she wanted to send a message to everyone in the gymnasium: Elijah Ingram was a St. Anthony Friar, and nothing he had done changed that.

"The first thing they're going to see in that gym is you and me hugging," Sister Alan said.

Elijah wore a green Celtics cap, a white bandana beneath it, and as he walked into the gymnasium, every eye burned into him. Once he stepped into the gym, the first familiar face he saw was that of a beaming old man, one who never packed political correctness or tact in his training bag.

"Elijah, I knew that girl!" Doc said. "I used to go out with her when I was in Pittsburgh."

Elijah just shook his head and laughed, comfortable in the knowledge that some things at St. Anthony never did change. Whatever happened, Doc was going to bust his balls. All in all, it felt good to be back among family.

"I needed to be here," he said later. "This is a place that will always be a part of me, the one place that I know I'm going to get love no matter what."

On the court, there was little Friars love for Palacios, who grew exasperated with the ball-hawking Derrick and Beanie constantly collapsing down low to help Barney with him. The small St. Anthony guards were like a pack of dogs barking up his leg whenever the ball found Palacios's hands. Whichever way he spun, there was a Friar with feet planted, willing to sacrifice his safety and absorb the hit for an offensive foul. When Palacios passed the ball out of the collapsing defense, the St. Anthony recovery to cover his teammates was swift, the guards covering every corner of the floor, denying everyone.

Palacios finally lost his cool late in the third period. He had been held to just eleven points—five of which had come within the first ninety seconds of the game—when Barney bodied up to him, bringing Sean rushing to jar the ball out of Palacios's massive hands. Palacios, tired of the physicality of the game, tossed Sean backward, earning himself an offensive foul. The great Palacios finished with eighteen points, the rest of them meaningless baskets in the fourth quarter, as St. Anthony distanced itself for a 60–48 victory. Otis played several minutes, but didn't score. He looked rusty and felt out of sync. "It's going to take time, but it was nice to be back with the fellas," he would say in the locker room.

Jay Cyriac, a 76ers scout, scribbled his final thoughts in his notebook and left the gymnasium. Seton Hall University's talented young assistant, Brian Nash, shook his head incredulously about the kind of job St. Anthony had done on Palacios.

"That's why Bob Hurley is who he is," Nash said. "They swarmed Palacios. They never let him get his feet underneath."

Watching his players get a snack for the road out of the vending machines, the Rev. Stelzer sounded like he was suggesting that Our Savior had been worked over a little by hometown Jersey City officiating. "They did a nice job of swarming Palacios and beating him up," he said. "The atmosphere here helped allow them to do it."

It was a common complaint among vanquished visitors of St. Anthony, just like those teams who lost to Duke, the Lakers and the Bulls dynasties. Maybe there was something to the idea that tradition and intimidating presences on the sidelines and court give teams more than a benefit of the doubt, but on this night, Palacios wasn't much of a match for Hurley. After the game, Elijah trailed the Friars into the locker room. And just before he ducked through the door, he reached up and pulled his bandana off, as though he were walking into church.

"Just respect for the man," Elijah Ingram explained.

Wherever they went, whatever happened in life, there was something comforting for his past players to know they could always come home to St. Anthony and find that things had never really changed. Always some solitary star the Friars had to shut down, always the warm embrace of family.

And always respect for the man.

CHAPTER 17

IT WAS ONLY a matter of time. Bob Hurley and Ben Gamble had been waiting for someone to do this to St. Anthony, and more importantly, waiting to watch the Friars' response. All along, they knew the best way to challenge their team was to *challenge* them. Elizabeth High School slapped a full-court press on the Friars, bodied chest to chest all over the floor, sending an unmistakable message: They were unbowed by St. Anthony's ranking and record and reputation.

Everywhere Hurley looked in the opening minutes at the charter school gym on Thursday night, one of his players was getting pushed off the ball. Going backward. Or getting up off the floor. For the first time, someone else was dictating the terms of engagement. Elizabeth was determined to take the Friars back to the streets, pure and simple.

"The one thing about St. Anthony teams is that they'll put opponents away really quick, if you let them," Elizabeth coach Donnie Stewart said later. "They're like the old Mike Tyson. One hit, and they'll take you out in the first round."

Elizabeth had exploded out of its corner throwing haymakers. Derrick tossed a pass into the backcourt for a turnover. Another pass zipped through Sean's hands and out-of-bounds. Sean dribbled to the basket, leaping into the air and leaning into defenders, grimacing when no foul came. This would inspire Hurley to tell him at halftime, "Why isn't there a call? Because no referee in the world is going to blow the whistle and bail out a *fucking idiot* who's up in the air for some unknown reason." The quick, ball-hawking Elizabeth guards would be poisonous to Sean, holding him without a basket. Beanie and Lamar would lock him up in practice often, but now it was happening in the games, too.

The Friars turned the ball over again and again, but Hurley never called a timeout to settle them down. To prepare for the game, Elizabeth's coach had called his old boss and mentor, ex-Elizabeth coach Ben Candelino, for advice on strategizing against Hurley. One of the tips that stayed with Stewart turned out to be exactly true. Hurley wouldn't come to the rescue of his players. He didn't call a timeout. He didn't make any adjustments. "He's stubborn, in that way," Stewart would say. "He wants to see his kids work out of it themselves."

Yes, Hurley wanted to see his leaders take over on the floor, fighting through the turbulence with patience and poise. This wasn't a tact that Hurley would have the luxury of employing in a lose-and-go-home circumstance, but now, on February 12, with him gearing his team toward the state tournament, he was determined to let them bob up and down in the water, gasping for air, before he tossed them the life preserver.

Maybe the stagnancy was the product of a fourth game in seven days for the Friars, a tough stretch of Raritan, Niagara Falls and Our Savior that had left them with tired legs and a belief that Elizabeth, despite a 14-3 record and a respectable ranking of twelfth in the state poll, would be something of a breather with the countdown to St. Raymond's just seven days away. Whatever the reasons, Elizabeth did Hurley the favor of turning the first half into a referendum on the Friars' will. They were the perfect test at the perfect time for St. Anthony. A tough, urban school with an enormous enrollment of 5,400, Elizabeth's players wore cornrows, headbands, and a steely resolve where so many St. Anthony opponents harbored a hesitancy.

While St. Anthony ran crisp, sound offensive plays, Hurley was hardly a rigid system coach frowning on the creative impulses of his players. Especially with a small, guard-oriented team, he implored Derrick, Beanie, Sean and Otis to make plays on offense. He wanted them to play with so much swagger, so much command of the circumstances, that they could take a man off the dribble to the basket to create for teammates and themselves. To be that big-time college point guard, this was the part of the game where Sean still sorely struggled, where Hurley was working hardest on developing.

To give themselves a workable advantage heading into halftime, the Friars scored eight straight points to end the second quarter, taking a 31–23 lead into the locker room. Hurley laid into the team hard, finishing his blitzkrieg this way: "They didn't come here to ask for our autographs. Are they just going to smack us?"

The Friars answered the coach's call in the opening minutes of the third, ripping off fifteen straight points on the way to salvaging a 63–44 victory. Even so, St. Anthony wouldn't salvage a clean getaway.

"I knew we were going to get killed in that locker room," Sean said.

After the final buzzer, the Elizabeth players wouldn't stop tugging at Hurley's heart. One by one, they shook his hand, called him "Mr. Hurley," and told him it was an honor to compete against St. Anthony. Wonderful. The St. Anthony kids must have been wondering why the Elizabeth players didn't bring Hurley an apple, too. As the coaches passed, Hurley told Stewart this had been the first time all season that an opposing team had played harder than his own. Once Elizabeth returned to its locker room, Stewart told his players what Hurley had said, and everyone cheered. Elizabeth had lost by nineteen points, suffered through twenty-three straight St. Anthony points, and Stewart told his kids he had never been prouder of them.

Without a word, next door, the St. Anthony players sat on the benches and floor in the cramped locker room, waiting for the assistants and Hurley to file in and close the door behind them. It wasn't long before Hurley stood before them, tapping the toe of his right shoe and saying nothing. His eyes darted from player to player.

The kids would've rather stared back into an eclipse than into those rabid eyes.

"You are who you are," Hurley finally said. "These are the personality and character flaws of this entire group. When this season is done, we'll go back to the one simple thing: If this ends up anything short of a state championship, you're just going to be a bunch of people that all the adults will remember as the worst class in St. Anthony history.

"I have never been around more poorly individually motivated people. Ever. This reminds me of what juvenile probation used to look like on Thursdays up at the county building, where guys would just drag their ass in. Lamar Alston's life is dragging his fucking ass from one place to the next. No spirit. No fucking enthusiasm.

"What happened today was very simple: They got into Mercer's chest. And Mosby's chest. And McCurdy's chest. And what happened? Everybody went, 'Ohhhhh nooooo, one of *those* games.' They couldn't wait to come here and play us.

"And who are you? You're the willing victim. You stand there and you let people get in your face. My prayers are for your families. When you leave this place, the structure that it gives you, how many of you can handle this tough world? My blessings. I hope it works out for you all. But I have real strong reservations of nearly every one of you, because when you have obstacles in your path—academic, social, athletic, emotional—you will not have the mental toughness, the self-discipline, the passion, to overcome it."

It had stayed with him the way the Elizabeth kids went out of their way to show him respect after the game, the way they showed the game itself respect with how they competed against St. Anthony. They weren't good enough to beat the Friars. They didn't have enough talent. Still, they had wanted to play that game against St. Anthony far more than his kids had wanted to play them.

"I'm afraid to even ask this, but does anyone even know the name of the Elizabeth coach?

"Huh, anyone?"

Nothing.

"Lamar, what's the coach's name at Seton Hall Prep?"

Nothing.

"Barney, what's the coach's name at Seton Hall Prep?"

Blank stare.

"Ahmad Nivins, what's the coach at Seton Hall's name?"

Another blank stare.

"Bob Farrell is the coach of Seton Hall Prep. He's coached in the McDonald's All-American game. He's won state championships. He's had Brevin Knight in the NBA. You must never read a fucking newspaper. Part of having SAT scores that are very, very low is that you don't even read the sports page."

Hurley grabbed a chair from the showers, and sat down. This told the team everything that it feared. They weren't leaving soon. This wasn't ending, but just beginning.

"I have contempt," Hurley started again. "I have nothing but contempt for you all. You make me sick. You have no passion. You're not going to make it. You're such a sorry-ass bunch. I can say to you that the state championship is a month and a day away, and know what you can do?

"Go back to your miserable fucking existence.

"Go back to not fucking caring.

"Go back to being *cool*.

"My frustration is this: I would just love to beat your ass. Because somebody should've beat your ass growing up. I got my ass beat a bunch of times. I came from a very good generation, and if I did something to embarrass my father, he kicked the shit out of me.

"And what did I learn? Well, I learned first that I didn't like getting the shit kicked out of me. And the second thing I learned as I got older, never would I want to do something to embarrass my dad. Because he was a hero of mine.

"A hero of mine.

"I think of the families here, and they must come home and their heads must be fuckin' spinning. I look around here and I want somebody to go out and accomplish something. Go out and every fuckin' day get away from the crowd and be your own person. But it can't happen. Because you're a bunch of miserable fucking adolescents. You look for somebody to tell you, 'Ah, that's OK . . . You've got car keys and a steady girlfriend, but you've got no SAT scores and no grades and no fuckin' future.

"Now, teams are coming into our building and they want to fucking get us. They want us here. So, go ahead, read your press clippings. But at least give the sport the respect to know who's in it."

His rage dissolved into a long, exhausted groan. He turned to his assistant coaches, all of them standing stoically behind him.

"Oh my God. How bad is this?"

It looked like it was over. Hurley breathed out, and picked up his clipboard like he wanted to leave—only to have Gamble sigh and say incredulously, "I can't believe they didn't know Bob Farrell."

"I could go further," Hurley threatened. "You want to take this thing further?"

Some of the kids shot glances at Gamble, as if to tell him, *What did you have to say that for?* because they knew that it just got Hurley all wound up again. They had just bought ten more minutes of his wrath.

"How many of you know the name of the coach at St. Peter's College?"

Now, Lamar Alston did know his name: Bob Leckie. In fact, Lamar half-raised his hand, only to quickly put it down. He was pretty sure it was Leckie, but he would be damned to let himself guess wrong and invite that heat. He just played dumb like everyone else.

"Not one person," Hurley said, scanning the room.

"Put your hand up if St. Peter's College was good enough to allow you to work out in their gym every day last spring?"

Several hands went up. Marcus. Otis. Beanie. Barney. Derrick. Lamar.

"Five of them were in the gym every day and they don't even know the man's name. Some of you guys are getting recruiting letters from him and you don't even know the man's name?"

Hurley turned to Gamble and shook his head, two Jersey City gym rats wondering where the time had gone, how a generation of St. Anthony players could be so unaware of a basketball world that surrounded them.

For Hurley, the complete disconnect between his players—between a generation of kids like them and the world in which they competed—was symptomatic of a greater disregard. He believed that for most of his players, basketball wasn't God. It was video games and cell phones and mindless television shows and it broke his heart. It killed him.

It always got back to the fact that they just didn't love the game the way he did. Didn't respect those in it. He couldn't get over that. He would *never* get over that.

How could they not spend the day as nervous as him?

How could they not devour the morning sports page?

How could they not know Bob Farrell?

"This is such a different city now," Hurley was saying now. "I wore a letter sweater when I was a kid in Jersey City. You wore the amount of stripes for your varsity year. Like Marcus Williams would have four stripes on his sweater. That was a big deal. Now, if you've got four chains around your neck, it's a big fucking deal. Those guys used to come in and see me in probation. I used to laugh at those guys. It's called chump change in life. You settle for one thing. You've got it now. And you spend most of your life in jail.

"A very good friend of mine is in jail; a kid who Ben and I tried to counsel before he went away. He made a huge mistake in his adult life. I keep taking books that I want him to read so that he has something to do while he's in prison.

"Do you all understand that there are people all over the place who made just one decision. *Just one decision in life* . . .

"God, we must have these kinds of discussions three times a week now."

Hurley breathed into his lungs now, and let loose with something that was as much a plea as it was a command. Somewhere along the way, this had become no longer about a lousy first half, about backing down to Elizabeth, about the way they had played the game. He had six weeks left with his seniors, if they could make it to the Tournament of Champions finals. This was one of those nights when Hurley knew he was the last line of defense for them, the last voice that held the authority—that probably even cared enough—to call them out.

His eyes were wide now, his face red, that square jaw jutting toward them.

"I'M TALKING ABOUT AMOUNTING TO SOMETHING. . . .
SEPARATE YOURSELVES FROM THE FUCKING CROWD. . . . BE
FUCKING SPECIAL."

The thunder of his voice hit the concrete walls like a freight train,
shaking the room and standing the hair on necks at attention.

"And what is it? Every fuckin' day, here we go, these eight or nine
guys that are the same.

"*Mediocre.*

"However, over here," he said, extending his arms to cover the coaching staff, "you're surrounded by greatness.

"When you're finished playing here, remember why you fuckin'
won. . . . Why you fuckin' won.

"You don't even know the names of people. I could tell you the names
of the high school coaches in Jersey City in 1965. At Lincoln High School,
John Ryan. At Bayonne High School, Bernie Ockene. Lou Campanelli at
Marist High School. Tony Nicodemo at Ferris. At Snyder, Al Ardizone. At
Dickinson, Sam Kaplan. At Memorial, Tony Boccheri.

"I can tell you names of people from forty years ago, because when I
grew up, coaches were *big*. You lazy motherfuckers don't even know the
names of coaches."

With one final sweeping measure of the room, Hurley climbed to his
feet, spit out "You're all shit," and stalked toward the door, leaving the St.
Anthony Friars, now 19-0, in a sobered silence.

OUTSIDE THE LOCKER room, Sister Alan was waiting at the scorer's table
with an exhausted collection of family, friends and college recruiters.
"When these seniors graduate," Hurley snapped, walking past her, "their
parents all owe us a cruise."

After the players finished dressing and left the locker room, they found
Melissa Hurley waiting in the gymnasium, passing out red-and-pink-
hearted plastic bags of sweets for Valentine's Day. The coach had already
passed out his Valentines, a swift kick in the collective balls.

Meanwhile, Hurley stood with Gamble and Jim Carr, the Rutgers
assistant, still seething. Carr was a family friend, going back years. He had
dubbed Hurley "Jack Palance with a whistle," and this was surely one of
those Palance moments.

Around him in the postgame milling, everyone looked a little askew at
Hurley. Of course, none of them could've possibly known the reasons why

he was *still* rattling off the names of high school basketball coaches from the 1960s. He just stood there, mumbling, "St. Michael's, Union City . . . Mike Rubbinaccio . . . Bill Kuchar at St. Mary's . . . Bob O'Connor at St. Al's . . . They were the coaches when I was a kid. I mean, I knew the jayvee coaches' names."

Soon, everyone cleared out of the gym. Through the front doors and into the parking lot, Chris had convinced her husband to grab a burger and keep the postgame P.J. Ryan's streak alive for the season. Walking to the car, the wind whipping snow past his face, Robert Patrick Hurley's voice remained the most relentless in the Jersey City night.

". . . Hank Morano was at Emerson. Bill McKeever, Union Hill. Matt Sabello, North Bergen. . . ."

Over a burger and fries, Chris Hurley would be treated to a roll call of every high school coach in Newark in the 1960s. And after that, he worked his way down to the Jersey Shore.

"They don't know the name of one coach on our schedule," he said, shaking his head between bites.

Maybe Hurley should take the St. John's job.

After all, the kids in the Big East know who Boeheim and Calhoun are.

THE NEXT MORNING, it was just a matter of time until someone was thrown out of practice. The mildest of indiscretions had promised to be turned into capital offenses and someone was going to go today. In the unbeaten national championship season of 1989, when Bobby, Jerry Walker and Terry Dehere practiced hard every day and blew teams out every night, Hurley tossed players out of practice in a regular rotation to simply combat complacency. Sometimes, throwing them out was a spontaneous combustion of emotions. Sometimes, it was calculated to stir a particular player. This sure seemed to be one of those latter days.

Hurley told his players that he was treating the Elizabeth game as a loss, as if his tirade the previous night had left any doubt about that. He told them that the unbeaten Friars were destined for a colossal March collapse. With a long Presidents' Day weekend for St. Anthony that started Thursday morning and extended until Tuesday, Hurley made the strategic decision to use the St. Peter's College gymnasium for this 10:00 A.M. Saturday practice, minimizing the chance of a sluggishness after his players would've spent a mindless day hanging out.

St. Peter's was glad to have the Friars using the facility for practice, and eager to accommodate St. Anthony's wishes to move the much-anticipated St. Raymond's game there next Thursday. After all, they were recruiting several St. Anthony players. For the biggest game of the regular season, St. Anthony could accomplish two things by moving the game out of the comfortable confines of the charter school: sell many more tickets, and give themselves another chance to play in the college gym the state used for the northern sectionals of the Parochial B state tournament.

What worked against the players that day was the length of the court, a wider and longer surface that promised to make a hard day of running unbearable. Hurley guaranteed Lamar a grueling workstation to start practice. "Alston's going to die today," Hurley said with a wry smile near mid-court. "Look who I have him with—Otis, who can't wait to come back. And Marcus, who's trying to get out of the doghouse. A nightmare for Alston."

Hurley turned and walked toward mid-court. "This is judgment day for the cool guys. The bullshit is over. Nobody is just going to get in the game anymore because they have a uniform. You play because you deserve to play.

"Guys are going to lose their jobs over one thing that bothers me. One thing. What is your job every day? Please me, all day, for one month from today. Then, if I never see you again, you'll have a jacket that says state champions.

"If you guys fail this now, you don't fail me—you fail all the group."

When Hurley tossed that out—*failing the group*—there was no mistaking the impending target of his red-hot poker. He motioned to Beanie, and ominously warned, "I'm watching him like a hawk."

Beanie's heart sank.

Sooner or later, he knew this was coming.

"What game is up for us Sunday? St. Dominic's of Oyster Bay," Hurley continued. "That's when Ahmad Mosby left us last year. Right there, right at this time of the season. And I'll bring it up regularly now, because I want to know if we've had any *character development* here."

They were coming up on the anniversary of Beanie's personal meltdown as a junior. This was a threshold the senior still had to cross with Hurley, a cementing of confidence that his coach could count on him down the stretch this season. When he had cracked a year ago, the championship dream had crumbled. In this season, so much of St. Anthony's success had centered on Beanie's resolve, on an ability to turn Hurley's heat into fuel. It was the anniversary of the walls closing in on him, the pressures reaching critical mass and exploding. This was Hurley's way of telling him they had returned to that crossroad, telling Beanie that it was time to declare himself once and for all. Hurley had been proud of Beanie's progress, showing it at different times—sending him out as appointed captain to pick up a team trophy at St. John's and declaring him the true MVP over Sean at the PrimeTime Shootout.

Hurley believed he had to keep Beanie thinking that every day was an installment in winning back the coach's ultimate trust. Hurley kept on him, because he refused to let Beanie's past failures, his demons, become the pink elephant in the gym. The Friars were too invested in Beanie now, too dependent on him, and Hurley was testing his resolve now. He wanted to know they could count on Ahmad Mosby.

"I hope we're not the same group that I worked with last year," Hurley yelled. "I want to know that we've grown. But I'm watching close."

The rage welled within Beanie, and he would've loved to simply slug Hurley. For Beanie, he could never move past the fact that his life had never before included a man disciplining him. By the time they were seniors, most of Hurley's players could compartmentalize his digs, let it go on some level, but every biting word bore itself into Beanie's soul.

Once The Faa saw the score of the Elizabeth game in the morning paper, he made his way over to St. Peter's, figuring that the entertainment value would be at a premium. Halfway through the practice, he arrived with a personal over-under prediction of four Friars having been thrown out for varying offenses—real or imagined. He was close. By the time he arrived, Lamar, Shelton and Linoll had gone out the door.

"Anybody think I'm screwing around today?" Hurley yelled.

"NO!" the players barked back, never missing a step in a monkey in the middle drill.

"Anybody want a piece of me?"

"NO!"

Hurley nodded approvingly. The sneakers kept squeaking, the bodies dripping sweat and the push for the state championship—one month away—had begun in earnest.

One more month, the seniors had jackets, and they never had to see him again.

At this point, to the kids, it sounded like a pretty damn good deal.

To the side of the doorway inside the St. Dominic High School gymnasium, Rob Pavinelli watched a junior-varsity game and waited for the St.

Anthony bus to work its way over the Long Island Expressway. St. Dom's had a proud basketball heritage in its quaint north-shore town of Oyster Bay, including the development of a scrappy young guard back in the 1970s named Rick Pitino.

"Right now," Pavinelli, St. Dominic's coach, said wistfully Sunday afternoon, "I wish I had a player good enough to send to Coach Pitino at Louisville."

Pavinelli was a trim, young-looking forty years old. His team had played St. Anthony six straight years and lost six straight times. "Maybe you beat him once," he said, "and then you can say, 'Hey, how many people have beaten Bob Hurley?'"

In his house, Pavinelli kept a framed picture of himself standing between two of the greatest high school coaches ever—Hurley and DeMatha Catholic's Morgan Wootten.

"I would be lying if I didn't say that I looked up to [Hurley], because I do," he admitted. "He's the standard-bearer for high school coaches. When you talk about high school coaches, you talk about Bob Hurley and Morgan Wootten.

"There are some other programs who have as much talent as St. Anthony's does, but he just gets kids to do exactly what he wants them to do. Especially in these times, that's the big difference. Kids have changed a lot in the last five or six years. But he still gets them to do exactly what he wants them to do."

All week in practice, Pavinelli tried to simulate the St. Anthony pressure by using seven defenders on the floor against his five offensive starters.

"You just don't see man-to-man half-court defense—in your face, denying every pass—like they do it," Pavinelli said.

Just then, Hurley walked into the gymnasium, beating the team bus to another game. To Pavinelli, there was something regal about having him visit St. Dominic's every other season for a game, a sense of basketball royalty descending.

"What I really admire is that there are no airs about him. He could be a real asshole, and he never is. He comes in, he beats you and he's never condescending. He'll tell you why he beat you. He'll help you. One time we played them out in California, and we played very well. They were up 18–6 after the first quarter and we went to the zone. And after the game, he tells me, 'You probably should've started out in the zone.'

"Most guys would just shake your hand and say, 'See you later,' he said. "He's not like that. He's always looking to teach and help."

★ ★ ★

MAYBE NOBODY NEEDED Hurley's help right now as much as his discombobulated junior, Sean McCurdy. At practice Saturday, Hurley watched him trying to integrate a step-back-and-shoot move into his decaying arsenal, and told him, "Sean, your game is so screwed up right now, stop trying to add things. Do less."

Sean had been anxious for the game. His scoring average had kept on the decline, and going without a field goal against Elizabeth visibly shook him. He tried to take to heart Hurley's lessons of doing a little bit of everything on the floor, but a part of him resisted. He was a scorer to the core.

Bob McCurdy had made the drive down from Connecticut, as tired as ever from shuttling between St. Anthony games in Jersey and his oldest son Mike's games at Southern Connecticut State in New Haven. His parents lived on Long Island, in Deer Park, about thirty minutes west of Oyster Bay, and they had also come to watch Sean with an aunt and cousins. Cindy McCurdy had family friends from Connecticut sitting in the next section of bleachers. Within the coaching staff, there was a belief that the more family in the stands to see Sean, the worse he played.

His father had tremendous respect for Hurley, always trying to defer to the coach's expertise in basketball matters involving Sean. Cindy had passed her ex-husband an article that longtime St. Anthony chronicler Jim Hague had written in the *Hudson Reporter*, honoring Sean as the county high school player of the week for his performances against The Hun and Niagara Falls. In the story, Hurley, only half-jokingly, said the difference between his performance last season and this one was that Sean no longer went home after practice and did extra shooting on his own. Hurley loved the diligence, but believed that Sean constantly undid the proper form and mechanics taught to him in practice by shooting unsupervised. Upon returning to the gym the next day, Sean would've regressed back into his bad habits.

This made Sean's father bristle a bit. There was a constant push-and-pull for Sean between Hurley's instructions and his father's nightly questions on the phone about whether he had gone downstairs in the apartment complex's gym for extra shooting.

Hurley worked relentlessly with Sean to make him a complete guard. One staff member described him as a "driveway player," a kid who played so much basketball alone that he struggled within the context of the teammates surrounding him. Sometimes, the ability to react instinctively to a defender was missing. As another St. Anthony coach said, "He plays the way he lives up in that apartment: all alone."

The scouting report on Sean clearly had circulated: Pressure him on the dribble, trap him and watch him pick up the ball and panic. He would try to split the defenders on the way to the basket, leaving his feet and getting caught in the air with nowhere to go.

Hurley was on him hard. Near the end of the half, Sean forced his way out of a double-team, never lifting his eyes to find an open teammate. He missed a difficult, off-balance leaner, leaving his father in the stands to understand what would happen to his son next.

"He's out of the game," McCurdy predicted. And he was right.

Hurley wasted no time sending Beanie back on the floor for Sean. When a player made a mistake, they could count on Hurley breathlessly reaching for one of his substitutes and hurtling him toward the scorer's table. This was a fact of life for St. Anthony, the way he coached the game.

"If you're worried about making a mistake, about coming out of the game to get chewed out, it's tough to play," McCurdy said.

As much as Hurley believed Sean had regressed, had been burdened with too much needless stress about impressing college coaches to earn that big-time scholarship, his father had a different vision of his son's struggles.

As Sean returned to the court for the start of the second quarter, his father lifted his forefingers to his mouth and whistled. As Sean looked up, his father flapped his wrist back and forth to his son, the universal sign for keep shooting. This had been a time-honored family adage, a belief about what a McCurdy did in good times and bad times: Just keep shooting.

"They're not running many plays for him to get shots," Bob McCurdy said, staring straight ahead, his eyes fixed on Sean defending a St. Dominic player. "He has to create his own shots. Plus, the ones he's gotten haven't fallen. And once they don't fall, you're hesitant to shoot them."

If this was the assessment of the father, it sure wasn't that of the coach. Of course, this was a common push-and-pull of high school sports. There were times the father cringed over the ferocity of Hurley toward Sean, saying later, "I think that maybe less could be more with Sean," or worrying, "Coach Hurley went a little too far with him." Yet, McCurdy still eventually deferred to the coach. He knew the schools recruiting Sean wasn't just a direct correlation to his St. Anthony pedigree, but the reason. "He only has Sean's best interests at heart," he said.

"What I have to realize is that Coach has had a hell of a lot more success his way than I've had mine. Hey, I have no track record as a coach. I'll keep my faith with him."

After reentering the game on the next possession, Sean missed an open three-pointer and committed a needless foul with eleven seconds left in the second quarter. It was right there, in front of the St. Anthony bench. "What are you doing?" an exasperated Hurley pleaded. St. Anthony was winning by eighteen going into the locker room, but Sean's struggles were descending into a spiral.

After a 68–35 victory, the tension in the gymnasium continued to escalate. Cindy confronted Tom Pushie, charging the St. Anthony assistant coach with shooting her a nasty glare on his way to the halftime locker room. He denied it, but she insisted two people sitting in the stands had witnessed it, too.

The mild confrontation played out beyond earshot of Bob Hurley, but it eventually found its way back to him. In his program, just about everything did.

THE FINALISTS FOR the Naismith Memorial Basketball Hall of Fame's Class of 2004 were released in Springfield, Massachusetts, on Sunday, a list of the finalists for consideration appearing in Monday morning's papers.

In 2000, after Morgan Wootten became the third high school basketball coach in history to be inducted into the Hall, there was a general consensus that the next would be Bob Hurley.

"Those are the two that stand out first in my mind," Syracuse's Jim Boeheim would say.

A telephone call to Robin Deutsch, an official at the Hall of Fame, uncovered just one stumbling block.

No one had ever filled out the simple form to nominate Hurley.

"We would love to get one from him," Deutsch said.

For most basketball immortals elected into the Hall, the actual nomination process was an afterthought. Five years after retirement, NBA players were eligible for enshrinement. Assuredly, they had public relations departments and agents carefully cultivating candidacies. Twenty-five years into coaching careers, the Bob Knights and Mike Krzyzewskis had sports publicity departments to furnish every nugget of relevant information to the Hall's committee. International players had foreign basketball federations. Besides, the biggest names in basketball had accomplishments and records that spoke for themselves. Their candidacies were too high-profile to slip through the cracks.

Before Wootten, there had been two exclusively high school coaches enshrined: Passaic High of New Jersey's Ernest Blood, who had a 159-game winning streak between 1915 and 1924, and Bertha Teague, an Oklahoma high school girls coach inducted as a "contributor."

Sooner rather than later, a nomination form on Hurley's behalf needed to be submitted to the Hall of Fame's screening committee, which ultimately would approve its advancement to the true gatekeepers: an annual rotating committee of twenty-four trustees, inductees and media that needed sixteen members to pass a nominee onto enshrinement.

When boys basketball coach Ralph Tasker of Hobbs, New Mexico, who retired with a 1,122-291 record, came before the committee in the mid-1990s, Mike DeCourcy, a decorated basketball writer for *The Sporting News*, wasn't the only member who simply had never heard of him. Wootten still hadn't been elected, and most agreed that he should go into the Hall before any high school coach.

"There are basically two reactions to candidacies," DeCourcy says. "With Tasker, it was, 'Why should he get in?' With Bob Hurley, with his name and reputation, you ask, 'Why shouldn't he get in?' What will help him, too, is the way people remember Bobby. He was a poster boy for what his father was as a coach."

If it took Wootten until the end of his career in 2000 to finally get into the Hall of Fame, Hurley didn't dare suggest that he deserved it any earlier in life—if at all. Hurley never played for a coach who left a complete and indelible mark on him. One that he had played against did, however. Hurley was a sophomore guard for St. Peter's Prep on a trip to Hyattsville, Maryland, in the winter of 1963, a loss to defending national champion DeMatha Catholic that left him remembering mostly the aura of the man standing on the sideline. Wootten had turned into a legend around Washington, D.C., and it wouldn't be long before he was the most famous and respected high school basketball coach in the country. DeMatha was a magical name, inspiring reverence the way Notre Dame, the Yankees, and the Celtics did.

And eight years later, when St. Anthony hired Hurley as coach, he never dared tell people his private mission for the job. Yet, in his heart, Hurley understood what he wanted his basketball program to be.

"I wanted to run St. Anthony just like Coach Wootten did DeMatha," Hurley says. "He always talked about his seniors going to college, not the championships or the games won. He always talked about the important part of this job."

After forty-six seasons, Wootten retired in 2002 with a 1,274-192 record and five national championships leaving behind Hurley as the unparalleled dean of active high school basketball coaches. Wootten's Hall of Fame profile called his .869 winning percentage the highest in scholastic basketball history, but with St. Anthony 20-0 on the season, Hurley's career record stood at 816-91, an .8996 winning percentage. With three more victories without a loss in the current season, Hurley would raise his winning percentage to a surreal .900.

"People say, 'Well, Hurley's had good players,'" Boeheim says. "Well, he beats other teams with good players by forty points."

The two most storied high school coaches in history never did meet on the court. DeMatha and St. Anthony had planned to play a game in 1993 at St. Anthony's holiday tournament, but Hurley was 2,500 miles away at Bobby's bedside following the crash. St. Anthony assistant George Canda coached the DeMatha game, losing by a basket to Wootten.

"DeMatha is going to finish 1-0 under Coach Wootten versus St. Anthony and that's the way it should be," Hurley says. "I would rather leave him up on the pedestal. Everything I did, I modeled after him. For the longest time, he *was* high school basketball."

Nine years earlier, Hurley had made a most favorable impression on officials at the Hall of Fame. The USA Basketball Federation was desperate to make sure its pre-collegiate team beat a team of international stars in the inaugural Nike Hoop Summit in 1995, and it commissioned the coach it best believed could deliver preparation on short notice: Hurley. The U.S. players had no concept of international rules, court dimensions or style. Hurley had to immerse himself, as well.

The Basketball Hall of Fame hosted the game at the Springfield Civic Center, and the U.S. Junior Select roster was star-studded, including future NBA lottery picks Kevin Garnett and Stephon Marbury, Antawn Jamison and Shareef Abdur-Rahim. Hurley had three days to prepare for the game, and insisted on holding serious practices. Most of his players just wanted to hang out in the gym and shoot, causing a clash of cultures.

"This isn't an All-Star game," Hurley reminded them. "I don't have to play any of you."

Eventually, they warmed to the workouts. Marbury loved talking guard play with Hurley. Whenever Hurley would call out the "fist"—the three-quarters court trap that they used at St. Anthony—the American star's eyes lit up. "It meant they were going to get a turnover and a dunk," says Doc Miller, who worked with Hurley as a trainer on the team. The U.S. won, 86–77, and Hurley allowed himself to imagine returning to town for his induction ceremony someday.

For a coach who never had to have a gymnasium, nor leave Jersey City, to build his coaching legend, it would be the completion of a most unthinkable journey.

MARCUS DRESSED ALONE in the back of the Neptune High School locker room, the solitary St. Anthony player remembering the despair felt within these walls two years earlier. Down here on the Jersey Shore, the Friars' chase for a perfect season and a shot at the 2002 *USA Today* national championship were vanquished with a heartbreaking loss.

In a far corner Marcus tied his sneakers on an empty bench. Neptune had won eighteen of its nineteen games in the season, and had a throbbing, sold-out gymnasium waiting for St. Anthony outside the locker room. What's more, Neptune had the memory of its fans storming the floor two years earlier, trampling the Friars on the way to a stunning, two-point victory that stood as the only blemish on St. Anthony's way to the Tournament of Champions title and its number-two spot in the *USA Today* poll.

Among these Friars in the locker room, only Marcus had played in that 2002 game. Only he knew the regret of how one misstep, one loss, could stay with you for the longest time. All along, he had wanted an unbeaten senior season. He wanted to make St. Anthony history.

"This is one of the St. Anthony rivalry games right here," Marcus said softly. Beyond the row of steel lockers, he could hear the laughter of his teammates as they dressed for the game. "I know Coach Hurley is going to look at me as a go-to guy, as somebody who is going to keep us under control on the court. We played them in the summer down here and we beat them, but they're going to have everybody on their side here: fans, referees, everybody. Everybody is talking about the St. Ray's game, but we need to know this game is more important. It's the one we're playing tonight."

Just minutes before the opening tip, with fans spilled into doorways and the obstructed-view corners of the gym, a rail-thin six-foot-eight man stopped by the St. Anthony bench to visit with Hurley. It was New York City playground legend Lloyd Daniels, forever remembered simply as "Swee' Pea," one of the epic talents and cautionary tales in basketball history.

After his ill-fated try to get eligible at UNLV—where he would be busted for crack—and a near-fatal shooting on the streets of New York, Swee' Pea ended up a shell of his past greatness. Even then, he was still good enough to bounce around the NBA for a few seasons.

"The greatest talent to ever play in White Eagle," Hurley would say later. Lloyd Daniels always did love the runs there. All around New York, they had treated him like royalty on the playgrounds. Only, nobody wanted his autograph at White Eagle. They would knock him on his ass, like anyone else. Swee' Pea always appreciated that about Jersey City.

At the last minute, Cindy McCurdy changed her mind about sitting in the row of seats behind the St. Anthony bench. Sister Alan and Sister Felicia had already taken root there. With Hurley within arm's length on the bench, Cindy sensed it might be best for everyone's evening if she found a seat across the gym.

"Coach doesn't like my yelling," she said, picking up and moving into the bleachers across the floor.

"Good idea," Sister Alan said.

For most of the game's early minutes, it felt like the 2002 St. Anthony team unraveling again. The stomping students and fans had St. Anthony, in Hurley's words later, "folding up like a cheap suit." All that noise, all that hostility, had bubbled over in the gym, just as Marcus had promised his teammates.

Tonight, it would be Derrick who held the Friars together, the tiny point guard slowly, surely rising with confidence and command of the team. It could be a nightmare for a young point guard to learn his lessons under Hurley, a process that Gamble had once described to a flustered Elijah Ingram this way: "St. Anthony is the New York Yankees of high school basketball, and our point guard has to be Jeter." Despite Derrick's flurry of three-pointers and jump shots, St. Anthony was trailing going into halftime for the first time in the season, 27–26.

"If Derrick Mercer doesn't make those three threes," Hurley barked at them in the locker room, "where the hell are we right now?"

Unlike two years earlier, St. Anthony would refuse to let Neptune stay in the game in the second half. Marcus scored on a slicing layup to start the third, immediately taking back the lead. Then Derrick went back to work. Those stubby, chiseled legs chased the ball everywhere, pressuring Neptune into three consecutive turnovers. After stealing a pass, Derrick sped down the floor, finding Barney on a clever bounce pass that resulted in a three-point play. Moments later, Sean fed Derrick in the corner, and the Neptune defense still seemed skeptical of his shooting touch, offering him just enough space to loft yet another three-pointer through the net. After Otis popped a three, it was 37–29, and the Friars were on their way. As Marcus promised, he would be the steadying influence, scoring thirteen points, grabbing nine rebounds, and most importantly, holding Neptune's top scorer, DJ Simms, to only six points.

Afterward, people congratulated Derrick's father, Derrick Sr., on the best game of his son's career, a nineteen-point performance, but his dad deflected it, insisting, "He was all right. The last thing he needs is to get a big head. He's five-seven. He needs to keep working."

All he had ever wanted was for his son to get an education under Hurley, a chance to be instilled with the discipline and determination he had been missing as a young man growing up in Jersey City. Derrick. Sr., a security guard at No. 6 school, never missed one of his son's games, staying in the background and trusting whatever Hurley believed best for his boy. American University assistant Kelvin Jefferson had scouted Derrick at the PrimeTime Shootout, leaving breathless over the possibility of recruiting the point guard to the school in Washington, D.C. Jefferson couldn't wait for his head coach, Jeff Jones, to see Derrick Mercer and fall in love with him, too.

Yelling at Derrick in the preseason once, Hurley barked to him, "I've never had a father who cared more about seeing his son be successful as yours does. How the hell can he want it more than you?"

This was Hurley's kind of parent, all the way. And now, as the packed Neptune stands began to thin late in the fourth quarter, the St. Anthony starters grabbed towels, leaned back on the bench and settled into watching the final moments of a satisfying 63–48 victory. Only the action was no longer playing out on the floor. Something else had started to steal the bench's attention—along with that of those remaining in the stands.

Across the court, Cindy McCurdy's arms flailed in the air, insisting to the cop trying to drag her out of the stands that he had it all wrong. In the row behind the St. Anthony bench, the one she had abandoned moments before the opening tip, simultaneously, Sister Felicia and Sister Alan groaned. Cindy had gotten herself into a scrap with a Neptune fan, and at the end of the St. Anthony bench, Greg Bracey stopped chatting up with

Doc and hustled across the floor to spirit her out of trouble. He talked the cop out of ejecting her, and stood to the side with her the rest of the game.

The way things were going for Sean, it was about the worst thing in the world that he could've seen. He needed less anxiety, not more. Everyone quickly turned their gaze to him on the bench, gauging his reaction. He sat stone-faced, unmoved, refusing to react at all. No big deal, he would insist later. No big deal.

Afterward in the locker room, Sean stopped Edem, the student-manager responsible for keeping stats, and asked him how many assists he had for the game. Sean had scored just six points, and understandably searched for something to take out of the night.

Edem pulled the pencil out from behind his ear, counted the assists in Sean's score-sheet column and answered him. "Two."

"No way," Sean snapped. "I had more than that."

Edem shrugged. What could he tell him?

On the way out of the locker room, Gamble and Pushie described the late-game scene in the stands to Hurley. Even they had stopped watching the game to take it in. Hurley never noticed it, but then, nobody locked into a game like he did. After Hurley's postgame radio interview courtside, Cindy was standing with Chris Hurley and some St. Anthony fans in the emptying gym.

Cindy tried to make light of the spectacle with Hurley, saying with a dismissive laugh, "That's the last time I try to defend your honor, Coach."

Hurley couldn't bring himself to crack a smile.

"Nobody needs to defend my honor," he said.

The biggest game of the season so far, St. Raymond's, was less than forty-eight hours away, and Bob Hurley was thinking about getting home and getting to work on it.

"He doesn't need this bullshit," Gamble said, walking toward the St. Anthony bus on a snowy night. "None of us do."

CHAPTER 18

AFTER A LATE night and early morning of studying tape of St. Raymond's games and an eight-hour shift at the prison, Ben Gamble showed up at practice a sorry sight Wednesday afternoon.

"I'm watching St. Ray's and thinking, 'They should never lose a game,'" he said.

Hurley moved up practice to 3:30 from the usual 4:30 start, giving the players' legs a little extra recovery time for Thursday night's game, which itself had been moved to a later start of 8:00. After St. Raymond's, St. Anthony would finish its regular season against St. Joseph's of Montvale and North Bergen. The Friars wouldn't lose to those teams, and even Hurley couldn't scare them into believing that that was possible.

So, this undefeated regular season run had come down to beating St. Raymond's, one of New York's most successful and talented teams. All around New York and New Jersey, everyone had been talking about this game. More than that, family and friends, schoolmates and teachers had been telling the St. Anthony players: Beat St. Ray's, and you're going unbeaten this season. Beat St. Ray's, and you're chasing history now.

"I had my eye on this game all season long," Sean had said. "To me, this is the hump game. If we get past that, we could run the table."

Sean wasn't alone in that thinking, and Hurley knew it. This was a delicate time for the Friars. He considered his team too immature, too fragile, to go into the game consumed with protecting an unbeaten season. The consequences of losing hung over everyone's head, leaving Hurley determined to soften the significance of the game. He wanted the pressure to be on the performance, on playing well and preparing for the postseason.

Most of all, Hurley wanted the Friars to play like they had nothing to lose. Even though this team, especially these seniors, believed they had *everything* to lose. To a man, they knew they weren't just chasing a state championship. If they cleared St. Raymond's, the most imperfect St. Anthony team was chasing the perfect season.

"I won't be surprised if we lose tomorrow," Hurley told them at the start of practice. "And if we lose, I wouldn't be surprised if that might jar this group. Our goal should not be an undefeated regular season. I don't want us to lose sight. Our goal is to win a state championship. So if this loss makes guys who haven't been concentrating suddenly realize we're fragile, I'll call in today and say we'll forfeit.

"I'm worried about us winning the rest of our games and going to the state tournament. I'm just not sure about you guys."

All of his players were sitting behind the basket, leaning against the wall, and most of them had been around Hurley long enough not to doubt the sincerity of his message. He would no sooner choose to lose a game than he would break-dance in the middle of Journal Square.

"If you're not ready to come here tomorrow and play, stay home sick from school. Because we can't put guys in this game who aren't ready to play a six-eight forward [Gavin Grant] going to N.C. State, a six-five forward [Brian Laing] going to Seton Hall, a six-nine center [Frank Elegar] going to Drexel, a junior guard [Ricky Torres] that the entire Big East is recruiting. The little guard they have is just a regular high school player—the other four are not.

"Now, look around at each other. We're up against it.

"This is a state tournament game for us tomorrow. If we play well and they beat us, we can just say, 'OK, we played well. They were better than us. Now we're ready for St. Pat's or Paterson Catholic in the state tournament.' If we come in tomorrow, and we do that dumb shit—Sean dribbles the ball five hundred times for no reason, Otis isn't getting deflections on defense, and on and on, we'll get beat badly. Everybody has to play his best tomorrow, because if most of you were at St. Raymond's, you would be on the bench.

"Except for Derrick Mercer, everybody here is playing against a better player tomorrow. So here's what it is: some very, very good players over there against hopefully eight or nine guys here who are gonna bring it."

Hurley told the team about losing to St. Raymond's in 1993, in double-overtime at the Armory, when St. Anthony was undefeated and number one in the nation and the Friars' Rod Rhodes was rated as the best high school senior in the country. "After that, we crushed everybody in the state tournament," he said, his way of dismissing the loss to St. Ray's as nothing that stopped the Friars on the way to the ultimate destination. Hurley had suspended Rhodes for the first quarter of that game, but he still scored forty-two points. Longtime St. Raymond's coach, Gary DeCesare, had finished the night with four players on the floor, because eight St. Ray's players had fouled out. "Twenty-seven free throws for Rhodes," DeCesare wistfully recalls.

Hurley also told them the story of how in 2000 an official's controversial call sent St. Ray's All-American, Julius Hodge, to the line in the final seconds for two free throws. Both dropped, and St. Raymond's had a historic upset of St. Anthony in Jersey City. DeCesare still remembers Hurley chasing the official off the court, telling him he would never work one of his games again.

Hurley then told his current St. Anthony players, "Our next game was Dajuan Wagner and Camden and we smacked them. We beat everybody else the rest of the season."

His point was simple: "This is nothing more tomorrow than a game to get ready for the state tournament. Nothing more."

Jersey kids always had to travel to New York to prove themselves, but the success of St. Anthony had gone a long way to turn the tables on that rite of passage. "We always played that game late in the season," says DeCesare, who would later leave St. Raymond's to take an assistant's job at the University of Richmond. "I used it as a measuring stick of how we were going to do in the New York City playoffs. If we played St. Anthony tough, or even beat them, we knew we were ready to run the table in New York."

St. Anthony had a long history of playing the New York City powerhouses, public and parochial. In the battle of New York and New Jersey, it would be a Connecticut kid the Friars needed to get going again.

In practice, Hurley deemed that Sean was holding the ball too long in the offensive sets, searching for his own shot at the expense of sharing with teammates. Hurley stripped him of his black starter jersey and demoted him to the second-team white.

"It's all about you, McCurdy," Hurley snapped at him.

"What about us?

"WHAT ABOUT US?"

Most of all, Hurley still wanted Sean to learn to play with poise. He was playing too fast, too rattled, too manic. With the laboring grimaces Sean made more and more, he looked to his coach like someone trying to bench-press too much weight. He let himself get trapped in double-teams.

He pounded the ball into the floor on the dribble, going nowhere fast. Too often, his hands were where the ball went to die in the St. Anthony offense.

Hurley wasn't angry that Sean had gone into a funk, as much as angry that he was doing all the wrong things to get out of it, angry that he wasn't listening to Hurley about basketball as much as Hurley believed he listened to his family. He knew in Sean's estimation that shooting and scoring were still his standards for success. To get him to be a complete player, the kind Sean wanted to become by moving to Jersey City, Hurley still needed to deprogram his basketball value system and replace it with St. Anthony's own.

"Don't do us any fucking favors and commute from Connecticut," Hurley blasted. "We'll coach who we have here."

Five minutes later, Hurley threw everyone out of the gym. Sean dressed the fastest, blew out of the locker room and climbed in his Jeep Cherokee to drive home. This was the scene every day: Sean driving away, and his teammates cutting through the Newport Mall on the way to buses and trains. From his cell phone, Sean told Erman to go back to New York and forget staying with him in the apartment. Even with his mother gone to Connecticut again, he wanted to be alone.

"He's supposed to be the normal kid here, but he might have the most dysfunctional life of them all," Hurley had sighed one night earlier in the season.

It never seemed so true. That night, Erman had called Melissa Hurley to tell her Sean was alone in the apartment. Her father told her that Sean needed someone there, that the kid could not stay alone.

It turned out to be a good thing. Melissa and Sean had a long talk, the kind they hadn't had since his sophomore year, when she had watched him regularly. Sean wasn't just losing his own confidence, he feared, but something in his mind, worse: his coach's.

"Relax," Melissa told him. "Bobby and Danny used to get thrown out of practice three times a week. He didn't even throw you out, did he? He threw out the whole team, right?

"Sean," she assured him, "you'll be fine."

"ARE WE GOING to break even?" Bob Hurley asked, his eyes scanning the empty rows of wooden bleachers rising from courtside at St. Peter's College.

"Stop it," Sister Alan warned him. "Just worry about coaching the game."

For St. Anthony to break even on the gym rental, it needed 1,500 fans to purchase tickets. For now, Hurley sat on the bench, his clipboard resting on the seat beside him. For the past forty-eight hours, the coach had been a harried wreck. He had worked hard to insulate his players from the pressure of winning this game, grateful to absorb all of it himself. At three o'clock that morning, he had been up pacing, driving Chris crazy.

As Erman had come to understand, it was best to stay clear of Hurley in those nervous minutes before tip-off, especially when he was sitting alone with his thoughts on the bench. There had been newspaper stories in the *Chicago Sun-Times* and *Louisville Courier-Journal* that week on Erman's Horatio Alger story. At courtside before the St. Raymond's game, a New York *Daily News* writer approached Erman about setting up a time to interview him for a story.

No, no, he said. That wouldn't be a good idea.

The last thing Erman wanted was Hurley suspecting him of self-promoting, trying to be the star of the show. Hurley had been so good to him, so patient with emptying out his basketball mind to every one of Erman's questions. Hurley had even given Erman responsibilities of traveling to scout opponents and entrusted him to handle a bulk of the early recruiting for the underclassmen.

Erman never regretted his decision to quit the law firm and chase his basketball dream at St. Anthony. Never once. Every morning, he still woke up on the floor of that cramped apartment at 5:00, rolled off that inflatable mattress and couldn't wait to see what Hurley had to teach him that day. Sure, Erman was broke. Too much of his $421 a week ended up as bus fare and McDonald's for the kids, or went toward settling his skyrocketing cell-phone bill returning calls to the college recruiters on behalf of the juniors. Anyway, he loved it. Erman had never felt so fulfilled, so useful, in his life.

"I was a lawyer for one of the best firms in the country, surrounded by people who were supposed to be the best and brightest," he says. "But I've never been in a situation where I've been around someone who's the absolute best at what he does. Coach Hurley is one of the greatest basketball minds ever, and he's completely accessible. He'll talk all day to you, about anything you ask. I used to be in a profession where there were jerks who it was like pulling teeth to get them to share information. And they weren't even close to Coach Hurley in their fields. This is unlike any education I've had in my life."

Bernie Fitzsimmons, the St. Anthony development director, made copies of the newspaper stories, circulating them throughout the incoming crowd at St. Peter's.

Enough of this, a sheepish Erman said. Enough.

Suddenly, Erman was sitting unsuspectingly beside Hurley on the bench about forty-five minutes before the game, when a *Daily News* photographer asked Hurley to slide over and pose for a picture.

With his assistant coach.

"No, no!" Erman pleaded to the photographer, but it was too late.

The photographer dropped to his knees, and started snapping away. Hurley even managed a smile for those photos, which in Erman's mind would never, ever see the pages of the tabloid. He was never doing the interview for that story. There was one star at St. Anthony, and it sure as hell wasn't the lawyer with Louisville basketball posters hanging in his environmental science classrooms.

Sister Alan had her own agenda for the St. Raymond's game: keeping this unbeaten season alive. During school that day, she sought out Sean in a corridor, telling him that he looked tense, that he needed to calm down.

"Just relax and have only one voice in your head: Bob Hurley," she had advised him. "And block everything else out."

As Sister Alan watched Sean stretching in warm-ups, she said, "He's no dummy. He knows what I'm talking about. His mother just keeps talking about the schools recruiting him, all of the stuff she's filling his head with. The kid needs to be left alone."

She had been far less subtle with Barney. After the players had finished stretching, the five-foot-three nun tugged the six-foot-five center by the arm and gave him a little extra motivation for the ball game.

"You'd better play well tonight, or I'm telling your father about you driving your girlfriend's car all over the place."

"*What?*" Barney said, stunned.

"Don't worry," she assured him. "I know all about it."

Downstairs in the locker room, Hurley told the players of a rumor circulating that the St. Raymond's coach had suspended a player for the game. Hurley was standing in the middle of the room, trying to turn it into fuel for the Friars' ferocity.

"Anybody who would be disrespectful enough to get suspended before a game like this, well, your hair should be standing up on your neck right now," Hurley said, with a thick layer of contempt in his voice. "When the six-foot-eight, long-armed kid goes up and gets the tip, that might be the only time they have control of this game.

"Let's get out and get 'em."

When they reached the court, the six-foot-eight, long-armed kid, Gavin Grant, was wearing street clothes on the St. Raymond's bench, suspended for reportedly talking back to his coach in practice. Still, St. Ray's had the two most talented players on the floor, Laing and Torres, and there was no suggesting that this would be anything but a stern test for St. Anthony.

Barney Anderson scored St. Anthony's first eight points of the game, and even sacrificed his body to take a charge from Elegar, St. Raymond's center. St. Anthony struggled to get in sync offensively, but started to get going in the second quarter, when Sean finally began making plays again. First, he hit a free-throw-line jump shot, something it seemed he hadn't done in weeks. And at the other end, Sean did something that St. Anthony hadn't seen from him all season: He blocked a shot.

Finally, Sean had a little momentum going. He wouldn't stop. About a minute later, he scored on a driving layup, and turned back quickly to anticipate the direction of St. Raymond's inbounds pass. He guessed perfectly, stealing the ball and firing a pass back out to Beanie. Without hesitating, Sean curled back toward the basket, where Beanie gave the ball back to him on a gorgeous feed for a lefty layup. Everybody was standing in the gymnasium now, cheering wildly, the bleachers bouncing with the pounding of happy feet.

St. Raymond's called a timeout, Sean and Beanie slapped hands, and St. Anthony had a 14–6 lead.

It was still early in the second quarter, and Hurley had worked himself into a full sweat. He worked the stick of gum in his mouth like a jackhammer. All over the floor, the Friars were denying St. Raymond's passing lanes and sliding into position to draw offensive charges. When Beanie drew his second charge on a Torres drive to the basket, St. Raymond's coach, Oliver Antigua, complained to the official, "Every time they fall, it's not a charge. They're flopping!"

Beanie had a little actor in him, no question. Moments later, Derrick picked off a pass on the St. Anthony press, dribbling to the basket for a twisting layup that was met with a hard foul. The shot dropped into the net, his free throw was good, and the three-point play pushed the Friars to a ten-point lead with a little over three minutes left in the half.

Hurley turned to Gamble on the bench, incredulously telling him, "I just had to throw my gum away. I chewed it so damn hard, it turned to paste in my mouth."

Meanwhile, Barney stayed on course for keeping those car keys by trailing Otis on a breakaway to the basket. Since returning after he broke foot, Otis had little lift on his jumps. His layup bounced hard off the backboard and popped into the air off the rim, but Barney had his back. He leaped into the air, snatched Otis's miss in mid-flight and slammed it back through the rim.

Barney sprinted off the floor for halftime, his thirteen points and inside presence far and away the difference in the seven-point lead. Sister Alan struggled to hide a smug smile. After all, it wasn't just Hurley who knew the right buttons to push with the kids. This was St. Anthony basketball. They always did have to be a little more creative to gain an edge.

After the break, Barney stayed ferocious, dunking again to begin the third quarter. Marcus made consecutive slicing layups in traffic. St. Raymond's hung in there. Torres, the gifted junior scorer, and Laing, the sculpted six-foot-five senior, traded baskets in the third quarter. Still, the St. Anthony man-to-man made St. Raymond's run its offense far from the basket, frustrating them to the point where they too often simply flung whatever they could to the rim.

Down the stretch, it looked like St. Anthony was on the brink of blowing a wobbly St. Raymond's out of the gym. The usually explosive St. Ray's still had just thirty-three points with four minutes and twenty-five seconds left in the game. They trailed by twelve points, but St. Anthony then turned the ball over a few times and missed a few free throws. They were stumbling to the finish line and Hurley was seething. They had constructed a big lead, breathed out and relaxed. Suddenly, Torres hit a long three-pointer with a minute and a half left, and St. Raymond's had climbed back to within 47–41.

From there, Sean brought the game home for St. Anthony. At times, he still looked rattled and pressing, but in the critical moments of the fourth quarter, he steadied himself. He scored six straight points—including four at the free-throw line—to push the Friars out to a 53–41 advantage with 41.3 seconds left.

Hurley sent a substitute into the game to replace Sean, greeting him back on the bench with a firm handshake. But those final 41.3 seconds would turn out to be far shakier than Hurley wanted to see out of his players. Ahmad Nivins hacked one St. Raymond's player going to the basket, and let another dribble past him like a matador. Beanie stepped to the free-throw line with twenty-three seconds left and missed both shots. With eleven seconds left, he was back again. He cradled the ball for a long time in his hands, looking strangely unnerved given that the victory was secure, that there was no pressure shooting the ball.

After missing another, Hurley lost it. "GROW UP!" he screamed toward Beanie on the floor. "JUST SHOOT THE DAMN FOUL SHOT. THERE'S TEN SECONDS LEFT IN THE GAME!"

To no one's surprise, Beanie clanked the final free throw, his fourth straight in the final seconds of the 54–46 victory. Hurley turned to Gamble and muttered, "Fucking Mosby," and walked down the sideline to shake hands with St. Ray's.

Soon, the St. Anthony players were racing down the staircase to the locker room, screams of "Yeah, baby! . . . Number one!" echoing off the walls. They moved like a gathering stampede, thundering toward the state tournament, toward the perfect season, toward St. Anthony history. Outside the locker room, Sean waited for Beanie. As Sean reached out his hand to congratulate him, Beanie's shoulders slumped. He was still livid over Hurley calling him out in the final seconds.

"Don't sweat it, Beanie," Sean said, trying to calm him down. "Forget the free throws."

"Fuck him," Beanie snapped.

All the St. Anthony players rushed into the locker room, as thrilled as they were relieved. All season, this game had been circled on the schedule. And they had done it. They had beaten St. Raymond's. Even with Grant suspended for the game, St. Ray's still had several Division I talents on the floor. Barney roared into the locker room, slapping five with Derrick Mercer and pounding Sean on the back. He had given up five inches in the middle and still scored twenty-one points. They sat down on the wooden benches, waiting for the coach to offer his congratulations for a job well done.

"YOU FUCKING CLOWNS!" Hurley screamed, exploding through the locker room, looking like a linebacker chasing down a quarterback. Backs stiffened. Eyes batted and blinked, upper lips bit down. Marcus whipped his head around, ending his lighthearted ribbing with Otis.

Hurley marched down the middle of the room, stepping between the benches that hugged two parallel walls of lockers. He stopped at the chalkboard, turned around and noticed the door was still open.

He called for someone to shut it.

Now, Hurley started for real.

"STATE TOURNAMENT ATMOSPHERE . . . STATE TOURNAMENT GAME. . . . FOUR FOUL SHOTS. . . .

"And every one of his free throws hit the basket and flew off."

Hurley glared down at Beanie.

"Four in a row," Hurley said with utter disdain.

Hurley stood up straight and let out a long sigh. He rubbed his hand over his mouth, stroked his chin and stared down at the floor. He looked up again. His voice was pleading now.

"You don't get it. This is your standard for winning. You won by eight. They weren't that freakin' good. We should've won that game by fifteen, easy."

Hurley stood by Beanie, who sat with his shoulders slumped, those long, bony arms dangling down.

"Listen to me: It can't be his standard. It can't be. And it can't be the standards for most of you here. It's got to be the standards the school has set over the years for what is championship play.

"THIS IS NOT CHAMPIONSHIP PLAY! THIS IS JUST A VIC-TORY!

"How many of you understand the difference?"

Hurley lowered his voice to a raspy whisper.

"Nobody would. And why would nobody know right now?"

Hurley nodded over at Gamble. "He knows."

He pointed to Marcus. "He knows. He had a uniform when older guys did it.

"Why wouldn't any one of you know right now?"

Together, everyone said, "We've never won."

"Right," Hurley said, nodding with them. "You've never won.

"But here's what you don't understand: It's never about winning here. It's about performance, and that performance was not acceptable. It is for you sloppy asses, who will go into school tomorrow and get your seventy-fives back from tests. You'll do a paper and you'll get a C-minus. This was supposed to be one of New York City's best teams and they should've gone out of here with a freakin' whuppin'.

"Because they weren't good enough. And we had them on the ropes, numerous times. And we couldn't put them away."

Hurley just couldn't get over the final four minutes of the thirty-two-minute high school game. His rage was with Beanie, from whom he wanted desperately to see poise in the stretch run of the season. He couldn't get over his senior guard freezing in those final seconds at the free-throw line, so devoid of composure. He did not want to believe Beanie was cracking again. But he feared it, and Hurley was determined to stop it right there, to rage against the kid's demons.

"Freakin' Mosby. This is a character issue right now. Well, you better

fuckin' grow up. Because if this continues in the North Jersey championship game, we lose.

"Or we have to sit you."

Hurley called everyone into the center of the room for the postgame
prayer. They all surrounded the coach, hands rising to touch in the air, the
season rounding third and heading for home.

One more time, Hurley calmly reminded them. "It is not acceptable to
just win a high school basketball game any old way.

"Hail Mary, full of grace . . ."

St. Raymond's coach Oliver Antigua met with reporters upstairs in the
Yanitelli Center, saying of St. Anthony: "There's no question they're the
best defensive team we've seen. They don't let you run any of your stuff.
We started throwing up bombs from everywhere, because that's all we
could get. They play harder than any team I've ever seen in my life."

Hurley shuffled off to Bergen County to scout St. Joseph's of Montvale
on Friday afternoon, leaving the team to Greg Bracey and Erman for
weight training and conditioning in the gym. Bracey backed his SUV into
the side parking lot of the charter school, and he and the players carried
barbells and ropes, medicine balls and pulleys into the gym. When Hurley
wasn't there, the kids treated the lower-level assistants like substitute teachers. "No discipline at all when Coach Hurley isn't here," Sean said, dutifully shooting free throws at the end of conditioning. Sean had watched
Marcus, Shelton and Lamar walk out early, leaving Beanie to finish the job
Hurley had told them to do.

Beanie wore a white do-rag under his black cap, a silent act of dress-
code rebellion on a day he knew Hurley wouldn't see him. He did his job,
and that was what mattered now. He did what was asked. Hurley wanted a
hundred free throws? He gave him a hundred free throws. In fact, nobody
had been a more diligent practice player for the Friars. All season, Hurley
watched Beanie run so hard in sprints, constantly pushing to beat his
teammates, that he believed Beanie had gotten quicker over the course of
the year.

Hurley had told Beanie earlier, too, but Beanie wouldn't let himself
hear that over the screaming. After the workout, Beanie was catching a ride
to his grandfather's house. And once again, he was fighting that feeling of

persecution, a belief that everyone kept unjustly calling him out. The list of perpetrators was long—the Sisters, his teachers, and always, his basketball coach. Just about anyone in authority. The past week hung over Beanie like an anvil, beginning with Hurley dangling the disintegration of his junior season over him, and ending with Hurley berating him over the final moments of the St. Raymond's victory.

He stared out the passenger-side window at Marin Avenue, talking about a debt that stayed unpaid to the program, a second chance with Hurley that came with reminders of a penance still unserved, a redemption still unclaimed.

"Why does he have to keep bringing that up?" Beanie asked. "I'm here now, right? I mean, last night, I played a wonderful game. I had no turnovers. I was getting everyone else shots. So why does he have to get on me about four free throws at the end of the game? Why does he always pick me out?"

When it was suggested that Hurley had been hard on a lot of players lately, including Sean, whom everyone had long believed had a free pass, Beanie scoffed, "Not like he is on me. Whatever I do, he's going to bring up last year.

"Why do I have to keep going through this with him?"

Hurley was never going to throw his arm around Beanie, tell him he believed he wouldn't crack, wouldn't let down the team again. That wasn't happening. Instead, he was testing Beanie every day, letting him know that he was watching, that people were counting on him. If nothing else, Beanie knew this: An unbeaten season could go a long way toward pushing it back in his coach's face, toward cementing a legacy for him and the seniors.

"If we do that, he can't say nothing." Beanie stared straight ahead, nodding in agreement with his words. "He can't say *nothing*. I think about that all the time. If we go unbeaten, he can't say nothin'."

"I want to go undefeated, but I don't know if it's going to happen."

Asked why not, he replied, "I don't think anyone can beat us in New Jersey. But we can beat ourselves. Even with that, I get tired of hearing him say that we're going to lose to St. Pat's. We haven't lost to anybody yet. He's really confusing."

"I still don't know him," Beanie said. "I don't know him at all."

As the car turned down Montgomery Street, crossing over the line of demarcation in Jersey City between the promise of the downtown waterfront development and the poverty and decay of the old city neighborhoods, Beanie talked about college, about getting away.

Ramapo, the powerhouse Division III program nestled in the cushy suburbs of Mahwah, about forty minutes north of Jersey City, still recruited him the hardest. Chuck McBreen or a member of his coaching staff had attended almost all of the St. Anthony games, hanging around outside the locker room to, as McBreen laughingly called it, "try to pull teeth to get Beanie to talk." They hung in there, banking on the belief that Beanie would pass on junior college far from Jersey City, a two-year way station to his Division I dream, and opt to stay close to home. They were banking on the belief that Beanie was one more Jersey City kid uneasy about moving too far away from these streets.

Beanie had his mind set on Pensacola, one of the schools sending him a steady stream of recruiting mail. The Pensacola coach told him of the Pell Grants worth $2,500 a semester. It sounded like an amazing proposition to Beanie. "You don't even have to use it for books," he pointed out.

He was so close to getting out of Jersey City, so close to making it to the state tournament he missed a year ago. Until they won it all, Beanie had to live with the burden of his unraveling being the difference between a championship season and something unacceptable at St. Anthony.

Still, no one had to tell Ahmad Mosby about burdens. He carried a lot of them. He carried them like a sack of rocks. His father, his brother, his uncle, all locked up or dead. One last Mosby trying to make his stand in Jersey City now.

It was dark a little after 6:15 on Grand Street, where a working girl staked her claim on the cracked sidewalk. Beanie was climbing out of the car, outside his grandfather's house.

"I want to get away from Jersey City," he said, unfolding himself out of the front seat and throwing his bag over his shoulder.

"There's nothing here for me."

CHAPTER 19

DANNY HURLEY WAS going down and he was going down hard. All hell was breaking loose at the state prep-school championship game, with Lawrenceville drilling St. Benedict's, and he had decided that he'd be damned if he was going to go out like the referees tried to send him. He had been tossed for screaming "You're awful" to an official, and the more he started to think about that, standing in the corridor outside the gym at South Brunswick High School, the more unacceptable it had become.

If the old man's kid was going down in a championship game, he was going down like a Hurley: throwing haymakers. It kept getting worse by the minute. One of his assistant coaches had been ejected, and his star player, J.R. Smith, had fouled out and lobbed one of his sneakers into the stands. And the worst of it was still the end-zone dance Lawrenceville Prep was doing on St. Benedict's dream of a third state prep-school title in his three seasons on the job.

Danny Hurley was six-foot-two, with wire-rimmed glasses and a charming, cynical disposition that his coaching friend Rob Lanier described as Richard Lewis with a clipboard, a reference to the self-tormenting comedian. On this late February Sunday afternoon, Danny was angry and embarrassed and had become more like his old man growing up than anyone could've believed possible.

"This is a farce!" Chris Hurley yelled out of the stands.

Her husband dipped his head, tugging on the brim of his baseball cap and casting a weary eye at the court. The moment the elder Hurley had ascended the bleachers late in the first quarter, every eye in the section seemed to follow him. He was still the standard by which they judged his son's work. And once everything began to unravel, Bob wanted to go down on the floor, scoop up his son and spare him the indignity of leaving in such shambles what had been such a spectacular season.

Nevertheless, it wasn't over, because there was no way a Hurley went down without the last word. So Danny stepped back inside the doorway of the gymnasium, turned to the two game officials beneath the basket, and took them on one at a time.

"You're an ass," he yelled to one.

"And you're a little troll," he said, pointing to the second.

Before he could work his way to the third member of the officiating crew, a South Brunswick policeman stepped up to him with a warning. "Another word, you're leaving in cuffs," he said.

What a disaster. A 29-1 season finished in a wreck beyond recognition. His mother was on the cell phone to Melissa describing the scene, and through it all, nobody seemed to notice the teenager walking back and forth behind the St. Benedict's bench, wearing a Duke No. 11 jersey. It was fitting. The jersey was the result of a business deal that Bobby tried to bring Danny into with him. To capitalize on the throwback jersey craze, a company offered to share the proceeds with Duke and Bobby. Bobby worked out an agreement whereby the company had to give Danny $1,000 to release his old Seton Hall University jersey, No. 15, for sale, too. Bobby was still looking out for his little brother, but Danny told him to keep the money, and in turn, he'd keep his pride. No way did he want to start walking into Jersey shopping malls and see those unsold Seton Hall jerseys on the bargain rack, dropping from 20 percent off, to 30, to 50 and on down.

"Whatever money I would've pocketed," Danny laughed, "I'd rather hold onto my last piece of dignity."

It was never easy being Danny Hurley. He had won two straight prep-school championships since taking over at St. Benedict's in 2001, and yet the whispers walking out of the gym were predictable: Danny Hurley sure wasn't Bob Hurley. The Internet message boards lit up the next day, anonymous postings insisting that his father never would've lost a title game like that. Danny was 29-2 for the season, having won tournaments in three states, and now 75-12 in his three years at St. Benedict's. His kids were getting scholarships, his program was beating the best in the country, and it still didn't matter. Whatever Danny Hurley had done in his basketball career, it would never be enough for some people.

He wasn't Bob now, and he wasn't Bobby then. He spent his entire childhood fighting for his own identity in the shadow of his older brother.

Bobby was one of a kind, one of the most popular players in modern college basketball history, the All-America and Final Four MVP every small white kid believed he could become. Bobby's story was a fairy tale. Danny couldn't be Bobby, any more than any kid in America could be him.

Eventually, people had to shake their heads and wonder if Danny was just some sort of a basketball masochist. After all of his struggles, what did he decide to do?

Become a high school basketball coach in northern Jersey.

"The first time I saw Danny coach, it reminded me of Bob when Bob first started out," Chris Hurley says. "Bob has mellowed out a lot, but Danny still has that youthful living and dying with every play."

Danny Hurley was the class clown, the "Bohemian," Sister Alan says. He was the wisecracker in the back of the room causing everyone else to lose it, while he kept a straight face. Jerry Walker, the St. Anthony and Seton Hall star, always believed that Danny had more natural ability than Bobby, but just never worked like him. Truth be told, Danny grew up watching Bobby sacrifice his childhood and decided that it wasn't for him.

He was two years younger, a sophomore when Bobby was a senior and playing point guard for one of the greatest high school teams in history. He was two inches taller and left-handed, more of a shooter than a playmaker. Danny had a magnificent high school career, one of the best in state history, but it wasn't Bobby's. Bobby had been 115-5, winning four state titles, a national championship, and at the end of his senior year, earning co-MVP of the McDonald's All-American game with Shaquille O'Neal.

"Bobby always viewed himself as the best player on the court, whereas I always felt like the little brother," Danny says. "I was always being compared to him, but Bobby was Bobby. There were no comparisons to him. He was just Bobby Hurley, great guard at St. Anthony. All people did was compare my game with him, and you can say that you don't pay attention to that stuff, but as a fourteen- or fifteen-year-old, of course you do. It took a lot of self-confidence from me."

When Danny was a junior at St. Anthony, Bobby was the freshman bringing Duke to the Final Four. As a St. Anthony senior, Danny missed a three-pointer at the buzzer in his father's only Tournament of Champions defeat in school history. It was a difficult shot, rimming in and out, and St. Anthony had been underdogs in the title game. Danny had done a remarkable job to keep the Friars in the game, but it was typical: St. Anthony finished his senior season 31-1, and No. 2 in the country. Bobby had been 32-0, and No. 1 as a senior. For anyone else, it would've been an amazing career. For Danny Hurley, well, it wasn't Bobby.

Danny had an offer to play for Duke, but nobody in the family believed it would be a wise choice. He picked Seton Hall, where two of his old St. Anthony teammates from Bobby's class—Terry Dehere and Jerry Walker—had stayed close to home to play for coach P.J. Carlesimo. From the beginning, Danny had a hard time at Seton Hall. Bobby had turned into a college matinee idol at Duke; Danny struggled to just get minutes on the floor as a freshman.

Everywhere Seton Hall traveled in the Big East, the chants were relentless, "Bob-bee's Better . . . Bob-bee's Better," and it wore Danny down. Eventually, he still preferred the road torment over the Seton Hall home games in the 20,000-seat Meadowlands Arena. It was one thing to get taunted by opposing fans, but when the Seton Hall faithful turned on Danny, it floored him and the family.

It got so bad that Chris Hurley would settle into her seat with a routine announcement to the potential tormenters in her section: "I'm Danny Hurley's mother."

It was a declaration that everyone had better watch their mouth. Bob stopped sitting in the stands altogether, choosing instead to stand in one of the portals to the lower bowl of the arena, just to keep from punching people out.

"I never imagined that adults could be that angry about the sport," Danny says. "Playing in the New York-New Jersey area is hard because they treat the colleges like the pros. They're not real forgiving. The media was tough, too. This wasn't Bobby getting covered in the Durham paper, where it was just, 'Well, the kids gave it the old college try.' This was a pro mentality, and that was tough to deal with."

After Danny had arrived on Seton Hall's campus outside Newark in the fall of 1991, he would regret not moving into the upperclassman dormitories with Walker and Dehere. He ended up living with the freshmen, spending far too many nights out drinking. And when he wasn't an immediate star at Seton Hall, everything started spiraling for him. If Bobby had a bad game, Danny knew, he would come back to campus, turn on the lights to the gym and take 400 extra shots. Danny would come back, close his door and lose himself in self-loathing.

"There was just something about his mental makeup that was different than me," Danny says. "He just had a tunnel vision that I didn't have."

His Seton Hall teammates started to worry about his drinking, the worst of it coming one night when those dollar drafts turned into Danny smashing a campus golf cart into a concrete wall. At the beginning of his sophomore season in December 1993, there was an afternoon-evening doubleheader at Madison Square Garden featuring St. John's and Seton Hall in the afternoon, and the Knicks and Sacramento Kings in the evening. Hurley night at the Garden. "Just what I needed at the time," Danny recalls. He played dismally, missing all six of his shots, and told Bobby later that night he couldn't breathe anymore. He had stopped going to classes, stopped returning calls to close friends, stopped leaving his room for anything but basketball practice.

"Bobby, I'm done," Danny told him. "I'm packing it in."

In the days after the Garden doubleheader, Danny's world turned darker. He wouldn't eat. He wouldn't go out for anything but basketball practice. He felt like he was on the brink of a breakdown. As much as he could, Danny had steered clear of contact with his parents—especially his father. He didn't want Bob Hurley see his son the way he had become depressed and demoralized. The players his father had sent away to college were always calling him with problems, but Danny didn't dare. "It would've been tough for him to see me so weak," Danny says.

Bobby had always been his protector, and he always regretted missing the warning signs of Danny's spiral. Bobby felt such guilt over never truly understanding the burden of being his big brother. As much as Bobby believed he had been there for Danny, it wasn't until the aftermath of his own car crash and inevitable drags from lottery pick to journeyman guard that forced Bobby to see the world through his brother's eyes.

A diminished Bobby Hurley discovered what it was like to chase the legend of a young Bobby Hurley, something Danny had done most of his life.

"Before then, I don't think that I could identify with his problems," Bobby says. "I never really understood what Danny was going through. A lot of people in the area who wanted to see me do well didn't always give Danny a full chance to succeed. The expectations were ridiculous for him. What Danny needed was for us to be spaced out three or four years, instead of eighteen months. Then, things might have been different for him."

By December 11, 1993, Danny had stopped going to classes, moved out of his dorm room and finally had it publicly declared that he would take a leave of absence from the team. On December 12, Bobby had his car accident, and his parents rushed off to Sacramento to nurse him back to health. As one family friend put it, "Danny couldn't even have a tragedy to himself."

Reaching his brother's side in California, Danny was inconsolable in the hospital room, sitting and crying for hours. For hours, Danny tried to understand why it wasn't him in the bed, why God had chosen this to happen to Bobby. This was the wrong Hurley son, Danny cried. "I was just this guy who couldn't even finish his college career without quitting," Danny would say later. "I felt so worthless."

With his parents staying in Sacramento with Bobby, Danny, on leave at Seton Hall, helped coach the St. Anthony team. When he finally came home, Bob Hurley was so run-down that he eventually contracted pneumonia, so Danny took over the St. Anthony team with George Canda, his father's assistant, and coached them until Bob was well enough to take over again.

Carlesimo left for the Portland Trail Blazers before the start of Danny's senior season at Seton Hall, replaced with an old Jersey City playground legend, George Blaney, whom Bob Hurley had grown up idolizing. He was a kind, soft-spoken man, the perfect tonic for Carlesimo's hard-driving ways. Danny finished his career at Seton Hall with a strong senior season, restored with a newfound self-worth beyond basketball. He curbed the nightlife, earned his degree and passed on chances to play pro ball in Europe, to get into teaching and coaching.

Two years after graduation, Danny joined the coaching staff at Rutgers, where Kevin Bannon had been hired as head coach to invigorate a perpetually downtrodden program. One of the biggest problems for Rutgers had always been convincing the rich talent base of recruits in New Jersey to stay home and play for the state university. For the most part, Rutgers was a school synonymous with failure. The hiring of a Hurley son was the next best thing to getting Bob himself to take the Big East job, which was never happening. Bannon believed Danny could get his father to send some top St. Anthony recruits to Rutgers—something that had happened just twice in a quarter-century. What's more, the Hurley name would have credibility recruiting up and down the Eastern seaboard.

"Danny was a better coach than anyone on the staff," says ex-Rutgers assistant Rob Lanier, now head coach at Siena College. "He was young, just out of college and most of us had been in the profession for a few years. But all his life, he had so many things ingrained in him from one of the best basketball minds in the world. Nobody taught the game better than him. Nobody thought it better than him. From a technical stand-point, he was far superior to the rest of us."

It wasn't long before Hurley and Lanier realized they had misjudged their wisdom in hitching their coaching careers to Bannon. He turned out to be a grown-up frat boy using the perks of his job to make it one big party weekend. Yet, it wasn't all immature revelry. Some of the behavior was downright disturbing. Actually, the incident most connected to Bannon's four seasons at Rutgers would end up a Trivial Pursuit question: What school's head coach held a naked free-throw-shooting contest? The answer was Rutgers, where, as young assistant coaches, Danny and Lanier were so mortified, they had to walk out of the gym as Bannon encouraged his players to take off an article of clothing for every missed shot. At the end, two players and two student managers had to run naked sprints in the arena. Lawsuits were eventually filed.

"The whole time, I'm thinking, 'How am I going to tell my father about this?' " Danny says.

His own college playing career had torn away a good deal of his ideal-istic beliefs about the business of big-time basketball, but his experiences at Rutgers obliterated the rest. In the end, Danny found a perverse sort of satisfaction in the way the Rutgers program imploded. Bannon was fired in 2001. Danny lost his job in the head coaching changeover, the best thing that ever happened to him, he believes. In his mind, it saved him from a college fast-track life that would have demanded constant travel and strains on his family. He had been brought up to have a father home for dinner at night, the way his dad had with his own father.

"The first year of my son's life, it was just horrible," Danny says. "At first, I would come home and see him do things that he hadn't been doing when I left for a trip. And then, I would start coming home, pick him up and he didn't know who I was.

"By being a college coach, I was being a worse dad than mine was for me. You want to be a better dad than your father was. And that was hard. I wasn't exactly traveling around the world doing God's work, either. I was traveling around making nice money and basically being a salesman. It was pretty pathetic.

"My father didn't just have a job, but did a service to the community. He reached the hardest of souls in his job in probation. He saved so many of our friends growing up in Jersey City, guys who had parents who were in AA, or on drugs, or not around at all. For me, it had a profound impact, and it's a lot of the reason I struggled at the college level. I listened to him too much. I was probably destined to coach high school because I spent so much time listening to him."

He found peace of mind as a high school coach, turning St. Benedict's Prep, a boarding school in Newark, into a national power. He teaches history, coached basketball and brings his players into his family, the way his father had with the St. Anthony kids. His roster included kids from Puerto Rico, Africa, the Dominican Republic and points up and down the East Coast. The St. Benedict's players come home to Freehold with Danny on the weekends, eating dinner with his family and doing homework at his kitchen table.

"When I was burying my head on my desk at Rutgers, I didn't realize what I was missing. I didn't realize the feeling you got when one of your high school players calls you from college and tells you how great it is, and how much maybe you've affected his life getting there. That's what I learned from my dad. That's why college coaching sucked for me. It was just a business. It was misery because it's everything that's anti-Bob."

Danny takes money out of his pocket to buy his foreign players clothes when they have nothing to wear in the winter. He woke up at four o'clock during the season to monitor the team's morning study hall. He never rules out the possibility of coaching in college again, but he has a good life at St. Benedict's. Danny Hurley has found a place he can make a difference, a place where he figures he probably belonged the whole time.

"I always thought Bobby and me maximized ourselves. It was meant for him to be a first-round pick, make a ton of money and play in the NBA. It was meant for me to be a coach, to try and do some of the same things my dad did."

No, it was never easy being Danny Hurley. But along the way, the more Danny discovered Danny for himself, it got easier all the time.

CHAPTER 20

THE BASKETBALL PLAYERS crammed into the narrow photocopy room next to the main office at St. Anthony. The upperclassmen called down during eighth period on Tuesday. Marcus. Otis. Shelton. Lamar. Sean. Derrick. Barney. One by one, they straggled in to find Sister Alan with her arms folded, her eyes giving nothing.

Awaiting everyone's arrival, Sister stood silently. The quiet made everyone uneasy, eyes nervously darting back and forth at one another. All of it became too ominous for Otis, who finally cracked, "I didn't do it," leaving a bemused Sister Alan sure he was about to roll on one of his teammates for some secret indiscretion.

Allowing a smile, Sister Alan then looked up and turned serious.

"I just want to tell you all that you have a chance to do something so special. You have something so precious right now. Don't do anything to jeopardize it. This is the hardest part of the year: dealing with school, with the pressure of the games, your coach. . . .

"You've all come so far," she said. "Just realize I'm so proud of you all."

She could see the mood change immediately, the slumped, unsure postures transform into proud, puffed chests. What Sister Alan didn't tell them was that she had decided to put off a scheduled CAT scan until Friday morning, March 12, the eve of the Parochial B state championship game in Toms River. She made an appointment to review the results with Dr. Fong on March 15.

"I haven't had chemo in a while because of the infection," she said. "But I told God, 'I am not going to miss the championship.' If something's wrong with me, it has to wait until after the tournament."

One of Sister Alan's regrets was how much her sickness had kept her out of the lives of these seniors the past couple of years. Across so many days and nights, when it felt like she was losing her own fight, they had given her the gift of this basketball season. The kids never realized how they had carried her through the season, how much those couple of hours a night in the gymnasium brought her back to the old days at St. Anthony, a pain-free place when there was just joy. The nights when she wasn't well enough to make it to the gym, when she had to get telephone updates from Margie, none of them could ever understand how far away she felt from the love of her life.

"These seniors, I didn't think they had the character to work thi hard," she would confess. "I figured at some point they were going tc crumble. I'm keeping my fingers crossed. This is the group that I've most preached to: 'Don't do anything stupid in school, don't get yourself in trouble and destroy the chemistry.'

"Beanie has been the craziest these four years. Every time it looked like he turned the corner, I'd praise him and he'd do something stupid. It got to a point this year where I told him, 'Beanie, I'm afraid to even tell you that I've seen such a change in you, because I fear tomorrow you're going to do something stupid and get suspended.'

"As the season started, I told him that he's the one I could just kill. If he had the marks, he could really go somewhere. Because he's a smart kid who just never worked hard. And Otis, he's another one. Much smarter than people think. That's why I'm hoping this coach from Pensacola takes Marcus right away. Marcus is slow. He is really slow. And I said to Marcus, 'Would you like to go there?' And he said, 'I'll go anywhere to get out of Jersey City. Pensacola would be a nice change.'"

What Sister Alan did want the kids to understand, especially the seniors, was how the relationship they had with Hurley would someday change. At their ages, they couldn't understand why he had to be so demanding, so unbending—nor how one day they would be so grateful for it. For the seniors, they were just weeks away from that transformation in the coach-player dynamic. As hard as it was to believe sometimes, the taskmaster would turn into a loyal friend. And that stayed consistent from the best player on the team all the way down to the kids who barely played.

She wishes the seniors knew the story of Tennyson Whitted, a 1999 graduate of St. Anthony. His father, Charles, had died when Tennyson was three years old, leaving behind his wife, Gwendolyn, and son. She never recovered, spending years in and out of her son's life. For most of his life, Tennyson's grandmother, Emily Whitted, raised him in Jersey City.

Often, Tennyson considered transferring out of St. Anthony, something his public school friends were always encouraging him to do. He played behind three future Division I guards, and it was clear he was never going to play meaningful high school minutes for St. Anthony. "Why was I getting yelled at by Coach Hurley when I wasn't even playing?" Tennyson had wondered. "At times, I just thought he didn't think I was any good, that he didn't like my game at all."

And then one afternoon during his junior year, Emily Whitted was waiting on the front step of their apartment building when Tennyson came home. His best friend, David Jones, had been murdered. An argument over a bicycle had escalated into the killer returning to the scene with friends and firepower, driving past, leaning out the car window and letting loose with a hail of bullets into David's torso, leaving him to bleed to death on a Jersey City street.

A memorial service was held at the Boys Club, where all his friends grew up. David Jones didn't go to St. Anthony. He didn't play basketball. For those reasons, the image of Bob Hurley standing in the congregation of the service, weeping for another life lost on those streets would stay with Tennyson forever.

After the ceremony, Hurley sought out Tennyson and reminded him that he wasn't obligated to attend basketball practice that day, and whatever he needed—to talk, to cry, to eat a hot dinner—Bob and Chris Hurley would be there for him.

But Tennyson didn't just want to go to basketball practice, he needed to be there. Even in the coach's most scorching practices, it was still his security blanket. Tennyson stayed his four years, earned solid grades, and Hurley repaid his loyalty: He found him a chance to play at Ramapo College. As a junior and senior, Tennyson would lead all of Division III in assists and steals. In his final season, he took his team to the Elite Eight of the NCAA Division III Tournament, within a missed shot of the Final Four.

"It wasn't until I got to college that someone said to me, 'If a coach doesn't yell at you, he probably doesn't care about you,' " Tennyson says now. "Coach Hurley probably yelled at me because he expected more of me, because he didn't think I was doing all the things I could do. Looking back, he probably yelled because he wanted me to know he was watching me, that he truly cared. You never understand that when you're playing for him, but I do now."

Sometimes, these bench players are the kids who require the most investment from Hurley, because it could be so easy for them to drift. After

Hurley had helped him get into Ramapo, Tennyson expected his relationship with Hurley to come to a close. "Why would he ever continue to care
for me, when I never did anything for him?" he wondered. "I hardly ever
played. I mean, I never won one high school basketball game for him."

His freshman year at Ramapo, Tennyson's coaches were so impressed
with his complete knowledge and understanding of the game that he won
the starting point guard job. Early in the season, Ramapo traveled to play
New Jersey City University, at a time when the St. Anthony season was
getting under way. Friends stopped over at the game, but when Tennyson
dribbled out for layup lines, he glanced up, searching for familiar faces, and
his heart just stopped.

There was Hurley, giving a knowing nod from his seat in the bleachers.
So nervous to impress him, Tennyson had a sloppy triple-double: twelve
points, ten rebounds and ten turnovers. Hurley waited for him outside the
locker room, told him he was proud of his progress, and, as always, offered
some suggestions on his game.

Throughout Tennyson's four years of college, Hurley kept in close
contact with him, getting him summer jobs and camp positions. After the
coach's own camp in the Poconos, Hurley would slip him something extra
in his paycheck, understanding he had no family to support him, no one
else to really help him out. After college graduation in the spring of 2003,
Tennyson went to Atlanta for a pro tryout before European team scouts.
Prior to the trip, Hurley had been on the telephone with him, offering
advice on how to impress the scouts. Truthfully, Hurley wanted him to get
the playing out of his system and get on with what Hurley told Tennyson
was his calling: "You were destined to be a high school teacher and coach,"
he said.

Tennyson had thought so, too. And yet, to hear Bob Hurley tell him
that, well, Tennyson couldn't lie. It gave him goose bumps.

All through his college years, Tennyson had an on-again, off-again
thought about getting a tattoo on his shoulder, perhaps something honoring his late father and slain friend. Each time he considered the possibility,
he remembered what Bob Hurley always told his teams: He lost a little
respect for a man with a tattoo.

He never did get one, and he figures he probably never will.

In Tennyson Whitted's mind, the consequences were too grave.

"I never want my coach to lose any respect for me."

★   ★   ★

THE APPLAUSE THUNDERING inside the locker-room walls of North Bergen High had come on the coach's cue, with Bob Hurley telling his team, "An unbeaten regular season is a hell of an accomplishment." He was allowing the Friars, now 24-0, to give themselves a standing ovation.

They were the fourth team in St. Anthony history to finish a regular season without a loss, with the previous three tearing through the state tournament to finish undefeated state champions. The '89 and '96 teams, brimming with All-American high school players, won *USA Today* national titles.

Even without its best offensive player, Otis, through the heart of the season, St. Anthony kept winning with its defense. As much as ever, Hurley was the reason for the respect afforded the Friars in the national poll.

The Friars had closed out the regular season with convincing victories over a fine St. Joseph's of Montvale team and North Bergen to earn them a first-round bye in the Parochial B state tournament. It was now Thursday, February 24, and they wouldn't play a state tournament game for eight days. Even then, the first-round game promised to be a mismatch against a low seed, and foremost on Hurley's mind now was finding ways to continue to challenge his players.

Hurley told them they would be scrimmaging Parochial A top-seed Seton Hall Prep on Monday in Jersey City to prepare for the tournament. His coaching staff was floored that he had agreed to such a meeting. Why give Seton Hall Prep a chance to figure out how to beat St. Anthony when it would matter for real? This could only harm St. Anthony, and help them. After all, Seton Hall was still number two in the state, and on a collision course for a rematch with St. Anthony in the Tournament of Champions title game. Since losing to St. Anthony in mid-January, Seton Hall had been unbeaten and moved into the *USA Today* poll at number twenty-one.

Otis suspected Hurley had his reasons. "Coach is getting psychological on them," he declared with a wink, tapping two fingers to his temple.

MONMOUTH UNIVERSITY COACH Dave Calloway met with his top assistant, Geoff Billet, on Friday morning to hear him out on one more rave review of the two St. Anthony juniors whom they had been scouting for several months. Billet had gone back to the Jersey Shore campus after the North Bergen game, comfortable in believing that Derrick Mercer and Barney

Anderson were two kids with the talent to keep Monmouth competing for NCAA tournament bids.

Billet had invited Derrick and Barney down to the small, private Division I school for that night's sold-out game against St. Francis College of New York, a meeting to decide the regular season champion of the Northeast Conference. Before they made the trip, Calloway called Hurley, telling him Monmouth would officially offer Barney and Derrick full basketball scholarships. Calloway knew that it was several months too soon to expect decisions, but he wanted both players to know how badly they wanted the teammates together at Monmouth in the fall of 2005.

This was a big deal. These were concrete offers. It was ironic: Sean and Ahmad were the two juniors getting recruited the most feverishly among major conference schools, but Derrick and Barney were ultimately the two most indispensable members of the class. Hurley called Sister Alan to tell the two kids at school, and then called over to the No. 6 School, where Chris Hurley taught kindergarten and Derrick Sr. worked as a security guard.

He couldn't track Derrick Sr. down, but one of his employees in the Recreation department, Rex Turso, found him on his cell phone in the school a few minutes later.

He told him the news of Monmouth's offer.

"Rex, stop lying," Derrick Sr. warned. "Stop lying."

"Derrick," Rex reasoned, "why would I make up Monmouth?"

Derrick Sr. was a beloved, engaging man, five-foot-six with a quick, penetrating smile. Ever since Derrick fell in love with the game as a young kid, his father dreamed of sending him to St. Anthony for Hurley. As he closed his cell phone in the hallway of the No. 6 School, he remembered all those people who told him he would regret sending his son to St. Anthony, that he would never be big enough, never good enough, to get off the bench. He remembered the crate that Doc Miller nailed together for him, the one Derrick used to do a hundred step-ups a night, to work on his leg strength and leaping. He remembered the overtime shifts to pay the St. Anthony tuition and the summer basketball camps bills for Derrick. He remembered those nights laying awake in the two-family house, fearful of the spiraling streets outside his bedroom window, where the pushers had grown so numerous on Stevens Avenue, so brash, that his two kids could no longer walk to Gusto's, the corner store, without stepping around dealers leaning into the rolled-down windows of stopped cars.

Derrick Mercer Sr. remembered it all, and in the middle of work, in the middle of an impossible dream for his five-foot-seven son, the tears filled his eyes.

THE FIRST OFFICIAL work of the postseason on Friday consisted of conditioning and weight lifting, and Hurley marveled over watching Derrick run roughshod over each of the eleven stations set up on the court. Each stop lasted forty seconds on, followed by twenty off, before moving to the next challenge. The stations included push-ups with hands balancing your body on basketballs, a tip drill on the backboard, and defensive slides across the paint and back. Because of the incredible speed that Derrick's feet generated, and how hard he had to work to move side to side with those short, stumpy strides, his feet were always ripping through the sides of his sneakers.

"Derrick will finish this workout and then want to go defend someone full-court," Hurley said.

As Derrick and Barney were leaving the floor after an hour in the gym, Hurley congratulated them on the scholarship offers.

"Did you call your house?" he asked Barney.

"No," Barney said. "My mother isn't home from work yet."

"She'll be so excited," Hurley promised. "That scholarship is worth about $150,000."

He knew the price of a Monmouth education immediately, because he had recently stopped signing the checks for Melissa's tuition bills there.

The chase for the state championship began in earnest the next morning, Saturday, February 28, at St. Peter's College. Waiting outside for Hurley to arrive at the Yanitelli Center, there was an uneasiness running through the team. Nobody had a bigger pit in his stomach than sophomore Linoll Mercedes. He had blown off conditioning on Friday, signing himself out of school in the late afternoon, telling Erman he had an appointment for therapy on his injured right arm. Of course, no one had remembered him hurting his right arm.

Before practice, the seniors teased Linoll. Marcus and Otis were fascinated with his death wish, knowing there was a better chance that the coach had cookies and punch waiting inside than him believing Linoll's tales of woe.

Hurley was nothing short of a madman this time of year, and anyone getting in his way of preparation for the state tournament risked life and limb. Despite the fact that St. Anthony was ranked first in New Jersey and was the favorite to win the Parochial B state championship and the Tournament of Champions, they were still coming off a season in which they had lost to archrival St. Patrick's.

"They've got our belts," Gamble said, inside the gym. "We've got to get them back."

They were halfway through practice when Hurley lost his patience with Linoll over a matter of effort, declaring loudly, "It is safe to say that Linoll has wasted an entire basketball season of his life. You're never going to get this back. Everybody your age has picked up one year on you with your shit attitude.

"And by the way," Hurley asked him. "Why weren't you here yesterday?"

Everyone had been waiting for this one.

Marcus and Otis fought a smile, enjoying every minute of it.

"I had to go somewhere with my parents," Linoll said, barely audible, eyes darting down to the floor.

"And who did you tell about it?" Hurley asked.

"Erman," Linoll mumbled.

Erman?

Suddenly, the rocks began to jar at the peak of Mount Hurley, the first few pebbles trickling down, the bigger boulders loosening, and soon the rockslide gathering speed, until Hurley's temper tumbled down like disaster in a red-faced avalanche.

"You told Errrrrr-man?"

"ERRRRRRR-MAN?

"IS THAT WHAT YOU CALL HIM?

"GET THE FUCK OUT OF HERE!"

For some strange reason, Linoll barely budged.

He just stood there on the sideline, all arms and legs and hangdog face. Hurley had turned around, but whipped back when he heard Marcus bark to Linoll, "Get out of here, man."

Hurley stomped his foot and screamed, "GET OUT OF HERE BEFORE I PUT MY FOOT UP YOUR ASS."

Linoll moved now, searching quickly for his gym bag in the pile of jackets and belongings stacked on the sideline.

"ERMAN?" Hurley repeated again, still incredulous over Linoll addressing a coach by merely his last name.

"ERRRRRRRR-MAN?" he screamed, letting the name roll off his tongue.

"YOU DISRESPECTFUL LITTLE SHIT!" Hurley finally yelled, just as Linoll had picked up considerable speed and beat it for the gymnasium doors.

Now, it was senior Justin Lewis's turn. He had slipped into practice ten minutes earlier, about an hour and fifteen minutes after it had started. This was the team's twelfth man, somebody in danger of getting left off the tournament roster of sixteen, with several promising underclassmen brought up from the 22-1 junior varsity.

"Where were you?" Hurley asked

"The bus wasn't running, Coach."

"The bus wasn't running?"

From mid-court, Hurley yelled to a cluster of players standing on the sidelines.

"Where's Qaysir?"

Quickly, Qaysir Woods stepped forward. For the first time this season, he sensed something good happening for him. He was a string-bean six-foot-three and he hadn't practiced all that well, hadn't remembered plays when Hurley put him in games, and certainly hadn't endeared himself to Mrs. Hurley on the trip to California when he loaded up on a tray full of desserts at Hometown Buffet.

"Qaysir, what time did you have to get up this morning to get to the train?"

"Five-thirty."

"How about that?" Hurley said. "Five-thirty.

"Give Qaysir a round of applause."

For the first and only time in his high school basketball career, senior Qaysir Woods earned a standing ovation. Throughout his two years at St. Anthony, he had wondered if Hurley knew the lengths he traveled every day to be a part of his team. He lived in Plainfield, thirty miles west of Jersey City. While the rest of his teammates were still sleeping, Qaysir awoke to a 5:00 A.M. alarm, pulled a sweatshirt hood over his head, and started the mile and a half walk to the Plainfield train station. From there, it was a thirty-minute ride into Newark, where he transferred trains and started on his way to Jersey City.

After practices ended around 6:30 in the evening, he ran several blocks to catch the PATH train at the Pavonia-Newport Station, being sure to make the connection to the 7:45 New Jersey Transit train from Newark to Plainfield. After another long, cold walk in the darkness—just like the one he took in the morning—Qaysir would arrive home at 9:00.

Then he'd eat, do his chores and his homework, and be in bed by 11:00.

During Qaysir's junior year, Tony DiGiovanni, the St. Anthony teacher and former assistant coach, lived in an apartment next door to White Eagle when the team still used the bingo hall for open gym and summer-league practices. DiGiovanni would arrive an hour early to open the gym, and Qaysir, the kid who came the farthest, the kid guaranteed to never play a meaningful minute of varsity basketball at St. Anthony, was almost always sitting on the steps, waiting for DiGiovanni to unlock the doors.

"On the weekends, I stay over Barney's house a lot, and I can see the difference between what I get for rest and the other players do," Qaysir says. "That extra sleep they get really helps them."

Still, Rutgers-Newark, a satellite to the Piscataway campus with its own fine Division III basketball program, had been faithfully recruiting Qaysir off his St. Anthony summer-league performances and practices.

In that one moment Saturday morning, in the one standing ovation Hurley made sure Qaysir would hear in his St. Anthony career, he finally knew the answer to the question that dogged him every day.

"I guess that was his way of telling me he did know," Qaysir would say later. "It all hasn't been for nothing. He noticed."

Hurley missed nothing. And Justin Lewis was thrown out of his gym, too, that Saturday morning.

Afterward, Hurley hustled over to the Armory to run a basketball clinic for close to a hundred Jersey City kids. This was part of his job as Recreation director, but he never needed to be on the city payroll to spend his free time conducting these clinics around town. Hurley had been doing it forever, and it never failed that he would see some talented seventh or eighth-grader everyone had been telling him about, and Hurley would feel like he was falling in love for the first time all over again. There wasn't a young basketball player in Jersey City running up and down that floor who didn't want Hurley's eyes on him, who didn't want the chance to someday be the next St. Anthony star.

Still, Derrick Sr. walked on clouds. He had the time of his life on the trip down to Monmouth the previous night, immersing himself with little Derrick and Barney in a wild campus arena atmosphere, complete with the trimmings of March Madness. After the game, the Monmouth coaches brought the three down to their winning locker room and gave them a taste of that championship feeling.

Derrick still wanted to wait for the big-time schools to court him. If they were recruiting Sean, he couldn't understand why they wouldn't eventually recruit him, too.

"I want to go to a school where Dick Vitale is going to scream my name," Derrick would tell friends.

Derrick Sr. simply wanted his son to attend a school where he could get a good, marketable degree. He didn't care about conferences, or televised games, or big-time reputations. For him, basketball was merely a means to an end. Knowing that affording a private university like Monmouth would've been impossible on his salary, this first scholarship offer felt like cashing a lottery ticket.

"You don't know how much of a burden that is off me," Derrick Sr. said. "I just want him to get a good education. I mean, I was a knucklehead in school. I just wanted to party, just hang out. I've tried to teach him the value of getting a good education.

"The biggest thing is, though, I can't get over what Coach Hurley has done for my family. He won't admit it, but I owe everything to him. If there was ever anything in the world that I could do for him—anything at all—he would just have to ask."

A little later, Hurley walked along a sun-splashed sidewalk on Montgomery Street toward his car, the chain-link fence to the parking lot to his right, and the drugstore and Burger King across the street. This was one of the days the Phil Jacksons and Pat Rileys, the Krzyzewskis and Knights, could never have on the job. They would never know what it felt like to take a five-foot-nothing kid like Derrick Mercer and make his family's dreams come true.

"I can imagine how much fun it was for big Derrick and the kids, going down to Monmouth last night," Hurley said. "All of the effort you put into things, the confusion, the uncertainty, and in that one moment, your hopes are all realized. Big Derrick is a wonderful guy. He's been coaching kids all over Jersey City for as long as I can remember.

"And then Barney calling his parents, and letting them know that college has been paid for—once they know that, it puts everything in its place."

Behind him, the armory was packed with kids playing ball, just like in the old days. In front of him, there was the final push for a national high school record-tying twenty-fourth state championship for St. Anthony, which would be his twenty-second as head coach. There was something else at work here, too: As little as Hurley dared to speak of it, it was unmistakably shiny and real. The Friars were playing for history now.

Hang around the possibilities of a basketball season, and you never know where they will take you.

SETON HALL PREP coach Bob Farrell could've called one of the New York City powers for a scrimmage to stay sharp when faced with an eight-day layoff before its opening tournament game, but he didn't. He called Hurley. When Farrell suggested that St. Anthony come to his gym in West Orange for the game, Hurley laughed.

"You called me," he told Farrell. "You come to Jersey City."

The gamesmanship never ended with them. And with five days until the start of the tournament, on Monday, March 1, no one around the St. Anthony coach completely understood his angle for agreeing to scrimmage them. Hurley reasoned his team needed to be constantly challenged. They had to be tested. "Our goal is a Parochial B state championship," Hurley explained. "If we play Seton Hall Prep now, it helps us to our goal. Will that help them a bit? Yeah, it will. But it will help us, too. Here's the thing: Our group needs to have something that is always going to make them work. If there isn't a carrot, our seniors don't internally lead."

Gamble just shook his head and shrugged when asked about it. This was one of those times he just had to trust Hurley's instincts for always navigating them out of harm's way in March. Through the years, Hurley had been such a dominant postseason coach—winning twenty-one Parochial state titles in thirty-one seasons, and eight of the nine Tournament of Champions that St. Anthony reached since that format was introduced in 1989—that Gamble had to defer to his judgment. If anyone deserved the benefit of the doubt, it was Bob Hurley.

Like the rest of his staff, Gamble feared the scrimmage would give Prep's junior guards a chance to face that vaunted St. Anthony pressure defense again, and possibly, become more clear-minded and confident in combating it. Most of all, this could give Seton Hall Prep an opportunity to believe they could beat St. Anthony, something they hadn't done since the 1990–1991 season.

Even The Faa had wandered over to the gym for this one. The old baseball coach and scout was nursing a dip in his cheeks and gripping a fungo bat in his weatherworn hands.

"This is a chess match between the two coaches," he said, grabbing a chair and sitting down at the scorer's table. The scrimmage had been closed to the public. There were whispers all over North Jersey that they were playing in secret in Jersey City, and what people wouldn't have given to watch how it played out.

Another player relegated to spectator was Sean McCurdy, who had sprained an ankle in Saturday's practice and had been told to stay off his feet for several days. Sean wore his Reebok Iverson jacket and a fresh brush cut. He sat a few feet from the end of the St. Anthony bench, next to Chris Hurley.

For the first time since returning from his injury, Otis was back in the starting lineup with his boys, Marcus and Beanie. Add Barney and Derrick, and the seniors couldn't help but notice that this made it an all–Jersey City starting five.

With Sean on the sideline, everyone could see the crispness and fluidity with which the ball moved for St. Anthony in the scrimmage. There was one fast break where each of the five players touched the ball on the way to a layup, the kind of bang-bang-bang perfection that had been spotty that season.

St. Anthony took a two-by-four upside Prep's head, scoring the first fifteen points to start the scrimmage, letting them come back to tie it, and scoring a stunning thirty-six of the final forty-seven points for a devastating victory.

The seniors' bond seemed to be growing in strength and surety into an impenetrable wall under their leader, Marcus Williams. For most of the season, Marcus had been the most openly dismissive of Sean's importance to the team's success. To him, this small sampling against Seton Hall Prep was deeper validation.

"We were distributing the ball more," Marcus said afterward. "Sometimes, Sean has those games where the ball just stops in his hands, where he shoots a majority of the shots and everybody else just rebounds. Today, we shared the ball much better and there wasn't anybody breaking the offense. We stayed together as a team.

"The difference without Sean was noticeable to us, but to Coach, I don't know. Coach Hurley has a mind of his own. He's probably got something that he thinks will work better for us."

The coaches did notice the difference, but they also knew the team had functioned well without several individual parts throughout the course of the season. They knew how poorly Sean had been playing, but Hurley's intentions weren't on burying Sean for the state tournament. Instead, they wanted to get his head straight and get him playing well. They wanted to keep coaching him.

As for Seton Hall Prep, "The score was misleading," Hurley cautioned later. Clearly, he was trying to soften the ramifications and dissuade his players from believing somehow that they had just assured themselves of the Tournament of Champions title before the Parochial B state tournament had even started. Gamble confessed that the scrimmage went "exactly the way Coach Hurley wanted," meaning Hurley saw an opportunity to pound Prep into submission and did it. Prep looked shell-shocked leaving the gym. This idea had completely backfired on Farrell. If he had hoped to convince his team that it had closed the gap on St. Anthony, they had to wonder now whether they even belonged on the floor with the Friars.

"They're gone now," Otis said. "If we play them again, they know what will happen to them. They just froze. They couldn't do anything.

"All of us know what we just did. We can taste it right now."

As for Sean, the scrimmage made him defiant over the doctor's orders to stay out of practice for two or three more days. "There's no way," Sean said. "I'll be back sooner than that."

Nevertheless, it was clear that for all the famous college basketball schools recruiting him, for all the credibility the stage at St. Anthony had brought his reputation on a regional and national level, Sean McCurdy was back where he had started with the team. He needed to prove himself all over again to the Jersey City kids.

"To them," Gamble said, "he's still from Connecticut."

CHAPTER 21

THROUGHOUT THE WARM-UPS before the opening state tournament game, Marcus stole glances at the entrance doors of the charter school gymnasium. Always the portrait of poise, Sister Alan had known him too long to mistake the concern in those eyes.

Poor Hawthorne Christian had earned the chance to be the sacrificial offering in the Friars opening-round game, but the most pressing drama surrounding the night wouldn't be the 79–25 destruction delivered to them, but the final count on the mothers attending the St. Anthony Senior Night ceremonies.

Sister Alan grabbed Marcus's arm on the floor, trying to assure him.

"Don't worry if she doesn't come. Mrs. Hurley will walk out there with you."

The ceremony was brief and simple, the parents of the seniors invited out to center court, where the senior son would hand his mother a bouquet of flowers. With mere minutes to spare before the ceremony started, Marcus's face lit up.

"She's here!" he yelled over to Sister Alan. "She's here!"

But no player appeared prouder to have his mother in the gymnasium than Otis, who had thought about this night since starting out at St. Anthony. All season, he had reflected on the evening when Earleen Campbell would finally come watch him play ball. She had never been to a St. Anthony game, and to him, this was a chance to share in something that had meant as much to him as anything in the world.

For his senior theology class, Otis had written a paper detailing the influential people in his life. He wrote about his mother and earned an A-plus.

Everything I do is for my mother. I don't ask my mother for anything that much because I know that she doesn't have a lot of money to be giving me. She is a very hard working lady and I love her for that. I want her to get to the point where she doesn't have to struggle any more in life. I think that if I work my hardest and do my best I can help her with everything so she can just live care free.

Earleen would have the time of her life watching Otis play ball that night, saying later, "It was wonderful to see him so happy on the court."

When the Friars gathered for practice on Saturday morning—St. Mary's of Elizabeth, a twelfth seed, awaited them at home Monday night—there were no more bouquets in the gymnasium. St. Mary's had some athleticism and talent, a step up from overmatched Hawthorne Christian. Hurley promised two tough weekend days of practice, with his eye on the Parochial B North Jersey championship, on Wednesday night, March 10, against the winner of Paterson Catholic and St. Pat's. The winner of the North title almost always beat the South champion for the Parochial B title.

As the team gathered at mid-court for the start of practice, Hurley told them, "As soon as I blow the whistle, it's on you to show me how important this is to you."

The next two days were a symphony of fundamentals, from figure-eight dribbling around folding chairs, to drilling over and over the split-second transition from defense to offense, offense to defense, the blink-of-an-eye exercise that separated St. Anthony game after game from its opponents. They practiced gang rebounding on the boards, outside shooting sprees and setting screens.

Everyone was constantly winning and losing jobs, switching from starter black jerseys to white. There was an urgency to every pass and catch, every decision a Friar made on the floor.

This was the best of Bob Hurley, the teacher, the reason his former assistant DiGiovanni sat and scribbled furiously everything he saw in his notebook. In the fall, DiGiovanni and Erman had traveled to North Carolina, Duke and UConn to observe practices. Three stops, three Hall of Fame–caliber coaches, and DiGiovanni still insisted that here with Hurley, "These are the best practices—the best teaching—happening anywhere in basketball."

Everyone knew Hurley wanted St. Pat's. Oh, how he wanted them. He wouldn't say it, but it wasn't necessary. After all, the rest of the team wanted St. Pat's, too. St. Anthony and St. Pat's were the Hatfields and McCoys of North Jersey basketball. There was little affection between the two programs, and there was no mistaking the fact that next Wednesday night Hurley wanted to avenge the end of last season's tournament defeat to them. Kevin Boyle used St. Anthony as his model for success at St. Pat's, learning from Hurley that coaching championship high school basketball had to be a twelve-month-a-year job. They had beaten St. Anthony for the Parochial B title twice, including 2003 and 1998.

Boyle was himself an intense, hard-driving coach, responsible for con-structing a national power at the small Elizabeth school. He was considered an excellent bench coach and an aggressive pursuer of the best talent available—and even, in the minds of some, of those unavailable. There was no telling where the next St. Patrick's star would surface. The *Newark Star-Ledger*'s Steve Politi had referred to Boyle as the "Darth Vader" of New Jersey prep basketball, and his St. Patrick's program as the "Evil Empire," the black hat in the power struggle with Bob Hurley and Seton Hall Prep's Bob Farrell for state supremacy.

St. Pat's had been wildly inconsistent in the season, but still had a tough, scrappy team that Hurley didn't dare discount. So much of the weekend's practices were geared toward preparing for the possibility of St. Patrick's, with the understanding that the St. Mary's team they would face would be an opponent the Friars could control with ease.

As Hurley worked on breaking full-court pressure on Saturday—something he knew St. Patrick would slap on them—Shelton Gibbs strug-gled to make the first pass advancing the ball down the floor. Hurley howled in frustration, but privately seemed grateful for an opening to insert himself into the action. The more hyped Hurley felt, the more he needed to work it off alongside his team. Before long, Hurley was drenched in sweat, dribbling into traps and firing passes into the routes he taught them to take to beat the press.

His players were never sure what to do in these situations. How hard do you take it to Coach? How close do you get when defending him? When Barney couldn't catch one of Hurley's blistering passes down the sideline, one that flew beyond his reach and out-of-bounds, his new fifty-six-year-old teammate screamed, "BEND YOUR KNEES AND BE PREPARED TO CATCH THE PASS!"

Nobody dared tell Hurley that maybe, just maybe, Yao Ming couldn't have climbed a ladder to catch that one—or, in fact, many of the series of forty-foot passes that Hurley had sent sailing high and wide. Of course, Hurley had grown frustrated with Barney's lack of fire all afternoon. Still a small team, so much of what they did hinged on him protecting the inside.

"If not for long arms and being six-foot-five, you would be home watching television," Hurley snapped at him.

Then, caught out of position on the press, Barney recovered late to stop a breakaway basket and dropped Ahmad Nivins to the floor with a cross-body block.

"Go home," Hurley bellowed. "Get out of here. You're hurting a teammate because you're a lazy-ass."

It was state tournament time and the Friars were favorites. Hurley was determined to make himself the toughest opponent his team would meet in March. He was searching for a reason to turn the heat up and found it with a failed formation on an out-of-bounds play. Marcus knew it cold, but it didn't matter. Marcus was supposed to make sure everybody else knew it cold, too.

"Who's eighteen here?" Hurley demanded.

Under the basket, Marcus Williams raised his hand.

"Let's go, Marcus."

The sneakers stopped squealing, the balls stopped bouncing. There was just Hurley, leaning in with his chin now, making his way toward the toughest kid in the gym.

"You and me, we're going to go into the locker room. Come on, you wanna go into the locker room?"

It was an old, familiar dance with Marcus, one they had continued for four years in the program. Somewhere in Jersey City, there had to be some kid, on some playground, who one day would take Hurley up on his offer to throw down, but he had yet to pass through the doors of St. Anthony.

Marcus Williams respectfully declined the invitation. There may have been a part of Marcus—a part of them all—that wanted to take on Hurley for the Tough Guy Championship of Greenville, but it would have to wait until the season was over.

"Who else wants a piece of my ass?" Hurley growled.

Hurley stalked back to the middle of the gym, leaving Marcus behind. He rubbed his hand over his wristwatch, the way that, everyone knew, he did when something got him going good; when Bob Hurley wanted to take on the world.

"We're playing the biggest games in your careers tomorrow, and hopefully Wednesday, so what should we do? Just throw everybody out of practice because you're all so good? Yeah, you're all so fucking good."

He turned back toward his reserves standing at the mid-court line, who were merely spectators to the mistakes that started him on this tear.

His eyes stopped on junior Robert Bullock, guilty of the crime of just standing there staring back at Hurley in his line of vision.

"BULLOCK! I try to coach you every day," he boomed. "You got a fucking problem with that? I hope not," Hurley said, answering himself. "I hope not."

He turned back to everyone now. "I'm fifty-six years old," he began, "and when I can't kick anybody's ass in this building, I'll be seventy. Just know something: I don't drive up to practice every day saying to myself, 'Gee, I hope Barney's ready to play today.' It never registers in my head, because Barney better be fuckin' ready to play. If he's not, then another child is going to play.

"Because what am I going to do?" he asked them.

"I'm going to coach whoever is here.

"So get a drink of water, and get your ass back out here ready to be coached. Or get your shit and start running so I don't put a size twelve up somebody's ass right now."

After that, all you could hear was the thump, thump, thump of sneakers hitting the floor, the Friars running for the fountains in the hallway.

Son of a bitch, he *wanted* St. Pat's.

OUTSIDE THE GYM on Sunday afternoon, everyone stood in shorts and T-shirts, drinking in the warm March sun. Walking to his Jeep Cherokee, Sean sweated out his starting job for Monday night's game against St. Mary's. Hurley had held him out of the Hawthorne Christian game to give his ankle more time to rest. And after his first full workout in a week, it felt tender again. He had practiced well, the coaches agreed. He had been patient, not trying to force his offense into the flow. Hurley didn't tell him, but he planned to play him off the bench for Monday night's game. He did it with Otis's injury, and he would do it with Sean's. How life as the sixth man instead of a starter would affect Sean's psyche was the furthest thing from Hurley's mind now.

"That's up to him to figure out," Hurley would say. "It isn't about the individual. It's about the team."

A half an hour after practice Sunday, Sean bounded down to the lobby of his apartment building carrying a ball under his arm. He looked awful. After his mother left him on his own overnight, Sean had battled the coughing and wheezing of a chest cold, getting only two hours of sleep. After watching the Duke–North Carolina game Saturday night, he had closed his eyes on the couch—only to wake up a couple of hours later, agonizingly alone.

"I couldn't go back to sleep," Sean said through a raspy voice. "I was coughing. My head was spinning. I looked at the clock and it's 1:30 and I'm saying, 'What the hell?' I was wide awake, because I was just so sick."

He was still sick, Sunday afternoon, but Sean McCurdy hadn't moved to Jersey City to lay on his couch, blow his nose and watch the Nets-Lakers game. He hadn't moved here to hang out at Newport Mall with his teammates, or to find a semblance of a social life as a high school student. He moved here to be a basketball player, and basketball players lived in the gymnasium.

It was a gorgeous stroll down the pathway to his complex's gymnasium, the wind picking up a little, blowing the masts on the small sailboats floating on the Hudson. A lot of nights, Sean made this walk in the darkness, just him, his jump shot and his thoughts until they closed it up at 10:00.

Sean had stayed late the other night, setting a personal record with sixty-six straight free throws made. Sometimes, he came downstairs to work on his shot. Sometimes, it just gave him a chance to clear his mind. He dribbled the ball to the left, and swished a shot. And another. He was moving briskly around the three-point line, popping the shots one after another, and talking about the *Sports Illustrated* cover boy that week, Sebastian Telfair of Lincoln High in Brooklyn.

"Sebastian Telfair is going straight to the NBA, huh?" Sean said, pump-faking an imaginary defender and hitting another. "Do you think a point guard can go straight to the league? He's so small. I don't know." Telfair was five-foot-eleven, so Sean had an inch or two on him. That was probably all Sean had on him—an inch or two—but in his mind, it was something, anyway. It was a start. Upstairs in the apartment, Sean had taken down the New York *Daily News* photo of him rising to try and block Telfair's shot at the 2003 PrimeTime Shootout. It had been replaced with Sean taking the ball to the basket in the San Diego tournament, a much warmer memory.

In Cindy and Sean McCurdy's mind, college was a necessary step on his way to an NBA career. Nobody else at St. Anthony ever talked about the NBA—just scholarships, just getting out—but this mother and son were on a mission. There weren't too many six-foot-one guards with limited quickness in the pros, but that sort of reasoning didn't resonate with them.

Sean did consider the possibility of coaching someday, "but only if I don't make it," he said.

"And I'm going to make it," he quickly concluded.

Back upstairs on the fourteenth floor, Sean emptied a box of chicken nuggets into the microwave. Cindy had gone to Connecticut for the weekend, and the apartment looked as it would, with a seventeen-year-old living alone. Dirty dishes were in the sink, clothes on the floor, ripped open and untouched recruiting letters scattered on the dining room table. By the typeface on the envelopes, he could tell the difference between the personal correspondence and the form letters.

One of his favorites, the University of Notre Dame, whose assistants scouted Sean in San Diego and stopped in for a practice in Jersey City, had written out a card celebrating the Fighting Irish's recent Sweet 16 season and assuring him an ample opportunity to let the world see the talents of Sean McCurdy. "I hope you have watched our games of late because we allow our guards so much freedom to play," he wrote.

Now there was a college coach after Sean's heart. *Freedom.* Every recruiter sold starry-eyed high school guards on fast and loose college offenses, freewheeling systems where they could fire shots to the rims fast and furious, beefing up scoring averages and getting plenty of notice for the pros. Everybody preached freedom.

Ironically, St. Anthony players had traditionally been the prospects whom colleges recruited on the belief that they had been taught by Hurley to fit into a winning, team concept. There were no Friars scoring twenty-five and thirty points a game in high school. Terry Dehere became the all-time leading scorer in Seton Hall University and Big East history with 2,494 points, but had averaged only thirteen points a game his final season at St. Anthony. The recruiters knew that Sean wanted to hear something else—major shots, major production. And college recruiters were programmed to tell prospects what they wanted to hear.

Inside the fridge, there was enough lettuce left in a baggie for a salad. The only problem was there weren't any clean forks left. Digging deeper, Sean ferreted out a plastic fast-food fork.

"I knew this would come in handy," he said.

Just then, Cindy McCurdy called from Connecticut.

"How are you feeling?" she asked Sean.

"OK," he said.

"Did you practice today?"

"Yes."

"Did it hurt?"

"No," Sean said.

"Are you starting tomorrow?"

"Hopefully," he concluded.

Starting was important to Sean, much more so than it was for Otis. At St. Anthony, they were so conditioned to always think of the team that no one else ever seemed to consider stats and scoring. No one even knew the 1,000-point scorers in the school's history. There were no banners for them. Just state championship banners, just winning.

Nevertheless, Sean feared the perception that he was something less than the star at St. Anthony. In fact, this was one of the most star-free teams in school history.

"I wish I could score a little more," he confessed. "I wish I didn't have those droughts that I had. But there's nothing I can do about that now. All I can do is help my team win, but also, do what I need to do for myself personally. If we win and I only score three points, that's not really attracting the college coaches. But at thirteen points a game—I mean, I would like to score more than thirteen—but at least that's still the high man on the team."

He stabbed his fork into his salad, and stuffed a bite into his mouth.

"But we're winning. That's the only thing that really matters."

He sounded like he was trying to convince himself.

"I am happy," he said, sounding less than sold. "I am happy. I mean, kids at other schools are averaging seventeen, but you've never heard of them before. But you've heard of everybody on our team."

Cindy called back.

"When are you coming home?" Sean asked her. "I feel like crap. I mean, you can stay up there, but I just need medicine."

Call Melissa, Cindy said, and see if she could bring something for him to take.

"All right," Sean said.

Ever since the story on Erman—in which Hurley was quoted as calling his assistant Sean's "Mr. Mom"—had run in the *Chicago Sun-Times*, Cindy McCurdy hadn't invited Erman back to stay with Sean when she was out of town. But whoever stayed with Sean, he still spoke with his father on the telephone every night, and Bob McCurdy would kid his son, "If it's thundering out and you're scared, you can call me." It was his way of telling Sean that whatever the miles were between them, whatever the distance, whoever the non-flesh-and-blood watching over him in the apartment, he never wanted him to feel too alone in Jersey City.

"Sean calls me a lot at night just to talk," Doc Miller says. "My instincts as a father told me that the kid was lonely and I needed to try and stay close to him. That kid is something else. Except for little Bobby, I'm not sure I've ever seen a kid at St. Anthony who wanted it as badly as he does. And that's saying something, with the kids who've come through here. That's saying something."

And for that, Hurley held a profound respect for Sean. He lived to coach kids who loved basketball like he did, who had come to St. Anthony yearning for Hurley to get the most out of them. Whatever issues Hurley had with Cindy's theatrics, whatever introduction of overzealous suburban parental involvement she had brought to his program, he never let it cloud his admiration for her son's commitment.

Sean McCurdy didn't just learn how to play the game of basketball at St. Anthony, he learned how the *game was played*. If nothing else, Sean became an unscientific experiment in the high school basketball industry itself. He was a fascinating study in how reputations were made, how scholarships were won and lost, how recruiters' perceptions of players were tailored to the right pedigree, the right coach, and in his case, the right color. The stampede for colleges to recruit a good white player was thunderous.

"I started going to Five-Star Camp when I was in the sixth grade," Sean said in the kitchen. "I was nobody. I was just some little white kid nobody knew. The summer that I decided to come here, before my sophomore year, I went to Five-Star and I was playmaker of the week. It wasn't like they didn't know who I was, but they didn't care. They thought I was still from Connecticut. But when I came in last year, coming from St. Anthony's, people were just kissing my ass. 'Oh, you're Sean McCurdy.'

"Kids were saying, 'Oh, I see you on TV all the time.' [Camp co-owner Howard Garfinkel] saw me play this year a few times. He always liked me a lot. In the past, he always knew he would get my father's money three times a summer. But now he can see that I'm a player."

For Sean McCurdy, little else mattered.

BRUCE SPRINGSTEEN'S "GLORY DAYS" boomed on the P.J. Ryan's jukebox, drowning out the sound on the television hanging high in the far corner of the dining room. Quickly, Hurley had moved past the 88–39 victory over St. Mary's, immersing himself for a moment in the final seconds of the NCAA tournament bid on the line between Virginia Commonwealth and George Mason. Hurley had a rooting interest—he was pulling for the young VCU coach, Jeff Capel, the point guard who had replaced Bobby at Duke.

As Hurley downed a chicken sandwich, his eyes stayed on the screen. Between bites, he declared of Capel, "There's some Krzyzewski in there."

Tom Konchalski had come to the St. Mary's tournament game to evaluate the underclassmen players on St. Anthony for his ratings report. He had the seat next to Hurley in the corner booth now, alongside Chris and Melissa. Konchalski had considered his every visit from Queens as an installment in the seniors' saga, and he was catching up with Hurley on the soap opera.

"I'm like Father Flanagan with this year's team," Hurley said. "But I'll tell you: The most pleasant surprise of all has been Mosby."

But there was one bit of redemption that wouldn't come Ahmad Mosby's way his senior season: a second chance to beat St. Patrick's. St. Anthony could forget about the blood war with its bitter rival because Paterson Catholic, a tall, talented, albeit young team, had blown them out Monday night in Paterson, setting the stage for an unexpected Wednesday match-up for the North Jersey Parochial B sectional title game at St. Peter's College. It still took a minute for the information to digest, a moment to get past the idea that all that ill will wouldn't be spilling out on the court again.

Erman, Ling and the assistant junior-varsity coach, Todd Dagosta, had called to let Hurley know, while driving back from Paterson, with a scouting report and videotape.

"I'm glad it's not St. Pat's," Chris said. That fact alone promised to make living with her husband far more tolerable for the next forty-eight hours.

Outside P.J. Ryan's, a long way from sleep on his inflatable mattress, a longer way from his old fifty-eighth-floor office in the Sears Tower, Erman tossed his schoolbag into his Civic's trunk and slammed it shut. It was 11:00 now, and he planned to stay up late writing out his scouting report to fax to Hurley in the morning. By three in the morning, Hurley would be turning his apartment upside down for his own notes on Paterson Catholic taken at a game he saw earlier in the season. Finally, he realized they were back in his Recreation office. By 4:30 in the morning, Ben Gamble would be awake in Roselle watching tape of the Paterson Catholic-St. Pat's game, scribbling notes before he had to leave for the start of his 6 A.M. shift at the prison.

All of this sure beat preparing law briefs, Erman laughed outside P.J.

Ryan's. As he climbed into his cluttered Honda, he joked, "Tomorrow feels like a movie day in environmental science: *Finding Nemo*, I think."

THE SUN FINALLY fought its way out from behind an overcast gray sky, a warm light burning down on the unruly sight in the St. Anthony parking lot. The seniors were shadow boxing and wrestling, Qaysir was getting tossed onto the hood of a parked Lincoln Continental. Justin Lewis was sucker punched in the stomach.

In the middle of it all, Marcus Williams served as traffic cop. He lorded over his teammates, offering backup to spare one player a mild beating and letting the next get slammed into the brick building.

Marcus always said this was his team. He was right. He always called the shots.

This was Wednesday afternoon, March 10, and Paterson Catholic waited for the North Jersey title just a few hours away. Qaysir had been the one senior to remember Coach Erman's directive to the players: They were all expected to be in room 102 for a quick meeting at 3:15 before riding together to a waterfront restaurant for the team meal. It was 3:20 now.

"We better go inside," Qaysir warned. "Or we're going to get in trouble."

Marcus shot back an incredulous face, rolling his head back in laughter. "As long as Sean's out here, how we gonna get in trouble?"

No one could convince Marcus that there wasn't a double standard protecting Sean McCurdy at St. Anthony. Sean had moved into that big, spacious apartment on the waterfront, but Marcus's Jersey City was down on the streets, down in Curries Woods, and Sean didn't know that Jersey City. Sean represented opportunity to Marcus, the kind that he never had in life. His father had run off, his brother was locked up, and there was a part of him that deeply regretted never taking full advantage of the opportunities at St. Anthony. Hurley told him everything he needed to do—the road map for life, he called it. He had the road map. And Marcus never followed it.

Yet he was the ultimate team-player for the program, willing to do anything for the greater good. Marcus still suspected Sean would only be willing to do anything for Sean. Those MVP awards? The big-time recruiting? All the shots the coaches let him take and miss? He couldn't stand it. To Marcus, this was the bottom line: Sean was an outsider. And the deeper they got into the season, the worse Sean struggled, Marcus did less to disguise his disdain.

Whatever Marcus had to say about him, Sean wasn't listening. He was thirty feet away in the parking lot, busy taking a recruiting call from the assistant coach at Clemson University. Beginning in March, college coaches were allowed to make one call a month to a junior player. Clemson was an Atlantic Coast Conference school, and the assistant coach was calling him from Greensboro, North Carolina, where the team was preparing for the conference tournament. The assistant, Frank Smith, had even put Sean on the cell with the head coach, Oliver Purnell, who noted how he remembered playing against Bob McCurdy back in the '70s.

Erman finally came storming out of the school, wondering why the team hadn't come to the classroom like they had been told. Erman, wearing his game-night best, the maroon St. Anthony polo shirt with khaki pants, seethed over discovering the lawlessness prevailing in the parking lot.

"Marcus!" Erman yelled. "Can you be a fucking leader?"

He moved toward Marcus, Erman's slight, bespectacled frame supporting enough anger to make even Marcus take notice. This was a rare show of emotion out of the typically mild-mannered Erman, and it stopped the kids cold.

"It's the biggest game of the fucking season and you can't lead!" he yelled at Marcus.

The reprimand surprised Marcus, but he played it cool, like he had heard the line a thousand times in his four years at St. Anthony. Because he had.

"Every game is the biggest of the season," Marcus fired back. "Let's just fuckin' play the game, you know?" he said, sounding exasperated.

"Just fuckin' play the game."

In Marcus's mind, he was prepared to play. When there had been an important game at St. Anthony these past four years, no one had to come looking for Marcus Williams. He was always there, always in the middle of everything. He was tired of hearing the program was due something more out of him, something he hadn't been giving. Marcus had heard all of Hurley's speeches, all of his inspiration and condemnation. No, Marcus Williams didn't lead in the classroom, and he didn't lead in the locker room, and he sure didn't lead out here in the parking lot on game day. He led on the basketball court, and Coach Erman and Coach Hurley, and Bobby Hurley and David Rivers, and the whole damn history of St. Anthony basketball wanting him to uphold some standard of sainthood would have to live with that.

Just before they climbed into the school bus, Lamar reached out a hand in support of Marcus, insisting loud enough for everyone to hear, "I'm my own leader. Nobody needs to lead me." Marcus and Lamar laughed and embraced, the old dysfunctional Jersey City Boys Club crew staying united until the end.

Every day, Marcus usually stopped by Darren Erman's sixth period environmental science class to chat with his coach. The kids liked Erman, because he was sincere. They knew he cared. They could spot the phonies, and they knew he had a good heart. Ultimately, who else would've walked away from all that money as an attorney to come work with them? When Marcus had come by earlier that afternoon, Erman had told him, "You can't just act like a leader one hour a day, or one practice. Because nobody is going to respect you. You have to do it all the time, in everything you do."

As the team piled into the bus for the short drive to the restaurant, Sean was walking in the opposite direction, looking to catch a ride with someone who followed the team.

Erman pointed Sean toward the bus. "Be a part of the team for once, will you?" he snapped.

Sean hung up on Clemson and dutifully climbed aboard. He was still feeling the effects of the weekend bug, but wasn't planning to tell Hurley about it. Otis had thrown up in school, sick himself, but there was no way he was sitting out this game. Since returning after he broke his foot against Our Savior, he had continued to struggle. He was nowhere near the player who won the MVP in the San Diego tournament. The shooting guard position, once the deepest on the team, had become suspect.

"Damn," Sean would say on the drive over, "I'm nervous about today."

At Rosie Radigan's, whose owner, Rich McKeever, was a friend of Hurley's, Sean watched his teammates heap mounds of pasta and salad onto their plates. Before every home game, they had dinner there. But like his coach, Sean was too tense to eat. He kept his eyes on the mounted television in the corner, watching his favorite college basketball star, Marquette's Travis Diener, play in the Conference USA tournament.

After the team finished eating dinner, McKeever carried out a small chocolate cake with a lighted candle plopped on top. Erman had tipped him off that it was Beanie's birthday—his eighteenth—and soon everyone was singing "Happy Birthday" to him.

"Hey, Mosby," Sean yelled across the table, doing his best Hurley impression. "You're eighteen now. Let's go in the locker room."

Beanie laughed and puffed out his bony chest.

"I ain't afraid of him," Beanie boasted. "We're gonna fight."

"Make a wish," McKeever said. Only it was too late.

Beanie had already blown out his candle.

IN A SMALL training room in the basement of the Yanitelli Center at St. Peter's, Doc twisted and twirled the tape around the ankles of several St. Anthony players. Out of the corner of his eye, Doc would insist, he noticed the Paterson Catholic trainer stealing a peek at his genius. With this being such a big game and all, Doc was determined to do his part by refusing to reveal one of the secrets of St. Anthony's success.

"I didn't do anything fancy with the tape jobs," Doc would brag later. "None of the good shit until the guy was gone, anyway."

After all, this was the game. This was the de facto Parochial B state title. This was where, against St. Pat's a year earlier, so much seemed to unravel for the Friars. Obie Nwadike, the six-foot-four senior captain, had been hurt, Beanie had blown up, and Derrick was still too young to run the team. All that, and St. Anthony still had a one-point lead with a little over a minute left in that loss.

All along, Gamble and Pushie had insisted there would come a game in March when the team would lean on Lamar, when he could be the difference between winning and losing. With Sean and Otis sick and struggling, this night would be his redemption.

"This is the reason I came to your house that Sunday morning," Gamble told Lamar in a private moment. "Don't let me down."

Lamar nodded. He knew. He knew Ben Gamble, a Jersey City kid himself once, had the most to do with his second chance. He knew Gamble had gone to the wall for him. They needed everybody for Paterson Catholic, a 21-4 team built around two six-foot-seven twin sophomores named Jerrell and Terrell Williams, the kind of long, fluid athletes who promised to present problems for St. Anthony. They could pass over the pressure and do damage on the boards.

For many years, Paterson Catholic had always been one of the major obstacles on the way to the state title. They were forever stocked with major college prospects, but never had the coaching to compete with Hurley.

In 1995 and 1996, Paterson Catholic had the number-one-rated player in the country, six-foot-ten, 240-pound Tim Thomas, who would go on to play one year at Villanova before becoming a lottery pick in the 1997 NBA Draft. Even with talented teammates surrounding him destined for UConn (Kevin Freeman) and the University of Virginia (Donald Hand), Hurley's swarming, pressure defense had frustrated Thomas no end. In St. Anthony's unbeaten national championship season of 1996, when they ended Paterson Catholic's eighteen-game winning streak, Thomas had missed fifteen of twenty-four shots and never managed a dunk on the Friars.

On the eve of this game, Hurley had told his players, "All the older guys, this game is part of being able to get off the hook, part of being able to have an identity in the school. If you don't win, what will simply happen is that Paterson Catholic will soar up the state rankings. Seton Hall Prep will become number one in New Jersey. We will have had a great year and then we'll just drop like a bad stock. People will forget about us.

"Is that pressure? Yes, it is. But every time you play this time of year, there's pressure. How do you respond to pressure? [By doing the] little things in the game the coaches have talked to you about."

In the moments before taking to the floor, there were no ominous overtones, just a message of belief. St. Anthony was the better team, Hurley told them. "We built this schedule so we would have nothing but tough games to prepare us for this."

He wouldn't want to play all those talented young Paterson Catholic players next season, but this wasn't next season. This was St. Anthony's season. This was now.

"Keep the heat on them," he said in the locker room. "Get out there and get warm. Get yourself sweaty like a boxer. Let's see if we can knock them out in the first round. But if it's a long game, our bench and our conditioning is going to get us there."

Hurley had wanted the Friars to deliver the knockout punch on Paterson Catholic, and his players did the damnedest to deliver it. Off the opening tap, the Friars came out just like the worst of what the Elizabeth coach feared—the young Mike Tyson—climbing all over Paterson Catholic. Right away, the three-quarter-court trap found its first victim, with Derrick and Sean smothering point guard Nick Eaton into a panicked pass out-of-bounds. Moments later, Derrick stripped Eaton near mid-court, instantly throwing the ball down the floor to Sean for a layup.

Marcus reached around one of the Williams twins under the basket, stealing a pass and going end-to-end for another basket. Shelton Gibbs hit a baseline jump shot. Paterson Catholic couldn't get into its half-court offense, with the Friars closing and locking down everywhere on the floor. Paterson was wobbly, its eyes wide like quarters. Before they could break a sweat in the Parochial B North championship game, they were down 12–0 to St. Anthony. Most of the 2,000 fans were standing and screaming on the wooden bleachers in the Yanitelli Center, making the surroundings even more intimidating.

They were on the brink of getting blown out of the gym, out of the season. Maybe they were a year away. And maybe they had just been destined to end the season at the hands of Hurley, just as five past Paterson Catholic teams had done against St. Anthony. All year, it had been so easy for the Friars. They had hit good teams with fast and furious combinations to the body, leaving them dazed and prone on the court, and now they were beginning the destruction of Paterson Catholic.

Paterson Catholic was too talented to let that happen. They gathered themselves, began getting the ball inside to the Williams twins and did damage that way to St. Anthony. What started St. Anthony sputtering, and allowed Paterson Catholic to score nine of the next eleven points, centered on what had become a recurring theme for the Friars: the fragile psyche of Sean McCurdy.

He looked like a kid begging for an ulcer, his face flushed with angst. Part of it, surely, was the cold he couldn't push past all week. His entire disposition translated into hesitancy and uncertainty, something he couldn't afford in the fever-pitch speed and magnitude of this game. Early in the second quarter, Sean was called twice for traveling. Then he missed a three-pointer badly. Every time the ball touched his hands, everyone on the St. Anthony sideline held their breath, except Hurley.

"Relax, Sean," Hurley yelled to him. "Relax."

He had only wished it was so simple. Soon, Sean had the ball on the fast break, with teammates on the wings for the makings of an easy basket. But he was too frazzled. He sent it sailing out-of-bounds.

Sean was a mess, and time had run out to let him play through it. Hurley had no choice. With a little over six minutes left in the second quarter, Sean was finished for the rest of the half. Lamar checked into the game.

St. Anthony had Paterson Catholic on the ropes, but they hadn't taken them out. They were too talented to let hang around in this game, Hurley

feared. The last thing in the world he wanted to give that young team was
a sense that they belonged in the game, that maybe they could steal it. With
a 27–17 lead closing on a minute until halftime, with six-foot-seven Jerrell
Williams back on defense, Beanie's body shimmied to the right, and sens-
ing the defender committing the wrong way, he delivered a good old-
fashioned playground juke—purely instinctive to the moment, borne out
of brimming confidence. It got Williams going the wrong way, and Beanie
snapped a quick pass to a cutting Lamar for a lefty layup with sixteen seconds remaining.

After Paterson Catholic rushed down the floor and missed, Beanie was
on the break again, his eyes searching for the hot hand running with him.
He found Lamar again with a perfect pass to his left and his sweet lefty
stroke banked the ball into the basket to make it 31–17. Who would've
believed that the season could come down to Lamar Alston bailing out the
Friars?

Ben Gamble did, for one.

As the Friars hustled downstairs to the locker room, relieved that they
had created some distance with Paterson Catholic, Bob McCurdy marched
across the floor to find his ex-wife, Cindy, in the bleachers. His frustrations
could be understood on some level. He had been traveling back and forth
on flights for business that week, waking at 4:30 for the commute to New
York and later in Jersey for Sean's games. He had grown increasingly frustrated with the severity of Hurley's style toward his son. And now seeing
Sean sitting on the bench left him seething.

According to her, when he reached Cindy in the stands, he said, "Do
you think that I'm going to give you that money so that Sean can sit on the
bench here?" Before the end of the night, her ex-husband had her so flustered, she would say later, that she told herself, "We're leaving tonight and
never coming back."

As far as Bob McCurdy was concerned, she wouldn't be bringing Sean
out to Indiana for his senior season. As he had promised, Bill Shepherd
raised the possibility of Sean playing for a third high school in four years at
Muncie Central. Already, Sean had told his mother there was "No way I'm
leaving Coach Hurley," but she didn't discourage her brother from making
the call to her ex-husband.

To no one's surprise, the idea wasn't well-received with him.

"Not in a million years," Bob McCurdy would say later. "This is
insane. It's not like he's LeBron James or Kareem Abdul-Jabbar. He's got

the greatest coach in the world here. There's no way I would allow him to move to Indiana. I would absolutely stand in the way of that."

As long as Cindy and Sean stayed in Jersey City, the issue of financing the dual households was a growing source of trouble. She estimated that the cost of three years in New Jersey would reach $150,000. Her credit cards were maxed out. She was struggling to meet her $2,900-a-month rent in the high-rise condo and the cost of maintaining the house on the golf course in Milford.

As Sean stayed on the bench for longer stretches in the game, she raged against a season that had turned all wrong for her son. This wasn't part of the plan. As she would tell people throughout the year in fits of frustration, and would be heard saying again, "I'll pull my son right out of here."

If she didn't mean to put pressure on Sean, it was increasingly difficult to believe that that wasn't the end result. To Sean, his every misstep on the floor felt like a betrayal of his mother's mission to use St. Anthony as a stepping-stone to the bright lights of big-time college basketball. The burden was consuming him. There were some games where his eyes darted from his mother on one side of the gym, to his father on the other, to Bob Hurley on the bench. Around the program, the coaches and parents could see it. Everyone felt for him.

Sean started the third quarter, but Hurley brought him back to the bench when he was called for an illegal screen a minute and a half in. He gave him a second chance a minute later, when St. Anthony had its biggest lead of the game, 37–21, but as Paterson Catholic started to make its move Sean just looked lost. Hurley turned to Lamar again, and this time, stayed with him.

In the stands, Cindy was furious, but her son clearly could no longer function on the floor. As Hurley would never lose sight of, this state tournament game wasn't for the McCurdys. It wasn't to impress the recruiters from Indiana and Notre Dame and Georgia Tech. It wasn't for Sean's scoring average. Whatever hysterics the McCurdys' move had brought to Jersey City, they had to understand: This was about St. Anthony basketball, and that meant it was about winning.

And winning the game would soon be in real peril. Marcus picked up his third foul with 2:23 left in the third quarter, and his fourth eight seconds later. He had to sit. Barney had gone to the bench with his third foul, too. Suddenly, everything was shaky. Paterson Catholic slowly climbed back as the Friars' two best inside players sat on the bench. Eaton hit a gorgeous floater over the outstretched arms of Ahmad Nivins, and it was 44–38 after three quarters.

This was the whole season right now. Here was Paterson Catholic, out of nowhere, feeling like it had nothing to lose and pushing St. Anthony to the limit. Somewhere, St. Anthony had to make a stand. With seven minutes left in the game, Paterson Catholic's Jonathan Moody drilled a three-pointer to bring them within four points, and now Hurley had to turn his season over to the player he trusted the least, Lamar Alston.

About twenty rows up in the stands, Joe Boccia aimed the family video camera down to the floor as Lamar dribbled with complete confidence and control, working his way through the Paterson Catholic defense and delivering a perfect pass to Beanie for a layup. With Marcus in foul trouble and Otis still bringing little to the floor, it was the two outsiders, Lamar and Beanie, the two kids whom Hurley once would've never brought back, playing a two-man game to hold the season together. They knew each other's moves like they did the stops on the Jersey City bus line, able to anticipate where the other was going an instant before he did.

Moments later, Beanie beat his man on the dribble, getting fouled and earning a trip to the free-throw line. Unlike the end of that St. Raymond's game, there was no hesitation. He grabbed the ball, bounced it twice and swished the free throw. And then the second. This was the poise that Hurley had preached for so long. In the most important interlude of the season, everyone could see the calm washing over Beanie.

The kid had faced his demons, and for now, he had his peace.

Marcus had come back into the game with four fouls, Hurley trusting him to stay out of harm's way for a fifth that would've ended his night—and possibly his high school career. With a little over five minutes left, and St. Anthony clinging to a five-point lead, Marcus, the best defensive player on the best defensive team in the state, would steal the ball out of Jerrell Williams's hands and hit Derrick on the move. From across the floor, Derrick fired a hard bounce pass to Barney, who twisted his body in the air, absorbed a Paterson Catholic foul, and muscled his shot into the basket. He would miss the free throw, but St. Anthony had a 53–44 lead with 4:45 left. They had some breathing room.

In the end, they would hold on for a 65–54 victory.

Afterward, Hurley was the most relieved man in the locker room. This was March, Paterson Catholic had won twenty-one games, and deep down, he was glad that the Friars had been tested. "All I can say is that we survived. We survived," he told the team. "If you're going to brag about this one, you don't understand the difference between how you play, and winning and losing."

He turned to Sean, who was hunched on the edge of the locker-room bench, staring back hollowly at his coach.

"Sean," Hurley said, calmly, "I don't know if it's having been out with the ankle injury. Or being sick. Or just being completely out of it. You have to be able to develop poise in your life—an inner peace. When everything is going on in the gym, you can just get rid of it all. And just be playing, and hearing your teammates' voices. And your coach's voice.

"For you and Otis, why am I finding out now that you were sick? This isn't the NBA. If you're sick, maybe you shouldn't have played. We don't have to play sick people here.

"It's already under forty-eight hours to the state championship game—Saturday at noon. All the kids who are seniors: This is the game for you all."

Hurley started for the locker-room door to meet the reporters waiting outside, turning back before leaving with a final thought.

"Enjoy it."

Eventually, Sean would trudge gloomily out of the locker room. With Sean on the bench, his father had left the gym before the game's end. Chris Hurley walked over to Sean, trying to comfort him.

"You're going to be OK," she said.

St. Anthony had reached the Parochial B state championship game on Saturday, but it seemed to be of little consequence to a McCurdy family in crisis. They couldn't share in the joy that Derrick Mercer Sr. and Shelton Gibbs Sr. felt watching their sons chase a state championship for storied St. Anthony, a joy the fathers understood was independent of however the kids shot the ball that night, or how long they were in the game. In Jersey City, no one sent his kid to play for Hurley believing the reward would come with shots and scoring—you could send your kid anywhere to get that—but rather learning to win together, learning to be a man. Finally, Cindy McCurdy was beginning to understand what she had gotten into with Bob Hurley, but then again, so was he with her. For everyone, it was a bold new world.

"Sean is not happy," Cindy shot back at the reassuring words the coach's wife had offered her son. "He is *not* happy."

This wasn't part of Cindy McCurdy's master plan, and one thing was for certain: In the aftermath of St. Anthony's biggest victory of the season, no one was as joyless as she.

CHAPTER 22

HIS ARMS FOLDED, dreads flowing to his shoulders, Greg Bracey leaned back against the side gym wall and watched Hurley drill the offense on snapping passes to teammates. Bracey had been a conditioning coach for two of the best high school coaches in Connecticut history, Vito Montelli of St. Joseph's of Trumbull and Charles Bentley at Warren Harding of Bridgeport. They were disciplinarians in the mold of Hurley, and Bracey understood the species, the method behind the madness, and had lost track of the hours he had spent trying to explain it all to Cindy McCurdy. Trust the track record, he told her. Trust why you brought Sean to St. Anthony in the first place.

After returning home from the Paterson Catholic game a night earlier, Bracey had gotten Cindy's blow-by-blow account of the family's meltdown over Sean's benching. Bracey stayed with Cindy and Sean several days a week, commuting to Jersey City from Connecticut. He devoted significant time working Sean out in the gym, the weight room, and running him on the Connecticut beaches.

Bracey now rolled his eyes, shook his head and wondered when the pressure would be throttled back on Sean, when it would ease up.

"Sean is still young," he said. "He's still learning. So what the hell are the expectations? His team is number two in the nation and he's being recruited by the top schools in the country. What the hell do they want from him?"

Bracey nodded over to Hurley on the floor, saying with a wry smile, "There's a lot of pressure in this gym—if you haven't noticed. And all it's about is getting these kids to handle the pressure.

"But last night, his parents saw what happened with him as a punishment. And they take it personal. It ain't personal. St. Anthony is an attitude. Don't think that the other kids don't catch the same hell Sean catches when they have problems—and maybe more.

"None of these kids have been pampered. In Marcus's life, he's a family man. Lamar has his issues. Barney has the girls. They're not thinking about basketball when they leave this gym. It's what Sean goes home with twenty-four hours a day. And Sean has never really learned to manage his emotions.

"Everything in that family is basketball," Bracey said. "Everything. Last night, he wasn't in synch. He was taking NyQuil, and it was having an effect on him. Just accept that. Don't start pointing fingers at the man. That's what [Cindy] doesn't understand. I don't want to hear from her like last night, 'I didn't bring my son all the way down here, spend all this money, for him to sit on some bench. I'll take him right out of here.'

"First of all, where are you taking him? And second of all, you're too emotional. You don't see it for what it's worth. The father is emotional. He doesn't see it for what it's worth. The kid is having a bad game. Why embarrass him? The kid is sitting. He'll be stronger for it. If you notice, one game to another it's been one or two players. It's always been someone different. All except Marcus, because he's the rock. Everybody else has been up and down.

"Coach Hurley looks out for Sean and she doesn't see that. He is going to look after him, makes sure he gets to the best school."

"The bottom line is this: He would've never gotten the looks he's gotten from college coaches if he hadn't come to St. Anthony—no matter what he did in Connecticut. They should be thanking him."

And with that, Bracey pursed his lips, shook his head and turned his gaze back to Hurley on the practice floor. St. Anthony prepared for St. Rose of Belmar, the Parochial B South winner over Wildwood Catholic. They would meet at the Ritacco Center in Toms River, a new facility set to host four of Saturday's six state championship games. Those six winners would be seeded for the Tournament of Champions on Sunday, with the top two seeds getting byes in the first round.

A new day had done little to soothe Sean's state of mind. After another missed shot on the practice floor, his shoulders slouched, his face flummoxed with that familiar look. Sean was struggling to see the broader basketball picture, especially during the state tournament, a time of the year when everyone's sense for doing a little of everything on the court had to be heightened.

Hurley blew his whistle, grabbed the ball and stopped everything. He had tired of the Sean McCurdy soap opera. He had lost his patience.

"When my shot isn't falling, I can go to the offensive boards," Hurley said, stepping toward Sean. "I can defensive rebound. I can set good screens. I don't have to say, 'Oh shit, my shot isn't falling.' Know what that's about? Immaturity. There are a lot of things involved in basketball. It's not going to be just about whether Sean's making his jump shot.

"Do you think I give a shit about whether Sean is making his jump shot?" he asked. "NO!"

"Five things in basketball: Rebound. Defend. Dribble. Pass. And shoot. Five things. If one doesn't work, try the other four. I'm tired of this baby shit, '*Oh, my shot isn't falling.*'

"FUCK YOU AND YOUR SHOT!

"Do you got it?

"DO YOU GOT IT?"

Sean nodded. Yes, he got it. And he was getting it from everywhere now. In a private moment after practice, Hurley considered the contrast of his junior backcourt, Sean and Derrick. For now, they were going in different directions. The more Derrick became comfortable running the team, the more Sean looked like a lost soul.

"The recruiting has been something that's made Derrick feel good about himself," Hurley would say after practice. "Having Monmouth say they're going to offer him a scholarship has been great for his confidence. As for Sean, he puts such pressure on himself instead of just listening to us and just relaxing and playing. We've had a million kids recruited. This is not the time to worry about that stuff. You worry about that stuff during the month of July. That's when the colleges are going to make decisions about you. This is not the time.

"The difference between them? It's a Jersey City thing. I've known Derrick Sr. since he was a high school player himself. There's a trust there. There's an understanding that this is all going to work out, because it's all worked out here for years."

JUST BEFORE HURLEY left his office for practice on Friday, less than twenty-four hours before the Parochial B title game in Toms River, he called Judge Thomas Olivieri's office at Superior Court. The judge's secretary answered, telling Hurley the judge was sitting on the bench.

"I just wanted to tell him the kid who had gone through his court, Hank Rivers, is going to school now and playing today at 4:30 on ESPN," Hurley said. "I just wanted the judge to know that."

The secretary told him he would love to hear that news, because the judge and she had just been lamenting the rash of repeat names in the newspaper lately who were all in trouble again.

Ordinarily, Hurley didn't do reclamation projects. He wouldn't take kids with rap sheets. "But this was different," Hurley says. "This was the Rivers family."

The Riverses were St. Anthony royalty. Hank was the nephew of David Rivers, the All-America for Hurley in the class of 1984, who went on to become the all-time assist leader at the University of Notre Dame and a first-round pick of the Los Angeles Lakers. His story had a lot to do with the introduction of St. Anthony High School to the nation. His father, Willie, kept two jobs, working as an exterminator and a chandelier hanger. Mamie Rivers, his mother, was a hotel maid. Together, the Riverses raised fourteen children, including David, a wizard of a six-foot point guard out of the Lafayette section of Jersey City. The short, narrow outdoor court on Virginia Avenue was famous for producing great ball handlers, because the young kids growing up there were forced to learn how to get through tight spaces and get to the basket. Hurley still tells the stories of David running three miles in the pouring rain to the Eagle—too poor to pay the bus fare, and too proud to ask his coach for a ride.

Between his sophomore and junior seasons at Notre Dame, where he had developed into one of the best players in the country, David was thrown through the windshield of a van and into a ditch on a rural Indiana road. After nearly bleeding to death, doctors saved him on the operating table. Still, he was running within weeks and back on the court for the Fighting Irish. At thirty-eight years old today, he still plays professionally in Europe and has had several successful business ventures in the States.

A younger brother, Jermaine, had been destined for stardom at St. Anthony, too. Then, he started getting horrendous headaches late in 1987, his sophomore year of high school. They wouldn't go away. They took him to the doctors, worked him over with tests and discovered a massive, inoperable brain tumor.

Time would be short for Jermaine, so Hurley helped raise the money to fly him to South Bend to surprise his brother at college. When Jermaine was wheeled into practice, the whole gym stopped. Once David turned to see who had stolen everyone's attention, there was his little brother. His head had swollen so large that David could barely recognize the kid smiling back at him. He dropped his basketball, rushed across the gym and squeezed Jermaine in a long, tearful hug.

Eighteen months after his diagnosis, Jermaine Rivers died. He was seventeen years old.

With the Rivers family holding such a special place in Hurley's heart, he felt compelled in 1998 to reach out to the troubled Hank Rivers. He had been running with a gang calling itself NFP—Niggers From the Park—and well before his eighteenth birthday, he had been busted for everything, from peddling drugs, to guns, to stealing cars. He was sent away for the first time at fourteen years old. He was entrenched in two of the hard-core drug pockets in Jersey City: Arlington Park and Stegman Avenue.

After sitting down with the Rivers family, Hurley stepped between Hank and an eighteen-month sentence for car theft, telling the judge, "Give me a shot with him." If Bob Hurley believed he could salvage the kid, the Hudson County courts were glad to spare the space in the juvenile detention center at Jamesburg. The judge agreed to suspend the sentence and Hank started classes at St. Anthony with a promise.

"If you mess up one more time," Hurley told him, "I'll have to let you go."

When Hank Rivers had arrived at St. Anthony for the second semester of his sophomore year in 1998, Hurley let him work out with the team. First, he had to prove his staying power in the classroom and community. He wouldn't get a uniform until his junior year.

Often, they worked one-on-one in the gym, Hurley flooding Rivers with the fundamentals of basketball and life. Hurley worked on his value system and character at the same time he worked on the six-foot-eight Rivers' low-post moves.

"He was trying to tell me about something bigger than Jersey City, instilling in my head that I didn't have to be stuck there for life," Rivers says now. "He always told me this, and it was true: The people you're hanging with aren't your friends, and they ain't gonna be there with you when you're locked up in a cell."

Under Hurley's watch, Rivers stopped hanging on the street corners. He stopped running with NFP. As a junior, he became the starting center for the Friars. Hurley gave him his own maroon-and-gold St. Anthony sweatsuit, and he wore it everywhere. These were his new gang colors, and ultimately, his lasting loyalty.

"For the first time in my life, being at St. Anthony, I felt a part of something major," he says. "When you play there, everybody in Jersey City knows you're doing something big. Real big. You don't need to go home at night and be a part of no gang. You've got family at St. Anthony. I felt like I was at home, like I didn't have to go hang on the corner."

As a senior, Hank had already turned nineteen years old, leaving him ineligible for high school basketball in New Jersey. Hurley sent him to New York to play with the Riverside Church team and, upon graduation, found him a scholarship to Southeast Community College in Nebraska. After earning his associate degree and averaging twenty points a game there, he earned a full ride to Stephen F. Austin University in Texas.

"When I come home from college now, it's like everybody is stuck," Rivers says. "Nobody is moving nowhere. I still see the same people, in the same spots, doing the same thing. It doesn't take long and I'm ready to go back again."

There were still days he woke up in his dormitory room, wondering how his life had wound its way to Nacogdoches, Texas, three hours east of Dallas, two and a half north of Houston, and a world away from Jersey City.

"If I never met Coach Hurley, I don't know where I'd be," he says. "Actually, I do know: either coming or going to prison. Or I'd be dead. He was the best thing to ever happen to me. He taught me a work ethic, taught me leadership, taught me to live your life the right way.

"I never thought this would be true, but I miss his screaming sometimes. Just to hear him say, 'Get your ass over here,' I miss that so much. I wish I could go back and play four years for St. Anthony. You leave there, and nobody ever pushes you in the same way again."

HURLEY WOULD TELL the team a snippet of the Hank Rivers story as they stretched for Friday afternoon's practice. He worked his way through a short, mostly mental preparation for the game with St. Rose of Belmar the next day for the Parochial B title. Afterward, with the players slouched against the back wall, he set the stage for the seniors' chance to finally be remembered as something more than what his preseason description had been: the worst class in school history.

If they played the right way, played together, they would beat St. Rose. Hurley didn't try to sell them on anything different. There were monumental challenges still waiting out there in the Tournament of Champions, but all along, he measured vindication for the seniors on the traditional Parochial B state title. The Tournament of Champions hadn't started until 1989, when the state high school association figured it was a way to capitalize on the popularity of the Bobby Hurley, Jerry Walker, and Terry Dehere St. Anthony machine. Now, the kids were the ones thinking past St. Rose, past Parochial B, and chasing that prize of perfection a week from Sunday in the 20,000-seat Meadowlands Arena.

"We started last year in April and May with cloth gloves on, dribbling around folding chairs," Hurley said. We did it for months. We got thrown out of White Eagle Hall for good on June 30th, and you started coming in here for open gym. We had already played the team camp at Rutgers. After traveling all over the place, we won the national tournament in Philadelphia. We played in the Jersey City Summer League. We went to summer camps. We've done a shitload of stuff. And it all put us where we are right now. Be the same as we are every day tomorrow.

"Go home and get ready for something that puts you in the history books," he told them. "Taste it tonight."

For the first time, Lamar Alston felt like a real part of the championship chase. He had played an immense role in the Paterson Catholic victory, his biggest step in the arduous process of giving Hurley a reason to count on him again. When Lamar had returned to the team in late January, Hurley had resisted playing him. The less the team counted on him, the coach had thought, the less chance he could have of letting everyone down. Through it all, Lamar stayed prepared, waiting for his opportunity. He had one of those jump shots that seemed like he could swish even when rolling out of bed in the morning. It was always with him. More than that, Lamar was the player nobody wanted guarding them in practice. He had those long arms, that strong, sturdy body.

Behind all that, he had perhaps the most fragile soul on the team. The biggest issue in his life—reconciling with his birth-father—was still a source of angst for him. "I've been trying to sit down and be the father in the relationship," Lamar would say. "If I don't talk to him, he won't speak." Along the way, he tried to realize that the man he had long been at odds with, his disciplinarian stepfather, Joe Boccia, had been there every step of the way in his life. Now, if nothing else, Lamar said, "I know who was there and who wasn't there."

For all his confusion about where he belonged in the world, and with whom, Lamar felt his greatest sense of belonging in this senior class, with Marcus, Beanie, Otis and Shelton. Those were his boys. He had started high school at Marist in Bayonne, but had found his way back to St. Anthony as a sophomore, back to the Boys Club crew that once set out to conquer the world.

After practice, Lamar talked in the hallway outside the gymnasium. "My opportunity came in that one night against Paterson Catholic," he said, a Cincinnati Reds cap pulled down tightly on his head. "And I was ready for it. The biggest thing is that I'm just happy to be back here. I'm a part of this again. All of us seniors, we been playing with each other, and against each other, since we were little kids. We went to nationals in AAU and came close to the championship. This will be the first time that we've accomplished something this big on our own: a state championship.

Lamar flashed a satisfied smile now, the kind that comes when you've wandered out of the woods and come into the clear.

"We ain't gonna stop with Parochial B, either. We're taking this thing all the way to the T.O.C. Because then, it'll mean that we're not the most messed-up senior class Coach Hurley has ever had."

Hurley hustled out of practice at a little after 5:00, rushing to a spot on a StairMaster in the ground floor fitness room of his high-rise. He turned the television to ESPN, finding the Stephen F. Austin versus University of Texas-San Antonio game for the Southland Conference's automatic NCAA tournament bid starting the second half. Hurley started climbing and locked his eyes on the six-foot-eight, 230-pound center for Stephen F. Austin, keeping his team in the game almost by himself.

Every year, there were so many twists and turns on the road to the Final Four, and Hurley, his aching knees churning, his breathing growing heavier, found himself thinking back to the whole, remarkable salvation of Hank Rivers. As he pumped his legs, he made a promise to himself: The way Rivers was playing, Hurley wasn't climbing off that machine until his kid fouled out, or won or lost the game. Around Hurley, in the exercise room, eyes kept darting to the soaked, grunting fifty-six-year-old man climbing a mountain on those steps. For forty-five minutes, it was like Hurley was alone with Hank Rivers again, back in White Eagle, laying out all the lessons that would give him the habits and the heart to chase a better life all the way to Nebraska, and to Texas, and now, to the cusp of carrying a college basketball team to the NCAA tournament.

There was a little over a minute left in the game when Hank Rivers grabbed a teammate's missed shot and powered the ball back into the basket only to be whistled for an offensive foul, his fifth and final of the game. That was the end of the season for Stephen F. Austin University, a 74–70 loss, and Bob Hurley finally slowed the StairMaster to a stop. No one in the room could tell if that was simply sweat streaming down his cheeks, or perhaps, the tears of a proud old coach.

★ ★ ★

BLUEBIRD BUS NO. 5404 rumbled outside the front doors of St. Anthony, its engine spitting and moaning a little after nine in the morning on a clear blue Jersey City Saturday March morning. Marcus Williams peered out from his customary seat in the back row and locked a steely glare on Qaysir Woods.

"Take your do-rag off," Marcus commanded.

Three rows ahead, Qaysir acted like he didn't hear the order. For a moment, he kept staring straight ahead, figuring that Marcus wouldn't stay after him.

"*Right now,*" Marcus said, slowly spitting out the words to suggest that he wouldn't be asking a third time.

Qaysir glanced back to see a stone-faced Marcus burning his eyes into him, and without a word, he quickly reached up, ripped the rag off and shoved it into his gym bag. Whatever had happened these past four years, whatever everyone had expected Marcus to be and whatever he had done or failed to do, he was now in the stretch drive of completing an unassailable legacy of winning. With a chance for his third Parochial B title in four years, and maybe his third Tournament of Champions, Marcus was locked into his leadership role. Nobody else on the bus had ever been a part of winning these kinds of championships, and he was determined to let nothing stand in the way.

All the way in the front, Gamble had a *Star-Ledger* opened to the preview of the game. That afternoon, St. Rose of Belmar, 23-4, from down the Shore, would try to do something no team in the state's history had ever done in seventeen tries: beat St. Anthony in a Parochial B title game. (St. Anthony's five other championships under Hurley had come in the early 1970s, when they played in the defunct Parochial C division.)

On the way to the Turnpike, the bus passed the Statue of Liberty, standing in all her majesty in the harbor. They were going downstate for the championship game Saturday morning, and hoped to work their way all the way back north again—Friday night for the T.O.C. Final Four at Rutgers University in Piscataway and Sunday, March 21, for the title game at the Meadowlands Arena in East Rutherford, just a couple of miles from Jersey City.

"If we take care of business today," Gamble said, "Coach will look at everything after Parochial B as gravy."

Then he laughed.

"Until tomorrow, anyway."

The Jersey Turnpike and Garden State Parkway would turn into a drive down memory lane from the basketball season, the signs for Elizabeth, Neptune, Asbury Park and Trenton blurring past on the sign posts. Behind them, three buses of St. Anthony teachers and students rolling toward Toms River accompanied the team for the game. Sister Felicia steered her car in the back of the pack, leaving Sister Alan back at the house. Sister Alan had gone for more tests on Friday, and they had knocked her out. There was a victory party set for The Astor Bar on Montgomery, a restaurant/bar owned by Margie Calabrese's family, and she was hoping to meet everyone there in the late afternoon. Assuming they beat St. Rose, of course.

The Ritacco Center was just like Hurley advertised: a sparkling new 5,000-seat arena connected to the affluent Toms River North High School. A state-of-the-art electronic scoreboard hung suspended over the court. On a far wall, there was a video board offering in-game replays. Hurley herded his players into a bright, spacious locker room with a blue floor and a big, wide chalkboard.

In the arena, St. Peter's College assistant coach John Coffino climbed a few rows up behind the St. Anthony bench. He wondered whether anyone had seen Boccia, Lamar's stepfather, who usually perched high in the stands videotaping the games. Lamar had a meeting scheduled for the Monday after the T.O.C. title game, with Bob Leckie, the head coach. The St. Peter's coaches had been encouraged by Lamar's progress. They always knew he was talented enough, but had wanted to monitor how Lamar handled the second chance Hurley had given him.

Near mid-court, Cindy McCurdy studied Sean closely in warm-ups. Now feeling healthier, Sean was determined to push past the drama that had surrounded the Paterson Catholic game. Because St. Rose didn't have the athleticism and quickness to pressure St. Anthony's guards, Hurley and his coaches were hopeful this opponent would be a good opportunity for Sean to restore some confidence. Early in the game, Hurley was committed to running some plays designed to get Sean some easy, open shots.

"We've got to get Sean going again," Cindy said, nodding toward her son on the court. "I'm not trying to put too much pressure on him, but I told him, 'If you play like that, I can't afford to live down here.'"

She laughed uneasily, trying to diffuse the harshness of her words. When asked about the source of the burden on her son that seemed to mushroom as the season wore on, Cindy wondered whether she had done a good enough job of shielding him from what she said had become her mounting financial struggle of living in Jersey City. Soon she came to an entirely different conclusion about what had happened to Sean against Paterson Catholic at the Yanitelli Center two nights earlier.

"I think it's the gym over at St. Peter's. Even last year, Sean has never played well there.

A few feet away, Hurley had been impatiently biding his time on the St. Anthony sideline, counting down the final minutes until he would return to the locker room with his players and give his final instructions and thoughts. Before then, like always, Hurley studied the opposing players in warm-ups. His routine was to double-check the scouting report against what his own eyes told him, watching who made and missed shots, who looked confident and who didn't. Just trying to pick up something, anything, near game-time.

Quietly, an elderly man stood between the bottom row of the bleachers and the backs of the folding chairs on the St. Anthony sideline. He waited without a word. Waiting for Hurley to notice him.

Almost always, this was a time Hurley never wanted to be bothered, his mind completely immersed in the moment. He had arrived in Toms River a little harried, having spent his morning at a budget meeting of Jersey City municipal department heads, taking his turn to make a presentation to the mayor about Recreation. It wasn't until 10:00 that he left, and the way her husband had sped down the Garden State Parkway, Chris was privately preparing an impassioned plea for the state trooper she was sure would pull them over. He made the trip in an hour—terrific time, really.

Despite all that, when Hurley glanced up to see the man standing behind the bench, his trance was instantly vanquished.

Hurley's eyes lit up, and he reached quickly to embrace George Newcombe, the man responsible for giving him his first coaching job in 1966. An old fireman out of Greenville, Newcombe was the one who asked Brian Hurley, a member of his St. Paul's Parish grammar-school team, to ask Bob if he had any interest in taking over for him. Now Hurley was on the cusp of coaching a basketball game that could give St. Anthony twenty-four state titles in its history—twenty-two on his watch—a total that would tie the national record with Cheyenne, Wyoming. And a man he hadn't seen in more than a decade, who had retired and moved out of Jersey City years before, had come to watch Bob Hurley chasing in 2004 what he had first caught in the winter of '66–'67: a championship season.

"That was thirty-eight years ago," Hurley marveled to Newcombe.

"God, Bob, it's good to see you," he said, gripping tightly to Hurley's handshake now.

They talked for a moment, promising to catch up when the game was over.

Hurley was shaking his head on the walk to address the players waiting for him in the locker room. Thirty-eight years and Bob Hurley had never lost his love for that moment in the locker room with his boys, the unspoken bond of months and years of shared sacrifice and devotion. He had done it so many times, come to the crossroads of so many championship games, and maybe most fulfilling was how each time it felt for Hurley like the first time. Because for the players in the locker room, it often was the first time.

Hurley gave them his final pregame instructions. They knew everything St. Rose did. They were prepared. Ultimately, this game wasn't about stopping St. Rose, it was about just being St. Anthony. .

Now his players were sitting in three rows of folding chairs, feet tapping on the floor, necks rolling back on shoulders to stay loose.

"Yesterday, I was watching Hank Rivers play in the championship game to go to the NCAA tournament. I got on the StairMaster and I had to stay on there until he either fouled out or the game ended. And I was still on the thing when he fouled out, because I was so proud of what he did.

"We kick you in the ass all the time because we want to see you do well," he continued. "And this is one of those opportunities now."

After punctuating the prayer with a thundering cheer—"One, two, three, HARD WORK!"—the players hopped and hollered, moving eagerly toward the door.

Hurley unwrapped a stick of gum, folded it into his mouth and started trailing his assistants toward the floor.

"Hey, Coach," Doc said, sidling over to him. "Did you hear we beat Delbarton in hockey last night?"

What?

Hurley had a glazed, befuddled look in his eyes, because on the way to the floor for the Parochial B state championship game, Doc couldn't possibly be telling him about St. Peter's Prep beating Delbarton in a hockey game.

Doc reached out to shake his hand, and Hurley obliged, congratulating his old trainer on the big hockey upset. Hurley understood that Doc Miller

had to be the only man alive who could've pulled that stunt, at that
moment, and left the coach laughing.

A FEW MINUTES into the game, up 7–0, Hurley called an out-of-bounds
play in which a screen on the baseline would seal Sean alone in the far corner. He'd receive a skip pass and shoot an uncontested three-pointer. The
setup worked perfectly. Sean caught the ball, letting loose with an arcing
shot that somehow hit the side of the backboard and bounced away.

Moments later, when St. Rose knocked the ball out-of-bounds again.
Hurley called the play again. Only, this time, it was for Otis. Once again,
the screen was set. The pass skipped over the St. Rose defense. With time
to gather himself and take the shot, Otis rose in perfect symmetry, letting
the ball roll off his fingertips at the apex of his leap. Just like Hurley taught
him.

The ball hit the side of the backboard and bounced out-of-bounds.

That hadn't happened twice in the season to St. Anthony, and now it
had happened on consecutive possessions. Nothing was going well for
them. The way St. Anthony struggled to turn St. Rose turnovers into easy
baskets, the way passes tipped off teammates' fingers, the way shots rattled
off rims, it was clear that St. Anthony had a case of the big-game jitters.

At the end of the first quarter, Otis couldn't hear the bench counting
down, causing him to dribble out the clock without a shot. That hadn't
happened all season, either. The Friars were winning, 17–12, but a loud St.
Rose cheering section, covering several regions of the stands, screamed
wildly. They were thrilled to still be in the game.

A little later, Otis had the ball on the break, dribbling down the left
side with a St. Rose defender closing the angle on him and the basket. He
still hadn't recovered his lift, his explosion, since coming back from the
injury. In a lot of ways, Otis was a shell of his old self. He had struggled to
get back into shape. On this drive to the rim, he should've kept dribbling
hard down the left side and gone straight up for the rim with his left hand.
He didn't. In taking the ball under the basket, and trying to come back out
on the right for a reverse layup, his body became discombobulated, and he
missed the shot badly. St. Rose grabbed the rebound and passed the ball
down the floor. There, Sean Mullin, the nephew of the great St. John's and
NBA star Chris Mullin, hit a three-pointer to bring St. Rose within two,
19–17.

Hurley called a timeout. And the Ritacco Center exploded with cheers, most of the several thousand there wondering just how long St. Rose could hang on in this game.

Hurley snapped at Otis as he walked past. "SHOOT THE LEFTY LAYUP!"

Enough was enough, Hurley told them. Enough of the nerves, the uneasiness—it was time to play now. The longer they let St. Rose stay packed in that zone defense, the longer they let them run those methodical half-court plays on offense, the more dangerous this game could get for St. Anthony. They needed to turn up the heat, and turn it up now.

When play resumed, Beanie beat a St. Rose dribbler to position on the baseline, absorbing an offensive charge. Then, Marcus made a three-pointer. Lamar popped one, too. Sean scooped up a loose ball in the back-court, and passed ahead to Lamar for another basket. Then, Sean hit a long three-pointer. It was 30–19, and Hurley said to Gamble on the bench that St. Rose "can't play the way they want down double [figures]." Sooner or later, he knew, they had to stop running those long, patient offensive sets, and come out of that passive zone and challenge St. Anthony man-to-man. They had to make the game faster for a chance to get back into it. But by trying to speed the game up with inferior athletes, they would only be inviting a worse beating.

Everybody was making plays for St. Anthony now. Marcus grabbed a rebound away from two defenders and laid the ball back into the basket. Derrick made a steal and scored on a layup. Sean beat his man to the bas-ket, and banked the ball home. And with six seconds left in the half, Mar-cus hit another three-pointer. It was 41–19 going into halftime, with the Friars closing out the final five minutes on a furious run. They had outscored St. Rose 22–2 after Hurley's timeout.

Back in the locker room, Hurley began with a simple question:

"Who can honestly tell me they struggled in the beginning of the game because they were too nervous?"

In the three rows of folding chairs facing him, several hands fired into the air. Otis. Sean. Marcus. Derrick. Almost everyone.

Hurley laughed.

"Sports are amazing," he said.

St. Anthony would defeat St. Rose 74–38 for the Parochial B state championship, the twenty-fourth in school history and the twenty-second with Bob Hurley as coach. Marcus had scored twenty-two points to earn the MVP of the game, and when it came time to accept the championship trophy in the middle of the floor, the state high school officials asked for a St. Anthony senior to come and get it.

That wouldn't do, Hurley thought. That wouldn't do at all.

"The five seniors," Hurley said, waving his hand toward center court. "Go and get it."

So Marcus, Beanie, Otis, Shelton and Lamar would stand side by side for the trophy presentation and then stay out there to pose for pictures. Beanie held the trophy in his hands, held it high in the air, and the cheers came tumbling down out of the stands. Marcus hugged Lamar, and Shelton slapped Otis's hand, and together they laughed and smiled in the middle of the arena.

Through it all, though, there was no leaping around and celebrating, no sense that this was the end of the road. Hurley may have measured a successful season with a Parochial B state championship, but no one else was buying it. Maybe this victory got them off the hook with Hurley, but not with themselves. As Otis carried the trophy back to the locker room, he said, "We finally won something. But we ain't done yet. We ain't finished with this season."

Danny Hurley Jr., six years old, came running into the locker room, standing at his grandfather's side as he began to address the team.

"This has been as rewarding of a year as I've ever been involved with," Hurley told them.

All the smiles on his players suddenly turned serious, those words stopping everyone cold. The most rewarding year ever? Others had been telling Hurley something and now he had begun to believe it, too: He had probably gotten more out of this team than any other he had ever coached. This could've been the best coaching job he'd ever done, and as his son Danny said, "That's like trying to sit around and compare Jordan's fifty-point performances to each other."

It wasn't long until Hurley's eyes stopped on one of the seniors sitting on the floor, the missing face in the team photo working his way back into good graces. Hurley couldn't help but think of himself as a better man, a better coach, for allowing a lost kid like Lamar to find his way.

"Lamar came back to his senses, came back to basketball, and has a chance in his life to taste this," Hurley said.

Amazing, Lamar was thinking, how he had come back so far in the coach's eyes, that he was actually using his first name again. No more Alston.

He was Lamar again.

"He almost blew it," Hurley told the team, "but he came back and this will turn out to be something he'll remember the rest of his life."

Gamble and Pushie smiled. Lamar's success belonged to them, too.

"When I know that you guys are nervous about this, it tells me you're still kids," Hurley said. "And we want you all to be just kids. Our season is going to continue. We're not done. But as far as our place in history, our seniors, we're in.

"We have a state championship."

There would be no practice on Sunday, but Hurley wanted the team dressed in the maroon St. Anthony sweatsuit and gathered at 12:30 in Lincoln Park on Kennedy Boulevard. Together, they would march through the streets of Jersey City in the St. Patrick's Day parade.

"We're going to walk all the way up to Journal Square and let everybody clap for us tomorrow," Hurley said. "The hair on my neck is standing up right now, because that's where we want to get our recognition: back in Jersey City. *USA Today* means nothing. We want to go back to the city. We want people to see this accomplishment. Jersey City loves to see some success, and quite often, we're the only success in the sports world."

They would practice again on Monday, Hurley told them, maybe scrimmage against a New York City team on Wednesday to stay sharp, because undoubtedly, as the top seed, they would have a bye in the quarterfinal round of the Tournament of Champions. St. Anthony would advance directly to the tournament Final Four at Rutgers next Friday, where the semifinal doubleheader usually packed the 9,000-seat arena. It was a wonderful atmosphere for high school basketball, and a tournament Hurley tried to treat like house money.

In the Parochial A North title game, Seton Hall Prep had struggled to beat Don Bosco Prep and would play St. Augustine of Vineland for the state championship that afternoon in Toms River. Seton Hall would lose that game, ending the speculation that Prep was on a collision course with St. Anthony. (After they had collided in that closed-door scrimmage, no one surrounding St. Anthony believed Prep was ever the same again.)

"But when is all of that?" Hurley said, dismissively waving his hand in the air about the Tournament of Champions. "That's forty-eight hours away from worrying about.

"Let's enjoy this."

Across the locker room, Hurley talked with reporters. Someone asked him where this team stacked up in St. Anthony history. They still had two

games left before a possible perfect season, so Hurley was hesitant to pre-
scribe a permanent place in lore for the team. But he did say, "I've never
had a team that from the beginning of the season to the end could will
things through with their defense. We've just been a remarkable defensive
team."

As Hurley worked his way into the hallway, accepting congratulations
along the way, he couldn't stop thinking about the opening moments of
the game, about how nervous his players had been, about how human they
all were. So much of what he taught his teams centered around poise, and
this team had almost always had it when it was needed. This was something
else, Saturday. When all his players' hands went up in that locker room at
halftime, the innocence of it all had touched Hurley in a surprising way.

In the corridor, Hurley visited with Danny and Monmouth assistant
Geoff Billet, telling them all about his players' halftime confession.

"We managed not to screw them up," Hurley said. "In this crazy
world that we're in, we managed to let them still be kids."

The team climbed back into the bus, driving back for a party at the
Astor, across from the Armory, on Montgomery Street. Hurley climbed
into the Camry with Chris, setting out on a far more leisurely drive home
than the scramble to get down for the game had been. She punched numbers into his cell, dialing up all the usual suspects before handing it over to
her husband so he could talk to them.

She called Bobby at Madison Square Garden, where he was scouting
the Big East Tournament for the 76ers. And then she dialed The Faa.

Hurley had clear driving on the Turnpike, a Mets spring-training game
on the radio and a sense of satisfaction about Lamar Alston.

"Ben and Tommy stuck their necks out on this one," Hurley told
Chris.

He knew that Lamar had the meeting scheduled with St. Peter's, but
wasn't convinced that was the best course for his future. "I'd like to get
him to a school up in New England, like a Stonehill or a Merrimack,"
Hurley said. "He could be a good Division II player up there. That's a
good league. Those are good schools. I don't know if St. Peter's is the best
place for him. He's one I'd like to get away from Jersey City."

After about an hour, the coach, forever sending his players out of Jersey City, made his way back there once again, turning off Exit 14C, crossing the Casciano Bridge and feeling the warm embrace of home as soon as
he could see the faded, green steeple of St. Paul's Parish—where, growing
up, he had attended Mass—rising over Greenville. Over at the Astor, Sister

Felicia, Sister Alan, The Faa and all the coaches, players and their families were waiting for Chris and him.

But in the quiet of his car, late on Saturday afternoon, Bob Hurley would take another look at that steeple and think about the neighborhood fireman who sent his little brother for him that day, asking Hurley to begin a coaching life on that snowy lot of the parish blacktop, a coaching life that could've taken him to the biggest and brightest stages in college basketball. He thought about it all, about all the people and places basketball had allowed him to see. All of it unforgettable, all of it beyond his wildest dreams.

But the best part of all, the best part *still,* was, wherever the game took him, wherever he left them all talking about his team, about the way Bob Hurley still coached those boys, he always found his way back home, back to Jersey City.

"Nineteen-sixty-six to 2004," he said softly, his eyes lingering on St. Paul's for a few moments. "Astounding."

They would all sit for hours at a long table that evening, ultimately leaving just the Hurleys, the Sisters and The Faa remembering old teams and old times. Hurley would even grab the back of an envelope and scribble that out-of-bounds play with Sean and Otis that he couldn't get over, wondering about "the genius coach who actually called for it a second time." They would all laugh, listening to Hurley dismiss the Tournament of Champions as just "something extra" they had to do after the Parochial B, because once Hurley brought the team down to the T.O.C. luncheon on Monday afternoon, got a look at all the other state champions and coaches obsessed with finding a way to beat St. Anthony, all that talk would go out the window. He'd be hell-bent on winning it all, always.

WHAT BEN GAMBLE wanted was to reach into the big, soft chair in the hotel lobby, grab the kid by his shirt collar and snap his ass awake. However tempting, he resisted the urge. Instead, he sharply snapped, "Lamar!"

Nothing.

"Lamar," Gamble barked, a little louder this time.

Still, nothing.

"LAMAR!"

With that, Lamar's head jerked, his eyes dizzily blinked open, and he finally stirred out of his slumber. Dragging himself to his feet, he clomped sluggishly across the lobby carpet, marching past the assistant coach's glare and into the banquet room for the Tournament of Champions luncheon. His shirt was untucked, his bushy hair unkempt, and Gamble warned him, "You'd better get yourself together. You're representing St. Anthony."

In Gamble's estimation, Lamar looked like someone "who had been out all night drinking and was trying to sleep it off." But he decided to spare Lamar a bigger problem, declining to disclose the scene to Hurley in the banquet room.

Hurley was already in a horrible mood, anyway. All the way down from Jersey City on the school bus, he had been seething over several players, including Marcus, his supposed leader, who had shown up dressed sloppily that morning, wearing sneakers instead of shoes. He sent Marcus home to change, with Derrick Mercer Sr. driving him to the luncheon.

Throughout the lunch program, Gamble had more cause for concern. Seeing Lamar like that made him wonder whether something was up, whether Sister Alan's warnings and his own private misgivings could yet come back to haunt the team.

Still, they weren't far from the finish line. In less than a week, the season would be over, and Gamble and Pushie would be in the clear for recommending Lamar's reinstatement. They were almost there.

Back in Jersey City on Monday afternoon, Hurley would run the team through a light practice. There was just one thing he needed to see. He couldn't help himself.

Hurley had everyone line up in the corner with a basketball, and one by one, take a shot. They were to aim for the side of the backboard.

No one hit it.

CHAPTER 23

WINTER HAD BLOWN back into northern Jersey, the warm, welcoming mid-March weather turning blustery once more. All the momentum of spring seemed to be blowing away in the swirling snow outside St. Anthony on the Eighth Street, another storm just when everyone had hoped the harshness was behind them.

The storm had inspired Hurley to change practice time, and near noon on Tuesday, March 16, he called Erman at school, instructing him to alert the players to the 3:15 start. Between the end of the seniors' eighth-period-less school day at 2:15 and the time the players needed to be dressed and on the practice floor, there would be little time for detours.

When Hurley arrived a little after 3:00, everyone was there but two seniors: Otis and Lamar. There was no issue with Otis. Still sick, he had been excused from school at midday and had gone home to bed. His virus had lingered for well over a week, and Hurley had grown frustrated that no one had seen fit to take him to the doctor. Finally, an appointment had been made for him to get checked out on Wednesday. At that point, no one could be sure of his status for Friday night's T.O.C. game at Rutgers, between the winner of Raritan and Haddonfield High School.

Lamar was a different story. When Erman told him of the change, Lamar suggested nothing that would've indicated a problem. Shortly into the start of practice, Gamble arrived from his shift at the prison, still needing to change out of the blue shirt and black pants of his corrections uniform. As he did that on the sideline, Hurley walked past him and said simply, "No Lamar."

Gamble looked up quickly, instinctively scanning the court to see for himself. Damn it. After that scene Monday at the luncheon, he knew something wasn't right.

All at once, Gamble felt equal parts embarrassed and angry. Despite all the levels that Gamble and Hurley's relationship had evolved over the years, and the fact that the coach considered his longtime assistant much more his peer than his pupil, Gamble still got a sinking feeling at that moment, the one that came over most of his players. That sense that he had let Hurley down.

Ultimately, it wasn't Gamble and Pushie who had let Lamar back on the team, but rather Hurley himself. No decisions affecting St. Anthony basketball were ever made without Hurley's blessing. He was on the line, just like his assistants. And everyone was feeling they had been burned.

That night, Gamble called Boccia. Although Erman had called the stepfather from practice trying to gather Lamar's whereabouts, Boccia still hadn't spoken with his son as of 8:30 that night, and like everyone else, he had reached the breaking point with Lamar.

"I'm giving up on him," he told Gamble. "Everybody stuck their neck out for Lamar and now he pulled this stunt."

Gamble just listened. There wasn't much left for him to say. They had been over this territory again and again. "You know what the deal is," Gamble told Boccia. "Coach has probably already made the decision that he's not going to play Friday."

Gamble wondered something else: "Do you know that he wasn't at practice last Tuesday? He went home from school, saying he was sick."

As far as the father knew, Lamar hadn't missed any practices. At least, practice was where he told him he had gone.

"He lied to both of us," Gamble said.

Gamble hung up with Boccia and called Hurley with the story.

There was no discussion.

"That's got to be it," Gamble said.

"He's done," Hurley decided.

The next morning, Lamar, one of St. Anthony's most repeatedly tardy students, arrived at school well before the homeroom bell, marching directly into the main office with the intent, he said, of calling Hurley to explain himself. He had a story. At that moment, Hurley was on the line with Margie Calabrese, telling her to pass along a message to Lamar. The coach wanted back his uniform and his Reebok Iverson jacket.

With less than a week left in his high school career, he had been thrown off the team. For good. If he had only hung on for that week, Lamar would've had Hurley as an ally for life. To Hurley, this had been a devastating betrayal. Those calls to Merrimack and Stonehill for scholarships would never be made. Lamar Alston was on his own.

He stood there, strangely stunned, somehow still thinking he could get on the telephone and give his side of the story. Typically, Lamar said, he didn't bring his practice gear to school, usually returning home after his final class, gathering it up and driving over to practice. But his parents had taken away use of the car because he had been constantly disobeying them at home. He had had girls over to the house when it was just him and his younger brother at home, Boccia said. He had been staying out late. He had been living too fast.

And with the snow Tuesday, the buses were running late, stuck behind plows in some instances, and it wasn't until a little before four that Lamar made it home to pick up his clothes. "If I tried to catch the bus back across town at that point, I would've been getting to practice when everyone else was leaving," he explained.

His stepfather hadn't bought it. All he had to do, Boccia insisted, would've been to call him at work and tell him his problem. "I would've been angry that it had come to that, but I would've gotten him over to practice. I would've come get him from the office." Once again, though, the two of them had been at odds and Lamar just closed out the world. He chose the worst possible route, calling no one—not Hurley, not Gamble, not Erman. Not anyone. He had lit a fuse to his St. Anthony career and blown it to bits. There was a strange, sad, self-destructive bent to it all.

That afternoon, Hurley had invited one of New York's top teams, Xaverian of Brooklyn, to Jersey City for a scrimmage. Before they arrived, Hurley pushed his broom end to end, sweeping Lamar out of the program, out of his life, once and for all.

"As soon as he had some success, there was responsibility for maintaining it," Hurley said, stopping for a moment on the baseline. "And that's when he runs. It goes back to the same things. He's never had a job. He's never had it very tough in life. Things have been done for him."

His best friend on the team, Marcus, said, "He's crazy. I told him that the first time he quit. To come this far . . . I mean . . . Lamar is just crazy."

After finding out that he had missed practice on Tuesday night, Boccia called Derrick Mercer Sr. in a panic. "You need to call Lamar," Boccia implored him. "He listens to you."

He did call him, but Lamar never picked up. In the lobby outside the gymnasium, Derrick Sr. tried his cell phone again.

That time, Lamar answered.

"Where are you?" Derrick Sr. asked him.

"Newark," he replied.

"Newark? What the hell are you doing there? If I was you I would go see Coach Hurley. Take your father and mother with you and ask for another chance. Please, Lamar. *Please.* This is your future. If the colleges see this, do you think they're going to take a chance on you? How do you think you're going to get to college at the end of the year? What do you think the coaches here are going to say about you? You've got to be a man. You've got to step up, Lamar."

Derrick Sr. hung up the telephone and sighed. "Do you believe this? He said he was too scared to come to practice yesterday when he was already late."

He had done what he could for Lamar. Everyone had.

"That's his life. He made the decision. He's got to live with it."

After the scrimmage, Hurley drove down to Toms River to scout the Tournament of Champions quarterfinals with Chris, Erman and Damel Ling in his car. As everyone else gabbed, Hurley was busy reconstituting the team in his mind. Lamar was gone, so Shelton had to play more minutes. Otis had checked out at the doctor, and would be fine for Friday night's game.

"Did you read the *Ledger* yesterday?" Chris wondered from the backseat. "They had three ways to beat St. Anthony's."

In her own protective way, she sounded annoyed by the story's premise. "Do you believe that?"

"Three ways?" Hurley said. "I can give you fifteen."

He steered down the Jersey Turnpike, passing the unsightly fuel refineries in Elizabeth, and laughed to himself. "Man, we are a flawed team."

If nothing else, St. Anthony was a diminished team without Lamar. In the end, basketball had used Lamar, the way he never allowed himself to use it. To commit so much, to come that far and then leave high school without Hurley's blessing for the life beyond St. Anthony was maddening. To think of the possibilities that could've been there with a degree out of a Stonehill, or a Merrimack, was heartbreaking. All his life, Lamar always had an opening for another chance, but this time it was over.

When Hurley arrived at the Ritacco Center, Gamble was in the bleachers, taking notes on the Raritan-Haddonfield game. Lamar Alston was still on the assistant coach's mind.

"We figured that we would play St. Pat's and we would need him at that time," Gamble said. "It happened to be Paterson Catholic, and there's no question: He pulled through when we needed him.

"I can't speak for him anymore. Coach Hurley is not going to speak for him. And when that happens, especially with our program, everybody is going to know there is a problem with this kid. Everybody is going to know the kid has been thrown off the team twice in one season. That's a warning sign. And he may be so stubborn and ignorant, he may not even ever realize what he's blown.

"If he can't make a commitment now, at eighteen, doing something he supposedly loves, what's going to happen when he has to do it to take care of himself and his family?

"Hell, my conscience is clear. There's nothing else that I can do."

Gamble stared straight out on the floor, where Raritan was on its way to a victory and a rematch with St. Anthony in the Final Four on Friday night.

"My conscience is clear."

Before getting on the Turnpike heading back to ward Jersey City, Hurley stopped at a gas station. As the attendant filled the tank, two men walked up to the driver's-side window, waving a five-dollar bill and asking Hurley to jump a dead car battery.

"We're trying to get to Jersey City," they said.

"Jersey City?" Hurley said. His eyes lit up. "I'm from Jersey City."

"I grew up in the Heights," one guy told him.

"I'm Bob Hurley."

"Bob Hurley?" the man said, turning to his buddy.

"Bob Hurley!" the other burst out.

"Yeah, yeah . . . I'm from Greenville," Hurley said. "My father was a Jersey City cop."

"Bob, we're at a gas station," Chris noted. "Can't the gas station worker do this for them?"

He glanced over to the passenger seat, incredulous. "Red," he said, "they're Jersey City guys."

That's all he needed to say. She knew she had no comeback for that.

After they hooked up the jumper cables under his hood and started the car, Hurley steered back onto the road, the snow smashing into the windshield. Chris was dozing in the backseat and Hurley was pushing for the Tournament of Champions. Still, Lamar was lingering in his rearview mirror. He was still trying to figure out that damn kid.

"He came to the parade Sunday, but he didn't come to practice," Hurley said, shaking his head.

All the way to the end, this senior class had tested Hurley's faith in ways that thirty-two seasons on the job had never done. Sometimes, it seemed the record was a liar: Twenty-eight and oh felt like anything but perfection. For all the issues with Lamar, all of Hurley's theories, there was still something baffling about it: How did a kid get so close and just blow himself up like that? They just kept teaching Hurley that they really never were close. He had to keep telling himself. They were never close. They always had miles to go.

Hurley stepped on the gas pedal and steered through the snowy night.

The coach knew the road well, but it was still hard to see where they were headed.

ON THURSDAY, HURLEY STARTED TO turn the heat back up, catching Shelton coasting through a drill and raising his voice for the first time since the Parochial B championship.

Hurley walked to Shelton and exaggeratedly dragged a finger across his chest.

He held it in the air.

"You're not even sweating, Shelton," Hurley said.

He stepped back now and started talking loudly, for the gymnasium to hear him.

"This could be his last high school practice. He's barely sweating. How long have we been out on the floor?" Hurley asked.

"How long?"

"An hour," the team responded.

"ONE HOUR!" Hurley barked back. "Guess what, Shelt? You've done this too many days in high school. This is why we pick up the phone and call schools for you, and college coaches tell us they watched our games and you showed them nothing. That's why nobody is recruiting you.

"Every day," Hurley screamed, "if you don't work at it, somebody else is. You think Calhoun's working at Raritan today? You think Johnson's working at Raritan today? I know they are.

"But Shelton Gibbs isn't."

Hurley was on a roll now, and it was time to clear the air. He had things on his mind and it was time to get it all out there.

"And Lamar Alston isn't with us today. Do you want me to put you in that category, Shelton? Do you want to be in that category with the motherfucker who took playing time from you, playing time from Otis? Jerked everybody around . . . Walked away from it?

"We played somebody who turned out to be a piece of shit."

And that was the last time the St. Anthony High School Friars ever heard their coach bring up Lamar Alston.

TWO HOURS LATER, Boccia was driving through the streets of Jersey City, talking on his cell phone and wondering where his son had gone. He had thrown Lamar out of his house that week, sending him to live with his grandmother. Next, Lamar had stopped going to school. Now, no one had seen him for two days.

Lamar was on the lam.

"He's running now," Boccia said, "but I can't have him in my house anymore. I can't have him around my younger son. His excuse with practice was that, 'If I'm late, I don't want to go in and have him yell at me.' That's been Lamar's habit in life. It's always been, 'Stroke me the right way and I'll give you what I want to give you. Don't stroke me the right way and I'll have an attitude. And then I'll say the consequences were too harsh.' Well, he can't blame anyone now. He put himself in this position.

"He let everybody down. He let Ben down. He let Pushie down. Coach Hurley is disappointed. The thing is, as a leader, a disciplinarian, if Hurley allows that to slide, he won't have his success rate. His regime will collapse. Other coaches in the state would probably allow Lamar to continue with all kinds of antics. He could've gotten away with much more and played. I know Coach Hurley and Ben are focused on a mission right now. Once that mission is complete, if in any way they can help me with Lamar, I know they will."

Joe Boccia sounded more hopeful than sure.

CHAPTER 24

HUNDREDS OF ARMS were swaying side to side, feet were pounding on the wooden bleachers, and they had a hold of Barney Anderson now. Behind the basket, rows and rows of the rabid Raritan faithful had lured his gaze past the shiny rim and into the blurring madness. He dribbled once on the free-throw line. And again. He looked wobbly, like he was liable to fall over sideways. Every second that he stood squeezing the ball in his hands now, wishing away that lump in his narrowing throat, the rumble rose in the Rutgers Athletic Center.

Someone needed to settle St. Anthony down. Someone needed to get a grip on this game. Someone needed to stop the bleeding. Everyone screamed louder and louder, waved those arms faster, and faster, and Barney looked like he was staring into the lights of a chugging, churning locomotive. He dipped his knees, flicked his wrist, and his shot never reached the rim. "AIRRRRRRRRRRRR BALLLLLLLLLL," they screamed now. There were 3,600 people in the 8,500-seat Big East Conference arena, but it sounded smaller and smaller with the noise, sounded like the walls were closing in on the St. Anthony Friars.

The team bus had clipped the concrete corner of a Jersey Turnpike toll-booth lane, flattening a front tire and stranding the team for thirty precious minutes, and everything had seemed so rushed, once they arrived in Piscataway for the Tournament of Champions semifinal game. From the bus ride to the warm-ups to the coach's pregame talk, everything felt out of rhythm for the Friars.

They were still screaming "air ball" when Barney bricked his second shot, and the Friars were unraveling like nothing seen this season. For starters, perhaps Barney had come to the state's Final Four with a false

sense of security to meet the talented six-foot-seven Qa'rraan Calhoun of
Raritan in the middle. After all, Barney had made eleven shots without a
miss in the Friars 73–55 victory over Raritan in February, obliterating the
reedy Calhoun with his strength and conditioning under the basket.
Maybe everyone had been feeling a little full of themselves with that beat-
down in the memory bank, but any sense of security had rapidly disinte-
grated into uncertainty, beginning with Barney.

For some confounding reason, he struggled to catch the simplest of
passes anymore. Barney bobbled balls. Dropped them. Or missed them
entirely. He had suddenly become like one of those baseball pitchers who
has lost his ability to throw strikes, a mental block that had come without
warning. Barney had been the poster child for the problems, but everyone
shared a part in the pounding.

Nothing would drop for St. Anthony. Beanie was called for carrying
the ball. Sean missed a layup on a backdoor cut, Otis missed a layup on the
break, and Marcus missed *two* straight under the basket. They were running
Hurley's plays to perfection, getting the shots he wanted in the offense, but
nobody could get the ball to fall. Everyone sat stunned, watching, wondering what the hell had happened to St. Anthony. Calhoun was cracking on
Barney, the way Barney had done to him in February. He had been scoring, smacking shots out of the air and electrifying the evening.

Raritan had the ball for the final shot of the quarter, and its talented
point guard, Marques Johnson, swished a long three-pointer with eight
seconds left. The Rutgers Athletic Center exploded, the Raritan Rockets
picking up fans throughout the building, everyone glad to climb onboard
the underdog's bandwagon. When the buzzer sounded, Raritan's players
leaped and fired fists into the air as they left the floor, met at mid-court by
their roaring, red-faced coach, Sean Devaney. It was 15–5, Raritan, and
suddenly St. Anthony was down double-digits for the first time this season.

St. Anthony had missed seventeen of nineteen shots to start the game.

The noise was deafening as the Friars staggered back to the bench, the
tide of the season turning in one lost quarter of basketball. For the first
time, everyone would find out how well St. Anthony could take a punch,
how well they would react to adversity.

Hurley flashed back to a Tournament of Champions game more than
a decade earlier, when St. Anthony was down double-figures to McCor-
ristin High of Trenton. The opposing players had preened past the St.
Anthony bench, eyeballing and taunting them, sending the St. Anthony
huddle into hysterics. "They demeaned us," Hurley would recall later. "By

halftime, it was a tie game. We ended up winning the game because that was unacceptable. We play our ass off, but we don't do that to you. Once they did that to us, there was no more strategy involved in the game. It became just a matter of disrespect. And they paid for the disrespect."

In the huddle, Hurley shouted over the buzzing building. "Freakin' layups. Layup, Sean. Layup, Marcus. Layup, Barney. Layup, Otis. Everything we run, we're getting layups." From there, he told everyone to sit back, breathe out and treat themselves like boxers between rounds. There was nothing to diagram on his clipboard to get his team out of trouble. They were playing in a college arena, the stands were hopping and it was natural that the players were hyped. Everyone needed to gather himself and understand that, by staying together, by staying with the plan, they had to believe they would get back into the game.

Hurley wanted to lure Raritan into a running game, understanding that Jersey City legs would eventually wear out the legs of the Jersey Shore kids. To that end, Hurley sent four St. Anthony players to the offensive boards on every shot, guaranteeing it would leave them short on defense. This way, St. Anthony would entice Raritan to try and take advantage of favorable fast-break possibilities. Fool's gold, all the way. If it cost St. Anthony a few baskets early, the hope was that it would wear down Raritan later.

"Stay together," Marcus told his teammates, climbing off the bench and starting back for the second quarter. "Yo, everyone stay together."

The Friars settled down. Finally, Sean made a layup on the move. This time, Barney swished two free throws in the face of those wild, waving hands in the background. And now, it was Marcus Williams's time.

Hurley had moved Marcus, his best defender, onto Calhoun. It was six-foot-two against six-foot-seven, but something had to be done, especially on the defensive end. With six minutes left in the second quarter, Marcus grabbed an offensive rebound after leaping three times to tip it in the air, ultimately out-willing Calhoun to the ball. He laid it over the center's long arms to bring St. Anthony back within five, 16–11. Moments later, Marcus fought his way around Calhoun to grab another missed shot and muscled that back over him for a basket, too.

At his size, it was remarkable the way Marcus could control a high school basketball game. To be six-foot-two and play as though he were six-foot-seven was a testament to his toughness and tenacity, to the innate understanding he had for angles and positioning on the floor. Marcus had developed an acumen for playing taller players on the outdoor courts of

Curries Woods, where, to get picked for games, he had to learn to cover bigger, older players.

Beanie worked with Otis to trap the point guard, Johnson, in the backcourt, leaving him squeezed and signaling for a timeout. The best hands on the team, Shelton, stole a pass, and found Beanie streaking down the sideline to make it 21–21 with three minutes left. The game had turned into a track meet, St. Anthony transforming that drill they did every day in practice—grabbing the ball and busting it down the floor with two or three quick passes for a layup—often without the ball ever touching the floor for a dribble. This was the old Boston Celtics fast-break, lightning-quick and purposeful passes without a wasted motion.

"They're so quick-striking. One miss, and boom, they're down the court with a layup," Raritan's coach, Devaney, said later.

Shelton would be a godsend for the Friars in this game. With those long arms and tireless legs, he could run all day. Reclaiming those minutes that Lamar's return had usurped from him, Shelton beat Raritan down the floor twice for breakaway baskets. It was like he was playing to make up for that lost time, and St. Anthony needed him like never before. In the final seconds of the first half, Derrick's pressure on Raritan's weary Marques Johnson turned into a steal. On the dead sprint, he passed the ball to Beanie, who beat the buzzer by an instant with his layup. The St. Anthony bench leaped into the air, sprinting across the floor for the locker room. They had turned a 15–5 deficit into a 29–27 lead at halftime.

When they arrived in the locker room, everyone was breathing heavily. Derrick, Beanie, Shelton and Marcus were sitting on stools next to where Hurley stood, and they were exhausted. They could only imagine the scene in the Raritan locker room. Without a word, Gamble grabbed a white index card out of Hurley's hand. He knew the sight of it looked different to the kids, and he wanted to make sure nothing in the world felt different about the game.

"We survived it," Hurley told them. "We survived a 15 to 5 first quarter, and we're up two at halftime. What do we have here? First, we've been off a week. And secondly, hey, it's a different time of the year. We've got ourselves in a ball game. It's something we've prepped for all year.

"Listen," he said, holding his right hand up in the air, "we've never been a team that's been up here all the time. We had a bump in this game, and the bump was good for our character. We're finding out about how we can count on each other.

"What does the crowd want? You heard it. Everybody jumped for the underdog. That's terrific. Those of us right here, and that little group of people behind our bench, versus the building. This is a nice setting, fellas. This is a nice setting."

Once again, Sean had been out of sorts. He had let a plodding but clever Raritan guard, Mike Nunes, beat him to the baseline for two layups. When Sean backed off him, Nunes buried a three-pointer. Sean picked up two consecutive fouls in the second quarter, and it was a good thing that Hurley didn't see him kick his chair on the bench before sitting down.

"Sean needs to be able to relax, go out there and function," Hurley said, sounding the usual call to calmness for his beleaguered junior.

The third quarter began even worse for Sean. Nunes scored on him again. Raritan had spotted the soft spot in the St. Anthony defense—Sean McCurdy—and Devaney appeared committed to exploiting him. On the other end of the floor, Sean gave the ball right back to Raritan. Hurley had seen enough and brought Sean back to the bench with a little over six minutes left in the third.

He would barely have time to wipe himself down with a towel before Hurley sent him back in thirty seconds later. It was 31–31, when Sean dribbled into the paint, the long arms of Calhoun closing fast toward him between the foul line and the basket. And just as Calhoun looked like he would reject his fifth shot of the night, Sean flicked a high, arching, teardrop shot over the center's reach. It swished into the basket.

The St. Anthony press aligned in the blink of an eye, and Marcus perfectly timed his lunge for the inbounds pass. He tipped it toward the corner, chasing the loose ball down near the end line. As he lost his balance, teetering on the brink of falling out-of-bounds, he had the presence of mind to call a timeout and preserve the possession.

About a minute later, Hurley called a play for Sean, a dribble handoff play the coach had just incorporated into the offense in the practice preceding the game. Freed just inside the three-point line, Sean swished a picture-perfect twenty-foot jumper.

He wasn't done. Now it was Raritan that was rattled. They couldn't get the ball inbounds again. Friars swarmed everywhere, hands and arms and quick feet covering every inch of the floor. Sean snatched a careless inbounds pass while moving toward the basket, dribbled twice and laid it in softly off the backboard, giving St. Anthony a 37–31 lead with 3:47 left in the third.

Raritan called time, and the ferocity flushed on Sean's face was unlike anything witnessed in weeks with him. He clenched his fists and flexed his arms straight down to his sides.

"YEAHHHHHHH," Sean screamed, slapping Marcus's hand on the way back to the bench.

In that one sequence, Sean had shown the spontaneity and instinct that had been missing in his game. For the first time in weeks, Sean McCurdy reacted, stopped thinking and *played*. And when he did that, he could be a dangerous basketball player. The Rutgers coaches sitting courtside exchanged knowing nods, relieved to see some justification honor the investment they had made in recruiting him throughout the season.

From there, it was all about Marcus Williams. For him, this was probably as close as he would ever come to starring in a Big East Conference arena, something that had seemed a given four years earlier. Now, Marcus wasn't so sure about his basketball future, but he had this moment, this tournament, this precious perfect season. And he would grab it by the throat, squeeze it tight, and make it his own.

After the Raritan timeout, they tried a third time to inbound the ball against the St. Anthony pressure. Marcus shadowed the passer, pressuring him into a five-second violation. After that, Marcus dribbled past Calhoun—again—for a layup. Calhoun was dragging, but Marcus had never seemed so spry, so fresh. Who was giving up the five inches here? It was hard to tell anymore. Marcus beat Calhoun to another loose ball, and halfway between the free-throw line and the rim, he tipped it to Derrick for a layup. Suddenly, it was 41–31 with two minutes left in the third.

Once again, the third quarter had belonged to St. Anthony. Once again, they had left a team gasping for air on the basketball court.

St. Anthony would dust Raritan for a 56–42 victory, hurtling themselves into the Tournament of Champions title game on Sunday night for the tenth time in its sixteen-year history. Marcus would hold Calhoun to just one basket in the second half. It was more than the best performance of his high school career; Marcus had delivered a clinic on playing all-around, dominant Bob Hurley basketball. He had barely reached double figures in scoring, but he had completely controlled the game.

He had ten points and four steals, but the true measure of his performance were his career-best eighteen rebounds and lights-out defense on Calhoun. Marcus had thrown the Friars on his back, determined to deliver the unbeaten season he had wanted since all the way back in the fall, back when the team looked unlike anything that had ever come close to greatness at St. Anthony. Back when Hurley branded the seniors the biggest cast of misfits and screwups in school history, back when the underclassmen were turning into wise guys and all hell was breaking loose. All the way back when Marcus Williams, the only one of these Friars to ever be a part of a championship season, insisted he knew the way.

Off the arena floor and down the corridor, the Friars were running to the locker room, toward that Sunday night at the Meadowlands that they had been chasing for almost a year now. Twenty-nine and oh, and only the winner of the Bloomfield Tech-St. Augustine game, beginning minutes later, stood between St. Anthony and the unbeaten season they had dared themselves to believe possible.

Inside the locker room, Hurley was thrilled and his players could tell. He was proud of the poise they had shown, proud of the perseverance to stay united when a jarring start to the game had most of the building turning against them. These Friars had developed into the ultimate reflection of the man standing in the middle of the room now. From beginning to end, perhaps no St. Anthony team had come further to reflect his resolve. Whatever came their way, they kept finding answers. Kept finding ways to win. They just kept coming at teams, like almost nothing Hurley had ever seen at St. Anthony. The Friars reached the Tournament of Champions title game without a loss, the imperfect team staying perfect.

On his way off the floor, Hurley told the team, a tournament official had told him he needed to pick players to bring to the press conference. "And when our games end," he confessed to the team, "I can never figure out who did what. I know Marcus should go in there. Otherwise, I'm never sure.

"I feel like I ought to bring all of you."

He told them that conditioning had played the biggest part in the game, that the longer it wore on, the less Raritan had left to answer them. One more time, they had ground a team down. They had out-willed them. What Hurley loved best was how the arena seemed to turn on them, and then how his team turned to one another to find a way to win.

"At 15 to 5, everyone in the building said, 'Ohhhh, they could lose this game.' And everybody jumped on that. It was a tribute to St. Anthony basketball."

Before leaving for the interview room, Hurley said, "For the seniors, tomorrow will be the last practice of your high school career."

He scanned the row of lockers and stools, before his eyes stopped on Qaysir Woods in the corner.

"Try to get through your last practice without me yelling at you."

Everyone laughed. So did Hurley. Even he couldn't hold back on that one.

Marcus, Beanie, Derrick and Sean walked with him down the hall. They sat in chairs on an elevated table, each with a microphone before him. There was a seat for Hurley there, too, but he passed on it. He sat down on the far corner of the platform, his feet dangling.

In this setting, Hurley was still in complete control. The state's high school writers loved talking to him, because he never held back. Whatever was on his mind ended up in their notebooks. He was what they called "a great quote." They asked him now about the poor start to the game, and Hurley replied, "In the first quarter, we felt like we played very well offensively, but we were unable to do something very simple . . ."

And without finishing his sentence, he glanced back to his four players on the podium, a cue for them to finish it for him.

All at once, all four said, "Make layups."

The whole room laughed. Hurley would have a ball holding court. From all parts of the state—and the nation, really—scholastic writers would call him on issues of amateur basketball, recruiting, and sometimes just to hear him spin his stories. Nobody seemed in much of a hurry to get back to the arena for the Bloomfield Tech–St. Augustine game, because once they got Hurley going, nobody wanted to stop him.

"Our guys play their asses off," he said. "Sometimes the decisions aren't the greatest, but we're attacking the whole way."

He talked about how hard they played the game, how they loved competing. He brought up the example of Seton Hall University's surprising NCAA tournament victory over the University of Arizona twenty four hours earlier, when a St. Anthony alum, Donald Copeland, had been inserted into the game to stop Arizona's star, Mustafa Shakur.

"Our guys like matchups," he explained. "Donald Copeland wanted to be in the game. He wanted to be guarding Shakur. That's a St. Anthony's attitude. It's all about winning. It's not about individual stuff. It's team. It's team. It's team. It's all about accepting challenges. We might get our ass beat, but you'll have to work pretty hard to do that.

"We're a bunch of urban kids who work really hard. And that's the reason we're good."

Hurley nodded over at Beanie. He had finished with twelve points and five assists, remaining a stabilizing force on the floor.

"He came to the school to play for me," Hurley said, "and we've been like what at times?"

Hurley did a roller-coaster ride with his hands.

"Up and down," he said, answering his own question.

"And where are we right now?" he asked back, over his shoulder.

"Up," Beanie said.

The whole room broke up.

Beanie laughed the loudest.

WITH A RARE early entrance for a Saturday afternoon, Marcus Williams beat everybody to the gymnasium for his final high school practice on March 20. He was forty-five minutes early, clutching his Burger King lunch in one hand and a maroon St. Anthony gym bag over his shoulder.

Along with his teammates, Marcus had stayed down at Rutgers to watch Bloomfield Tech and its explosive senior guards blow out St. Augustine, 76–59, setting the stage for Sunday night's Tournament of Champions final at the Meadowlands Arena.

For better or worse, the Friars had come to the end of a remarkable run. St. Anthony had lost just one game going back to the previous summer, a Jersey City summer league game when most of the team was away at AAU tournaments and camps, and the young kids had to play with Qaysir as the go-to man. Besides that, they had a winning streak that together numbered nearly a hundred victories.

"Since last summer," Marcus said, as he dropped a chicken strip into his container of sauce, sitting on a bench in the locker room, "I've known that I've got to carry this team on my back.

"I'll do it one more game."

If nothing else, Bloomfield Tech had won St. Anthony's respect last June, when they met in the Metro Classic at Seton Hall University. After going down by twenty points to St. Anthony, those dangerous Tech guards shot them all the way back into the game, even taking a one-point lead late before finally succumbing. To beat St. Anthony, an opponent needed three reliable ball handlers, and preferably, one great guard to absorb the Friars' pressure for his teammates. Bloomfield Tech fit the profile.

They were 25-7, a northern Jersey school whose star, Courtney Nelson, considered the best guard in the state, had grown up playing with the seniors on the Jersey City Boys Club team. Nelson had gone off for twenty-nine points against St. Augustine in the semifinals.

With him leading the way, Tech was the hot tournament team, fighting back from a sluggish early season when they had struggled meeting the preseason hype surrounding a number twenty-three *USA Today* ranking. Besides Nelson, who had committed to playing at the University of Richmond, Tech had two senior guards, DaShawn Dwight and Jason Wilson, signed with Division I Quinnipiac College. In the middle, Tech had a six-foot-nine center, Casiem Drummond, a sophomore already inspiring interest in the nation's college powers.

They were dangerous. And in a lot of ways, Tech was modeled after St. Anthony. Back in January, with Hurley watching in the bleachers at St. Benedict's Prep, Tech's Nick Mariniello was the young coach grateful to get a nod of approval from Hurley after his set play turned into a perfectly diagrammed basket.

"Our whole season was geared toward playing them in the championship game," Mariniello would admit. "And for a lot of people, we're all fascinated with how Bob's been able to sustain that success over such a long time. It's true greatness. As a coach, all I've tried to do is emulate what he's done at St. Anthony. He's motivated me in every way to be a better coach. After a lot of our games, I would tell our team, 'You guys want to play St. Anthony in the T.O.C. and they would've beat the guys out there we played by thirty.' They're the Yankees of high school basketball. A lot of people are jealous of them, but we're all trying to figure out a way to be like them."

The St. Anthony locker room started to come alive for the 1:00 practice on Saturday. Shelton showed up. And then Ralph and Miles, who had been brought up to sit on the bench for the states, came together from North Bergen, as always. Otis. Barney. Soon, Marcus, Shelton and junior Eric Centeno disappeared into a shower stall and started rolling dice. When Pushie brought a box of donuts into the locker room, Otis barked, "Hey, Coach!" loud enough for the dice players to understand that it was a signal to shut it down.

Someone scooped up the dice, but Pushie hadn't come snooping for suspect extracurriculars. Just simply to drop off breakfast.

When Hurley arrived a few minutes later, his eyes darted to find Barney. As almost everyone else stretched and shot basketballs, his oft-flighty center was standing in the corner, gabbing away with Qaysir. Once he gathered everyone for the Bloomfield Tech scouting report, Hurley started in immediately on his six-foot-five junior center.

"Barney, you were terrible yesterday," he said. "Just terrible. We could've lost that game. You were dragging us down. But my problem is this: If someone plays poorly, it can't continue. The individual responsibility is to get out before practice and be working on stuff.

"So I came in the door today and the first thing I wanted to see is what you're doing, how you're preparing to play well after you didn't last night. That's the way life is. I want to see someone who didn't have a good day bouncing back the next day to insure he has a better one.

"How about Barney now? How about what's happened to him?

"Suddenly, every time we give him the ball in the post, he's falling down. His legs are collapsing underneath him. I can't explain it, but today I know that if I'm him, I'm in here throwing the ball off the backboard and getting my balance. I know I'm in here working."

But the biggest burden for the Tech game belonged to Derrick. He had harassed and exhausted point guard after point guard throughout the late stages of the season, a tenacious defender who had American and Boston University joining Monmouth and a growing list of colleges that were recruiting him hard as a junior. Now, Bloomfield Tech promised to offer him his most formidable foe: best guard in the state, top-100 player in the country, Courtney Nelson.

"Derrick," Hurley said, "I don't think he can shake you off the dribble."

Derrick nodded back to Hurley. He was playing so well, so confidently, that he didn't believe Sebastian Telfair could take him off the dribble right now.

"He got twenty-nine points last night. Nobody we've played this year has gotten that on us."

Against the wall, the players sat and listened, never once hearing Hurley bring up the issue of an unbeaten season. It was on everyone's mind, but he insisted on keeping the Tournament of Champions title game like the preparation for every other one of their twenty-nine victories. Along the way, there was always some great player St. Anthony had to stop. They probably hadn't played a guard like Nelson since 2001, when Gamble had scouted Camden High School's Dajuan Wagner three times to study ways of containing him.

Wagner had scored one hundred points in a high school game, and finished his high school career with an ungodly 3,462 points.

"Coach Hurley had them boys like robots," Wagner, now a guard for the Cleveland Cavaliers, laughs. "I remember there were one or two of them around me anywhere I turned. They played hard. What I remember is that them boys didn't want to let that coach down."

As far back as Wagner remembered, it was the only game that he had ever fouled out of, a product of St. Anthony constantly going after him on the defensive end. Camden lost by twenty-three points, and Hurley's legend for game-planning against great players only grew. Nelson was no Wagner, but he was good. Damn good. And he could end the St. Anthony season in disgrace, if they let him loose.

Hurley climbed out of the chair he had positioned near the free-throw line and stepped closer to his players.

"A team needs anchors," he said. "We need something that goes in the water that gives us control. We need guys to be anchors tomorrow. Marcus is the anchor of St. Anthony. Derrick Mercer has been an anchor. Ahmad Mosby has been an anchor. And Barney has *not* been an anchor. We need guys who can go out and function. The pressure of the game is gone. The voices you hear are your teammates. You're working together. We can count on guys to do things. If we get the ball into Barney in the post, we expect to get a shot. We don't expect to throw the ball into the post and watch the guy fall down on his ass.

"That's lack of preparation. That's not being ready to play."

Late in the practice, Qaysir Woods mistook which direction Miles Beatty was cutting and threw a pass out-of-bounds. He made a face at the freshman, wondering why he had messed up his chance for an assist. There were five minutes left in the final practice of his high school career. Unless the game was well in hand, Qaysir wouldn't play against Bloomfield Tech. There was nothing else he could do for St. Anthony basketball. But it didn't matter. Bob Hurley couldn't stop himself. There were five minutes left, and Qaysir Woods deserved to be coached. He deserved to get his ass chewed out, just like Marcus Williams and Ahmad Mosby. He deserved to be held accountable, just like the players who promised to decide the perfect season on Sunday night.

Maybe John Wooden only coached his top seven players. Maybe Wooden wouldn't have said a word to Qaysir Woods, but then, Wooden never coached in Jersey City.

"QAYSIR THROWS THE BALL AWAY AND MAKES A FACE?" Hurley screamed. "THERE'S FIVE MINUTES LEFT IN YOUR HIGH SCHOOL CAREER AND YOU'RE STILL A BABY!

"WHY DON'T YOU GROW UP?"

After Hurley finished yelling at Qaysir, a most telling thing happened over in the corner of the gym. Marcus had come to the sideline, out of the half-court offensive sets they were working on, and walked over to Gamble. Nobody would've noticed him slipping out into the hallway. Nobody would've said a word. Gary Greenberg always talked about how Marcus used to walk over his mother at home, and he sure walked over his teachers in school, but this was the one place in the world that commanded his ultimate and undying respect. This was the place that taught him respect. There were just a few minutes left in his last practice and Marcus walked over to Ben Gamble and asked him a question.

"Coach, is it OK if I go get a drink?"

A few moments later, Beanie tossed a lob pass on a backdoor cut, the ball reaching Marcus in full flight to the rim. They hadn't made eye contact for one of these plays in forever, because Marcus simply didn't have the lift he had as a younger player. Marcus used to reach for the stars, but the older he got, something always seemed to be pulling him back to earth. Once the future of New Jersey high school basketball, he left everyone breathless with these sort of airborne dances. No, he hadn't done this in a long, long time. Yet now, the old man of St. Anthony basketball lifted and lifted those legs, catching the pass high over the rim with two hands and slamming it back through the basket.

"That's it!" Hurley said, clasping his palms together and laughing an incredulous laugh with everyone else.

The Friars were ready. Twenty-nine and oh, and one more test. One more night. All the other four-year starters in St. Anthony history had gone on to big-time colleges and the pros. That wasn't happening with Marcus Williams. Deep down, he knew this was probably the biggest basketball game he'd ever play for the rest of his life, because this was for St. Anthony history and only a kid out of Greenville, out of Curries Woods, could know what that meant to him. He had lousy grades and a beautiful baby, an understanding that his best chance to leave a legacy wouldn't come with Dick Vitale screaming his name, or NBA commissioner David Stern calling it out on draft night. It would come at the Meadowlands Arena, in the 2004 Tournament of Champions title game. It would come on a basketball court full of kids going on to bigger and better things in the world, but none of them would ever know more about winning, more about controlling that game, than Marcus Williams.

As he climbed over that rim Saturday afternoon, redemption in those legs, redemption in the air, for that fleeting moment, Marcus Williams felt like he was on top of the world. Twenty-nine and oh, and damn if he wouldn't give anything to deliver that perfect ending.

CHAPTER 25

WHEN THE KIDS climbed on the bus at 6:20 P.M. outside the high school, they were surprised to find a most familiar face in an unfamiliar place: Coach Hurley sitting five rows back, side by side with his wife. It would be a short, two-mile drive to the Meadowlands, just past the motel and fast-food alley on Tonnelle Avenue, to Route 3, and west toward the big white arena illuminated with the lights on the roadside. The digital sign hanging over the highway read: H.S. BASKETBALL TONIGHT.

"How about that?" Hurley said softly.

The Nets had played the Dallas Mavericks that afternoon, but now, the Tournament of Champions headlined a boys and girls doubleheader. Paterson Eastside met the Shabazz of Newark girls in the 6:30 game, and St. Anthony-Bloomfield Tech was at 8:30, live on the YES Network.

"I'm sure the NBA scouts will be here to see us tonight, especially with all the guys leaving for the draft this year," Hurley said with a wry smile, the bus rolling into the parking lot.

"Well, I know the Sixers will have a guy here," he said, knowing that Bobby would be at the game.

The bus was led down the garage entrance into the underbelly of the arena, where the team was ushered through the concrete corridors and into a visitors dressing room. In every locker, a metal hook held a state championship bag, including a T-shirt. On the chairs, there was a game program with a page of pictures and information about every team.

As the players and coaches filed in, unbuttoning jackets and setting them neatly in the lockers, Hurley told them to take a walk inside into the arena and watch the girls game.

"Take a look around and enjoy this," Hurley told them. "You got here by working hard."

Doc stood in the middle of the locker room, enjoying the fact that he had a genuine trainer's table on which to tape the boys. To him, these conditions did justice to his genius work. No more damn rushed tape jobs crammed between hot ovens and relish jugs back in the charter school kitchen.

"Put on a show, will ya?" Doc barked. "None of that down 15 to 5 bullshit, huh?"

Marcus and Beanie exchanged glances and laughed. They knew that they'd miss that old man. Against the cinder-block wall, Qaysir thumbed through the game program pages, searching for his face in the team picture. "Hey, there I am!" he said to no one in particular, as though there had been some doubt he would actually appear in there.

Outside, the Sisters were sitting in the baseline seats, just off the end of where the St. Anthony bench would be located. Sister Alan was holding an elastic band of fives, tens and twenties, along with a fistful of tickets for the North-South Senior All-Star game the next week down in Toms River. Marcus and Beanie had been chosen to play for the North, an honor accompanied by the responsibility of selling twenty tickets for the game. Marcus had delivered his share over to her, sparing himself the aggravation. Before the opening tip, she had sold ten.

While Marcus and Sister Alan had been waiting for the bus outside St. Anthony an hour and a half earlier, she kept telling him, "You're the only one who's been here before. You've got to keep these kids from being shaky."

Marcus knew, he said. He knew.

"I don't believe we're here," Sister Alan said now. She was looking out on the court, watching the Friars shoot at the far end.

"Never in a million years did I believe we were going to be here."

Perhaps the only thing more remarkable was that Sister Alan herself had made it to see the game. She should've been dead two years earlier, but she kept defying the odds, confounding the doctors, and pushing on. Another important appointment awaited her the next day, another check to see how the tumors looked, a road map to how soon she would return to chemotherapy. She had planned the appointment weeks ago, set against the Tournament of Champions final date.

The more Hurley and Gamble examined the game strategy, the clearer it seemed. Derrick had to get into Courtney Nelson's body, the way he had done to everyone else. He had to stop Nelson's penetration into the paint. He had to turn Nelson into a jump-shooter. For one more night, they would need to win it with defense. One more night, someone else would have the best scorer on the floor. And one more time, they would test the system against the star.

During warm-ups, Darren Erman worked on Derrick, appealing to that underdog in him. Erman was like a fight trainer, trying to prep his boxer. Understandably, Derrick had been baffled over the big-time recruiting lust for his classmate Sean, compared to the schools recruiting him. "You've got a golden opportunity to do something special," Erman told him. "This is the best guard in the state. If you play well, it will open a lot of doors for you. And you are going to go out there and shut him down, Derrick. That's what you do."

Once they were back inside the locker room, Gamble finished the scouting report and told the team a story, one that only Marcus remembered well. Two years earlier, St. Anthony was playing Shabazz of Newark for the Tournament of Champions title here. There were two seconds left, with St. Anthony clinging to a one-point lead, and Shabazz was inbounding the ball on the baseline.

"And if you ever look at that tape," Gamble said, "you can see Dwayne [Lee], and you can see Elijah [Ingram], and you can see Donald [Copeland], jumping up and down yelling, 'Lob! Lob!' because they knew what the out-of-bounds play was going to be, with two seconds left.

"So, we jammed the big man who was supposed to get the ball. They weren't able to get him the lob, because we knew the out-of-bounds play by just following the scouting report. They threw the ball out to another kid, Harper. He took a wild shot, and we ended up winning the state championship.

"Everything that you see here, you're going to see in a few minutes. Just follow the game plan, follow the tendencies, and we're going to be successful."

He waited for Hurley to make his entrance, and when he did, there was no call for a Knute Rockne speech. This wasn't an instance when Hurley had to convince an underdog that it could win, convince them that they could beat the team in the locker room down the hall. All they had to do was be themselves. He told them that, Saturday, after practice, and it hadn't changed. Everything they had done for the last year had prepared them for a chance to make history. All the weights and running, all the repetition and tirades, all of it, had hardened them for this title game.

Once again, Hurley sent the St. Anthony Friars into the final night of another New Jersey high school basketball season.

"We're in a professional building. The game is on television. And we're playing for the championship in our state," he said. "Do we need anything else?"

Everyone gathered in the middle of the room, arms reaching for the ceiling, Friar on Friar, flesh on flesh, waiting for Hurley to begin the prayer. The imperfect team on the threshold of finishing the perfect season. Marcus leaned into Sean, and Sean into Otis, and Beanie and Shelton, and everyone pushed together tighter now. Everyone surrounded Bob Hurley, pushing so close to him that they could feel the vibration of his voice.

"Four months. One more night. Thirty-two more minutes," he said. "Hail Mary, Full of Grace . . ."

The lights dimmed in the arena, the strobes burning down on the two benches for the introductions. There were several thousand people peppering the lower bowl of the cavernous arena, including Bobby and Danny under the basket wearing baseball caps. Across the floor, Rob Kennedy and Tate George, the YES Network broadcast crew, finished giving the keys to the game on air. Once the lights were turned on, the television cameras moved off the floor. Tech won the opening tip, and Derrick Mercer just lowered himself into a dribbling Courtney Nelson, one more St. Anthony guard looking to make his reputation in a big game against a big player. Derrick's palms were pointed upward. His knees bent so far that his rear end nearly grazed the floor. His chin jutted out into Nelson's kneecaps. Some players started out in this kind of defensive stance for dramatic effect, an impossibly tough position that lasted, maybe, one trip down the floor. Derrick was different. He could chase his man all night like this, and he had vowed that that was what he would do.

He dug in and started dogging Nelson, step for step, dribble for dribble. The best guard in the state against the kid too small to play for St. Anthony, the kid with the memories of those turnovers that cost them the St. Pat's game for the Parochial B title a year ago. If anyone had come to personify the defensive doggedness, the spirit of St. Anthony, it was Derrick.

It wouldn't take long for the Friars to jump Bloomfield Tech. Beanie made it 7–6 on a three-point play, a driving, determined basket and foul, and they were on their way. From the start of the game, Bloomfield Tech struggled to respond to St. Anthony's surety. The Friars were snapping the ball around the perimeter, patiently waiting for an opening in the Bloomfield Tech zone. Otis caught and shot—no hesitation, no second-guessing, no going back now—and swished a three-pointer.

Nelson tried to take the ball coast-to-coast, leaving a too-hard pass to

the six-nine Casiem Drummond, who fumbled it out-of-bounds. The
pressure had Bloomfield Tech unsettled, surrendering the ball again and
again. They knew what was coming, Mariniello understood: "There's no
preparing for it." Bloomfield Tech dribbled recklessly to the basket, trying
to get something to the rim. Wilson grabbed a loose ball and tried to leap
over Otis for a layup. His shot bounced into the basket, but Otis had position on him, earning the charge.

Meanwhile, Derrick and Beanie pushed the ball into the heart of the
Bloomfield Tech zone, collapsing defenders and threading passes to Barney
on the baseline. Finally, he was catching the ball and finishing plays. He
was an anchor again. His three-point play made it 13–6 with two and a
half minutes left in the quarter. As St. Anthony worked for the final shot,
Shelton dribbled hard to the basket, shoveling a pass in traffic to Barney
along the baseline. His layup dropped through the net as the buzzer
sounded, pushing the Friars out, 18–10.

"Courtney's it right now," Hurley told them in the huddle. "Courtney
is the offense."

The Friars had been finding little resistance attacking Drummond.
"Are they even challenging us inside?" Hurley asked. "Go up with your
best stuff."

Near the start of the second quarter, with his Friars defender hanging
all over him, Dwight squeezed the ball, swinging his elbow into the side of
Beanie's jaw to create some space. When he was younger, Beanie would've
made a spectacle of getting smacked in the mouth. Along the way this season, something had clicked. Something had hardened within him. Yes,
Dwight let him have it in the jaw. Beanie absorbed the blow and
backpedaled, but quickly thrust himself back into his man's body, as
though to suggest that he'd have to hit him harder. Much harder.

As St. Anthony took away more and more from his Bloomfield Tech
teammates—the drives, the passing lanes, the open shots and, over and over,
the ball itself, with its three-quarter-court traps—Nelson tried to do more
on his own. He tried to do too much. Derrick forced Nelson into a travel,
and then buried a three-pointer himself from the deep corner to make it
21–11 with 5:35 left in the half. Moments later, Derrick drew a charge on
the baseline. He was taking it to the best guard in the state, earning a reputation the way Erman promised it would come.

St. Anthony was everywhere, turning this performance into a clinic.
Beanie chased a loose ball into the television table, stealing another rushed,
sloppy pass that a smothered Bloomfield ball handler had flung into the air.

Sean glanced to his right on the fast break, only to pass left to Marcus, catching him in stride. He laid it into the basket, pushing the spread to 27–13 and inspiring Bloomfield Tech to burn a timeout.

After the timeout, Nelson found himself trapped in the backcourt, Derrick and Sean closing in on him. And for the life of him, Nelson couldn't find a Tech teammate. Everyone rotated perfectly for St. Anthony on the pressure, filling gaps, a synchronicity of months and months of training, the five fingers moving as one. The fist. That's what Hurley always said: the five fingers becoming a fist. All Nelson could see were St. Anthony Friars surrounding him, and he screamed for a timeout to the official.

Clutching his clipboard, Erman leaped off the bench, screaming, "They used another!"

At halftime, Hurley stood for a moment, silent, searching for something—anything—to be critical about. There was nothing. They were winning, 33–16, and this sure felt like an old-fashioned St. Anthony ass-kicking. After the St. Raymond's game, Hurley had asked the question: Who knew the difference between a victory and championship basketball?

Who knew?

Finally, they did.

"Make them have to chase us now," Hurley said. "They're going to come out and play us, and we'll have a chance to go past them. We attack anything that they run against us. We want to keep trapping Courtney Nelson. Can the other two guys for them break us down? Absolutely not.

"Sixteen minutes left now. Sixteen minutes left in the season. We're going to go out and smack them in this quarter, because we're going to attack everything that they do. Not one passive thing. Everything we do is attacking. If they score, we inbounds the ball and we're running their asses."

And they ran Bloomfield Tech's ass through the third quarter, the traps turning into steals, the steals into baskets, the baskets bringing St. Anthony back into its pressure and leaving Bloomfield Tech in a shambles, an experienced, explosive team reduced to rubble. It was a basketball clinic out of the old days at St. Anthony, one of those nights Hurley felt like a conductor standing before his symphony, transforming the disparate instruments and parts into something spellbinding.

Bloomfield Tech turned to a full-court press, but it was futile. Now Otis had confidence with the ball in his hands, blasting past the Tech defenders to find Beanie and Marcus for layups on the fast break.

"Way to go, Otis! You're waking up," Doc yelled on his way back to the bench for a timeout in the third quarter.

Everybody was playing well now. Sean hit a gorgeous off-balance shot from the baseline, and Derrick grabbed an offensive rebound in traffic and laid it back over the foot-taller Drummond for a basket. Marcus patrolled the middle of the St. Anthony press like a free safety, constantly picking passes out of the air.

To the end, Hurley was Hurley. When Sean had been careless with the ball and was subsequently pulled out of the game, Hurley was typically correcting him as he returned to the bench. Frustrated, Sean turned away, a spasm of unintended disrespect that was akin to a Friar pouring gasoline over himself and lighting the match.

Before Sean's shorts hit the seat, Hurley lurched toward him and warned: "If you ever turn away like that again when I'm talking to you, I'll knock your fuckin' head off."

With St. Anthony winning 57–38 with a little over five minutes left in the fourth, the last thing Hurley wanted to do was embarrass Bloomfield Tech. He told the guards to stand outside and play catch, turning to his delay game to burn minutes off the clock. "Simple plays the rest of the way," Hurley yelled to Marcus. "We don't need to be running anymore."

From the stands, a voice yelled out.

"Come on Hurley, let 'em play!"

Hurley spun around and barked back to the crowd, "Who's the lunatic over there that doesn't understand holding the ball?"

With under two minutes left and a 65–46 lead, Hurley cleared the bench, congratulating his starters one by one as they came out of the game. Marcus. Beanie. Otis. Derrick. The arena gave them a long, loud standing ovation. As little Derrick arrived back, Gamble teased him about how much better he looked as a junior without those goofy goggles from his sophomore season. "Hey," Gamble said admiringly, "you turned Courtney Nelson into a jump-shooter." Yes, they had never let him get to the basket, never let him create, never let him breathe. Another big star had felt the force of the Friars in a big game.

Barney stayed on the floor until he picked up his fifth foul with a minute left. As Tech lined up to shoot its free throws, Barney innocently took his position under the basket, waiting on the shot. The referee was trying to tell him it had been his fifth, but he appeared confused when Barney didn't respond to him.

"Our guy doesn't know," Hurley apologetically yelled down the floor to the ref.

"Come on, Barney Anderson," Hurley barked, waving his arm for him to come back to the bench. "You fouled out of the game."

Barney looked startled, and immediately started running off the floor. Everyone lost it on the sidelines, getting a good laugh at his expense. When Barney arrived back on the bench, there were Marcus and Otis and Beanie waiting to greet him, waiting to count down together the final seconds of the 67–55 Tournament of Champions victory.

The chase was over. Thirty and oh.

Perfection.

The kids spilled onto the floor, hugging and laughing, throwing themselves into one another. Sister Alan grabbed Marcus and squeezed him tight. Gary Greenberg wandered onto the floor and told Beanie he had never been so proud of one of his kids. Somewhere in the madness, Otis grabbed that championship trophy, grabbed it on a night he had played one of his best games since the broken foot, and held it in his arms.

Chris Hurley set down her pencil and closed her scorebook. Another championship season in the ledger. She walked down the courtside table, where the winning coach waited with a kiss.

The public-address announcer began to introduce the Most Valuable Player for the game, and Hurley called out, "Hey, Marcus, get ready to go."

Only, the voice declared, "Number thirty-five, Barney Anderson . . ." He had scored fifteen points, almost all by simply catching the passes on Derrick and Beanie's drives into the paint and finishing with layups. Of course, the MVP could've been Marcus that night. Or Derrick.

Most of all, they knew: The MVP was the St. Anthony way itself, the standard of the stubborn coach. Hurley called everyone to the middle of the floor, the Friars soon squeezing together for a championship photo, squeezing together until the faces were blurred behind hands holding fingers into the air, declaring once and for all, declaring forever, that they were number one. They were in the history books.

Thirty and oh.

In the locker room, they were soon spraying cans of soda, Ralph Fernandez shaking one up good and shooting a syrupy cola shower over the seniors. Gamble grabbed Otis and hugged him, saying into his ear as they embraced, "I'm so proud of you." And in an instant, all the cheering and celebration stopped in the locker room when Hurley walked through the door.

They had been waiting for this one. How they had waited for it.

"We've had four undefeated teams in four different decades," Hurley began. "We had it in 1974. We had Bobby's team in 1989. We had it in 1996. And here we are in 2004. You guys not only go down as state champs, as the Tournament of Champions winner, you're now one of four undefeated teams in school history. We'll finish the season in the *Star-Ledger*, the Madison Square Garden Network—all of them—number one in every single poll. And we finish second in the country to a school, Oak Hill, that has a new team every year.

"The accomplishment is unbelievable. For the senior guys who are leaving, we have our success. Now we want to be able to take this and put everything else in place. We've got to get guys visiting colleges now, get our futures in order. The underclassmen had a taste of it, but I don't know if you'll be good enough next year."

Hurley was already starting to coach next season.

"But this accomplishment . . ." Hurley paused, shaking his head, "is unbelievable.

"Ben, would you have believed this?"

Gamble flashed back to all the moments through the four years with these seniors, all the times the kids seemed like they wouldn't last one more day with Hurley, and maybe, he wouldn't last one more day with them. All of that, and Gamble just shook his head.

"Think about our scrimmages the first week of the season," Hurley said. "Think about how far we've come. By the time the season wore on, the older kids finally grew up. By the end of the season, this was vintage St. Anthony basketball. Today, we dominated this team. We dominated them. Everybody they've played lately, they've done this to. And we did it to them."

Bob Hurley said it again: "Vintage St. Anthony basketball."

And with that, the Friars roared now. They just roared. They let go in the locker room, the way that St. Anthony players never did. Because there was always something they were chasing here, sometimes something they couldn't see for themselves, something they had to trust to Hurley's well-traveled, well-worn map. Here they had arrived on the final night of the high school basketball season, 30-0 now and forever.

Hurley asked Gamble and Pushie to share some thoughts with the team.

"You'll remember this for the rest of your lives," Gamble told them. "I know I will."

For Tom Pushie, this was the end of the line. He was a stay-at-home father for his three kids, and the time away in Jersey City every day had become too much of a strain on his family life in Mahwah, with the two-hour round-trip commute. He had started helping Hurley four years earlier, when the seniors were freshmen. He felt like he was graduating with them.

Pushie breathed out. "I'm going to have a hard time getting through this . . ." he began. "Four years ago, I got a chance to coach here. But I told Ben about two weeks ago that I can't . . . do this . . . anymore."

His hand quivered over his mouth. The kids started clapping and cheering, trying to get Coach Push through it.

He started sobbing, saying, "I'm going to . . . miss it . . . I'm going to miss it so . . . much."

Hurley threw an arm around him, his eyes getting moist, too. He tried to put Pushie at ease, saying, "Three T.O.C.'s in four years, Tommy. . . . Not too bad . . . Not too bad."

Pushie kept going. "I'm sorry I'm looking like this to you guys. But I just want you to know . . .

"It meant a lot."

They all cheered, and Hurley took over again.

"We have to figure out how we're going to our honor ourselves now. We're going to go on one of those tours. We're going to go on to the state assembly. We're going to go pick up our banners. We're going to do a lot of things. And we accomplished it by doing what?

"Working our asses off."

In this moment, Hurley wanted to keep reminding them of the cause and effect, the relationship between the result and the commitment it took to get there. For his seniors, they would walk out of that locker room and never be coached by him again. He was done pushing and prodding, done with his work. For this class, Hurley just prayed this wouldn't be the end of accomplishments, but just the beginning.

"We're going to remember this the rest of our lives," he said.

At that moment, Marcus came running back into the locker room, finished with his postgame courtside interviews.

"Wow, Marcus live on television . . ." Hurley said, laughing, allowing Marcus to slide into the crush of bodies in the middle of the locker room as they pressed together again.

They thrust arms and hands into the center one final time, all for one, all for St. Anthony, all together a final time. Once more, they surrounded Bob Hurley and waited for the sound of his voice.

"Hail Mary, full of grace, the Lord is with you, Blessed art thou among women, and blessed is the fruit of thy womb Jesus. Holy Mary, mother of God, pray for us sinners, now and at the hour of our death.

"Amen.

"LADY OF VICTORY PRAY FOR US.

"ST. ANTHONY PRAY FOR US . . ."

And you heard every voice now, every voice, "ONE . . . TWO . . . THREE . . . HARD WORK!"

As Hurley gathered the four seniors to bring them with him to the press conference, Gamble reached for Barney's MVP trophy. "Let me see this thing," Gamble ordered. "Boy, that's a nice trophy they gave you for not boxing Drummond out all game."

And with that, Gamble could no longer fight back a smile and slapped Barney on the shoulder. Out of nowhere, the most stoic and even kid on the team dissolved into tears, crying and crying as he held that trophy tighter. Hurley had been looking for an anchor, and Barney had been relieved to give him one.

In the press conference, it was Marcus, Beanie, Otis and Shelton sitting side by side. Once again, Hurley sat on the side of the podium, letting his players sit on the stage.

"We've done so many things to put ourselves in the history books at our own school, it's staggering," Hurley told the reporters. "These four seniors all came in together four years ago. Marcus has been on three T.O.C. championships, but the other three kids were not part of any of this. But now, I'm so proud they're a part of it."

A reporter asked for a comparison of his unbeaten 2004 team with Hurley's best teams ever. "I've never had a better defensive team," he said.

"For this team to go undefeated, to me, they've achieved as much as any team I've ever had."

Marcus shot a look Otis. Beanie looked at Marcus. Coach Hurley said What?

"We surpassed anything we ever imagined."

Hurley turned back to his seniors on stage, asking, "Did any of you guys think we'd go undefeated?"

"No," they said.

Of course, they were just going along with him. All along, Marcus knew they would do it. He had always believed he could will it, and there were times in the season when that's exactly what he had done for St. Anthony.

"They jump into some heady company in St. Anthony history," Hurley said. "They're going to be in the midst of many historical St. Anthony arguments: an undefeated season and the Tournament of Champions. Everybody here has sacrificed something so that we could have a unique team of eight or nine guys. If you take some of the guys sitting behind me now, put them on other high school teams with the green light to shoot, you've got guys who would've averaged 18 or 20 points a game.

"The captain of the precinct attached to St. Anthony is Bob Kilduff. He was the captain of the '74 team, and now these kids will be able to walk up to him and get a little conversation going."

Hurley was smiling now, catching the glow of his kids' faces out of the corner of his eye.

"They can get in there with any argument."

Hurley stayed back in the press conference to do some television stand-ups, excusing the players so they could return to the celebration in the locker room. On his walk back a few minutes later, Hurley passed Beanie in the hallway. Around his neck, Beanie wore a nylon net the tournament officials had clipped off one of the rims.

"He glommed that net from me!" Hurley said.

Together, they laughed. The last Mosby man had never stood so tall.

On the ride back to Jersey City, in those final moments with this team, Hurley moved in and out of the darkness, the street lights lighting and dimming his figure in the second row of the school bus. The formula, Hurley called it. He still had it. Beyond the walls of the gym everything had changed, the culture and the families and a steady erosion of values trying to cut to the core of his program. It all had changed, but Bob Hurley never did. The St. Anthony way, his way, had never before survived such a test.

"The most rewarding season of my life," Hurley said softly, the noise way in the back of the bus, where the kids still hooted and hollered, drowning him out. This had been the season validating everything he held sacred: the discipline, the dedication, the honor. This had been the year that reaffirmed for him all the reasons to keep fighting for St. Anthony's survival, the reasons it still desperately needed him, the reasons Bob Hurley would stay forever. They were bringing another trophy back to the little brick school on Eighth Street, another busload of boys taking the hardest road to manhood.

"Tough kids," Hurley said of them. "For Jersey City, they're great examples of taking something, putting in the proper amount of time and dreaming the dream. And trying to be great.

"We play our asses off. We never had a technical foul the entire season, never any jawing with a guy from another team. We don't do that. We're about guys giving up individual stuff for the greater good of the team. We're about kids accepting challenges.

"They've done it in such a way that even people who don't like us have to grudgingly respect us. I mean, to look at the four of those seniors sitting up there in the press conference tonight, knowing how they accomplished it—just *knowing* how they did it. All the recognition they're going to receive now puts them through the roof, feeling great about themselves. They will now work harder at some of their deficiencies, so they can continue to move on. I've seen it in a million kids, and I know I'm going to see it again with them."

Hurley told the bus driver to take the long way into Jersey City, swinging by the Grove Street PATH station because it was too late on a Sunday night for anything to be running out of Pavonia–Newport near the school. It wasn't long before the bus was rolling down Newark Avenue, through the heart of downtown. He didn't mind sitting a little longer on the bus with the boys, with this season, with this team that had given him so much heartache and doubt, and finally, one of the greatest gifts of his coaching life.

All the way back in the beginning, back at the Boys Club on the eve of the first practice, Ben Gamble told the seniors, "Fellas, you've got some hearts to win over." What he had meant was that the biggest bunch of screwups in St. Anthony basketball history had one last winter, one last chance, to make a legacy.

Now, as the yellow school bus rolled home to Jersey City on the final night of the high school basketball season, on the last leg of a long journey, they had gone the distance for Bob Hurley. Finally, the imperfect team had delivered its perfect season, and won the heart of the toughest S.O.B. to ever walk in the gym with a whistle.

CHAPTER 26

THE ARCHITECTURAL MODEL sprawled on a folding table in the front of the school auditorium, an ambitious vision for the St. Anthony High of tomorrow, its detailed design before the eyes of a steering committee seated at dinner. Surrounded with trustees and administration, and accompanied by his wife, Bob Hurley fought the urge to blurt out his boyish delight about a part of the expansion and construction plans that he had long ago conditioned his brain to believe he wouldn't witness in his lifetime.

For months, it had been in the works. Still, the model mesmerized him.

This late April evening in 2004 was the launch of the first phase of a three-year plan to raise $20 million and transform the eighty-seven-year-old brick schoolhouse into a modern academic high school setting.

No more leaking roofs. No more winter coats in classrooms with broken-down radiators. No more science experiments backing up because of clogged and crumbling pipes that caused flooding.

Tom Rybak, an architect and a St. Anthony trustee, had been charged with creating the blueprint for the renovations of the existing school, as well as a design for the new structures surrounding it. There would be a science and library wing, a new cafeteria and guidance center, classrooms and offices.

Already, the campaign had $1.5 million pledged from corporations, charitable foundations and ordinary donors for the initial $10 million stage of the project. These would be the renovations, a roof, windows, science labs, an elevator, and something else, too.

What Hurley couldn't take his eyes off of—what he had worked to help shape for several months with the architect—sat in the middle of it all.

The Friar Center, they called it now.

The gymnasium.

The tenth gym where St. Anthony would play a home game in its three decades under Hurley would be its final home.

They were going to construct a gym with thirty rows of bleachers and 1,100 seats. It would have four locker rooms and two scoreboards and a mezzanine level to entertain big-shot donors and alumni for basketball games. There would be a training room for Doc Miller to tape ankles without dodging relish bottles and pretzels baking in the ovens. There would be glass trophy cases. Before everything else was built, there would be a gymnasium rising on Eighth Street, because the trustees knew it could start making money for the school immediately. It could bring them six figures of revenue a year with ticket sales, television rights, corporate rentals for adult pickup basketball games and leagues, and of course, those Bob Hurley basketball clinics that would bring coaches on pilgrimages from far and wide.

And they were building a gym before everything else, because, well, they owed the man who made it all possible. The school owed him its life.

At the dinner, the trustees gave a pep talk to the gathering before sending them out into the community with an orchestrated target of possible donors, from all walks of life and industries. A financial planning institution had prepared a glossy, eighty-page business plan, complete with cost projections, student families' financial statistics, and news articles on the school's story and mission. Donors would find out St. Anthony had made it through one more school year, short $150,000 of the $1.9 million budget for 2003–2004. The deficit would come out of a dwindling discretionary bank account of $600,000. Thirty-four percent of the operating budget had been reached with the tuition of St. Anthony families, of whom 60 percent lived below the poverty line of $16,000.

"If these kids and their families will work that hard to come here, shouldn't we work that hard to help them?" the president of the trustees, Tom Breen, said.

So, Hurley would give the last speech of the night, one more pep talk before the toughest test St. Anthony High School would face that year. Fortifying its future.

He wore a charcoal-gray turtleneck and sports coat and fumbled with the microphone for a moment before deciding he didn't need it. Just like he wouldn't need a note card to talk for the next twenty minutes.

"Sister Felicia, Sister Alan and I have been here a long time," Hurley began, "and I don't know how much more the three of us have left. I'd like to be coaching in that gym someday, but I don't want to be sitting in a rocking chair needing someone to tap me and say, 'Coach, the game is over. We won. Time to go home now.'

"I'd like to make it there when I'm still functioning at a high level, but I can't be real sure. But I'm sure about this: When people say, 'Well, you really need a gym at St. Anthony,' they're wrong.

"The basketball team doesn't need a gymnasium. We'll win anywhere we play. We'll make do, because we always have. But if you're a guy downstairs during lunchtime, you're probably on the verge of suspension most days. The weather is cold and you're sitting there with nothing to do. Chances are, something dumb is going to happen.

"The kids need a gym to go blow off steam. They need it for phys. ed. classes. We need a gym because Tom Breen tells me we can raise a lot of money renting it out. But we don't need it for the basketball team.

"We're going to still try to get these kids to the finish line with the labs and computer rooms we have here, with a structure that is far below what students are getting in other schools in Jersey City. The majority of our kids come from Lincoln and Snyder districts and they make a big decision: Either leave the neighborhood and come to St. Anthony, or make the simple choice to go with their friends to one of those high schools. The guys on my team leave them, come here and they go to college. Two of my best seniors this year came from Snyder's district, where 16 percent of the seniors passed the high school proficiency test. That's not a standard we have here.

"Two of the three seniors who were our best players this year grew up in public housing in Jersey City. And as we speak tonight, they're trying to fight cutting the cord with the world they know [here] versus the world out there. We're battling that every day. That is a reality. The principals of their grammar schools are ecstatic they're graduating from high school. That's not our goal. We're battling a couple of terrific basketball players to believe they can do more, and they're not necessarily sure they need to do any better.

"The school is not going to die. It used to be that the nuns' prayers kept the school going. And the nuns' prayers would keep this place going, but I really think the kids here deserve more than what they have.

"Whoever is here tonight, whoever has the time, the passion, maybe you would jump in and give us the help. Sister Felicia, Sister Alan, and me—who knows how much longer we have here? It would be nice to turn this place over to someone. One of the greatest things we could ever be able to do is walk through a new building and see kids have the same opportunities that others do.

"The kids at Snyder have the labs. They have all the necessary things. But they don't have the environment.

"We have the environment here."

AT EVENING'S END, Sister Alan stood ten feet away from the architect's model and marveled over the possibilities.

"I couldn't even react to this," she said. "It was so heart-wrenching. We dreamed about this for so long. You just keep plodding, and you wish maybe we wouldn't have to plod anymore. We've been here so long, I'd just like to know we can retire when it's time to retire—and the place will go on."

Sister Alan was determined to retire someday, to leave St. Anthony on her terms. She hadn't been back in radiation chemo since the infection that had hospitalized her in January. Following the Tournament of Champions victory in late March, she finally took the tests she had been putting off because of the basketball season. When the results came back, the doctor clutched them in her office and smiled at Sister Alan.

"You've got some friends up there," she said. "This is the best one you've had."

When it was time to leave the dinner on that warm April night, the stragglers lingering in the school auditorium were a familiar four: Sisters Felicia and Alan, and Bob and Chris Hurley.

Under a clear night sky outside, Sister Felicia stopped and gazed toward the empty parking lot.

"Can you picture it?" she asked. "Can you see the gym?"

For a moment, they all stared into the darkness. In some ways, they had been doing that together forever. After all these decades, all the years that St. Anthony stayed open on the nuns' prayers and the basketball coach's will, Sister Felicia would say it again.

"Can't you just picture it?"

Behind the decaying but defiant brick building, there was nothing to see in that dark downtown lot. Nothing except what the three of them always had the gift to see.

A tomorrow for St. Anthony High School.

★　★　★

THE BULLETIN BOARD inside the tiny athletic office listed the school's leaders in dragging ass for the academic year, and three of the top four were familiar names: Lamar Alston, Marcus Williams and Ahmad Mosby had combined for sixty-nine absences and ninety-five tardies, the three rarely in school once basketball season ended and Hurley held no more authority over them.

The memo stuck on a tack was an odd juxtaposition with the meetings inside several nearby classrooms, where coaches from Indiana, Richmond and St. Joseph's took turns introducing themselves to Sean McCurdy and Ahmad Nivins.

It was springtime, so the colleges were stopping into schools to begin their courtships of the junior class. This marked a return to the normal order of affairs for St. Anthony basketball, where the four juniors—Sean, Ahmad, Derrick and Barney—were well on their way to earning Division I basketball scholarships next fall.

The relative naïveté that the three Jersey City–raised juniors brought to these meetings contrasted with the savvy of Sean, who carried himself like a shrewd businessman. He knew what he wanted to hear. Nothing slipped past him. Recruiting was a game and he had learned to play it well. What it took sometimes was one flashy weekend to make a prospect a hot commodity, and that happened with Sean at an April AAU tournament in Houston. He had played point guard for his New York–based team and performed well. Suddenly, Indiana was hot on his trail, making a snap judgment that they couldn't live without him after watching the tape of his career game against The Hun School in January and scouting the Houston tournament.

Over that weekend in Houston, one Atlantic 10 Conference assistant coach believed Sean had compared favorably to the East's best junior point prospect, Greg Paulus of Syracuse, New York, who had already committed to Duke. Sean and Cindy had their eyes on the stars now, convinced Sean had punched his ticket to the big time.

That afternoon at the high school, Sean listened to the head coaches of two 2004 NCAA tournament coaches, Phil Martelli of St. Joseph's and Jerry Wainwright of Richmond, but each coach left feeling that Sean considered their schools well beneath his aspirations. They also knew it was early in the recruiting process, knew that the big-time schools could still cool on him, but neither he nor his mother ever considered that a possibility.

Cindy McCurdy had wanted to drop in for the Indiana visit, but Hurley directed her to stay away. "This is a chance for Sean to meet with the coaches one-on-one and get introduced to them," he had said.

Of course, Hurley didn't tell Larry Nivins and Derrick Mercer Sr. anything like that. He wanted them with their sons, educating themselves about the coaches and schools. Derrick Sr. would get so nervous for these meetings, he would literally start sweating. He never wanted to say the wrong thing and hurt his son's chance of the coach offering him a scholarship. Cindy was too entrenched in the recruiting for Sean's own good, Hurley worried, and she needed to step back and let it take its course.

Nevertheless, she was thrilled with how the early stages of Sean's recruitment had played out. All according to plan. All validating her vision. Indiana coach Mike Davis loved the idea of a winning player, out of a winning program. Politically, it didn't hurt Davis, who was African-American, to recruit a white player, especially considering he had gone away from the traditional crew-cut Indiana farm boys of the Bob Knight era, tapping increasingly into his own Southern roots for a different brand of Hoosier: black.

Davis had planned to fly to New Jersey for a few days to meet with Sean at school, but he had a recruit visiting campus and sent his young assistant coach, Dusty May, to make the presentation. May had been the biggest advocate on staff for pursuing Sean McCurdy.

Sean settled into a soft office chair, sitting across from May. Since the end of the season, Sean had bleached his hair blond, much to the dismay of Hurley. "He wants to impress these coaches into believing he can be someone to run their team as a point guard," he said incredulously, "and he shows up looking like that."

May wore a wine-red Indiana basketball polo shirt and an earnest Indiana farm-boy look, an ex–Bob Knight student manager who had moved up the coaching ladder. He started fast and laid it on thick.

"When I think of Indiana basketball," May declared, "I see Sean McCurdy. Tough. Passion for the game. Shooting. Defense. You're everything that we're lacking right now. Kids today are a different brand, but you're the brand that Indiana always won with. We want you. We want you to be at Indiana. The fans want you to be at Indiana. We have 16,000 at every game, and we play twenty to twenty-five games a year on national television. You're going to be a household name across the country. You can come in and play major minutes as a freshman. We're just recruiting a couple of other point guards—haven't offered a scholarship to any of them—but I can honestly say you're at the top of the list. You bring so many of the little things to the game that will help us win a championship. We were in the national championship game three years ago, and we're trying to get back as soon as possible.

"We're only recruiting kids we think we can win a national championship with."

Now, Dusty May was talking. The eager Indiana assistant had Sean
McCurdy wanting him to never stop.

"You're going to be a legend in the state," May said. "It's all over the
Internet message boards that we're recruiting you. You're going to be able
to make a lot of money when you're done. You're going to be able to get
a great job. I feel like you're going to be synonymous with Indiana basketball for a long time. When you think of Indiana legends, the Damon Bai-
leys, I think you can be to that level. I grew up in Indiana. I know what
Indiana basketball is. That's how I see you."

May knew his audience well, pushing all the right themes with Sean.
He had questions—Who else are you recruiting? What's your style of play?
What's Coach Davis's relationship with his players?—and May kept spitting out the answers, each one better than the last. Halfway through the
meeting, Erman walked into the room. He had been shuttling between
Ahmad's and Sean's visits, and asked a wide-eyed Sean, "Have you even
asked one question about academics yet?"

Well, no. He still seemed too busy playing over in his mind what May
had said about the way they let guards play at Indiana, how they aren't just
allowed to shoot three-pointers when flying down the floor on the fast
break, but were encouraged to. "Coach Davis will take you out if you
don't," May had assured him, and Sean nodded approvingly, enamored of
the Candyland being described to him.

Major playing time as a freshman, icon status, national television games
and all the three-pointers he could shoot? If it sounded too good to be
true, it probably was. Yet, this was what Sean McCurdy had been waiting
his whole life to hear. This was the reason he had spent all those solitary
hours in the gym, why he had left his family and friends and life in Connecticut for Jersey City and Bob Hurley.

"What does your mother think?" May asked.

"She likes the fact that it's Indiana," Sean said. "Her whole family is
out there. She's going to follow me wherever I go to school."

"Oh, OK," May said, sounding surprised.

"She says she wouldn't mind moving back there," Sean said.

"Anything else?" the coach asked.

"So I want to get this straight," Sean said, leaning forward in his
chair. "Are you saying that if Coach Davis was here, he would offer me a
scholarship?"

"I can't offer you a scholarship," May said. "But Coach Davis wants you. We just want the actual scholarship offer to be more formal. But we want you at Indiana. Period. I can't offer you a scholarship, but you have a scholarship offer. . . ."

Through the semantics, May tried to make himself clear.

"We want you at Indiana."

Once Sean had a chance to visit the campus in Bloomington, May seemed to suggest that Davis's offer would be a mere formality.

The McCurdys felt that was the perfect possibility for everyone in the family. Besides Cindy's family ties, Sean's father's stepson, Charlie Emerson, was on a football scholarship at Indiana. Bob McCurdy wanted Sean to pick the right school for him, but admitted that the destination of Bloomington, Indiana, would make life easier for everyone.

Sean and May discussed the possibility of an unofficial visit to Bloomington before the summer, and an official expense-paid campus trip once classes started again in the fall. As Sean rushed out the door, running late for the open gym over at the charter school, his mind raced with visions of Hoosier hysteria.

Cindy McCurdy was waiting there, anxious to hear how the meeting with Indiana had gone. As Sean had mentioned, she planned to follow her son to school, though Cindy hadn't told her ex-husband about the coupling of their son's college career and her relocation plans.

If it was Indiana, she figured she'd get a house and return home permanently. And if it were anywhere else, she planned on renting an apartment near campus. Greg Bracey planned to make the move with them.

"I'm not doing it because I want to be with [Sean] all the time," she explained. "I just want to be at every home game and all his away games. I want to be in the excitement of his college career.

"He and I have spent so much time by ourselves, he wants me to do this. He wants me to be there to share it with him. One [college] assistant coach asked him, 'Well, what about when you go pro?' And Sean said, 'Yeah, I want my mom wherever I am.'

"I think the reason he doesn't mind is because I'm not a nag. He calls Gregory his stepfather. They're close. He likes being with us. We don't crowd his space."

Because she was positive it promised to be spectacular, she didn't want to miss a minute of her son's college career. Also, Cindy had dismissed

Sean's struggles through the late season as purely a product of her son play-ing out of position, away from the point. After his performances in several spring AAU events, two recruiting services—Insiders and Rivalshoops.com—selected Sean as one of the top hundred high school players in the Class of 2005. The highest ranking had him eighty-second, and to Sean, that seemed a little low. He figured he should've been among the top five point guards in the country, and insisted to one scouting service that when he was playing well, no one could stop him.

"He didn't have the ball in his hands enough to create for himself," Cindy said, critiquing his inconsistent junior season at St. Anthony. "That's the magic of watching Sean play: how he loves to pass to his teammates. I really think he's going to be a good point guard. It's almost a waste for him to play [shooting guard].

"And when he gets to play the point, he plays like Bobby Hurley."

When reading recruiting Web sites after the season, Ben Gamble had seethed over comments attributed to the family about how the coach had used Sean, about how not having the ball in his hands had contributed to his struggling. Gamble found the notion to be downright "disrespectful."

"The reason Sean struggled had nothing to do with the way he was used at St. Anthony," he said. "And it bothers me to hear anything sug-gesting that.

"Sean was not a good enough ball handler to run our team," Gamble would counter. "He was not a good enough defender to lead our team. Where he used him [off the ball], that was the best way to succeed at this time in his career. If we put him at the point, it would've hurt the team. And it would've just discouraged him. He wouldn't have done well. I watched him too many times with no one around him, just dribbling all over the place without a clue.

"The quicker, athletic teams gave him a lot of problems. But we never gave up on him. We could've easily sat him and tried Otis a little more. He was listening to his mother sitting on one side of the gym yelling at him, and at the same time, trying to hear his coach on the bench giving con-structive instruction. That was a big part of the problem."

Cindy wasn't looking back, but full speed forward. Her directive in the recruiting process was simple.

"This is about finding a coach to get Sean ready for the NBA," she said. "I want a coach who is just going to say, 'You're my point guard and I'm giving you the ball for four years.'"

As for the NBA, she said, "That's what Sean wants. I really think it's possible now. If he has as good of a teacher in college as he's had in high school, he might really be able to do it."

Bob McCurdy had largely stayed out of the recruiting process in the pre-summer stages, but sounded surprised to hear of his ex-wife's plans to shadow Sean to school in the fall of 2005. He hoped it wasn't true. In fact, he sounded resolved to put a stop to it. No one had to tell McCurdy the long odds of playing in the NBA. He had lived it.

"[The NBA talk] is so premature it's almost funny," he said. "What you want the kid to do is choose a school where he can get a good education and play for a coach who can teach some life lessons. That's what it's all about. The NBA is not in my vocabulary. What it's about now is maximizing his God-given ability in the classroom and on the court. There's nothing wrong with the dream, but that doesn't mean you put everything else on the back burner and become a complete jock."

FIVE DAYS AFTER Dusty May visited St. Anthony, Cindy and Sean flew to Indiana to tour the campus and meet with Mike Davis. After May had watched Sean struggle in the two-hour open gym with his St. Anthony teammates after the school visit earlier in the week, he returned to Bloomington uncertain over the wildly up and down play of the recruit. Additionally, he had returned raving about an emerging Ahmad Nivins.

Soon, Sean found himself introduced to the forever-changing world of high school recruiting, where on Monday he could be the next Indiana icon, a legend from Terre Haute to Kokomo, and by that next Saturday, the next great Hoosier legend still couldn't coax a scholarship offer out of those Indiana coaches. Indiana had second thoughts on Sean, wanting to evaluate him further before offering the full ride.

This wasn't an uncommon practice, because scholarship limits for men's basketball made the awarding of them precious. Even so, the Indiana coaching staff still believed there was a good chance Sean would end up with them. Nevertheless, Cindy was livid. Within a week, she hustled Sean to the University of Maryland to meet with coach Gary Williams. He did offer a scholarship, and soon Sean was telling everyone that Maryland was far and away the leader to sign him to a letter of intent in November 2004. After all, Williams had a history of developing guards for the NBA, including the backcourt of Juan Dixon and Steve Blake. Together, they had beaten Indiana and Davis for the 2002 NCAA title. Williams could make Sean McCurdy a pro, the mother and son concluded.

If Cindy had hoped Maryland's offer would prod Indiana into countering with one of its own, it didn't. In fact, Indiana would completely reverse course. They were uneasy with how much of a priority she had placed on Indiana developing her son for the NBA. A parent overestimating the pro potential of a child wasn't an unusual development for college coaches, but the bigger concern had come with her plan to uproot to Indiana with Sean.

"She brought up that Greg would need a job out in Indiana," May said. "That was an area that I absolutely would never get into with any recruit. I just felt like it was time that we should cool it, and back off."

As a staff, Indiana watched him in a few games at the ABCD Camp in July, but like a lot of major college coaches, they were unimpressed.

Over the month of July, Cindy spared no expense, traveling with Sean on the summer basketball circuit. From the ABCD Camp in New Jersey, to Five-Star in Pennsylvania, to the Big-Time AAU Tournament in Las Vegas, college coaches and St. Anthony travel companions were stunned by the shadow she cast over Sean. It wasn't so much that Cindy McCurdy was seen everywhere as it was that she was *heard* everywhere. The gossip circle of college coaches and summer-circuit regulars spent the summer swapping more stories of her theatrics in the stands, her loud and emotional fits of frustration borne out of Sean's struggles to show he belonged among the best point-guard prospects in the nation.

It wasn't uncommon at Five-Star for Cindy to thank coaches for stopping by Sean's games to observe him, only for the college coaches to be too polite to break the news that they weren't there for her son. They were all chasing the rapidly developing Ahmad Nivins. Suddenly, coaches in the Big East, ACC, Big Ten, Pac-10 and SEC were hot on his trail, but Ahmad was nothing if not loyal, and underdog national power St. Joseph's University stayed at the top of his list. After all, Martelli had started recruiting him before everyone else. Sean had encouraged him to take the biggest offer that came his way, but then again, Sean and Ahmad had come to St. Anthony with different objectives. Ahmad loved the tight-knit St. Joe's campus, the genuine coach, Martelli, and the university's well-respected business school.

"In stock terms, the story of the summer was, 'Buy on Nivins, and sell on McCurdy,'" one recruiter would say.

The summer hadn't just delivered to the elite programs a reason to doubt Sean's worthiness for a scholarship, but the risk and reward of giving him the benefit of the doubt and offering one.

"It gets hard when a kid is being evaluated on something other than basketball, and that's what happened with McCurdy," one Division I head coach said. "She's part of the equation because she's made herself part of the equation. I believe this: Sean McCurdy is going to play at more than one college. Wherever he starts, he will end up transferring because she's just not going to find that perfect world she's looking for. It's a shame, because that kid has worked hard and sacrificed a lot in that whole situation, moving to Jersey City. But I think they're in for a rude awakening."

As the summer wore on, Sean still clung to Maryland as his top choice, but it turned into an unrequited love. More and more, Gary Williams and his assistants were absent in the stands for Sean's summer games. At the end of July, Maryland assistant Dave Dickerson called Bob Hurley and told him they were no were no longer interested in recruiting Sean McCurdy. The scholarship offer had been pulled back.

Hurley had stayed in contact with Sean's father during the summer, but had remained on the sidelines for the rise and fall of Sean under Cindy McCurdy. Sooner or later, Hurley knew the family would need him. And they needed him now. Massachusetts had been steadily recruiting Sean, and Hurley contacted University of Rhode Island coach Jim Baron and encouraged him to get involved with Sean, too. Arkansas had started showing interest when everyone was stopping, but the Razorbacks seemed an odd fit for his talent.

By staying in New England, Bob McCurdy and Hurley knew Cindy wouldn't need to move within a jump shot of her son's dormitory room. She could stay in Connecticut, and Sean, they hoped, could have a chance at a more traditional college experience.

"The recruiting process isn't what they wanted it to be, but it's time to deal with what it is," Hurley said.

LAMAR ALSTON WAS tired. He had been running the streets for weeks, running out on Jackson and Ocean avenues into the empty hours of the night, running angry from his past and frightened for his future. He was just so damn tired of running.

After imploding with Hurley just days before the Tournament of Champions Final Four, Lamar spiraled into an abyss of despair and depression.

"Poor L is way out there right now," Otis had said. "I'm worried about him."

Lamar lived with his grandmother on Jackson, where there were few checks and balances and little authority over him. From March until April, and then April to May, the days and nights were a dull, aching blur for him. When he was so moved, he went to school. Other times, he just hung out. He felt like he had hit a dead end in life.

"It hit him that he was out of chances," Joe Boccia would say. "It finally hit him that there were consequences for his actions, that Coach Hurley had done all he was going to do for him."

His old teammates had visited Madison Square Garden to get a picture taken on the floor before a Knicks game as the tri-state region's number-one team, been feted in the state legislature, and had a banquet where the state championship jackets were passed out to the players. The other seniors were visiting colleges, and all around Jersey City, people were asking Lamar what happened to him; how in the world could he get so close and throw it all away. Without Hurley's blessing, Lamar would be left sifting through a handful of non-scholarship Division III schools and junior colleges.

Hurley felt like he had given Lamar the chance of a lifetime to return to the team, only to have his trust betrayed. Lamar believed the punishment for missing the practice in the final week of the season was too severe. He denied ever blowing off that practice a week earlier, the one Gamble talked to his stepfather about, where he discovered Lamar's excuse to be bogus.

"It's just like Hurley to do that, just throw me away when I needed him the most," Lamar would say. "When all the schools saw that I wasn't playing in the T.O.C. games, that I left the team a second time, that was it. They didn't want me no more. After that, no school called me. That was the end of it.

"The only school that called me was Rutgers-Newark, and that's because two of my high school coaches from my freshman year at Marist were there. Hurley's got that much power. His word means that much. After that happened, I hated him. I hated him. I said, 'Fuck everything.' I didn't care about nothing anymore. Whatever happened to myself, to anybody, I didn't care."

Lamar desperately needed counseling now, but he had stopped it months ago. No one in his family made him keep up with it. He was lonely and scared, and all of it had turned into too much.

Finally, there was a night in mid-May when he decided enough was enough. He picked up a Glock handgun on the street, brought it back to his grandmother's house and took it upstairs to his room.

He lay the bullets out on a bureau and cradled the gun in his hands.

"I thought maybe I would put myself out of my misery," Lamar would remember.

For what felt like forever, he held the cold steel in his hands and considered the consequences.

The minutes passed as Lamar stood in the stillness of one more lost night in Jersey City, one more moment in a life that felt like a failure. If he had just gone to that practice, if he had just made it five more days, everything would've been different. In the fall, he would've been walking the tree-lined campus of one of those beautiful New England schools Hurley had in mind for him. Lamar never made it. Now, he stared into an abyss of loathing that threatened to consume him.

As he held that gun in his hands, he hated everyone and everything. He hated what he had done to put himself there, and hated what, he believed, awaited him.

Still, something in his heart wouldn't let him do it.

In the end, the bullets stayed on the bureau. He wouldn't load the gun. He couldn't.

"It wasn't worth it," he said later.

After a few more days in May, as spring began its burn into a long summer on the streets of Jersey City, Lamar was still unsure whether his life was worth living. But he did get rid of the Glock.

TWO WEEKS AFTER the Tournament of Champions, Bob Hurley drove Beanie, Marcus and Otis to Newark International Airport, checked them into a flight on the electronic ticket kiosk and shipped them off for a visit to Pensacola, Florida.

All along, this had been his hope for these seniors. Hurley had visited Pensacola Junior College himself in the fall, and believed this was his best shot to get them out of Jersey City, get each a two-year associate degree and a successful transfer to a basketball scholarship in Division I.

To him, the most critical step was getting these three seniors far away, off in a campus setting where, at the first test, they couldn't act on the temptation to run back to the familiar faces and streets of home.

"My thing with most of our guys is this: If I can get them out of Jersey City, get them out with some values in life, they'll grow up fast in that first semester away," Hurley says. "You can't just come home at the first bump in the road. If I can get them away to college, I don't care if they go there and put their left sneaker on their right foot. Because they're going to be forced to grow. They will come back to see me and they'll talk about how much they love college, how much they're enjoying their experience, and they're going to help me to establish things with the next group.

"They'll come back and tell the group that's still at St. Anthony, 'Boy, Hurley's demanding, but it's going to be fun when you get to college.' The thing is: It can't be fun now, or they'll never get to college."

When they returned, Hurley hoped to hear them tell him they wanted to accept the scholarships Pensacola had offered them. No one did. When Hurley heard the reasons Marcus and Beanie were giving for their uncertainty, he knew he had trouble. All season long, the Pensacola assistant, Terrance Harris, heard those two telling him how much they were looking forward to visiting Florida, how badly they wanted to get out of Jersey City.

"Every kid who comes from New York City and New Jersey, there always seems to be something pulling them back there," Harris would say. "We thought these kids would be different coming from Hurley's program. We thought that they would be mentally tougher to survive."

Hurley knew they were struggling to leave Jersey City. They just couldn't let go.

"They're afraid to take the next step in life," Hurley says. "Even though the two of them live in public housing, they're comfortable with the way they live. They've got to want something better—something more. They've got to want that for themselves."

For Otis, he simply wasn't comfortable with the proximity to the nightlife and beach. "I worried I wouldn't be able to concentrate there," he said.

The longer the three went without a decision, the more junior colleges across the country scrambled to court them. They were the best of what was left in the bargain bin, the kind of disciplined, well-coached players two-year schools didn't usually find coming their way. In the history of St. Anthony, it had never come down to a core of a senior class becoming the hottest tickets on the junior-college circuit.

Gamble set up a meeting at school with Otis, Marcus and Beanie to go over the schools interested in them. They would discuss where each wanted to visit, and the kinds of informed, educated questions they should ask of coaches and school officials on the trips.

When Gamble arrived at 2:00 one spring afternoon, Marcus and Beanie had gone home. Only Otis waited for him.

"Those two just bailed," Otis said later. "I took advantage of the opportunity. I can't wait around for Marcus and Beanie anymore. I can't wait around for nobody else to make their decisions. I've got to get moving with my life. I'm getting out of Jersey City."

Still, Gamble set up a travel itinerary for Beanie to make a recruiting trip to South Plains, a junior college in Texas. He even dropped a prepaid plane ticket off for Beanie in Jersey City on the day before the flight, reminding him of the identification forms he would need to bring to the airport. The next day, the South Plains coaches were planning to pick him up at the airport. Gamble called over to St. Anthony on a different matter, and mentioned to Margie Calabrese about the 10:40 A.M. flight out of Newark that Beanie had taken to Texas.

"Beanie?" she asked. "He's here taking an exam today."

When she went to ask Beanie why he had missed the flight, he told her, "I changed my mind."

When pushed further about the irresponsibility of just blowing it all off, he started his old defensive act: "Don't yell at me. Don't talk to me that way."

South Plains had lost the value on the flight ticket, and Gamble had to make the humiliating call to the school's coaches to tell them Ahmad Mosby never got on the plane. The coaches had questions for Gamble, but he had no answers for them. "Mosby was a coward for pulling something like that," Gamble said later. "How many more things could we do to help that kid?"

No one was surprised when Beanie skipped the postseason banquet.

"I know he doesn't want to face me or Coach right now," Gamble would say. In the end, Beanie picked the college he had resisted all season: Division III Ramapo. Once, it had been too small-time for his eventual ambitions of Division I, too close to the streets back home. Ramapo was a wonderful choice for uncomplicated St. Anthony reserve Tennyson Whitted six years earlier, but with Ahmad Mosby's talent and his issues, it looked like the easy way out. There were no basketball scholarships in Division III, so Beanie would end up with thousands of dollars in loans after his four years. It didn't matter to him. He knew Hurley didn't want him to go there, and that was all the more reason to rebel and choose it anyway.

"We got a steal," Ramapo coach Chuck McBreen said. "He's a mid-major Division I player who will be a 1,000-point scorer and an All-American for us—if we can just keep him eligible, and keep him on the right path."

All along, McBreen trusted his instincts that Beanie wouldn't want to stray too far from home, and he was right.

Marcus made trips to Pensacola, Barton Community College in Kansas, and Monroe Community College in Rochester, New York. He told the college coaches about Marcus Jr., and everyone told him it was no problem. With his Pell Grant money, he could send something home every month.

He had never wanted to stay in Jersey City. He knew he needed to leave, but in the end, for his own reasons, Marcus, like Beanie, couldn't cut the cord to Jersey City. He would pick Global Institute of Technology, a junior college in New York City. Marcus wanted his dormitory room to be right in Curries Woods. He planned to live at home and take the PATH into New York every day.

All Darren Erman could think of was the panic in Marcus that spring when he had to take the train to Madison Square Garden to get his picture taken for a Metropolitan New York All-Star team. The train would leave the Newport Square-Pavonia station in Jersey City and, within minutes, deliver him directly downstairs to the Garden in Penn Station.

"He must have called me five times that one day, trying to get me to go over with him," Erman said. "It was a straight shot, just a few minutes, and he would be there. And he did not want to go alone."

Marcus had lived in Jersey City his whole life, staring across the water to that Manhattan skyline and feeling like it was a world away. As much as anyone, Marcus needed to be far from home, isolated in a campus environment where he could concentrate on studying, because he would've had to work twice as hard to get through school with his learning disability. He needed access to tutors. He needed a roommate getting up every morning and going to class—not the sight of gangbangers smoking weed on the playground in his projects. The best-case scenario, Hurley had hoped, was getting Marcus his associate Degree, and then getting him into a physical education major at a four-year school.

For everyone who cared about Marcus, Globe Tech was the worst possible choice. "He's too far behind to survive any empty academic days in college," Hurley would say, and with Curries Woods and Greenville still his backdrop, they worried he'd be headed straight for them.

"How many days is he going to get up and take that PATH into New York for classes?" Gary Greenberg says. "What are the chances of him doing that? It's a shame. He barely came to St. Anthony every day. How's he going to get up and go to the train when it's raining, when it's cold? To me, this is a disaster."

Marcus heard it all, but insisted that staying home would be the best of both worlds for him.

This was for his son, Marcus Jr. This was a choice for fatherhood.

"Even staying close to home, I'm still going to have a mind-set like I'm away," Marcus insists. "I'm still going to take that responsibility to go to classes. By not having someone like Coach Hurley on my back, telling me what I need to do, I've got to coach myself. Everyone is saying that staying close to home isn't going to be good, but I don't want my son growing up without a father. I don't want him just seeing me coming back and forth to school."

Finally, Hurley had found out the truth about Marcus Jr., and it left him even more fearful for his future. He tried to tell him that the best thing he could do for his family was to get away for now, get a degree and give himself a chance to support them someday.

"He stopped being a kid and entered into an adult world far too soon—even before the baby, when he was dating a college girl in high school," Hurley said. "You just think that they would see these cycles in their own families and try to do anything in the world but repeat them. I just fear without a college degree, there isn't going to be much for Marcus besides chasing whatever tough, physical jobs are around town. He's a respectful kid with character and values. I'd go in with Marcus Williams any day of the week. I want the best for him, but I'm just not sure how this is going to work out.

"It hurts," Hurley said, thinking back on their four years together. "I wonder what more I could've done. When someone asks me where the guys from this team are going to school, I'm embarrassed. I try to explain it in general terms and move quickly to the juniors who are all academically qualified to sign with Division I schools in the fall. But I feel terrible. I know I did as much as could've been done, but you can't take an eighteen-year-old and put him in school like you bring a child to kindergarten. . . . In a lot of ways, it feels like failure with this whole group."

When, in 1996, the last unbeaten St. Anthony team had sent five seniors into Division I basketball, Hurley had been at odds with them through their senior year. The relationships deteriorated, because he knew he had to ride them hard to get them out of Jersey City and into the world. Both of Rashon Burno's parents had died of AIDS. They were a complicated class of kids with a lot of issues, Hurley said, but they all went away to school.

Anthony Perry had to sit out his freshman year at Georgetown as an academic non-qualifier, but graduated in four years. Burno had a year of prep school in New England, but earned a degree from DePaul University.

"None of them wanted to be the first one to come back home and have failed. But with this group, with Marcus and Ahmad Mosby, they set the bar so low for themselves. When it came to basketball, we never lowered it with them. But they can't translate that to their lives and it breaks your heart. If they fail now, it's almost the next logical step for them. If they drift off into the sunset never to be heard from again, so be it to them.

"Ultimately, they were maybe the biggest aberration of a group we had in thirty years here. The natural cycle of things has taken back over with the juniors, but this was just the strangest group we've ever had. It always gets back to that. The most dysfunctional class ever. We were like the Oakland A's back in the 1970s. All these issues and problems off the field, but you threw that ball up, and they played unselfishly. They played together. There were just flaws they could never get over."

OUTSIDE HIS BEDROOM window, a warm drizzle fell on Emory Street. Otis Campbell reached over to his bed stand, slipped a letter out of its envelope and held it in the air. "See this?" he asked, handing over a mock newspaper headline in the newspaper, screaming, "Otis Campbell leads Quinnipiac to NCAA Tournament." Beneath the celebration photo, the note told him this was the coaching staff's hope in two years: bring Otis back East on a basketball scholarship, bring him back for a fine business program at the Connecticut college.

"And Georgetown called the other day," Otis said, sitting on his bed. "They said they're going to keep their eye on me out at Hutch."

Hutchinson Junior College, out in the cornfields of Kansas. Otis had never felt such a peace as during his recruiting trip there. Hutchinson was one of the national junior college powers, with a history of sending its graduates to four-year schools on basketball scholarships. The silence was strange, the night falling on the campus, and it took a night or two to get used to the stillness. No sirens. No screams. No shots. Just a stillness that soon covered Otis like a warm blanket.

"Once I got out there, I realized that I would have a chance to grow," Otis said. "I would have a chance to become me—away from all these guys here, away from Jersey City. I don't want to have to depend on Marcus and Beanie anymore."

Today was graduation day at St. Anthony, and every few minutes, his cell phone kept ringing with his best friends. They were checking in with Otis, just checking out his wardrobe for the ceremony over at St. Anthony Church.

"If I wasn't going away to school," Otis said, "I wouldn't feel like I was graduating from anything today."

In the living room, his mother, Earleen, ironed a white dress shirt for graduation. Hanging near the ironing board, there was a certificate framed on the wall. High honor roll for the final marking period of his high school career.

He had come so far. Now, nothing could stop him. Together, the seniors had been a class of followers—never a leader among them. "Otis is the greatest miracle of them all," Gary Greenberg said. "From when he came to St. Anthony, Otis was the least likely kid to go away."

Said Otis: "When I was younger, I didn't think I could leave Jersey City. But I realize now there ain't nothing to stay here for. This is getting me one step closer to getting me to a good Division I school and getting me a degree. I've got nothing holding me back. I didn't mind getting on that plane by myself. I mean, I was looking forward to it. Just to have something new to look at. I'm tired of seeing the same stuff every day here. Same people standing on the street corners, same faces in the same places.

"If I went to New York City like Marcus, or Ramapo, if I don't like school one day, I could just get on the PATH, or a bus, and come home. If they don't want to stick it out, they can just bail. I'm not bailing. If you don't have that degree, you'll just end up like the rest of them, standing on the streets, doing nothing.

"I'm going to Hutch, and I'm going to stick it out. I've got to go out there and become a man. I know that if I could get through St. Anthony with Coach Hurley, I can get through anything in my life."

Since final exams had ended, Otis had been waking up early every morning and working out at Lincoln Park. All alone, he did the drills Hurley had taught him at St. Anthony, all alone in the morning air. Most of all, he heard Hurley's voice in his ear. He played his speeches over in his mind. Sometimes, it felt like a guardian angel to take with him.

"I got bigger things than Jersey City on my mind," Otis said. "I got plans."

He looked out the window, where the rain was still falling on the street.

"Coach Hurley can talk about my career, and how I went to Hutchinson, and then to a four-year college—how I kept following a dream and succeeded. I gave going away a chance."

Hurley had worked the telephones and gotten Dominican College, a small Division II school in New York State, to give Shelton a package of basketball and academic aid that left him with just $100 in fees to cover on his own. Over the summer, Hurley scored an internship for Shelton with a securities and trading firm in Jersey City, where Shelton proudly told of earning his own desk there. Qaysir Woods was going to Division III Rutgers-Newark, where he would play basketball. Justin Lewis had been accepted at several universities and would try to make Division I Fairleigh Dickinson University in Teaneck as a walk-on.

A little past 1:00 on June 5, Otis was leaving his house for the short ride to the church, when Lamar called him on his cell phone.

"You comin' today, L?" Otis asked him.

"No," he told him.

"Come on, Lamar!" Otis pleaded with him. "Come on, man. Where you at now, L? Just go over there. Don't miss this, man."

Lamar told him no. He wasn't graduating, anyway. He had to take summer school classes at St. Anthony to earn his diploma, but they did offer to let him walk with his classmates and accept an empty sheepskin. He was back with his parents, but told Otis he had gotten into trouble that morning for blowing off the SATs. He didn't think he'd make it over to the ceremony.

Otis still had a soft spot for Lamar. After all, they went back a long time. There was still a bond with that senior class. And there probably would always be.

"Lamar has just stayed away from all of us since he got thrown off the team," Otis said. "He didn't want to show us he was depressed. But we still had a job to do together. The seniors still had a job to finish."

A little after 1:00, Otis climbed out of a car on Sixth Street. Marcus and Shelton were waiting for him outside. Sister Felicia and Sister Alan also stood outside the church, shooing kids into the ceremony. The senior basketball players stood a block away, in little hurry to scale the steps into the church. This was the end of the line for them together, and they wanted it to last a little longer.

Marcus greeted Darren Erman on the sidewalk, telling him to come see him at Globe Tech next year.

"New York is going to be my city!" Marcus yelled, spreading his arms and holding them wide. "My city!"

Finally, a car pulled up to the corner.

"BEANIE!" they all screamed, and out popped Ahmad Mosby from the backseat of his mother's car.

Finally, there they were on that spring afternoon, together for one last time on graduation day, the old Boys Club team all grown up and waiting a little longer to walk up those church steps and into the rest of their lives. Marcus Williams. Ahmad Mosby. Otis Campbell. Shelton Gibbs.

"Come on, let's go," Sister Felicia called. It was time.

Throughout the graduation ceremony, they whispered to one another in church about how they missed Lamar, about how they needed him, to feel complete. Afterward, the Class of 2004 emptied out of the church, and the basketball players were thrilled to see the missing piece of the class picture standing across the street. Lamar and his parents stood there, gazing at the church, at the graduation that had gone on without him.

Lamar's cell phone rang. The mother of his three-and-a-half-year-old, Shamar, had put their son on the line for Lamar.

"Congratulations, Daddy," the little boy squealed. "Congratulations on your graduation."

And that would touch Lamar like nothing else had in this year. All together finally, the St. Anthony basketball class of 2004 stood on the corner of Monmouth and Sixth streets in Jersey City, at the intersection of the past and the future, and held on as long as they could.

Wherever life took them now, they always had the basketball season in which they made history at St. Anthony.

They would always have 30–0. And the voice in their heads.

Whether they loved Hurley, or loathed him, or were leaving, still unsure how they felt about him, they all took that voice with them.

"You have that voice forever, whether you want it or you don't," the fireman, Mark Harris, says. "When you're leaving, you're thinking maybe you're tired of it. Maybe you didn't understand what he was trying to do. But all of us, we still talk about it now: You will understand so much better when you're older. And you'll wish you could go back to that time. You wish you could go back with him again.

"But that voice, it's staying with you. You can fight it, but you're going to come to moments in your life when you'll hear him in your head. And every time, you'll be forced to think about doing the right thing. Every time."

★ ★ ★

ONE AFTERNOON IN the spring of 2004, Danny Hurley had the juniors on his father's basketball team in the St. Benedict's gymnasium. They were practicing for a combined St. Anthony-St. Benedict's AAU team to play in some tournaments throughout the Northeast. After watching them play ball for a time, he blew his whistle.

He wasn't angry. Just curious.

"If my father was in the gym, you'd all be playing a lot harder, wouldn't you?" Danny asked them.

Together, they all shrugged and nodded yes. Danny didn't take it personally. And when he talked, he didn't take it to heart that the St. Anthony kids were just a fraction of a second slower stopping everything when he had something to say. They were still respectful, but Danny knew that in Jersey City, that in Bob Hurley's gymnasium, "You always needed the neck braces when he opened his mouth and started to talk. No one would move an inch. No one would flinch. No one would take their eyes off him until he was done speaking. Anywhere else in society now, I don't know if that's a reasonable expectation for kids anymore. It's all changed. But over there, I bet you that hasn't changed at all.

"There are so many things that made him unique: growing up in Jersey City, thirty years as a probation officer, the unbelievable success he's had. So many things came together with my father that will probably never come together again with another coach.

"I don't know if there are any kids, or families of kids, or people in a city, who hold a coach in higher regard as they do Bob Hurley. I've got great players at St. Benedict's and I like to think I make a huge difference in their lives. But they won't ever look at me the same way those kids look at Coach Hurley in Jersey City. It ain't happening here, and it ain't happening in any sport, anywhere, ever again.

"Bob Hurley is the last one."

MICHAEL ROSARIO STOPPED over at the Recreation office at Caven Point at the end of the school year. He was the best eighth-grade basketball player and baseball pitcher in Jersey City, and he would sit with his future coach for a half hour and talk about it all. St. Anthony had the best class of incoming freshmen on the way since, well, four years ago, when the names were Williams and Campbell and Mosby.

"I can't wait to coach Rosario," Hurley would say throughout the spring. "Wait until that kid gets here."

Danny Hurley was right. Every year, he could set his watch by it. There was always some great eighth-grader his father just had to coach, just had to see through four years of high school. Maybe Rosario's will be the class who will finally get to play a home game in the new gymnasium at St. Anthony High School. Maybe he'll be the one to hear all about how Marcus Williams won three Tournament of Champions titles with never somewhere as beautiful as that new gym to play ball, and how Rosario needed to begin playing like he appreciated the place.

Georgia Tech sent a coach by the charter school gym later that day, and Hurley made sure Miles Beatty was on the floor, giving the assistant a reason to come back for his fabulous freshman guard.

Hurley had stopped over at the gym for a word with Miles.

"They're going to be back for you in a couple of years," Hurley had said, "but you've got to get your grades up. You don't want to be where Marcus Williams and Ahmad Mosby are right now. Your grades are going to be the difference. You can't let yourself end up like those seniors who are leaving now, those kids who left themselves too few options in life."

"I know, Coach," Miles had said. "I know. They're going up."

Back on the floor, Miles grabbed a rebound and turned down the floor, turning toward tomorrow on a sun-splashed Jersey City spring day when the St. Anthony kids played inside a hot gymnasium, working up a good sweat, working toward next season. Outside those walls, high school basketball belonged more and more to the shoe companies and summer-league coaches tearing at the fabric of it all. Everyone was promising something, but in here there were still just these assurances: The toughest S.O.B. they'll ever meet still knew the name of every basketball coach to ever blow a whistle in northern Jersey, and still believed there was just one old-school, hard-ass way to coach these kids. When trouble came walking down that sidewalk, Hurley wasn't crossing the street. Every day, he was walking straight into it. After all these years, he was still taking it head on.

There was a parable Hurley loved to tell about the summertime, about high school coaches out in the suburbs on the ninth hole of a golf course, bitching about Bob Hurley's style over in Jersey City.

"Some guy who's never been to Jersey City, who's never coached my kind of kids here, will be bitching all the way to the eighteenth hole while we're somewhere lifting weights, or running, or playing in front of a college coach earning kids scholarships. That coach will have been bitching about us the whole back nine, but somewhere on the eighteenth green, he's gonna say, 'Shit, though, St. Anthony is gonna be good again this year. Real good.'"

St. Anthony had a chance to be good, very good again, but Hurley had told those underclassmen in the celebration of the championship locker room that he wasn't sure if they would be good enough next year. He wasn't sure at all, but Hurley knew this: He was fifty-six years old, and he could still take a basketball team the distance. He could still get his kids to college, get them out the door with values and a voice to take with them for life.

All that, and he could still kick every ass in the gymnasium.

When the kids hustled out into the hallway for a drink of water between games on that warm spring day in Jersey City, Robert Patrick Hurley, out of Linden Avenue in the Greenville section of Jersey City, out of another time and place, reached for the broom and started sweeping.

AFTERWORD

As THE STEELE Canyon High School bench rushed the court, flooding the floor to celebrate what would be described as the greatest victory in San Diego high school basketball history, the St. Anthony Friars were left with a most unsettling and unfamiliar feeling: defeat.

For the first time in thirty-three games, St. Anthony had lost, 67–65 in overtime at the Holiday Prep Classic on December 29, 2004. The Friars had been ranked number one in the *USA Today* poll, but in the San Diego tournament had resembled nothing of the sort. They had committed thirty-three turnovers, missed pressure free throws and let a twelve-point fourth quarter lead disappear. Afterward, Coach Bob Hurley would praise the plucky Steele Canyon team to the *San Diego Union-Tribune* before allowing, "The number-one ranking was just hype. I'm embarrassed by the way we played. It's not characteristic of our team."

Although this kind of self-destructive loss would've been un-characteristic—even unthinkable—of last year's St. Anthony team, it would soon become apparent that it was hardly an aberration for this one. As magical as the 2003–2004 undefeated Tournament of Champions season had been, 2004–2005 would be disappointing, weighted with a crisis of chemistry and injuries.

On paper, this season's Friars should've been a bigger, stronger and deeper team—yet with far less psychodrama than their predecessor. Unlike that class of seniors who were so unsettled before the 2003–2004 season, their futures wildly unsure, the returning stars in the Class of 2005 signed Division I national letters of intent in November, solidifying college desti-nations before they ever played a game.

Barney Anderson, the 6'5" forward, chose Rider University in Lawrenceville, New Jersey, a member of the Metro Atlantic Athletic Conference. He had several offers, including St. Peter's College, Central Connecticut and Monmouth.

Ahmad Nivins, who had grown to 6'10", had turned down offers from the Big East, Atlantic Coast, Big 10 and Southeastern conferences to stay true to the school that had recruited him the longest and hardest: St. Joseph's in Philadelphia. "A lot of schools wanted me," Ahmad said, "but St. Joe's made me feel like they needed me."

Although tempted to wait until the spring signing period of his senior year to pick a school, allowing for higher profile college programs to evaluate him, the 5'7" Derrick Mercer ultimately heeded his father's advice and signed with American University in Washington, D.C. An excellent academic school in the prestigious Patriot League, the scholarship was worth $38,000 a year in tuition and fees. The American coaches believed that Derrick would be a four-year starter and the push they needed to make the NCAA tournament after falling one victory short in three straight conference tournaments.

The most drama of the fall signing period surrounded shooting guard Sean McCurdy, who took campus visits to the University of Rhode Island and University of Massachusetts, but felt blown away by his trip to the University of Arkansas. The Razorbacks were the final "big-time" school that was willing to extend a scholarship offer. It was a proposition that Sean couldn't resist, despite the fact that Arkansas played in the powerful Southeastern Conference, where athleticism and quickness spurred a blurring style of basketball that would more than test Sean's ability to defend bigger, taller and faster athletes.

As THE SENIORS started work for their final season at St. Anthony, the Friars were ranked No. 1 in several national polls. Yet, all that began to go awry within the first week of preseason practice when Sean fractured his right foot. Soon, he had a pin surgically inserted and he would never play a game his senior year. Ahmad Nivins missed several games at midseason with a stress fracture in his foot. Derrick Mercer struggled to shake a deep thigh bruise, forcing him to miss games and ultimately play in pain. Barney Anderson missed a final exam for the second straight season, costing him a one-game suspension.

In February, the Friars would lose three games in one week, which had never happened in the history of the program. One loss was in four overtimes to Dominguez High School of Los Angeles in Jersey City, one a blowout to DeMatha of Maryland, and the third to St. Raymond's on St. John's–bound Ricky Torres's three-point bank shot at the buzzer in the Bronx.

This had been a Friars season of nice, well-adjusted kids, and sometimes Hurley felt that the street toughness and swagger that Marcus Williams and Ahmad Mosby had brought a year earlier was missing—that desperation to will each other, whatever the circumstances, to victory. For last year's team, there was always something on the line. At times, they felt like they were playing for their lives, their futures. For all the headaches the 2003–2004 team had given Hurley away from the floor, he worried much less about them once they were on it. The next season had been the complete opposite—and would end with a crushing defeat to archrival St. Patrick's in the third-round of the Parochial B state tournament at the Dunn Center in Elizabeth, 67–51.

After the game, Derrick Mercer Sr. hugged his son and fought back tears. Ahmad Nivins chatted for a few moments with a St. Joseph's University assistant coach. Near the base of the bleachers, Hurley would tell Boys' Club director Gary Greenberg, "We've got to take back our city."

They were losing more young kids to the streets in Jersey City. The neighborhoods and grade schools that had fed the St. Anthony dynasty were generating fewer and fewer prospects. It was getting tougher to compete at the highest level with simply a student body of kids out of Jersey City and neighboring Hudson County towns, tougher to stay dominant in the rapidly changing climate of big-time high school basketball. Losing to St. Patrick's, with a far more geographically diverse roster, had been a sobering reminder to Hurley. High school basketball was changing again, and Bob Hurley was resisting it all.

AHMAD MOSBY HAD been a complicated kid, but he had always played his ass off for Hurley. Funny how time had dimmed some of his shortcomings for the coach, leaving Hurley nostalgic for the way he competed every night for him as a senior.

Trouble was, Chuck McBreen, the Ramapo College head coach, was having a far tougher time reaching his freshman guard. Beanie had been playing sparingly, largely because the team was ranked in the Division III national Top 20 with an upperclassmen backcourt, and partly because Beanie had been in his classic form: brooding, defying authority and threatening to blow a good opportunity.

During one of his early games at Ramapo, the defiant Beanie was in full blossom. After going to Newark the night before with his girlfriend, he hadn't gotten back in time for the morning shoot-around. His coach had benched him for the night. After the game, outside the gymnasium, Beanie talked for thirty minutes, sounding as though everyone was against him at Ramapo, especially McBreen. After one semester, Beanie was already threatening to transfer to a new school. He had been frustrated with his playing time, discovering that he wasn't the only Division I–caliber talent to slip through the cracks to Ramapo.

"This guy doesn't like me," Beanie said, nodding to the gymnasium from the hallway, talking about his coach.

When reminded that Ramapo had sent a member of its coaching staff to almost every one of St. Anthony's games during his senior year, desperate to recruit him, Beanie backed down a little, conceding that, yes, someone must have liked him there.

Truth was, McBreen loved his talent, but at times Beanie's attitude made the coach wonder if he was ultimately worth the trouble. Beanie always needed to know that someone believed in him, that someone thought he could make it, because he always struggled to believe he could, especially with the history of men in his family going down to drugs and crime.

Over the course of that first season at Ramapo, McBreen would reach Beanie and begin to get better performances from him in the classroom and on the court. Eventually, Beanie even repaired his relationship with the St. Anthony coaching staff. He even showed up at the high school and told the sisters that he finally realized how much the people there had cared about him.

MARCUS WILLIAMS LIVED in Globe Tech student housing on Staten Island, commuting to the lower Manhattan campus on a ferry each day for classes. The proximity to Jersey City brought Marcus back into town more than Hurley wanted—something that Hurley urged Globe coach Ken Wilcox to address—but Marcus somehow found a way to balance fatherhood with schoolwork and basketball and make it through his freshman year.

His responsibilities had grown. His girlfriend, Shameka, gave birth to a daughter in late August of 2004, joining one-year-old Marcus Jr.

To no one's surprise, Marcus made a seamless transition to the point guard position for Globe Tech, inspiring his team with the discipline, fundamentals, and winning disposition that too few players bring to the free-wheeling world of junior college basketball. In one game, down seventeen points against rival Monroe College in January, it wouldn't take long for a vintage Marcus to take over on both ends of the floor. He shut down the opposing point guard, stole passes, made shots, found teammates for easy baskets. As usual, Marcus did a little bit of everything.

After hitting a tough, leaning bank shot with six seconds left, he had brought Globe all the way back—until an opposing player hit a half-court shot at the buzzer to steal the victory.

In the hallway afterward, Marcus said, "Man, I miss Coach Hurley. I miss the structure there."

If Marcus was nothing else, though, he was adaptable. Called upon to play four positions on the floor at different times that year, he would lead Globe Tech to twenty-three victories and its first ever appearance in the National Junior College Athletic Association national tournament in Hutchinson, Kansas. All Marcus needed to do now was get through his sophomore year at Globe, get his associate's degree, and he would finally be on his way to Division I basketball.

FEW BACK HOME in New Jersey felt much disconnect with Otis Campbell in the fall of 2004, because during his first few months away at Hutchinson Community College in Kansas, he was constantly calling everyone. Their phones would ring on Friday or Saturday nights, with Otis calling to chat, often fighting through his homesickness.

Midway through the basketball season, Otis moved into Hutch's starting lineup—no small accomplishment considering the collection of talent on the roster—and the calls home became less frequent. Most important, Otis's sense of himself was right: Going far away to school, where there were fewer distractions, had forced him to immerse himself in his studies. By the end of the school year, he felt sure that he would eventually get a four-year degree, and then come back to Jersey City and get a job in one of the new office buildings going up on the waterfront.

LAMAR ALSTON WAS promising a triumphant return to New Jersey at Rutgers University-Newark, where he had hatched a plan to enroll for the fall semester of 2005, with his eventual designs on playing basketball. After living for a few months with his new wife in Alabama, and changing his mind on enrolling at a local college down there, he seemed determined to get an education and resurrect his basketball career.

"It ended all wrong for me at St. Anthony," Lamar said one day on the phone.

Rutgers-Newark coaches knew he would be a terrific talent for the Division III level, but were wise enough to Lamar's history to be skeptical. Lamar needed to take the SAT for the school's admissions department, but kept procrastinating. Eventually, the coaches were hearing more from his father, Joe Boccia, and less from Lamar.

Finally, the coaches were told that Lamar wouldn't take the SAT, ending the possibility of him going to Rutgers-Newark.

It became increasingly hard to reach Lamar on the phone by the spring and summer of 2005. There were some rumors that he would enroll at New Jersey City University in Jersey City for the fall semester, but no one could ever know for sure until Lamar showed up for the first day of classes.

As HIS SENIOR year progressed, Sean McCurdy, leaning on crutches and canes, spent more and more time with his mother back in Connecticut. He was often seen in the stands at the St. Joseph's of Trumbull games, where he visited with his old classmates and teammates. People who saw Sean there described him as thrilled to be back in that element, almost forlorn that he had ever left.

The McCurdy family and Bob Hurley ended on uneasy terms, after their relationship deteriorated over the course of Sean's senior year. At graduation in June, Cindy told Ben Gamble that if she could've done it all over again, she would've never uprooted and sent Sean to St. Anthony.

Looking back, Hurley had his regrets too.

"The whole thing reinforced to me what our mission is here, and who we serve," he said.

By the spring of 2005, Sean was anxious to leave for Arkansas, where he would start working out with the basketball team during summer school session. Bob McCurdy would be relieved when Cindy scrapped her plans to move near campus in Fayetteville.

Despite Sean's sluggish recovery from the broken foot, Arkansas coaches said they were convinced that he would play significant minutes as a freshman. They believed he could have an immediate impact, encouraged by the way Sean was unafraid to take charge with upperclassmen in the summer pick-up games. His college debut would be against his home-state

University of Connecticut Huskies on national television at the Maui Invitational.

SISTER ALAN CONTINUED to defy her doctors' original prognosis, seemingly willing her cancer into remission. In early 2005, tests showed that the chemo had isolated and reduced the tumor in her liver. That spring, she even felt well enough to take an Alaskan cruise with her sister.

Elsewhere, there had been hard times for members of the Friars family.

Doc Miller, the longtime St. Anthony trainer, had a recurrence of prostate cancer and had to undergo several hard-hitting bouts of chemo over the summer. At eighty-five years old, his body was struggling to rebound.

"I'm gonna beat this thing," he whispered one day on the phone, "but it's taking a lot out of me."

Before the summer was done, kidney trouble would be added to his ailment. He had to be hooked up to a dialysis machine. After that, he wasn't sure if he'd be able to work with the team next season.

And on April 7, 2005, Mark Harris, one of Bobby Hurley's teammates on the national championship team of 1989 and the Jersey City firefighter who remembered Hurley's lessons while confronting a rooftop blaze, died of stomach cancer. He was thirty-five years old.

His old coach spent several hours sitting at Harris's bedside in his final weeks. Mark Harris always said that never a day passed when something Bob Hurley had taught him didn't surface in his mind.

IN THE SPRING of 2005, Darren Erman had an offer to become a Los Angeles–based pro sports agent, but he hedged for months on making a decision. It was a tough choice, considering that his heart was still strongly rooted in basketball. After leaving St. Anthony's program, he had talked with several NBA executives about administrative positions that would utilize his law background, but had no firm offers. For the second straight summer, he coached professional players represented by the SFX Sports agency in a pro summer league, with his team winning the co-championship at the Global Hoops Summit in Las Vegas.

Finally, he turned down the agent's job to keep chasing his basketball dream, moving to Boston to be the personal workout coach for the Celtics'

Brian Scalabrine. Most days, Boston general manager Danny Ainge found Erman on a couch in the team's executive offices, almost holding vigil that some official within the franchise would find a job for Erman.

SISTER FELICIA LEFT her position as principal to take over as president of St. Anthony High School, overseeing the school's alumni relations and fund-raising operations. A longtime St. Anthony teacher, Ed Santana, would take over as the principal.

Before the start of the 2005–2006 school year, St. Anthony High School had raised two million dollars in pledges during the silent phase of an initial $10 million capital campaign to finance the first wave of construction of the school's new gymnasium and classroom facilities. Several potential million-dollar donors were interested in committing more money, but were waiting for another major donor or two to step up before they decided to do the same.

As much as St. Anthony kept trying to raise money for long-term projects, it still had to struggle to meet the annual operating budget for the school. St. Anthony's fight for survival forged on.

DESPITE SOLID SUPPORT in the nomination process, Bob Hurley fell short of earning enough votes to get on the final ballot for the Naismith Memorial Basketball Hall of Fame in his first try before the committee. UConn's Jim Calhoun and Syracuse's Jim Boeheim were the two men's coaches chosen for enshrinement for the Class of 2005. With more NBA officials than ever involved in the selection process, it wouldn't be easy for Hurley to become just the second high school coach in the modern era to make it. For most candidates, it was a long process to even reach the final ballot. For Hurley, it was harder because he had no public relations firm or marketing department submitting a proper application on his behalf.

St. Anthony will be young again in the 2005–2006 season, starting four underclassmen, including Miles Beatty, who already has Big East and ACC schools recruiting him. Hurley, at fifty-seven, isn't sure how much longer he can hold up against the increasing grind of fund-raising and coaching at St. Anthony. Hurley believes that he will coach his excellent group of sophomores, including Travon Woodall and Michael Rosario, through their graduation in 2009. He talks of perhaps retiring as coach of

St. Anthony sooner rather than later, leaving the program to Ben Gamble, and then joining his son, Danny, as his assistant at St. Benedict's Prep.

But in Jersey City, everyone will believe Bob Hurley retiring as St. Anthony's coach when they see it for themselves. If that gym is ever built, no one can imagine anyone else coaching opening night on Eighth Street.

Adrian Wojnarowski
September 2005
Glen Rock, New Jersey

ACKNOWLEDGMENTS

AFTER THE COACHES and players had returned to the locker room at the end of the Tournament of Champions victory, Bob Hurley turned to his team and declared, "There is no one happier in this room right now than Adrian. The Bad News Bears just went undefeated."

One thing was for sure: No one in that locker room felt any greater debt of gratitude. At a time in my newspaper column career when my cynicism covering pro and big-time college sports had maxed-out on the scandal and hubris of the times, my season with Bob Hurley and the St. Anthony High School basketball team reminded me why I dreamed of covering sports as a kid.

The Friars made every day a treasure for me.

Over several months of shuttling back and forth to St. Anthony, there was never a day speeding toward Jersey City when I couldn't wait to see what awaited me. When the season was over, Bob Hurley called it the most fulfilling season of his career. It will always be mine, too.

There is no writing a book without the help of many, but there was no writing this book without one: my beautiful wife, Amy. She gave up her own professional ambitions to support mine and, far more importantly, be the beacon in the lives of our children, Annie and Ben. She was a single parent for too much of the year, and she deserves a vacation. Until then, she gets my undying love and thanks.

My love and thanks also to the Wojnarowskis, the Bissonnettes, the Carrs, and the Quinlans, family all.

G. Gale Dickau taught me so much, but nothing helped me on this project more than her words forever ringing in my head. "Rewrite, rewrite and rewrite." Ever since sophomore English at Bristol Central High School, she has supplied a constant stream of encouragement, wisdom and friendship.

The Borg family and Vivian Waixel are marvelous people to work for at *The Record*. Executive editor Frank Scandale and managing editor Art Lenehan encouraged me to pursue the book from the beginning and always asked how it was going. Sports editor John Balkun and his assistant, Dave Rivera, were tremendously supportive. They allowed me the time I needed to see the book's reporting and writing to the end, and I'm grateful to them. They're pro's pros.

Dale Tepas pointed me toward St. Bonaventure University, and Father Dan Riley, O.F.M., helped me stay the course through it. Besides being great friends, Mike MacDonald and Kevin McNamee taught me to how to measure the qualities of character and caring in coaches. They both have them in abundance.

Authors who paved the way in this book genre were terrific sources of advice and encouragement, including Wayne Coffey, John Feinstein, Neil Hayes, Tim Keown, and Bill Reynolds.

As always, Mike Vaccaro and Les Carpenter were great sounding boards, but better friends. They've made me a better writer, and assuredly, a better person.

David Ramsey, Bob Klapisch, Ian O'Connor, Dan Wetzel, Mike DeCourcy and Mike Wise were good friends along the way. Seth Davis, John Akers, Chris Lawlor, Mike Quick, Tara Sullivan, Jim Hague, and Jay Gomes made invaluable contributions.

Rob Kennedy, Vin Vella and the rest of the Hoop Group treated me to a terrific week at the Bob Hurley Basketball School in the Pocono Mountains.

Margie Calabrese, Toni Bollhardt, Brother James and the rest of the St. Anthony family and faculty were welcoming and accommodating. The adult managers on the team, John Cicchetti, Harry Traina and Bob Sears always made room for me in the row behind the bench.

Sister Felicia and Sister Alan trusted a stranger to tell their story, and I owe them immeasurably.

The St. Anthony Board of Trustees were enthusiastic and encouraging throughout, especially Tom Breen, Nick Nicolosi, Bill Booker, Mike Slater, Kathleen Staudt and Bart Erbach. John O'Neil, Bernie Fitzsimmons and Gary Greenberg were great resources.

Greg Dinkin and Frank Scatoni of Venture Literary started out as my agents, but became much more. From the beginning, they championed this idea with expert counsel, editing and endless enthusiasm. Best of all, they provided perspective and calm for a first-time author.

Brendan Cahill, my editor at Gotham, was spectacular. His tenacity and touch made the final manuscript immeasurably sharper and smarter. His influence is all over this book. As an editor, Brendan is everything a writer dreams of working with.

Gotham publisher Bill Shinker believed in this story from the beginning and was encouraging throughout the process. Brendan's assistant, Patrick Mulligan, helped in every way possible. He was a pro, all the way through. Ray Lundgren designed a compelling cover, and Lisa Johnson, Kathleen Schmidt and Robert Kempe made committed contributions.

If you judge a coach by the company he keeps on his staff, then there can be no greater tribute paid to Bob Hurley.

No one helped me understand Bob and St. Anthony basketball more than Ben Gamble, who was generous in his time, memories and perspective. Between the end of the season and my deadline in August, hardly a day passed when I didn't call to review a particular point or episode in the season. Bob Hurley casts a long shadow, but Ben is a great coach and teacher of the game in his own right. He's an even better man.

Darren Erman was full of integrity and earnestness, looking forward, like me, every day to see what Hurley had awaiting us in the gym. Damel Ling never held those running pants against me. Tom Pushie and Dan McLaughlin made personal sacrifices to be a part of the staff, as well as help me along the way. Ben Richardville, Dennis Quinn and Todd Dagosta were in good spirits and humor every day. Tony DiGiovanni is going to be a coaching star.

No one can tell a story like Doc Miller. He's an original. That goes for Ed "The Faa" Ford too.

The families and players of the St. Anthony basketball team were fabulous. They allowed me into their lives and homes. They let me hang in the locker room, sit with them in classes, on school buses, and answered my questions when they were undoubtedly tired of doing so. They never made me feel like an outsider.

There wasn't one player whom I didn't root for, and won't be rooting for long after they've left St. Anthony.

The Hurley family was wonderful. Chris, Bobby, Danny and Melissa wanted this story told and did everything they could to facilitate that process for me. They are a study in how a family ought to keep watch on one another's back.

And finally a few words about Bob Hurley. He took a leap of faith to grant complete access to his world, and yet never once implored me,

"Don't use that in the book." He had such a strength of conviction in his methods and ways, and never flinched in letting me see it all. In the end, he trusted his genius and undying devotion to his players, past and present, would win out. And he was right. He gave me a front row seat to greatness.

He was relentlessly candid, kind and patient with me. More than anything else, Bob Hurley was compelling every day.

And for that, I'll always be grateful.

For information on donating to St. Anthony, please visit http://www.stanthonyhighschool.org.